Richard Guilliatt is a journalist and author. Born in the UK, he was a feature writer at the *Age* newspaper in Melbourne, Australia, before moving to New York in 1986 to work as a freelance writer. His work has appeared in many leading newspapers and magazines. In 2000, he won Australia's highest award for magazine feature writing, the Walkley Award.

Peter Hohnen was a partner in a prominent Canberra law firm for twenty years. A commander in the Royal Australian Naval Reserve for two decades, he was posted to Cambridge University in 1999 to study the law of the sea and the laws of armed conflict as a visiting fellow at the Lauterpacht Centre for International Law. His great-uncle, Alexander Ross Ainsworth, was chief engineer aboard the steamship *Matunga* when it was captured by SMS *Wolf* in August 1917.

www.rbooks.co.uk

RICHARD GUILLIATT & PETER HOHNEN

THE WOLF

HOW ONE GERMAN RAIDER TERRORISED AUSTRALIA AND THE SOUTHERN OCEANS IN THE FIRST WORLD WAR

CORGI BOOKS

For more information about this book
visit www.raiderwolf.com

TRANSWORLD PUBLISHERS
61-63 Uxbridge Road, London W5 5SA
A Random House Group Company
www.rbooks.co.uk

THE WOLF
A CORGI BOOK: 9780552157056

First published in Great Britain
in 2009 by Bantam Press
an imprint of Transworld Publishers

Published simultaneously in Australia in 2009 by William Heinemann
a division of Random House Australia Pty Ltd

Corgi edition published 2010

Cover design by Richard Shailer.
Cover photographs: SMS *Wolf* © Australian War Memorial,
H13505; *Wolfchen* seaplane © Australian War Memorial, PO5338-112;
sea © John Lund/Riser/Getty Images.
Cross-sectional representation of SMS Wolf on p. 5 by Paul Leigh.
Maps on pp. 6, 7 by James Mills-Hicks,
www.icecoldpublishing.com
Internal design by Midland Typesetters, Australia.
Picture-section layout by Midland Typesetters, Australia, and Sheree James.

This book is a work of non-fiction.

A CIP catalogue record for this book
is available from the British Library.

Addresses for Random House Group Ltd companies outside the UK
can be found at: www.randomhouse.co.uk
The Random House Group Ltd Reg. No. 954009

Typeset in Minion.
Printed in the UK by
CPI Cox & Wyman, Reading, RG1 8EX.

2 4 6 8 10 9 7 5 3 1

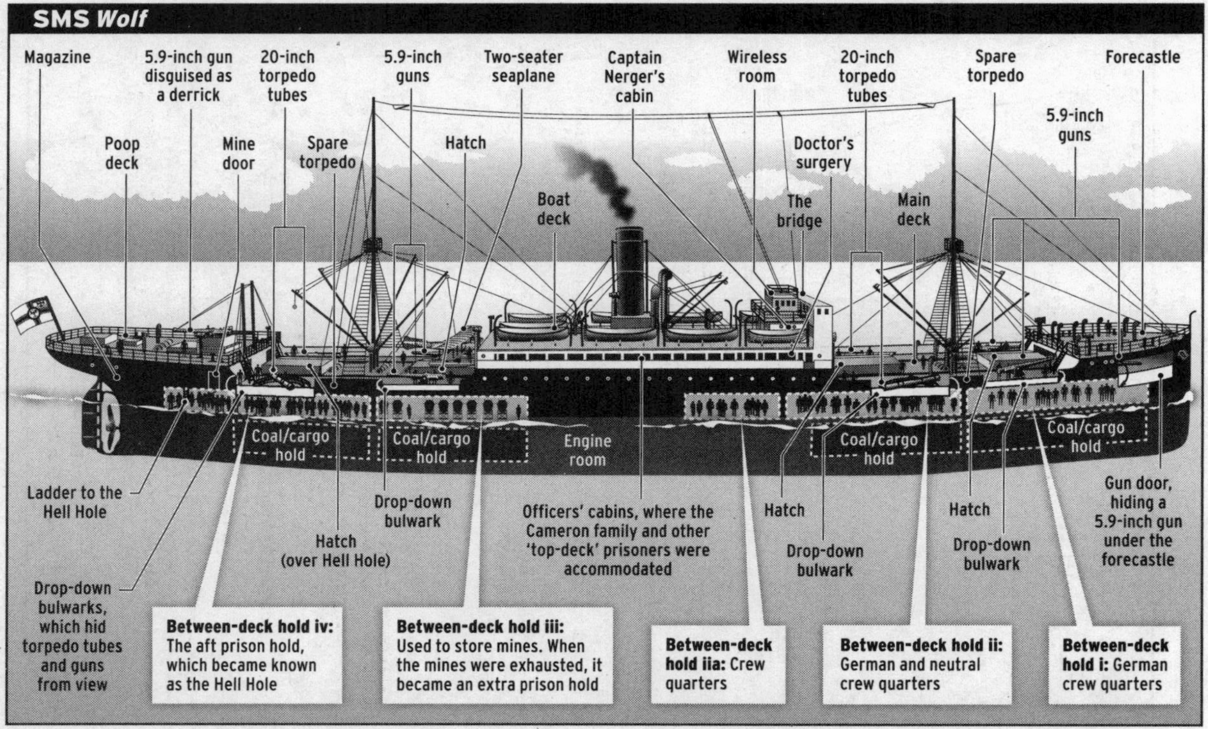
SMS Wolf
Magazine
5.9-inch gun disguised as a derrick
20-inch torpedo tubes
5.9-inch guns
Two-seater seaplane
Captain Nerger's cabin
Wireless room
20-inch torpedo tubes
Spare torpedo
Forecastle
5.9-inch guns
Poop deck
Mine door
Spare torpedo
Hatch
Boat deck
Doctor's surgery
The bridge
Main deck
Coal/cargo hold
Coal/cargo hold
Engine room
Coal/cargo hold
Coal/cargo hold
Ladder to the Hell Hole
Drop-down bulwark
Officers' cabins, where the Cameron family and other 'top-deck' prisoners were accommodated
Hatch
Hatch
Gun door, hiding a 5.9-inch gun under the forecastle
Hatch (over Hell Hole)
Drop-down bulwark
Drop-down bulwark
Drop-down bulwarks, which hid torpedo tubes and guns from view
Between-deck hold iv: The aft prison hold, which became known as the Hell Hole
Between-deck hold iii: Used to store mines. When the mines were exhausted, it became an extra prison hold
Between-deck hold iia: Crew quarters
Between-deck hold ii: German and neutral crew quarters
Between-deck hold i: German crew quarters

Cross-sectional artist's representation of SMS *Wolf*

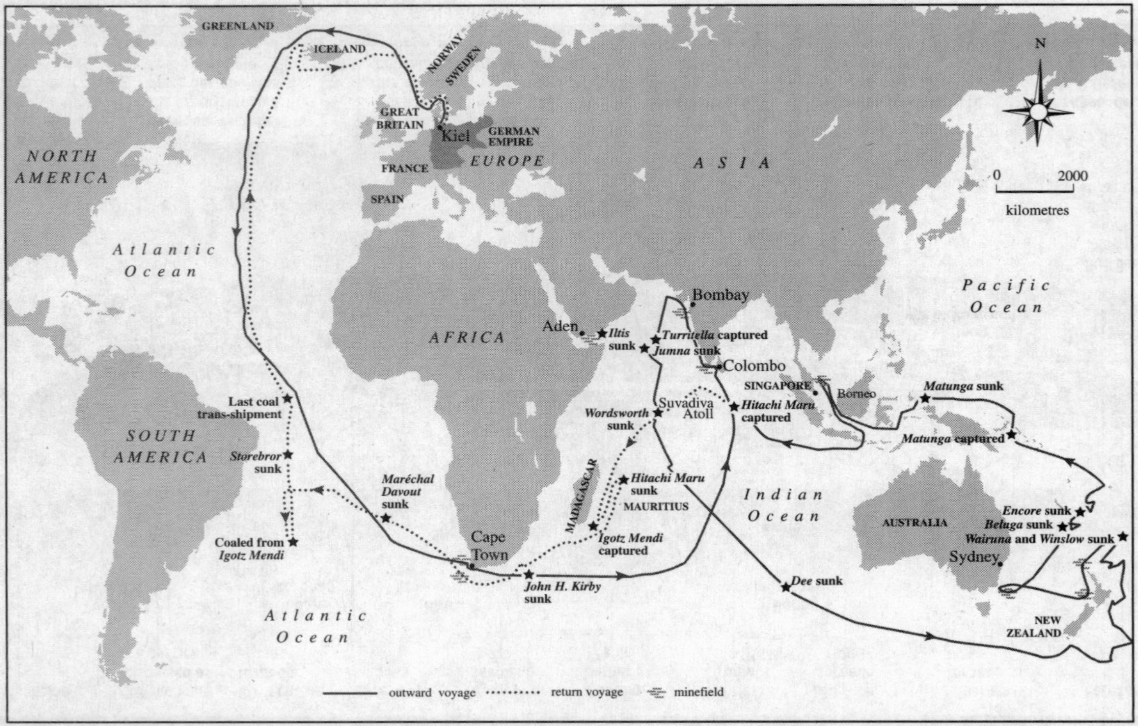

Voyage of SMS *Wolf*, November 1916–February 1918

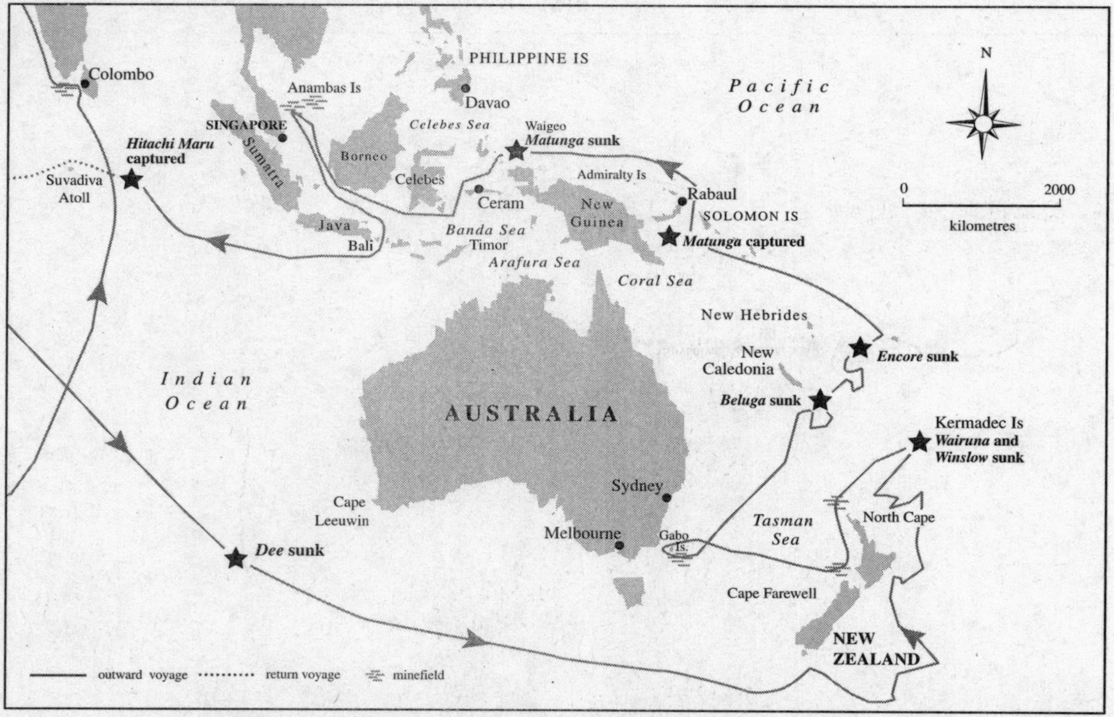

The *Wolf*'s raiding operations off Australia, March–September 1917

CONTENTS

PREFACE

The extraordinary voyage of the German warship *Wolf* is one of the least-known stories of the First World War, and yet, paradoxically, it is also one of the most extensively documented. More than 800 men, women and children lived on the ship at various times during her fifteen months at sea, and between 1918 and 1920 no less than seven of them wrote books detailing their experiences. By the early years of the Second World War, several other eyewitness accounts had been published. Yet few people today remember the *Wolf* beyond a devoted coterie of war buffs and maritime enthusiasts.

That neglect may reflect the limitations of most published accounts of the *Wolf*. Some were hastily and amateurishly written; most were subject to the censorious restraints of earlier times; nearly all of the German accounts were published during the war, with one eye on their propaganda value, and only one was ever translated into English. The early books were quickly forgotten, and the best of the later ones – the colourful memoirs of the former prisoner Roy Alexander and former crewman Theodor Plivier – are now more than seventy years old. The singular nature of the *Wolf*'s voyage – an odyssey across three oceans shared by an improbable mass of people thrown together to form a floating microcosm of the world – remains largely unknown.

This account, the first to tell the full story, began life when one of the authors, Peter Hohnen, delved into the experiences of his great-uncle, Ross Ainsworth, a young Australian merchant seaman whose ship, the *Matunga*, was captured by the *Wolf* off the coast of New Guinea in August 1917. Five years of research led us into the military archives of Britain, Germany, Australia, South Africa and New Zealand, and prompted a search to locate many of the scattered descendants of those who had lived on the ship nearly a century earlier. The material that was eventually unearthed – declassified documents, handwritten diaries, letters, faded black-and-white photographs and strips of silent film – yielded a story much richer and more intriguing than we could have anticipated.

On one level, it is the story of a daring military endeavour – a warship disguised as a civilian freighter, equipped with the most advanced technology of its era, sent on a suicide mission to the far side of the world. It is also the human story of how a multitude of people from warring nations coexisted in sometimes dire confines and discovered the commonalities that bonded them. And it is a story with political dimensions that were uncovered in government archives – a cautionary glimpse of how easily the press and the public can be manipulated towards xenophobic hatred when governments wield enormous powers of censorship and propaganda.

In writing this account, we have stayed true to the language and terminology of its era. Some of the racial attitudes expressed by those aboard the ship would cause grievous offence today, but because so much of the story pivots around the social interactions of those on the *Wolf*, it would be self-defeating to play the role of censor. We have likewise been faithful to place names that are now anachronisms, among them the following: Boeroe (now known as Buru), Bombay (Mumbai), Burma (Myanmar), Calcutta (Kolkata), Celebes (Sulawesi), Ceram (Seram), Ceylon

(Sri Lanka), Delagoa Bay (Maputo Bay), Madras (Chennai), Rangoon (Yangon) and Saigon (Ho Chi Minh City). Where imperial measurements for distance and weight were used in original sources, we have retained them.

Those who lived on the *Wolf*, both prisoners and crew, endured extreme mental and physical hardships during the course of the voyage, and it is not surprising that their eyewitness accounts sometimes contradict each other on the date, time and detail of particular events. In those instances, we have relied as much as possible on contemporaneous documents, in particular the daily war diary maintained aboard the ship by Kapitän Karl Nerger, a copy of which is held in the German military archives in Freiburg, and on declassified military files from various countries.

In the end, however, it is these first-person accounts, written in many different languages and from a multitude of viewpoints, that paint the most vivid picture of the *Wolf*'s strange and circuitous passage around the world in the years 1916–18. Through them, we get a palpable sense of the terrors and absurdities of the voyage, and of the war itself. Theirs is a remarkable survival story that opens a window into the turmoil that beset the world in those grinding final years of the First World War.

1

1

THE BLACK RAIDER

San Francisco Bay shimmered under a brilliant blue sky on the morning of 15 May 1917, yet Captain John Stanley Cameron was plagued by a sailor's nagging superstition as he guided his three-masted barque, the *Beluga*, out through the heads and into the Pacific Ocean. The spring temperature hovered around sixteen degrees Celsius, a mild westerly tugged at the *Beluga*'s sails and the old wooden whaler responded beautifully to Cameron's touch. Everything augured well for the ten-week voyage to Australia. But as he stood on the aft deck watching the brick ramparts of Alcatraz Island's military prison slip past on the port side, the skipper's mind kept returning to the ritual headcount he had performed aboard the ship shortly before casting off. With a load capacity of only 508 tons, the *Beluga* would normally have carried just Cameron and a crew of ten, but on this voyage he had brought along his young wife, Mary, and their six-year-old daughter, Juanita. Only as he prepared to cast off had he realised that the total number of people aboard her was now an unlucky thirteen.

When Cameron mentioned this bad omen to Mary, she laughed it off as old-fashioned nonsense more befitting a nineteenth-century salt than a skipper in this new age of industrial wonders. Mary Cameron had spent most of her twenty-seven years observing the paradoxically stoic but superstitious ways of sailors, for she had grown up in the Australian port city of Newcastle, north of Sydney, where her father was a stevedore and her mother ran a confectionery store on the docks. And Stan, although he was only thirty-two, was emphatically a seaman of the old school; his father, John, was one of San Francisco's venerated master mariners, and Stan had been venturing out to sea since he first stepped aboard the old man's whaler as an infant. He was among the last of a breed of merchant seamen who had learned their craft on sailing ships, reading their fortunes in the wind, the stars and other, less tangible portents.

Yet something deeper than mere superstition was at work in Cameron's mind, for the world was in turmoil as he and Mary set sail across the Pacific. Six weeks earlier, United States President Woodrow Wilson had proclaimed a state of war with Germany, officially ending his nation's tenuous neutrality to side with Britain in the 'grim and terrible' conflict that had turned the fields of France and Belgium into slaughtering grounds over the past three years. The president had confirmed an extraordinary tale the newspapers had been reporting for days – that Germany had attempted to enlist Mexico in a plot to invade Texas, New Mexico and Arizona. An intercepted telegram from Germany's foreign secretary, Arthur Zimmerman, had exposed the scheme, the last in a long line of provocations that went back to 1915, when a German submarine torpedoed the ocean-liner *Lusitania* off Ireland and killed nearly 1200 people, including 128 Americans.

War headlines had crowded the front pages of the San Francisco newspapers in the weeks before the Camerons set sail, and the city itself was swept with wild conjecture. The United States Navy had warned that German submarines might be lurking beneath the Pacific Ocean off the coast of California. The *San Francisco Chronicle* claimed U-boats were being constructed at a secret base somewhere on Mexico's south-western coastline, having been shipped in pieces from Germany. A submarine was said to have been sighted in the Gulf of California, only 700 miles south of Los Angeles. The military prison on Angel Island had been turned into an internment camp for German immigrants and suspected spies, among them the German consul-general in San Francisco, Franz Bopp, and two of his staff, who were charged with hatching a bomb plot. Four Indian immigrants who lived near the Camerons in Berkeley had been arrested as conspirators in a German-financed plot to send guns to revolutionaries in British India. Patrol boats were plying the bay night and day, on alert for possible attacks. 'The thrill of war', as the *Chronicle* put it, had finally come to the shores of the United States.

It was an inauspicious time to be taking a six-year-old child on a 7400-mile voyage across the equator. Yet the Camerons shared an impetuous spirit that went back to their whirlwind courtship nearly a decade earlier, when Stan had sailed into Newcastle harbour aboard his father's barque *Big Bonanza* in late December 1907. Mary's family still talked about the bewildering events of that Christmas, when Mary looked up from behind the counter of her mother's store to see a strapping six-foot-three American sailor with wide-set blue eyes, a rueful smile and a mop of light brown hair already coarsened by salt and sun. Whatever chemistry was triggered in that moment had been hastened along by Mary's high-spirited nature, for even at eighteen she was no introvert. Vivacious, oval-faced, with a thick mane of dark hair and a mischievous smile that dimpled her cheeks, she was one of eleven children in a noisy working-class family, and she sang on the stage of the Victoria Theatre and the local Wharf Labourers' Hall. In the days leading to Christmas, Stan had convinced his father to delay their departure from Newcastle and implored Mary's parents to let him take their daughter back to San Francisco. By Boxing Day, the young couple were married, and a day later Mary had walked aboard the *Big Bonanza* and set sail for a new life on the other side of the Pacific.

In the years since then, the Camerons had shared more than one adventure at sea, for Mary had chosen a shipboard life with Stan over the lonely existence of a shore wife. Eighteen months after their wedding, they had survived a terrifying ordeal off the coast of Alaska when their heavily laden whaler ran aground during a violent night-time snowstorm, which capsized some of the lifeboats carrying the 194 passengers and crew to shore. After nearly drowning in the raging surf that night, Mary had huddled on a desolate stretch of beach with the others, singing music-hall tunes to buoy their spirits until a rescue party found them. A year later, she was with Stan aboard the barque *Diamond Head*, en route from San Francisco to Seattle, when another storm nearly capsized the ship, snapping its mast and forcing them to seek shelter in a small cove.

Stan Cameron had hung up his skipper's cap shortly after that adventure, taking a port job around the time of his daughter Juanita's birth in 1911. He might never have returned to the sea had it not been for the war and Mary's fervent desire to see her family again. After years of begging and cajoling, her opportunity had finally come two months ago when Stan heard that the old *Beluga* was scheduled to take a shipment of benzine engine fuel to Sydney for the General Petroleum Company. Cameron knew the owner of the company, a rambunctious San Francisco millionaire called John Barneson who had hired Stan to sail his racing yacht *Edris* from Peru to San Francisco in 1912. The Camerons had named their second daughter after that sleek yacht, the fastest on the West Coast, and Stan had skippered her for Barneson intermittently since then. He also knew the *Beluga*, a reliable old barque that had been lying idle for several years in Oakland Harbor until she was recommissioned because of the heavy shipping losses caused by the war.

It was an opportunity too enticing to resist: he and Mary could leave four-year-old Edris in the care of a family friend in San Francisco and take Juanita with them on a paid summer cruise across the Pacific to see her grandparents for the first time. For Stan, the lure of returning to the sea was made even more irresistible by the money he could earn, for with freight-rates skyrocketing because of the war, merchant seamen were earning extraordinary wages. The crewmen of the *Beluga* were being paid sixty dollars a month, with a guaranteed minimum of ten months' work, and even at those rates Stan had found it so difficult to pull together a crew that he had been forced to delay his departure by a week and cross the bay to find a second mate on the docks in San Francisco.

With Germany and the United States now at war, Stan knew the *Beluga* was fair game for capture by any German submarine or warship he might encounter. And the newspapers were filled with terrifying accounts of the fate that befell anyone who fell into German hands. War correspondents claimed the Kaiser's troops had hacked off the limbs of children as they marched through Belgium; they violated nuns and crucified their enemies with bayonets. Only a month earlier, there were reports that the Germans were boiling down the bodies of the dead to make glycerine for their weapons. But Stan had spent enough time around Germans to wonder about such stories. His own crew was made up almost entirely of Swedes and Norwegians, many of whom felt as much cultural kinship with Germany as they did with the United States. They were the kind of veteran seamen whose presence was itself a reassurance.

'Seldom have I gone to sea under more favourable circumstances,' Cameron later recalled. 'A tight little vessel, a good deepwater crew of Scandinavian sailor men, plenty of good wholesome provisions and a cook who knew his business.'

If there were dangers in such a voyage, he could console himself that no American ship had yet been lost in the Pacific, despite the newspapers' overheated accounts of U-boat flotillas heading towards America. Like many of the city's merchant seamen, he was sceptical about such stories, and like many Americans he was ambivalent about his country's involvement in a conflict that had until recently seemed a distant struggle between the great powers of Europe. After three years of war, it was difficult to know what to believe. In Britain, Prime Minister Lloyd George was again promising imminent victory, yet in Washington there was talk that the English were on the brink of starvation. The Camerons had already lived through an age of upheaval: in their lifetimes, the automobile and the aircraft had revolutionised transport, the coal-fired steamship had supplanted the sailing boat, the wireless and the phonograph had been invented and the movie camera had made possible the silent wonder of the cinema. Assassinations and workers' revolts had convulsed Europe, and the United States had nearly gone to war with Mexico. This new conflict in France and Russia was yet more tumult, but it seemed so distant to Stan that when he later described the *Beluga*'s departure from San Francisco, he made almost no mention of it, and the only trepidation he could recall was the nagging thought of that unlucky thirteen.

As for Mary, no talk of war or bad omens could distract her from the excitement of returning home. This was to be another adventure, in an era when war itself was portrayed as an adventure, when newspapers spoke breathlessly of exciting battles and thrilling heroics on the frontlines. With her arm around Juanita, she clung to an optimistic faith as their sailing ship pulled clear of San Francisco Bay and into the heavier swell of the Pacific.

* *

The trade route from San Francisco to Sydney was the longest Stan Cameron had ever sailed, cutting diagonally across an ocean so vast that it was possible to remain at sea for weeks without seeing another ship or sighting one of the hundreds of islands scattered across the curvature of its surface. Stan fixed a course that took the *Beluga* well to the south-east of Hawaii, crossing the equator five weeks into the voyage at a point close to the ocean's geographic centre. The Pacific was a blank canvas out here: beyond the horizon, the Gilbert Islands passed by unseen as May gave way to June. The wind became cooler but the skies remained clear, and one day drifted into the next.

For Mary, the lulling monotony of the voyage was countered by the anticipation of her family reunion. In the decade since she had left Newcastle, all ten of her sisters and brothers had married and left home. Her younger sister Violet, who had been her singing partner on the stage of the Victoria Theatre at the age of twelve, was now a married woman of twenty-three. Her father was about to turn sixty and Mary knew from the letters they had exchanged that her mother, Jane, although only in her early fifties, was not well. Each day at noon, when Stan mapped out his chart, Mary would help him calculate their remaining distance to Newcastle.

'Then she would figure out just how long it would take, under various weather conditions, before she would be able to see her beloved Australia again,' he later wrote. 'Some days when we had a favourable wind and had made a good day's run in the right direction, she would be as happy as could be and singing all the time, but other days when we had made but little progress she would be way down in the dumps, and it would be extremely difficult to get a smile.'

Two weeks after they crossed the equator, the Camerons approached American-occupied Samoa – the customary stopover for ships en route to Australia – but Stan decided to press on.

On 9 July, the chart showed them less than a thousand miles from their destination, skirting just south of the islands of New Caledonia and about to cross below the Tropic of Capricorn. In nearly two months, they had still not seen another ship, but at two o'clock on that cloudless afternoon, Stan was on the quarterdeck supervising a maintenance crew high up in the aft mast when one of the sailors called down to him, 'Smoke-oh, on the port beam.' Cameron turned and lifted his binoculars to the south-west, scanning the horizon until he located the telltale grey smudge. In minutes, a black speck appeared, its shape slowly coalescing into the familiar angles of a steamship. From its course, Cameron judged it would sail directly past them, and he called down through the open skylight of the *Beluga*'s cabin to his wife and daughter, who rushed up to the aft deck to watch it pass.

Standing on the quarterdeck, Cameron strained through the binoculars to see the ship's flag as she approached, figuring her to be a British or Japanese tramp. She was a freighter, certainly, painted entirely black from hull to superstructure, and he judged her to be perhaps four hundred feet in length but without any obvious identifying features. He could make out the perpendicular bow slicing through the ocean, a three-tiered bridge set forward of amidships, a single funnel rising behind it, and derricks suspended skeletally above the decks fore and aft. But when the *Beluga*'s chief officer took the binoculars, he noticed something unusual.

'By God, Captain,' he remarked, 'I don't know her nationality, but she carries the largest crew I've ever seen.'

Cameron grabbed the binoculars back and took a closer look at the approaching ship, making out at least sixty crewmen in regulation man-o'-war sweaters standing behind the rails. For the first time, he sensed something awry about this encounter. He knew the British Navy had converted freighters into armed warships to supplement its forces and wondered whether this might be one, patrolling the Pacific islands from its base in Australia.

Just then, Mary and Juanita, who had gone below to change into their best frocks, re-emerged to greet the first new human faces they had seen in nearly two months. The little girl was waving cheerfully as the hulking black steamer drew closer, but it suddenly decreased its speed and turned towards them as a flag was hoisted from the jackstaff on its aft deck. Focusing the binoculars for a clearer view of the flag, Cameron felt a sudden chill in the pit of his stomach as he saw, framed inside the lenses, a black cross against a white background, a taloned eagle at its centre and horizontal black, white and red stripes in the top-left corner.

The German naval ensign flapped in the South Sea breeze as a second flag rose above the freighter's bridge, and Cameron swung the binoculars in that direction to see it spell out the three-letter international signal to heave-to and prepare to be boarded. He was still reeling from shock when two hinged iron sections of the black steamer's bulwarks suddenly crashed down, clanging against the hull as the barrels of two hydraulic guns swung out over the waves. With a hollow crack, one of the guns fired a shell, which arced over the *Beluga* and exploded in the sea beyond her, sending a plume of white water ten feet into the air.

It was in that moment that Cameron knew without doubt that this black freighter was a German commerce-raider and that his family had become prisoners of war, however incomprehensible it seemed on this empty sea more than ten thousand miles from the Western Front. Turning aft, he saw Mary twenty feet away, leaning against the wheelhouse with all colour drained from her face; from her look of transfixed terror, he knew that every story of Hun sadism she had absorbed from the newspapers over the past two years was now flooding her mind. Resting against her, his daughter had stopped waving and was looking back at him uncertainly.

Cameron shouted to his crew to draw in the *Beluga*'s sails, then rushed over to take Mary's hand. The look they exchanged was a wordless confirmation of their shared dread. The closer the black raider approached, the more flimsy and insignificant the *Beluga* seemed. The Germans were preparing to winch a launch off the port beam and Cameron hustled his wife and daughter into the cabin below, where they sat wordlessly on the sofa, staring into space. Juanita sensed the foreboding and began to whimper. When one of the *Beluga*'s crewmen called through the skylight that the launch was pulling alongside, Mary quickly rose, walked over to the bed and retrieved one of her husband's pistols from under the mattress. Stan would later say that the look of bloodless fear in her face stayed with him for months. 'Suddenly she threw both her arms around my neck,' he wrote, 'and drew my head into such a position that she could look into my eyes, and said, "Stanley, I want you to promise me that they will never get Juanita."'

As Stan Cameron emerged from the cabin, pausing to compose himself, he saw ten blue-uniformed German sailors leaping aboard the *Beluga* with pistols drawn. Standing on the quarterdeck, almost rigid with fear, he was disorientated when a young lieutenant strode up to him, saluted, and asked in perfect American-inflected English, 'Are you the captain of this vessel?' Cameron replied in the affirmative, and the German, after asking a few more questions about the *Beluga*'s origin and destination, announced with brisk formality, 'Captain, I take charge of your vessel in the name of the German Imperial Navy.' At this, he signalled his crew to haul down the American flag from the *Beluga*'s halyard and raise the German ensign in its place.

Amidships, the Germans were unpacking a black case containing twenty pairs of handcuffs and several small explosive devices, while the *Beluga*'s crew were searched for weapons. The explosives needed no explanation; under international 'prize' law, the Germans were entitled to seize the ship's cargo and destroy her as an enemy vessel. With as much surprise as relief, Cameron saw that the Germans were following the rules of sea warfare to the letter – having fired a warning shot to stop him, they had made no attempt to attack the ship and were now, with remarkable efficiency and discipline, taking a detailed inventory of his stores and equipment, signalling the results across to their captain aboard the freighter. The black raider, Cameron learned from the lieutenant, bore a name that required no translation: *Wolf*. Yet, as sinister as their vessel sounded, these men bore no resemblance to the savage 'Huns' of the wartime newspaper reports. Even the handcuffs proved superfluous, as the Germans directed the *Beluga*'s crew to help sort through the ship's supplies. The German officer introduced himself as Leutnant Ernst Szielasko and ordered the *Beluga*'s cook to come up to the quarterdeck, whereupon he requested a hearty meal for everyone on board and assigned one of his men to assist.

It was during this strangely amiable meal that Cameron, seeking any intimation he could get from the German officer about their intentions, discovered that Szielasko had been a merchant seaman like himself and had acquired his American accent while working on freighters operating along the West Coast of the United States. To Cameron's surprise, the German not only proved familiar with San Francisco but also revealed he had once been a crewman aboard the steamship *Roanoke*, on which Cameron himself had served. Szielasko explained that most of the *Wolf*'s crew were merchant seamen like him, from the German equivalent of the naval reserve. He assured Cameron that his family would not be harmed, despite being prisoners of war. His men, meanwhile, were fussing over Juanita so much that the little girl had quickly overcome her fear, ecstatic to have new company after eight weeks of tedium. Even Mary began to relax as she listened to Szielasko sharing sailing stories with her husband.

At sunset, the Camerons were finishing their meal when a signal from the *Wolf* sparked a rush of activity among the Germans. Szielasko told the couple a steamship was approaching from the south and the *Wolf* was setting off in pursuit, so the *Beluga* would rendezvous with the raider the following day. The barque's sails were unfurled, the raider's engines rumbled into life and in the fading light both ships moved off in separate directions.

Two hours later, Cameron was on deck when a freighter appeared in the moonlit waters to the north-east, heading towards Sydney. As she passed the *Beluga*, a Morse-lamp flashed on the ship's bridge, identifying her as the Australian cargo steamer *Fiona* and requesting the *Beluga*'s response. Cameron watched helplessly from the bridge of his captured ship while the Germans ignored the signal, and the freighter steamed past them heading south-west towards the very port he had come so tantalisingly close to reaching. In minutes, the *Fiona* disappeared into the darkness.

For Mary, the night passed torturously. Fearful for Juanita, distraught at being robbed of her reunion with her parents, she lay in the *Beluga*'s bunk unable to sleep, alert to every creak of the ship's hull and footfall of the German guards on the deck above.

In the morning, she and Stan rose to find no sign of the black raider. The Germans were sorting through the spoils of their capture, and Szielasko apologetically informed them they would be permitted to keep only essential items from their wardrobes, as most of their clothing was needed aboard the *Wolf*. The couple watched helplessly as their belongings were piled on the deck alongside the *Beluga*'s food stores, medical supplies, tools, a hundred cases of benzine and any remotely useful item the Germans could find.

In the course of that long, torpid day adrift in the Pacific, Stan Cameron learned several things that deepened his sense of foreboding about what lay ahead. The German navigating officer and boatswain proved as affable as Leutnant Szielasko – like him, they spoke fluent English and had worked as merchant seamen in the United States, until they returned to the fatherland to enlist when the war broke out. The clothing, they explained, was needed because the uniforms of the *Wolf*'s crew were disintegrating after more than seven months at sea; even Mary's long underwear would be handy for use as bandages. Cameron was incredulous to hear that, since leaving Germany in late 1916, the raider had never once pulled into port, instead plundering coal, food and supplies from the ships it had attacked. The crews of those ships were now held captive aboard the *Wolf*, but what plans the German captain had for them his men could not tell, for they knew little of their mission or where it would take them next. How the raider had come to be here in the South Pacific, Stan could not piece together, and how the crew had endured the voyage he could barely fathom. But it seemed from what the men said that they had already crossed the Atlantic, Indian and Southern oceans, and were now heading north towards the Dutch East Indies.

The Germans bantered amiably with Juanita and treated Mary with deference, for they had not seen a woman or child since leaving home. But for Mary this was hardly a reassurance, and the night again passed without sleep. At dawn the next day, she went above deck with Stan to find the hulking black presence of the *Wolf* standing three hundred yards distant. The raider had arrived silently in the pre-dawn darkness and four lifeboats were already being winched down to collect the benzine and other supplies stacked on the *Beluga*'s deck. Szielasko appeared and told them the *Wolf*'s captain had modified his instructions and would now permit the Camerons to take as many personal possessions as they wished, so Stan and Mary began searching through the piled stores to retrieve clothes, shoes, Mary's sewing machine and whatever else of value they could find. As they searched, they heard the drone of a motor and looked up to see a biplane appear in the distance, then descend slowly to fly a loop over the raider and disappear. It was, Szielasko explained, the raider's own seaplane, signalling the all-clear.

By one o'clock, the transfer of stores was complete and the Camerons were told to climb aboard one of the lifeboats with the crew. As they cast off from the *Beluga*, Stan was angered to see the deck rail of the *Wolf* lined with a procession of grinning German faces, filling Mary with renewed fear as they drew closer to the ship. With Juanita on his shoulders, Stan climbed the wooden steps of a rope ladder to the raider's deck; Mary followed, refusing the offer of a winched wicker chair, despite the heavy swell and her exhaustion. They were met by a grey-moustachioed senior officer who introduced himself as Kapitänleutnant Karl Schmehl, the first officer. Addressing Stan in perfect English, he said, 'Tell your wife and little girl that they have nothing to fear, that we are not the Huns you probably think we are.' To complete the incongruous courtesies, a cook appeared from the mess and leaned down to present Juanita with a glass of milk and a dish of pudding.

Taken below the poop deck, the Camerons found themselves in a walkway between decks, where they were led to their quarters – a cramped and unventilated storeroom, which a crewman was still cleaning out. As they peered into this iron-walled bunker, throngs of men shuffled past them, not just crewmen but prisoners of different nationalities – British, Indian, European, African – most with bare torsos and shaved heads, dressed only in ragged shorts or pants. Some were climbing up to the poop deck, where they exercised; others were heading back towards a hatch door that took them down to a hold, where the *Beluga*'s crew members had been taken. There appeared to be scores of these men, grimy and sweaty, casting dulled but curious glances at Mary as they trooped past. Pointing to the storeroom, the German first officer, Schmehl, said this would be the family's quarters if they wanted to stay together; alternatively, Mary and Juanita could be given a room below the bridge and Stan could remain here and visit them daily. Defiantly, however, Mary refused to be separated from her husband. Stan was wondering how his wife and daughter could possibly withstand the indignity of these quarters when the *Wolf*'s captain suddenly appeared before them.

Impeccably dressed in a spotless dark uniform, the German skipper was a trim and compact man whom Stan estimated to be around forty. Slightly built, with a squared-off face and hawkish nose softened by an almost feminine mouth, he carried himself with an air of implacable authority. In halting English and with utmost formality, he introduced himself as Kapitän Karl Nerger and apologised to Cameron for capturing the *Beluga*, saying he would have passed the ship by had he known a woman and child were aboard. Having revealed his vessel, he had been forced to take the Camerons aboard and would have to destroy the *Beluga*, but he would release them as soon as it proved possible to do so without jeopardising his own crew's safety. In the meantime, he would arrange a room for them in his officers' quarters, where Stan would be permitted to stay on the condition that he not speak to the crew or prisoners. With that, the captain withdrew, orders were snapped and the Camerons were led up to a stateroom on the berth deck. There, the crew rigged up a specially made hammock for Juanita and brought in the family's belongings.

In the relative comfort of this cabin, Stan and Mary sat on their bunk in bewildered silence. They had fallen into the hands of the feared Germans – but Germans with impeccable English and unfailing manners. Could these affable pirates, with their apologies and assurances, be taken at their word? They were still mulling over these contradictions an hour later when a crewman appeared in the doorway holding a wad of cotton batting. The *Beluga* was about to be fired on and sunk, he announced, and the family were advised to stuff their ears. The captain had given permission for Stan to watch from the boat deck.

Leaving Mary and Juanita in the cabin, Stan climbed a gangway to a vantage point high up behind the bridge, where the ship's six lifeboats were suspended from iron davits. Here, he looked backwards and saw the other prisoners on the poop deck, where they had gathered to watch the spectacle of the *Beluga*'s demise. In the fading light of dusk, Cameron estimated there were nearly a hundred men crowded down there. The *Beluga* was sitting at anchor two miles distant, her holds still filled with several hundred barrels of benzine. Twenty years earlier in Alaska, the little whaler had been burnt to the waterline in a horrendous fire and completely rebuilt to sail again, but there was to be no returning from this isolated spot in the Pacific. The *Wolf*'s forward guns erupted just as the sun touched the horizon, and Cameron flinched as 5.9-inch shells careened wildly around his little ship, falling harmlessly into the ocean fore, aft and beyond her. He counted eighteen missed shots and was silently marvelling at the Germans' lousy aim when a shell finally slammed into the old whaler's wooden hull, sending an angry shot of flame arcing across the orange sky. Suddenly, the little barque was ruptured by muffled explosions as canisters of benzine detonated inside her hold, some rocketing through the air, spraying plumes of red flame, others erupting inside her until fire blossomed slowly from the ship's centre and spread across the surface of the surrounding ocean like a molten tide.

Down in the stateroom, Mary Cameron heard the dull boom of the explosions through the wadding in her ears and hugged Juanita as the *Wolf* rocked from the concussion of the guns discharging. Even without witnessing the *Beluga*'s destruction, Mary's last vestige of stoicism crumbled with the loss of the ship that was to have taken her home, and something unravelled within her at that moment. On the deck above, Stan watched the spectacle with horrified awe. He would later record the scene in his memoir:

> The sea for miles around us was covered in burning petrol. The weather was almost calm, and occasionally a cat's paw of wind would come along and cause this flaming field of oil to run in various directions, opening a path of black water through a sea of flames. As soon as this cat's paw was over, the flames would run together again. When the spars fell out of the ship, the splash was not of water but a veritable cataract of flames. Even the Germans were impressed by the picture of three square miles of burning sea, leaping thirty feet high and raging for hours. God! It was a wonderful thing. In fact, the sight was so great that I did not realise that it was my own little home that was going up in flames.

Later in life, the terrible beauty of that spectacle would become one of Stan Cameron's recurring nightmares. It was as if their little sailing ship had been atomised, a remnant of a bygone world laid waste by the fearful technology of the new.

2

SUICIDE SHIPS

The chain of events that led the Cameron family into the path of the German raider *Wolf* had been set in motion two years earlier, many thousands of miles away on a calm afternoon on the Irish Channel, when an eighteen-year-old lookout aboard the British luxury ocean-liner *Lusitania* saw a phosphorescent burst of foam break the surface of the sea five hundred yards off the ship's starboard bow. As a thin line of bubbles tracked inexorably across the ocean's surface towards the ship, the lookout knew with certain horror what he was witnessing, but his cry of 'Torpedoes coming on the starboard side!' was lost on the afternoon breeze; even before he had run down to alert his brother below decks, the 30,000-ton liner was shaken as if by an enormous hammer-blow, followed seconds later by a rumbling deep within her core. The iron superstructure of the bridge began buckling and tearing in an eruption of flame, steam and smoke, and coal dust belched from the funnels and rained down on panicked passengers rushing to the upper decks. A complete power failure crippled the ship and she lurched thirty degrees to starboard, but the *Lusitania* kept moving, as if still on course for Liverpool. In the confusion that followed, an officer mistakenly halted the loading of the lifeboats and assured everyone the ship was safe.

The fastest ocean-liner on earth, the *Lusitania* was that day carrying more than 700 crew members and 1257 passengers, nearly two hundred of them Americans who had boarded in New York. Many felt the succession of explosions that shook the ship as cold water flooded into her engine rooms and blew her boilers, unleashing steam and scalding water at a pressure of 200 pounds per square inch. The heavy tilt of the deck to starboard made it impossible to launch lifeboats on the port side; passengers below were trapped in darkness and chaos. The *Lusitania* took eighteen minutes to sink, her bow striking the bottom of the channel in barely more than three hundred feet of water, so that those few survivors who had scrambled into the six lifeboats that were launched recalled watching the ship's immense stern and propellers rise above them and hang, suspended there momentarily, until they finally slid below the waves in a geyser of steam and smoke. Of the 1198 people who perished, thirty-five were infants.

The sinking of the *Lusitania* by the German submarine *U-20* immediately became the most reviled 'massacre' of the First World War. Kaiser Wilhelm II stood condemned as a murderer of innocent women and children, caricatured in Allied newspapers as a cloaked prince of darkness trailed by the ghosts of pleading naked cherubs. One hundred and twenty-eight American passengers had died, sparking a political crisis between Germany and the United States, which had remained steadfastly neutral since the war had begun. But the revulsion and horror that greeted the ship's destruction marked something more profound; it was the overturning of an old and enduring notion of warfare as a noble endeavour governed by rules of fairness and decency. War, German Field Marshal Helmuth von Moltke said in 1898, was part of the 'divine' plan that revealed man's noblest virtues. The torpedoing of a defenceless passenger-liner by an unseen submarine revealed the hollowness of such illusions and showed that technology had changed warfare irrevocably. New weapons had created their own rules.

As recently as 1907 and 1908, the great military powers had gathered in The Hague and London to set limits on the deployment of aerial bombs, sea mines, submarines, torpedoes and other mechanised weapons that augured a scale of carnage even generals feared to contemplate. These peace conferences, which had begun in 1899 with the lofty purpose of banning all new weapons, produced more than half a million pages of written deliberations and a vast array of painstakingly negotiated rules governing land and sea warfare. Their most ambitious achievement was the final Hague Declaration of 1907, a monument to 'Right, Justice and the Spirit of Peace and of International Concord', which was doomed to failure long before the assassination of Archduke Franz Ferdinand of Austria triggered the hostilities of August 1914. For, although all of the great powers had participated in the Hague deliberations, none had ever formally ratified its rules of war and few generals seriously contemplated abiding by them. The sinking of the *Lusitania* was by no stretch the first hostile act of the First World War that broke an international covenant.

Britain had planned, since at least 1911, that in the event of war with the Kaiser it would deploy its navy to create a 'distant blockade' of Germany and cut off the country's food supplies, notwithstanding that this would be entirely illegal according to rules of naval warfare that had been observed for nearly six decades. And when Germany invaded neutral Belgium in August 1914 – contravening one of the Hague Declaration's most fundamental tenets – Britain immediately implemented its blockade by dispatching its warships and minelayers into the North Sea. This had in turn spurred Germany's retaliatory announcement, in February 1915, that it would enforce a similar blockade against Britain by allowing its submarines to wage unrestricted warfare against every ship that ventured into the North Sea.

Behind the thundering indignation that each combatant hurled at the other for these infractions at sea, Britain's blockade and Germany's U-boat campaign shared a common purpose: to starve the enemy into submission. Britain's naval-intelligence chief, Sir Charles Ottley, had once predicted that the Royal Navy could cut off Germany's sea-trade so ruthlessly that 'grass would sooner or later grow in the streets of Hamburg and widespread dearth and ruin would be inflicted'. (The fact that Sir Charles made this comment less than a year after he helped negotiate the Hague Declaration suggests why it was doomed to fail.) Freighters destined for Germany passed through one of two narrow channels – either the North Sea between Scotland and Norway or the English Channel between Britain and France – which Britain aimed to choke off. Yet Britain itself, as an island nation that imported more than sixty per cent of its food, was arguably even more vulnerable to such economic warfare. British Admiral Sir John 'Jacky' Fisher had warned in 1906 that 'it's not invasion we have to fear if our navy is beaten. It's starvation.' Thus, both countries had always known that any confrontation between them might ultimately become a gruelling contest of slow economic strangulation, a trade war that would be fought entirely at sea.

Even six months into the war, that eventuality was taking shape. The horrendous and irresolvable carnage of Ypres and Lorraine suggested that, as Germany's Admiral Alfred von Tirpitz would later tell the Kaiser, the key to victory was freight. The problem for both Britain and Germany was that waging commerce war was no simple matter, for the oceans are the shared territory of all nations and thus governed by complex rules of engagement that had been developed over centuries. It was precisely these rules that Britain had broken with its 'distant blockade', invoking the wrath not just of Germany but also of neutral trading nations such as the United States. By using its navy to stop and search all freighters in the North Sea, Britain had deliberately contravened both the 1909 Declaration of London and the 1846 Treaty of Paris, which stipulated that naval blockades must be confined to within three miles of an enemy's shoreline. Even more egregiously, Germany's consequent campaign of indiscriminate submarine warfare had broken a long-accepted covenant that passenger-liners and neutral freighters should never come under attack from warships.

In response, both countries invoked the argument that modern weaponry had made the old rules redundant. Britain asserted that its navy could not possibly enforce a close blockade of Germany in an era of long-range cannons, mines, aircraft and submarines, all of which would decimate its ships. Germany argued that its submarines were similarly unable to comply with the prize rules of commerce warfare. Under those rules, which stretched back to the Napoleonic era, certain ships were guaranteed safe passage in wartime, specifically passenger-liners and the freighters of neutral nations. And while combatant nations were permitted to attack each other's trading ships, the civilian crews and passengers aboard these vessels were not to be harmed. A warship wanting to attack the freighter of an enemy nation was therefore obligated to act out an elaborate ritual of search-and-seizure: it would fire a warning shot, send across a boarding party, permit all crew and passengers to disembark and then tow the ship to a neutral port, where her status could be adjudicated by a prize court.

A submarine, Germany argued, could not possibly perform this tricky *pas de deux* because it contained no room for prisoners, carried insufficient crew to commandeer a freighter and was vulnerable to being fired on by ships that carried defensive guns. Furthermore, Britain's first lord of the Admiralty, Winston Churchill, had 'despicably' altered the customs of sea warfare by authorising Allied merchant captains to fly false neutral flags (a practice outlawed by the Hague Declaration) and by dispatching into the North Sea 'Q-boats' – heavily armed decoy ships that looked like freighters and flew false neutral flags but were designed to lure German submarines to the surface and destroy them. England had 'unscrupulously outraged all the fundamental principles of the old maritime law', thundered Tirpitz, leaving Germany no choice but to unleash its U-boats without restriction.

Tirpitz, in common with much of Germany's military leadership, was a man who gave little thought to the battlefield of public opinion: his sympathy for the men, women and children killed on the *Lusitania* was so limited that he later accused them of 'wanton recklessness' in boarding the ship. Later, it would be revealed that the *Lusitania* was carrying a secret cargo of armaments that may have ignited, hastening the ship's destruction. But in May 1915 the worldwide revulsion directed at Germany forced the Kaiser to rethink his trade-war strategy. The United States was in uproar over the deaths of its citizens. Former president Theodore Roosevelt was demanding that the country go to war against Germany. Newspapers were calling it 'a massacre', a 'crime' and 'the most momentous moral crisis since the crucifixion of Christ'. A retired United States admiral had called for the Kaiser, Tirpitz and the entire *Admiralstab* to be hanged.

Alarmed at the prospect of war with America, Wilhelm II defused the crisis by quietly ordering his U-boats to avoid attacks on passenger-ships and neutral freighters, leaving his admirals to ponder how they could starve the English if their submarine fleet was constrained by the damnable rules of war. The solution they turned to was a weapon as old as sailing ships themselves: the commerce-raider.

* *

In naval warfare, commerce-raiders played a role akin to piracy, earning themselves a place in the popular imagination that harked back to an older and more buccaneering era of sea warfare. Although subject to military command, raider-captains were lone operators who enjoyed enormous latitude for independent action and subterfuge. They were bandits, outside the conventional chain of command.

In the American Civil War, the Confederate Navy raider *Alabama* had attained folkloric status in Britain and America after an extraordinary two-year voyage in which she destroyed or captured sixty-five ships destined for the northern states, evading fleets of Yankee warships sent to destroy her. Captain Raphael Semmes, the commander of this sleek British-built sailing ship, was a veteran navy officer who affected a waxed moustache and an image of a Southern gentleman pirate. His modus operandi became the blueprint for the German captains who followed him six decades later: with his guns hidden behind bulwarks and a false flag flying from his mainmast, Semmes overhauled ships bringing supplies to the northern states, fired a warning shot across their bows, stole their cargoes and imprisoned their crews, then burned the ships to the waterline.

The *Alabama*'s 75,000-mile campaign of privateering ranged from Britain down through the Atlantic Ocean to Brazil, across the Indian Ocean to Singapore and India, then back via South Africa, achieving such infamy that it was commemorated in folk songs, fictionalised in dime-store novels and debated in hyperbolic newspaper coverage. After the ship was finally sunk by a United States gunship in June 1864, during an all-out battle off the coast of France that killed twenty-six of her crew, the *Manchester Guardian* exaggerated only slightly when it claimed that Semmes had single-handedly 'paralysed the commerce of a great nation'.

The aura of doomed romanticism that attached itself to raiders had been rekindled in the early months of the First World War by the exploits of one German warship in particular. In August 1914, the *Emden*, a medium-sized cruiser in the Kaiser's China fleet, was dispatched on a raiding campaign in the oceans around southern Asia under the command of her aristocratic captain, Karl von Müller. In just three months, Müller sank fifteen Allied freighters and staged daring attacks on the ports of Madras and Penang, where he set fire to oil tanks and destroyed a Russian and French warship, in the process earning himself increasingly adulatory press coverage, even in Britain. Prisoners released from the *Emden* described Müller as an affable gentleman who would happily converse in his cabin over a whisky and soda, and who assiduously observed the Hague rules of combat; he had left neutral ships unmolested, had rescued drowning crewmen from the French destroyer despite great risk to his own ship and took great care during the Madras bombardment to avoid civilian casualties.

The *Emden*'s exploits came to a horrific end on 9 November during a confrontation with the Australian light-cruiser HMAS

Sydney off the Cocos Islands, north-west of Australia, when a fusillade of shells from the *Sydney* ignited the raider's ammunition battery, engulfing her in an inferno that killed 130 men and horrifically injured scores more. In response, *The Times*, the *Daily Chronicle* and the *Daily Telegraph* published effusive tributes to Müller's chivalry and courage. 'It is almost in our heart to regret that the *Emden* has been captured and destroyed,' eulogised the *Telegraph*. 'The war on the sea will lose some of its piquancy, its humour and its interest now that the *Emden* has gone.' For its part, the *Chicago Tribune* judged the raider's exploits to be 'without parallel since the famous *Alabama* of the Confederate States was roaming the ocean'. The commerce-raider, in the eyes of these editorial-writers, was the antithesis of the devious and unsporting U-boat, a vestige of more gentlemanly traditions of warfare.

A less nostalgic view held sway in the German Navy, where the limited life expectancy of these ships was well known. Of the seven raiders Germany dispatched in the first year of the war, three were sunk after being attacked by Allied warships, one was destroyed by an internal explosion and three were forced to give themselves up in neutral ports. Although they destroyed 352,000 tons of shipping and caused significant disruption to Britain, the head of the High Seas Fleet, Admiral Hugo von Pohl, was dismissive of their role. Among ordinary German sailors, they earned the sobriquet *Himmelfahrtsdampfer* – suicide ships.

The problem with these early 'auxiliary cruisers', as they were officially known, was that they were either warships or converted ocean-liners, which consumed coal so quickly that they soon became dependent on fuel-ships and thus lacked mobility and range. In August 1915, a young naval-reserve officer named Theodor Wolf proposed a simple solution. Only twenty-nine years old, Wolf was a student of commerce-raiding and pointed out that an ordinary freighter, while much slower than a warship or passenger-liner, used far less fuel and possessed infinitely more storage space for both mines and prisoners. Such a ship could, unlike a submarine, be sent on a long-range mission and could operate within the Hague rules while maintaining its guise as an ordinary merchant steamer. Several months after the *Lusitania* sinking, Admiral Pohl grudgingly took up the suggestion, and in November 1915 a single-funnel 4788-ton freighter called the *Pungo* was recommissioned as the naval raider SMS (*Seiner Majestaet's Schiff* – His Majesty's Ship) *Moewe*.

Fitted out with two torpedo tubes and four guns, SMS *Moewe* cut a path of destruction through the Atlantic that surprised Pohl and prompted a rethink within the *Admiralstab*. The ship's weapons were cleverly hidden behind drop-down doors in the deck wall, which naval engineers had created by cutting out sections of the bulwark with oxyacetylene torches and reattaching them with hinges. Her masts had been rebuilt with telescopic mechanisms so they could be lowered and raised, and sheet-iron panels were carried on board to alter the appearance of her funnel and superstructure. In an era when identifying a ship was largely a matter of staring through binoculars at a silhouette on the horizon, the *Moewe* had been able to slip through the North Sea blockade and into the Atlantic under a false Swedish flag just before Christmas, carrying 500 mines and a crew of 219 men.

Her commander, an urbane and goateed thirty-six-year-old *korvettenkapitän* named Nikolaus Burggraf und Graf zu Dohna-Schlodien, laid minefields off Scotland, Ireland and southern France that destroyed three freighters and the battleship *King Edward VI*; then, disguising his ship variously as a P&O liner, a Swedish freighter and an Argentine transport, Dohna-Schlodien embarked on a raiding mission in which he sank seven British freighters, captured more than two hundred prisoners and seized £50,000 worth of gold bullion and cargo in less than a week. An eighth victim, the British passenger-liner *Appam*, he converted into a floating prison under the command of a junior officer, Leutnant Hans Berg, who sailed the *Appam* to the east coast of the still-neutral United States in early January to seek refuge under the United States–Prussia treaty of 1799.

The *Appam*'s arrival in Rhode Island's Newport Harbor on 1 February 1916 was a minor sensation that alerted the British Government to Germany's new commerce-raiding campaign. Aboard his prize ship, the garrulous Berg impressed journalists with his 'very pleasant manner' and boasted that the elusive *Moewe* was just one of nine surface-raiders being readied to wage war against British commerce. The *New York Times* praised the Germans' courteous treatment of women and their efforts to avoid casualties, judging the *Moewe*'s achievements to be 'as wonderful as any exploit of the *Emden*'. The *Moewe*, meanwhile, continued her raiding sallies in the southern Atlantic, and Dohna-Schlodien capped off his two-month mission by sinking six more ships and evading the blockade to return to Kiel, the first raider-captain to return his crew safely to port. For this achievement, the Kaiser personally bestowed on him the ultimate German military honour, the *Pour le Mérite*, colloquially known as the Blue Max. (Hans Berg was less fortunate: the *leutnant* and his crew were thrown into a Texas prison after the United States Government, signalling its deteriorating relations with Germany, refused to recognise the *Appam* as a legitimate prize of war.)

Berg's boast that Germany possessed a fleet of nine commerce-raiders proved only a mild exaggeration, for two more had already been dispatched in the weeks before the *Moewe* returned and at least one other was being readied. Their reputation as 'suicide ships' would, however, prove difficult to shake. SMS *Greif* was at sea only two days when her captain made the fateful decision to send a brief wireless message to Berlin, unaware that the British Government's most secretive defence-intelligence agency, Room 40, was intercepting all German military broadcasts. Having established the *Greif*'s position off Norway, Room 40 alerted the Admiralty, and a contingent of British warships was sent to destroy the raider, with the loss of all ninety-seven men aboard her.

Another raider, the ten-year-old freighter *Belgravia*, left Wilhelmshaven in north-west Germany on 26 February 1916 but ran aground on a sandbank in the mouth of the Elbe River as she headed out towards the North Sea. Weighed down by 600 mines in her stern and 7000 tons of coal in her holds, the ship buckled, broke her back and was towed ignominiously down the Elbe to Hamburg. Her captain, whose intended mission was to attack trade off India and South Africa, never even had a chance to perform the ritual rechristening of his ship with her raider-name. She was to have become SMS *Wolf*.

* *

By the time the *Belgravia* was scuttled in Hamburg, Admiral Pohl was dying of cancer and a conviction had grown firmer within the German military that victory against Britain could only be achieved by starving its people into submission. Nearly two years of land war in Europe and Russia had delivered a stalemate at horrendous cost. The encounter at sea between the two nations' naval fleets in May 1916 at Jutland had merely reinforced Britain's unassailable dominance. The German people were on bread rations as the British blockade cut off imports of food and agricultural fertiliser, and Pohl's successor, Admiral Reinhard Scheer, delivered some sobering news to the Kaiser a month after Jutland. 'A victorious end to the war at not too distant a date,' he said, 'can only be looked for by the crushing of English economic life through U-boat action against English commerce.'

While the Kaiser agonised about whether to resume unrestricted submarine attacks, Scheer authorised a new campaign by surface-raiders, the plan this time being to send raiders into the Atlantic, Pacific and Indian oceans. In Kiel, the *Moewe* was refitted for another mission under the command of Kapitän Dohna-Schlodien, while in Hamburg two new naval officers were selected to run the blockade. One was Count Felix von Luckner, a charming and debonair nobleman who would be given command of a 150-foot three-masted sailing ship rechristened the *Seeadler*. The other was a forty-one-year-old career officer, Korvettenkapitän Karl August Nerger, who was instructed to take charge of the crew of the ill-fated *Belgravia* and select a new ship to take its place as SMS *Wolf*.

In the highly stratified German Navy, Karl Nerger was something of an outsider. The son of a Prussian headmaster from the shipping city of Rostock, on the Baltic Sea in northern Germany, Nerger had contemplated studying architecture before deciding on a naval career at nineteen, and by twenty-one he had sailed to England, Sweden, Norway, the Mediterranean and India. By the early 1900s, however, he had fallen from grace in the eyes of the navy's social hierarchy by entering into a love affair with Marie Friedrichson, the dark-eyed daughter of a dockyard worker, who became pregnant by Nerger at the age of sixteen. The *Admiralstab* so frowned upon unions between its officers and women of a lower social caste that it routinely forbade them from marrying. Although Nerger's beloved Marie gave birth to three sons and a daughter between 1904 and 1910, the couple had never been granted a dispensation to marry.

But, in the eyes of at least some senior *Admiralstab* figures, Nerger had one quality that recommended him above all others for SMS *Wolf*. In 1900, he had served as first-lieutenant aboard the German warship *Iltis* when she was nearly destroyed by cannon fire while suppressing the Boxer Uprising in China alongside the British, French and Russian allies. Nerger had walked away unscathed from the mangled *Iltis*, even though the ship took sixteen cannon-hits, which killed eight men and severely wounded thirty, including the captain. Fourteen years later, Nerger had again come close to death in the Battle of Heligoland, one of the earliest First World War confrontations between the British and German navies. A contingent of British warships had subjected Nerger's ship, the *Stettin*, to a five-minute bombardment so ferocious that the surrounding sea was likened to a cauldron, yet legend had it that he strode up and down the bridge imperviously puffing a cigar, until the smoke cleared to reveal that only one shell had hit its target. 'For the completion of the tasks placed before SMS *Wolf*,' noted an *Admiralstab* memo, apparently in all seriousness, 'it is absolutely essential that the leader of the enterprise is not only efficient, but is also lucky.'

From the moment he came aboard the crippled *Belgravia* in April 1916, Nerger took to his new commission with a ruthlessly exacting eye. After searching among the laid-up freighters in the Hamburg dry dock, he chose a black-hulled modern merchant steamship of the Hansa line, the *Wachtfels*, and arranged for the navy to purchase her. The ship had barely been at sea since she was built in 1913, and her skipper had maintained her in such pristine condition that her brass fittings were polished to a mirror-gleam. Outwardly, there was little to distinguish the *Wachtfels* from hundreds of single-funnelled German freighters plying the world's trade routes. A little over 440 feet long and 56 feet wide, her white superstructure sat well forward, its three levels housing the bridge, captain's cabin, officers' quarters, wireless room and surgery. Behind the bridge rose a single funnel carrying smoke from a 2800-horsepower engine down in the bowels of the ship, where coal furnaces heated three boilers that pumped high-pressure steam to the pistons and through the heating system. Cargo holds fore and aft could be converted into crew and prisoner quarters, or bunkers for coal and mines. With a capacity of 5809 tons and a top speed of 10.5 knots, the *Wachtfels* could muster less than half the speed of a battle-cruiser. But Nerger had other priorities, for after inspecting the ship he had devised a raiding mission no one had ever attempted.

The *Admiralstab*'s instructions to Nerger were the same as those issued to the blighted captain of the *Belgravia*: to reach the Indian Ocean and create chaos along British trade routes. 'The approaches to the most important ports of British India and British South Africa, as well as the interconnecting trade routes, are to be contaminated with mines,' his operational orders stated. 'The chief ports are: Colombo, Bombay, Karachi, Calcutta, Rangoon, Singapore, Cape Town – the last-named port is to be mined first and, in addition, at least five ports in such sequence as may seem fit to the captain . . . After execution of the mining tasks, war on commerce is to be pursued until all resources are exhausted. The choice of operation is left to your own judgment. Main objective for attack is the grain trade from Australia to Europe, which continues throughout the year.'

With expanded coal bunkers, the slow and economical *Wachtfels* could sustain a six-month voyage without refuelling – enough to get her to India and back – but Nerger surprised his superiors by saying he wanted to stay at sea for a year. Such a feat barely seemed plausible given that Nerger would be forced to maintain radio silence and unable to pull in to port to refuel; even the Confederate Navy's *Alabama* had periodically docked in neutral ports to rest her crew and replenish supplies. The chief of the *Admiralstab*, Admiral Henning von Holtzendorff, was sceptical; such a long mission, he warned Nerger, could only be sustained by stealing coal and food from intercepted ships, and even then the crowding of prisoners and crew would become onerous. 'I wish you luck with that,' Holtzendorff said in his last meeting with Nerger. 'But the crew won't under any circumstances bear it. No commercial steamer has ever been at war for so long.'

Nerger was undeterred and set about countering such doubts. Where the *Belgravia* had been hastily prepared for her mission, he would take six painstaking months to transform the *Wachtfels*. The primary work was done at the navy dockyards in Wilhelmshaven, where the ship pulled in to port in early May with her new captain and crew, and a false name painted on her side: *Jupiter*. Below decks, navy engineers modified the cargo holds to create crew quarters and storage holds for torpedoes and mines. The iron walls and floors of an aft hold under the poop deck were fitted with latches and stays to accommodate hammocks, benches and tables in anticipation of several hundred prisoners. As with the *Moewe*, sections of the deck-walls were cut out with blowtorches and reattached as drop-down doors to conceal the guns and torpedo tubes. At the stern, a hatch door was fitted under the poop deck on the starboard side to allow mines to be dropped overboard. Nerger oversaw the work and browbeat the navy bureaucracy into meeting the costs of his demands. He insisted the ship's hospital be expanded and fitted out so that his two young doctors, Hermann Hauswaldt and Harald Runze, could undertake major surgical procedures. He asked for his wireless crew to be supplemented by a team of specialist code-breakers, necessitating enlargements to the radio room near the bridge.

Wireless technology at sea was little more than a decade old in the First World War, and many British merchant ships still used simple crystal receivers or crude magnetic-wire contraptions with a range of only a few hundred miles. By contrast, the equipment developed by Germany's Telefunken company was extraordinarily powerful; the Telefunken transmission tower at Nauen, west of Berlin, could send signals up to 5000 miles, giving it a reach that extended to South America and China, and Nerger requested that several of the company's most powerful receivers be installed on the ship. These would be essential to the success of the mission for, although the raider would transmit no signals, its team of seven radio-operators and code-breakers would at all times be scouring local wireless frequencies to ascertain nearby ship movements and warship deployments, and to pull from the air whatever news of the war they could.

Nerger had another ace up his sleeve to augment his ship's defences, but that was to remain secret until shortly before departure. In the interim, the raider was fitted out with weapons in preparation for crew-drills. Six hydraulically mounted guns were bolted to the deck behind the hidden flap-doors, two on each side of the foredeck and one either side of the aft; a seventh was fitted to the raised poop deck, disguised by a collapsible hatch made from tarpaulins and beams. Mounted on a swivelling chassis that enabled the twenty-foot-long barrel to be rapidly swung out over the ocean, each gun fired 5.9-inch-diameter shells and required a crew of four to load and aim. Three smaller two-inch guns were stored below for later use, along with 1400 shells and sixteen torpedoes. Torpedo tubes were fitted to fore and aft decks on either side. Camouflage techniques employed on the *Moewe* and

Belgravia were refined: telescopic masts were fitted; the funnel was encased in a fake outer shell whose height and girth could be altered; smokescreen tanks were installed on the poop deck; and paint supplies in the workshop were sufficient to recoat the ship in several different colours if required.

While Nerger was able to stringently control the fit-out, he had no opportunity to hand-pick his crew, which he inherited almost wholly from the *Belgravia*. Nearly all of these 345 men were drawn from the merchant marine reserves, a disparate bunch that included more than its share of misfits. Among the few career military officers were Nerger's second-in-command, Kapitänleutnant Iwan Brandes, and a thirty-year-old gunnery *oberleutnant* named Fritz Witschetzky. Tall and slim, with fine features and a mop of blond hair, Witschetzky embodied all the haughty qualities of the young Prussian officer class that would soon provoke outright mutiny in the German Navy. He arrived aboard the ship with his pet dachshund, Hans, a camera, a kit of watercolours and brushes, an easel and a journal in which to record his impressions of the voyage, later to be published under the title *Das Schwarze Schiff* ('The Black Ship'). Witschetzky's richly overseasoned account of his adventures would depict the *Wolf*'s crew as a stoic *bruderbund* of patriots who sang cheerful Teutonic shanties as they plundered the world's seas. 'A great bunch of guys,' he wrote, 'that was the crew of the *Wolf*.'

The feeling was not mutual, according to one of the men directly under Witschetzky's command. Theodor Plivier was a twenty-four-year-old firebrand merchant seaman who enrolled in 1914 and had already spent twenty-eight days in the brig for insubordination when he was assigned to the *Belgravia*. In later life, Plivier would become one of Germany's most outspoken communist writer-agitators; in 1916, he was one among thousands of young navy reservists who had grown weary of the war and resentful of the German Navy's grossly inequitable treatment of its officers and men. In Plivier's description, the Prussian officer class was a pampered and idiotic feudal aristocracy who guzzled champagne seized from French villages and gorged themselves on cooked meals even as food shortages were reducing ordinary Germans to a diet of watery turnip gruel. His scalding memoir, *Des Kaisers Kulis* ('The Kaiser's Coolies'), portrayed the officers' mess of a German warship as a grotesque circus where 'superabundance and ostentation prevailed, whilst prejudice and class arrogance paraded themselves . . . Every gathering and every banquet was unutterably stupid.' To Plivier, Fritz Witschetzky perfectly epitomised the 'smooth-faced asses' who rose through the ranks of the Kaiserliche Marine.

The bitterness of men like Plivier was in part a result of sheer boredom: many had spent the war confined to the Wilhelmshaven and Kiel docks toiling on warships that never sailed, for the Kaiser had decreed that the High Seas Fleet must be kept intact until war's end. Subsisting on meagre rations and enduring abysmal working conditions, their contempt for the naval hierarchy festered. 'Do you think I carried wine-buckets, ironed officers' trousers, washed sleeves foul with vomit, and grinned when gracious smiles appeared beneath caps worked with oak-leaves?' Plivier asked with rhetorical bitterness. 'No, no, don't suppose that.' In his eyes, being assigned to an auxiliary raider was the ultimate punishment, for the death rate on these ships was common knowledge. The *Belgravia*'s near-disastrous grounding had confirmed the crew's worst fears and revealed their disunity, for as the steam pipes threatened to blow and the lifeboats were launched, they had plundered the ship's food and liquor supplies and traded fisticuffs over the spoils.

To unite this fractious crew, Nerger drilled them relentlessly over several months, taking the ship north from Wilhelmshaven through the Kiel Canal to the shelter of the Baltic Sea, where torpedo and gunnery routines were practised for weeks on end, along with the elaborate rituals of stopping and seizing a prize ship. In Kiel harbour, more than 6200 tons of coal was winched aboard the ship one basket at a time – a grinding labour that took weeks, leaving the crew exhausted and the ship's white superstructure coated in black grit. By late October 1916, Nerger deemed the ship almost ready; its guise as a freighter was now so convincing that even stevedores coming aboard in Kiel failed to notice the guns and torpedo tubes concealed beneath tarpaulins.

Under cover of night in early November, the ship rendezvoused at sea with a minelayer, which laboriously winched across 465 horned contact-mines for storage in the aft armoury hold. Each of these egg-shaped blue-grey iron bombs weighed nearly four hundred pounds, half of which was tightly packed explosives, and the dangers of storing such a combustible cargo in close proximity to a coal furnace generating steam pressure of more than a hundred pounds per square inch needed no explanation. The ship was a floating powderkeg, a point that had already been brought home weeks earlier when white smoke had begun billowing up from the coal bunkers and Nerger had been forced to order the removal of the entire armament store and most of the coal supply until the fire was doused.

Neither the crew nor the officers had yet learned the details of their mission, but at least one mystery was resolved out here on the Baltic. An extra derrick had been erected on the back of the ship in Wilhelmshaven, and speculation about its purpose persisted right up to the November evening when a biplane hove into view, scudded across the waves on its floats and taxied alongside. The aircraft was a Friedrichshafen FF33E, the latest model of Germany's most reliable two-seater seaplane, and it was crucial to Nerger's plans. Although it had no fixed weapons, the plane's 150-horsepower engine could take it to an altitude of 3000 feet in seventeen minutes, and it could remain airborne for more than five hours. Just as the wireless room would be Nerger's ears, this reconnaissance aircraft would be his eyes, monitoring the surrounding seas for both hazards and opportunities. As the plane taxied alongside, the extra derrick was swung out, a cable was attached and it was hauled on board. Its occupants, pilot Paul Fabeck and naval *leutnant* Matthaus Stein, were soon supervising its dismantling and storage – a task that took just a few hours, for it was constructed largely of wood and cloth, the front of its fuselage being made of plywood panels, and the tail and wings just box-girder wooden frames covered in tightly stretched fabric. By night-time, all evidence of the plane had gone; its fuselage was stored in a wooden crate on the deck and its wings had been lowered into the mine hold.

The almost obsessive secrecy that Nerger applied to such tasks reflected his determination to avoid the fate of his predecessors. The British Navy's lightning attack on the *Greif* in February had fuelled a longstanding rumour in Kiel that traitors working on the German docks and inside the Kaiserliche Marine were spying for the enemy. The rumours had strengthened during the Battle of Jutland, when British warships anticipated German fleet movements with suspicious accuracy. Like many wartime conspiracy theories, this one was a myth, for British naval intelligence hardly needed spies on the docks.

In the first year of the war, the Allies had managed to obtain the principal codes used by Germany's military, merchant-navy and diplomatic personnel – a coup made possible by the fortuitous seizure of not just one but three codebooks, from a German diplomat's luggage in Persia, a German warship in the Baltic Sea and a freighter detained in Australia. Unaware of this massive breach of security, Germany had continued to use the codes or their variants for all wireless communication, and since Britain had severed every one of Germany's undersea telecommunication cables in August 1914, the Nauen transmission tower was the country's only efficient link with the outside world.

Consequently, the Royal Navy's resident intelligence genius, Admiral William Reginald 'Blinker' Hall, had spent much of the war working with a team of British mathematicians and academics inside Room 40 in Whitehall, decoding intercepted wireless messages that revealed crucial aspects of Germany's war plans, troop deployments and ship movements. It was the Room 40 team that would, in less than two months, decipher Arthur Zimmerman's telegram inviting Mexico to invade the United States.

Nerger knew only that he wanted no one, not even the senior navy personnel in Kiel, to be aware of his departure plans or his mission. Shortly after receiving his final orders on 18 November 1916, he organised a farewell banquet for his officers in the first week of December, and on 29 November he instructed them to make preparations for one final artillery drill in the Baltic the following day. But as the ship weaved through the buoys outside Kiel under a dense fogbank shortly after 10 am on that final day of November, Nerger assembled the crew and announced they were not returning to port – their raiding mission had begun as of that moment, and they were sailing for the island of Alsen to rendezvous with a U-boat. As the men dispersed, a bosun appeared on deck with a pot of black paint and a brush on an extended pole. Leaning over the bow, he blotted out the name *Jupiter*, his brush strokes rendering the ship anonymous and signifying her new incarnation as SMS *Wolf* as she prepared to run the gauntlet of the British naval blockade.

* *

At its narrowest point, the North Sea between Norway and Scotland's Shetland Islands spans less than two hundred miles, an ocean channel the British Navy had been patrolling since August 1914 in order to stop and inspect every merchant ship it encountered. It was through this bottleneck – which was also laced with British mines and patrolled by German U-boats – that the *Wolf* threaded its way under a British flag in the first week of December 1916.

Dressed like his crew in the winter woollens of a merchant seaman, Nerger did not leave the bridge for the first week of the voyage, taking meals and what sleep he could steal on a cot as the ship left behind its U-boat escort and headed north. To avoid the blockade, the raider would be forced to sail 800 miles north towards the Arctic Circle, then arc back down through the straits between Iceland and Greenland – a passage through minus-twenty-degree-Celsius air temperatures that would be an immediate test of the resilience of the engine-room boilers.

With 6000 tons of coal and more than a hundred tons of mines in her holds, the *Wolf* was so dangerously overburdened that her load-line was several feet underwater, and any experienced seaman would immediately have recognised something incongruous about this black and white freighter labouring through the grey swell of the North Sea like a blunt plough. But Nerger would later say, with a sailor's penchant for mysticism, that he never doubted he was guided by a 'lucky star'. And the mantle of good fortune that had draped itself around him in Heligoland and China seemed still in place, for the fog helpfully obscured the *Wolf* as she passed Norway, and a Force 10 gale that swept in as she moved away from the north coast of Scotland reduced visibility to near zero. By 10 December, the ship had reached the Atlantic Ocean undetected, having scraped through the ice floes of the Denmark Strait, where winter daylight lasted a mere four hours and Theodor Plivier watched immense icebergs drift past in the dim blue light.

Once past the blockade, Nerger retreated to his cabin above the officers' mess, the refuge in which he would spend most of the voyage when he was not on the bridge. Here, he took his meals alone, accompanied only by his silky grey cat, Eve, surrounded by his charts and a bookshelf filled with the works of Kant, Schopenhauer and other German philosophers. Although Nerger periodically joined the informal gatherings of the ship – he shared Christmas dinner with his crew off the west coast of Africa and participated a few days later in the sailors' ritual baptism ceremony as the ship crossed the equator – he remained a solitary enigma to most of his men. Plivier described him as 'the loneliest man on board. He had no social intercourse with anybody, not even with the officers. Once when he came into the mess whilst they were drinking on some festive occasion, his entrance cast a gloom upon the whole company; silence fell suddenly and the gentlemen sat facing one another like snow figures.'

Nerger's iron-willed demeanour was a product of necessity. The men under him knew nothing of their mission, wore no uniform and shared a fear that they might never see Germany again. To maintain discipline, he projected an aura of ironclad authority that could, as the crew soon found out, turn swiftly to volcanic anger. Some of the men openly questioned why an officer with such a stellar record had been assigned an apparent suicide mission. 'The admirals sent him to the sky-tripper, just as they did us,' mused Plivier. 'The devil alone knows why.'

Plivier was on deck on the morning of 16 January 1917, gazing at the monotonous vista of sky and sea that had greeted him every day of the ship's six-week southward passage, when the flattened hulk of Table Mountain broke through the horizon. The *Wolf* had arrived at Cape Town, its first minelaying target, after a 7000-mile voyage that had traversed the Atlantic from north to south. As word spread through the ship and crewmen were drawn up to the deck, a lookout called down the even more startling news that a convoy of seven ships was approaching from the south. Craning in that direction, Plivier saw smoke trails slowly form into a procession of ocean-liners making their way north, escorted by a British warship – the unmistakable configuration of an Allied troop-transport convoy heading towards Europe.

The *Wolf*, on its first real day of operations, was suddenly on high alert as men rushed to the hidden torpedo and gun placements and began priming them for action. Nerger stood on the bridge under a false flag of Britain as the convoy approached. His orders stipulated that he was to avoid raiding action until he had laid most of his mines, and even from this distance he could tell that an attack on the convoy would be suicidal folly. The warship was HMS *Cornwall*, a 9800-ton armoured cruiser that had sunk the *Leipzig* during the Battle of the Falkland Islands and carried more than twice the firepower of the *Wolf*. Nerger ordered his flag lowered and raised in greeting as the cruiser approached, and for a long and anxious moment there was no response even as the two ships drew closer, until finally the *Cornwall*'s flags returned the signal. The convoy – four recommissioned passenger-liners carrying several thousand troops from Australia, and two other liners carrying South African troops, labourers and more than five million pounds in gold bullion – sailed past the *Wolf* oblivious to the catastrophe it had narrowly avoided, for by nightfall Nerger was laying his first minefield in the sea lanes through which the ships had just passed.

Minelaying was an exercise in nerve-control that initially tested even Nerger's steely disposition. Each mine was a cast-iron barrel of explosives the size of a beer-keg, its metal shell embedded with eight lead prongs containing glass vials of sulphuric acid that, if broken, would ignite two-hundred pounds of TNT. Cumbersome and yet fragile, these ugly grey eggs had to be winched up to the deck in their wheeled trolleys, lowered onto rails and trundled to the stern of the ship to be dropped overboard through a hatch underneath the poop deck – an operation that by necessity had to be executed at night, with all lights extinguished and in shallow water close to shore. The whole procedure required an exact reading of the ocean depth, for each mine was connected to a measured anchor-chain that was released after launch, touching bottom so that the mines themselves were suspended twenty feet below the surface at precisely the depth of a large steamship's submerged hull. To attempt such an exercise in the busy shipping lanes of an enemy port while masquerading as a freighter was among the most dangerous assignments in naval warfare.

Nerger took the *Wolf* within twelve miles of the coast for his first drop south of Dassen Island, setting a slow course towards Cape Town. His intention was to lay seventy-five mines in a five-mile chain across the shipping lanes that radiated out from the port, but just after 9 pm he was spooked when the *Wolf* was caught in a blaze of light that proved to be the spotlight beam of a freighter passing to the north. It was a brilliantly clear night and all movement aboard the *Wolf* froze until the freighter passed out of sight. By the time the raider had drawn closer to Cape Town, a nearly full moon had risen and spotlights from the nearby naval station had begun strafing the surrounding seas and passing over the ship as the men trundled mines to her stern. From his roost, Witschetzky could stare through his binoculars at the lights on the city's main street, and Nerger became anxious about the possibility of encountering a patrol boat on such a brightly illuminated night. In fact, there were no patrol boats – a lapse that would cause some embarrassment to the Admiralty later. But, just after midnight, when another freighter passed by so close that its every feature was sharply defined in the silvery light, Nerger abruptly called a halt after the twenty-fifth mine had been dropped and shifted course to the south-west. It was pointless, he wrote in his log later that night, to imperil his mission at such an early stage.

Two nights later, after rounding the Cape, Nerger was again bedevilled by perfect weather as he attempted to lay mines in the heavily trafficked shipping lanes that fanned out from Cape Agulhas to Durban, Ceylon and Australia. After dropping thirty-one mines in a zigzag formation, with freighters passing close by throughout the night, he decided he had already tested his luck and turned the ship east into the lower reaches of the Indian Ocean. A new moon would be in the night-time sky over Ceylon in the second week of February, and Nerger had his sights set on being there. Only days later, as the *Wolf* turned north for the 5000-mile voyage to Colombo, the minefields off South Africa claimed their first victim.

* *

On the afternoon of 26 January, as his ship SS *Matheran* approached Cape Town on a calm sea, Captain Maurice Addy was writing letters in his cabin when a thunderous boom shook the 7654-ton freighter, nearly knocking the captain off his chair and blowing the hatches off the foredeck below. Addy rushed to the bridge just as the ship was rocked by a second explosion that, invisible to the eye, had ripped a massive hole in the aft hull below the waterline. Realising the *Matheran* was doomed, the captain ordered everyone into lifeboats as the freighter, loaded with salt, industrial supplies, mail and eleven racehorses taken aboard in

Liverpool, began listing off Dassen Island. In the flooded engine room, the crew miraculously scrambled clear of the onrushing water that surged through the gash in the hull; among them was an engineer who only a year earlier had survived a torpedo attack aboard the SS *Springwell* in the Mediterranean and later testified that 'the sensation on this occasion was just the same'. The *Matheran* sank within five minutes, and it was only after a passing steamship rescued Addy and his crew that the captain realised his steward had drowned while trying to escape.

News of the sinking galvanised the Royal Navy command post in Cape Town, for that very week an anonymous postcard had arrived in the mail bearing the message: 'South African mails will be blown up. Neutral vessels laying mines.' Vague as this warning was, the Admiralty's local commander nonetheless ordered the only neutral freighter in port, the Swedish steamship *Tasmanic*, to be detained and searched, and sent his only warships, the *Gloucester* and *Hyacinth*, out to investigate. Beyond that, there was little to be done except close the port, for South Africa in 1917 was a British colony that possessed no navy of its own, and Cape Town harbour was not equipped with minesweepers. The *Cape Argus* reported the destruction of the *Matheran* the following day. But this first reported attack on a merchant ship off Cape Town did not appear in either the *Cape Times* or in London, and in the absence of any official explanation, rumours quickly swept through Cape Town that some form of sabotage was involved. Within weeks, South African newspapers were accusing German-born immigrants of being behind the sinking.

Such speculation about German sabotage and plotting was endemic throughout the British Empire during the First World War, encouraged by a policy of government press control that frequently made it impossible to distinguish between myth, propaganda and fact. Details of ship sinkings, for instance, were routinely suppressed by the British War Office, which had assumed sweeping censorship powers at the outbreak of war when it seized control of every British cable company. This enabled it to intercept all foreign correspondents' dispatches and filter them through a team of censors, who worked around the clock in the London offices of the Official Press Bureau. In tandem with this censorship, the government's secret War Propaganda Bureau had enlisted popular writers such as John Buchan and Arthur Conan Doyle to compose a continual stream of pro-British stories and articles, which newspapers published – in the words of the press baron Lord Burnham – 'as a matter of courtesy'. These stories of plucky British heroism and unspeakable Hun savagery, often embellished with caricatures of monstrous German soldiers carrying despoiled maidens and dead children over their shoulders, constituted much of what passed for war reporting, as editors throughout the empire patriotically supported the war effort. The *Madras Mail* in India, for instance, openly informed its readers it had been instructed not to publish 'alarming accounts of disasters at sea' and was therefore expunging nearly all such stories from its pages, even those passed by the censor.

To Prime Minister Lloyd George, it was simply unthinkable that the British public should know about the realities of war. 'If the people really knew, the war would be stopped tomorrow,' he told the editor of the *Manchester Guardian* privately in December 1917. 'But of course they don't – and can't – know. The correspondents don't write and the censorship would not pass the truth.' Censorship and propaganda worked hand in glove, one shutting off unwelcome news while the other smoothed the public's brow with stirring tales from the front.

That this patriotic fervour often spilled over into outright racist hysteria may not have been intended, but it certainly helped sustain support for the war. In 1915, rioting crowds in London, Liverpool and Manchester had attacked German immigrants, following the sinking of the *Lusitania* and the publication of a report on alleged German atrocities in Belgium written by the former British diplomat Viscount James Bryce. The Bryce Report's shocking accounts of raped nuns and tortured children were later shown to be of dubious provenance, but the hatred they engendered would take years to run its course and inspired newspaper editors to wage anti-Hun campaigns of unbridled xenophobia. Outright fabrications – tales of crucified Allied soldiers and bodies boiled down for gun oil – received as much column space as genuine German excesses such as the execution of the British nurse Edith Cavell for espionage. The result was a hatred of all things German that took root across Britain, the United States, India, Australia, New Zealand and South Africa, and was targeted at German immigrants who were recategorised as 'enemy aliens', accused of disloyalty and interned by the thousands in concentration camps.

Distrust of German immigrants had been fuelled by the revelation in 1915 that United States law agencies had uncovered a loose-knit group of German agents who were attempting to ship arms to India, foment strike action at various American ports and plant time-bombs on freighters destined for Europe. The bombing of the Black Tom Island munitions store in New Jersey in 1916 was also believed to be German sabotage, and contributed to President Wilson's dark warning that 'the military masters of Germany . . . have filled our unsuspecting communities with vicious spies and conspirators'. Britain, too, had broken up a German espionage network in the early months of the war. But nearly all of these plots were executed by consular officials, soldiers or professional spies – a detail that became lost as the public succumbed to War Office propaganda dispatches warning that every German living abroad was a potential spy, each German butcher or baker enmeshed in a malign 'national endeavour' to sap the British Empire of its culture, freedom and strength.

With its large population of German traders and mining officials, South Africa was ripe for such fervid speculation. Anti-German riots had swept Cape Town, Port Elizabeth, Durban and Johannesburg after the *Lusitania* sinking, prompting the colonial government to announce it would intern all male 'enemy aliens'. More than 4500 German-born citizens had been imprisoned, and local newspapers waged vehement campaigns against 'enemy firms' such as Malcomess & Co., the second-largest retail merchant in the country, whose German-born chief executive was briefly interned until an army colonel on his board posted the extraordinary bond of £20,000.

Although a hastily convened marine inquiry found that the *Matheran* probably struck a mine, sabotage rumours persisted in Cape Town, and they were reignited when the British troopship *Tyndareus* struck the *Wolf*'s second minefield near Cape Agulhas only a few hours after leaving port on 6 February. Newly built and on her maiden voyage, the 10,500-ton *Tyndareus* was carrying 1005 soldiers from the 25th Middlesex Regiment, who were all evacuated with remarkable efficiency from the heavily listing ship, which remained afloat long enough to be nursed into dry dock. News of the disaster was immediately suppressed, but the city was further alarmed a week later when the freighter *Cilicia*, hugging the coastline as she approached Cape Town from the north, struck another mine off Dassen Island and was crippled.

In response, South African newspapers began speculating darkly about traitors working on the docks in league with visiting neutral ships and demanded the internment of all German-born citizens. Although the navy's suspicions about the Swedish freighter *Tasmanic* had come to naught and the presence of mines suggested that either a raider or a submarine was responsible, the *Rand Daily Mail* quickly pointed the finger at local Germans who had not yet been interned. 'Unless we are misinformed, there are officials of German descent still associated with the management of our docks and harbours, which does not seem to us to be a desirable state of things in war time,' the paper editorialised. '. . . The Union Government has hitherto treated enemy aliens with a leniency which we are afraid has not always been appreciated.' The *Cape Times* likewise demanded that all German-born men, women and children in the country be interned, regardless of their income or position, to prevent 'enemy action within our borders'. Not to be outdone, the *Star* concurred but demanded that imprisonment be extended to 'pro-German neutrals' – an apparent reference to Swedish and northern European immigrants, whom the paper described as 'the most dangerous people in South Africa today'.

Aboard the *Wolf*, Nerger would only later hear of these events, but he was about to foment a similar panic thousands of miles north on another continent, for by the time the *Cilicia* sank he was approaching Colombo after a four-week voyage through the monsoonal gales of the Indian Ocean. The *Wolf* had assumed a new guise during her passage north: the crew had painted over her white superstructure so that she was now entirely black. On the afternoon of 15 February, with the weather finally subsided, Nerger sighted the conical silhouette of Adam's Peak and ordered the crew to prepare for more minelaying.

As night fell and the mines were winched up to the deck, Nerger picked up the signals of several passing ships, including a Spanish passenger-freighter, the *C. de Eizaguirre*, which would prove almost eerily fated to cross paths with the *Wolf*. Steamer traffic into Colombo was heavy and a harbour spotlight at one point held the *Wolf* in its beam for thirty seconds as the crew huddled out of sight, but Nerger held his nerve and laid a string of fifty-five mines like a necklace across the sea lanes approaching the port.

He was heading north towards Bombay only a day later when he picked up an urgent wireless message that the 7175-ton British freighter *Worcestershire* had struck one of the mines and sunk with the loss of two crewmen, prompting local navy officials to close the Colombo port. The news was again suppressed in the press, however, and approaching ships were warned merely that an unspecified danger existed eight miles south-south-west of the harbour.

Nerger continued north, laying nineteen mines off Wadge Bank, a heavily trafficked spot between Colombo and Bombay, then sailed on to Bombay itself to drop another 110 mines in a crescent pattern across that port's approach lanes. In his captain's log that night, he puzzled over the local navy's reluctance to issue an explicit mine warning. 'It's strange that even now the reasons for the danger are not yet made known,' he wrote. 'Are they not known or is the administration in Colombo interested in keeping it secret?'

The following evening, the *Wolf* was sailing north towards Karachi when the wireless finally crackled with an urgent Admiralty alert – 'Beware of mines off Colombo!' – and a similar warning for Bombay. Unbeknown to Nerger, the British freighter *Perseus* had sunk off Colombo and a steamship leaving Bombay harbour had spotted one of the *Wolf*'s mines drifting on the surface and exploded it with rifle fire. Nerger had planned to plant another minefield off Karachi, nearly 600 miles away, thus completing a sweep of all three major British ports in the area, but realised now that all ships would be detained and the harbour on full alert. Hastily recalibrating his plans, he decided to deviate from his orders and suspend minelaying in favour of raiding sorties. 'I want to abort the exercise here and next go south to open the trade war at a convenient location, and to increase the coal supply,' he wrote in his log on the night of 21 February. The *Wolf*'s coal supplies were becoming depleted and Nerger hoped that in the southern Indian Ocean he could lay mines along the Australian coastline, where troop transports passed en route to South Africa. Then he planned to capture two ships, convert them to auxiliary raiders and return to India to lead simultaneous attacks on Rangoon, Karachi and Calcutta.

Nerger was not alone in wondering whether Britain's colonial authorities in India and Ceylon had deliberately tried to conceal the mine danger from local ships, for the editors of India's major newspapers were soon berating the government over its handling of the matter. As it had done with the *Tyndareus* incident in South Africa, the War Office had suppressed virtually all details of the *Worcestershire* and *Perseus* incidents, and in place of reliable information, wild rumours were soon sweeping India's ports. The government of Madras, where memories of the *Emden*'s raid three years earlier remained vivid, felt compelled to respond by releasing a statement that acknowledged the *Worcestershire*'s sinking but flatly denied it was caused by a mine – a remarkably bold falsehood given that minesweepers were at the moment criss-crossing the harbour entrance at Bombay and Colombo.

'As rumours of an alarming nature are understood to be in circulation in the city of Madras,' the statement asserted, 'the Government of Madras are in a position to state that the evidence to the cause of the sinking of the Bibby liner *Worcestershire* indicates an internal explosion. So far as the Government are aware, there is at present no reason to suppose that any hostile vessel is in the Bay of Bengal, and the military precautions that have been taken are purely of a precautionary character and afford no ground for alarm on the part of the public.'

The phrase 'internal explosion' needed no translation. Like South Africa, India was ripe with rumours of bomb plots and subversion during the First World War, for the British colonial government was fighting an increasingly militant independence movement and had imprisoned many radical activists in internment camps in the Indian cities of Ahmednagar, Bellarig and Belgaum. Most German-born Indian residents had been either interned or deported, among them more than four hundred missionaries and their wives and children. The public was therefore predisposed to accept the government's explanation that a bomb had been planted aboard the *Worcestershire*, even if the press remained sceptical.

The *Madras Mail*, abandoning its customary compliance, informed readers it had received reports that the *Worcestershire* sinking was caused by German 'piracy', possibly a submarine. In response, the government moved to censor all reporting of the matter, even parliamentary debate, prompting the *Times of Ceylon* to point out that such a move was superfluous because the Admiralty in London already wielded censorship powers that were 'absolute and completely outside the control of any local authority'.

It was the beginning of a pattern of censorship and misinformation that would blossom as the *Wolf* ventured into more distant and vulnerable reaches of the British Empire.

* *

When dawn broke over the Indian Ocean on the morning of 27 February, Karl Nerger was on the bridge of the *Wolf* staring through binoculars at the first quarry of his raiding mission: a British freighter that bizarrely appeared to be the mirror-image of his own ship. Nerger had been tracking the ship all night and now, 600 miles north-west of the Maldive Islands, he finally closed in and semaphored a signal to stop, ordering Fritz Witschetzky to send one shot across her bows from the *Wolf*'s forward guns. A contingent of twelve men was already clambering into the raider's motor launch to be winched overboard, and within five minutes the seizing of the ship had been executed as smoothly as the countless drills the crew had practised in the Baltic. The only unforeseen event had been the comic pantomime enacted aboard the freighter, for its officers had launched a lifeboat with such frantic haste that it nearly capsized, while above them a dozen Chinese crewmen shouted excitedly at the sight of their own officers abandoning them to the tender mercies of a motor launch filled with bayonet-wielding Germans.

At close range, the ship looked even more like the *Wolf*, from the profile of her bridge to the placement of the six lifeboats and the position of the derricks fore and aft. The name on her hull identified her as the *Turritella*, a British oil-tanker, but the raiding party led by Leutnant Karl Rose soon signalled back an explanation: she was in fact a German-built ship from the same Hansa production line as the *Wolf*, originally christened *Gutenfels*. Captured by the British in Alexandria at the beginning of the war, she had been recommissioned to run oil and supplies between Colombo and London, operating with an entirely Chinese crew under the command of a New Zealand-born skipper, Tom Meadows.

In a sentimental lapse he would soon regret, Nerger found himself reluctant to sink this 'fine German ship', even if she were carrying oil to Britain. Although the *Turritella* was of little use to him – she had an oil-fired engine and the only coal she carried was unsuitable for a ship's furnaces – Nerger had a superstitious belief that the *Wolf* had been guided to meet her sister-ship here in the middle of the Indian Ocean.

His second-in-command, Kapitänleutnant Iwan Brandes, adroitly offered a solution by suggesting he take a contingent of the *Wolf*'s men aboard the freighter, along with enough mines and armaments to convert her into an auxiliary minelayer under his command. Since the *Turritella* was a regular visitor to nearby ports, Brandes reasoned that he could lay mines close to Aden's harbour entrance without raising suspicion; furthermore, her Chinese crew were neutrals who could be recruited to remain aboard and work for the Germans at their regular pay-rate.

Within hours, the plan was being put into effect and, with due formality, Nerger issued written orders for Brandes to drop twenty-five mines off Aden before meeting the *Wolf* south of the Maldives. If Brandes was intercepted, he was to make for a neutral port or scuttle the ship but not, under any circumstances, allow the British to reclaim her. The young *kapitänleutnant* selected twenty-seven of the *Wolf*'s crew to join him on his newly commissioned ship, taking along a spare wireless set and one two-inch gun from the armaments store. The Chinese crew agreed to work for the Germans, and the *Turritella*'s contingent of seven British seamen were brought aboard the *Wolf* and became the first prisoners sent down to the aft hold, where some of the mines had been stored. As a precaution, Nerger ordered the seaplane assembled and launched on her maiden reconnaissance flight while the transfer of mines took place and his engineers modified the *Turritella*'s poop deck for minelaying. The plane's wood-framed fuselage and wings were bolted together on the deck and she was winched down onto the waves with her pilot and flight lieutenant balanced on the seafloats. After ceremonially breaking a champagne bottle over her propeller to christen her *Wolfchen* – Wolf Cub – the pair clambered into the cockpit and took off.

By the evening of 27 February, the *Turritella* was ready for her new mission, and the *Wolfchen* was recalled and brought back aboard. With a nostalgic flourish, Nerger had decided to rename this newly fashioned raider SMS *Iltis*, after the gunboat on which he had narrowly escaped death during the Boxer Uprising bombardment of 1900. The original *Iltis* had sunk three years earlier, scuttled by her own crew when the British and Japanese navies attacked the German garrison in the Chinese harbour of Tsingtao in the opening weeks of the war. But that was an omen Nerger chose to ignore as he watched her namesake disappear into the northern darkness, sailing towards Aden.

3

WARTIME SECRETS

Just after 10 am on 5 March 1917, a telegraph machine inside Admiralty headquarters at Whitehall spat out a brief and unwelcome one-page Morse dispatch from the British naval commander at Aden. 'German Minelayer "Turritella" sunk herself 12° 24'N, 43° 30'E a.m. 5th March,' read the opening sentence. The ten lines that followed informed the Royal Navy's senior command that the British gunboat *Odin* had intercepted the oil-tanker *Turritella* as she attempted to lay mines in the approach to Aden harbour earlier that morning. The tanker had been sunk by her prize crew of twenty-eight Germans, who had been retrieved from their lifeboats by the *Odin*, along with forty-six Chinese crew members, who told their rescuers the ship had been hijacked a week earlier by a German raider operating in the Indian Ocean and carrying a seaplane. Before the day was out, the news had been passed on to Britain's newly appointed first sea lord, Admiral Sir John Jellicoe.

The raiding career of Kapitänleutnant Iwan Brandes had come to a somewhat inglorious end in the entrance to the Red Sea only a week after he took command of the *Turritella*. After dropping his twenty-five mines on either side of the entrance to

Aden's port on the night of 4 March, Brandes had been making his escape when he encountered the *Odin*, a two-masted motorised sloop, in the early hours of the following morning. Despite the *Odin*'s puny size – she was barely a quarter of the *Turritella*'s tonnage and carried only a handful of four-inch guns – she was both faster and more heavily armed than the fully laden tanker, and as Brandes was chased east he had little choice but to order his crew to plant timer-bombs in the cargo bunkers and abandon ship. The *Turritella* sank in a cloud of steam and smoke ten miles from the coastline of British Somalia, and Brandes and his men were now being interrogated in the military prison in Aden.

From the *Turritella*'s Chinese crew, the British quickly gleaned a description of the black raider that had hijacked her; one of the Germans was found to be carrying a letter addressed to him via SMS *Wolf* in Kiel, and a Chinese crewman reported that Brandes's men had discussed the possibility of the raider making for Borneo in the East Indies, directly north of Australia. By 6 March, a report on the *Wolf* had been distributed throughout military intelligence and Whitehall, reaching as high as the first lord of the Admiralty, Sir Edward Carson, and sent to navy commanders in Colombo, Suez, Port Said, the East Indies, Bombay, Basra, South Africa, Zanzibar, Singapore, Australia and New Zealand. It contained a full description of the *Wolf*'s appearance and dimensions, including details of her drop-down bulwarks, torpedo placements, guns, derricks, seaplane and wireless towers, which enabled detailed sketches to be drawn up and distributed to naval patrols. The report speculated that the raider might have fifty mines left in her bunkers and be heading towards the East Indies.

The news that another German raider was at large could not have arrived at a less auspicious time for the Admiralty. A month earlier, Kaiser Wilhelm II had succumbed to the pleas of his admirals and ordered the resumption of unrestricted submarine warfare, this time with an expanded fleet of more than a hundred U-boats. By March, Britain was reeling from the onslaught, as shipping losses nearly doubled to reach 564,000 tons a month.

A freighter attempting a round trip from Britain to any port beyond Gibraltar faced a seventy-five-per-cent chance of being sunk; essential supplies of food and industrial raw materials were running low; insurance rates were skyrocketing and the available fleet of steamships was dwindling by the week. A run on the Bank of England's gold reserves so alarmed one treasury official, John Maynard Keynes, that he predicted the country could soon run out of money to finance the war effort. Arriving in London a few weeks later, United States Admiral William Sowden Sims would be shocked to hear, during a briefing at Admiralty headquarters, that Prime Minister Lloyd George's assurances of imminent victory were entirely false and that Britain faced inevitable defeat within months if shipping losses continued.

Now, compounding the Admiralty's travails, it was becoming clear that several German surface-raiders had broken through the blockade and were creating havoc along more distant trade routes. In December 1916, naval intelligence had learned that the *Moewe* was once again roaming the Atlantic, after a Belgian freighter captain reported that the raider had stopped his ship and allowed him to proceed as a neutral vessel. Since then, the *Moewe* – still under the command of Nikolaus Dohna-Schlodien, newly decorated and promoted to *Fregattenkapitän* – had enjoyed a second moment in the sun by sinking or capturing more than twenty ships and successfully sending one of them, the British freighter *Yarrowdale*, back to Germany laden with prisoners. In the very week that the *Turritella* was laying mines off Aden, the *Yarrowdale* had reappeared in the North Sea, recommissioned as the German raider *Leopard* – a short-lived mission that ended horrifically on 7 March when she was sunk by a British armoured cruiser with the loss of her entire crew of 319 men.

Three weeks later, wireless reports reached London of yet another raider, off Brazil. A French barque carrying the crews of several missing merchant ships had sailed into Rio de Janeiro's harbour, and the disembarking crewmen explained they had all been captured and then released by a three-masted sailing ship manned by a German raiding crew. It was the first confirmed sighting of the *Seeadler*, which had left Kiel three weeks after the *Wolf* under the command of Count Felix von Luckner, soon to prove himself one of the Great War's most charismatic self-mythologisers.

Britain's admirals were acutely aware of the havoc these free-lance marauders could create, for the exploits of the *Emden* and her sister-raiders in 1914 were still fresh in their minds. While U-boats were the primary threat, raiders had a mercurial quality that exacted its own psychological and tactical toll. Striking randomly, often far from the centres of combat, they stirred up press interest, created panic and disrupted shipping in distant parts of the empire, diverting warships from the main fronts of battle. During the *Emden*'s reign of terror, Winston Churchill had fired off furious missives warning that the press coverage was damaging the Royal Navy's reputation.

The sudden reappearance of the *Moewe* had forced Britain to suspend troop transportations from Dakar, Cape Town and Sierra Leone for weeks while twenty-four warships roamed the Atlantic conducting fruitless searches. Freight shipments had been delayed or cancelled in Atlantic Ocean ports along the entire American coastline from New York to Argentina, and even along the Pacific routes connecting Chile with Australia and California. The British had ordered all lighthouses and navigation lights in the West Indies extinguished. When false reports swept America in early April that a 10,000-ton raider had 'loomed out of the fog' only 200 miles from New York, market prices for steel, cotton and wheat plummeted.

In reality, the *Moewe* was by then already back in Germany, having sunk or captured 123,265 tons of shipping in four months. Flushed with success, Dohna-Schlodien held a press conference in which he airily ridiculed Sir John Jellicoe. 'I simply cannot understand why the English could not catch me on the way home,' he said with mock perplexity. 'Hitherto, we always recognised that the English navy bore itself very well and fought bravely. But now I must suppose that of late their leadership is no longer first-rate.'

The Admiralty's alert about the *Wolf* caused an immediate stir in Australia, whose navy officials had long feared that a German raider might appear off the country's vulnerable western coastline. Australia's major Indian Ocean port, Fremantle, was at the very south-western tip of the country, more than 3500 miles from where the *Turritella* had been captured. But on 7 March, Australia's prime minister, William Morris Hughes, made the dramatic announcement in parliament that all transports and troopship sailings had been cancelled due to the destruction of ships close to Australia. In an overheated moment – possibly explained by the fact that he had just called a snap election – Hughes claimed that the ships had been sunk 'within a few hundred miles of us, in the waters of the very ocean that lap[s] these shores'.

His navy minister, Joseph Cook, explained more accurately that a raider was known to be operating between Aden and Colombo. 'The raider is a large cargo steamer of about 4000 tons register,' Cook said, 'carrying guns and torpedo tubes. She also carries a seaplane.' It was a statement notable for being the only candid account of the *Wolf* that would be released by the Allies during the entire course of her raiding mission.

The British press had been permitted to publish a few limited accounts of the exploits of the *Moewe* and the *Seeadler*, but news was so tightly controlled that one Liberal parliamentarian had already noted 'a very strong impression in the City that we were not being told the whole of the activities of the raider or raiders that were known'. In other countries, news of the sinkings off Cape Town, Colombo and Bombay had already leaked out – Japanese newspapers, for instance, had reported in late February that a German raider was active off Ceylon. In the absence of official information, newspapers published a wild amalgam of rumour and speculation. From Brazil's *Jornal Pequeno* came a report that German raiders were now accompanied by miniature one-man submarines, a startling revelation that the *New York Times* embellished with an illustration of these tiny pedal-powered U-boats. The *Canadian News* contributed a fallacious story, reported throughout the United States, that a German raider was already in the South Pacific and had sunk a Japanese warship. In response, the governor of Hawaii, L. E. Pinkham, expressed fears that the island could run out of food. Rumours of a raider in the Pacific became so widespread that the Canadian Government announced it would no longer deny them because 'the manufacturing of these sensations is endless and the public seems willing to believe any story that is printed'.

Sir Edward Carson had assured the British Parliament in February that the government would never be a party to withholding information about raiders from the public and was pursuing a policy of absolute transparency. 'We are not, for any purpose of concealment . . . holding anything back,' the first lord said. The truth, as Carson knew, was that the government would do its utmost to prevent any information about the *Wolf* finding its way to the public, for a raider in the Indian Ocean presented a particularly thorny problem.

Immersed in the catastrophic shipping losses of the U-boat campaign, and with many of its Atlantic and Pacific warships still hunting for the *Moewe* and the *Seeadler*, the Admiralty was forced to call on the Japanese Navy for help under the Anglo-Japanese Alliance of 1911. On 9 March, the Foreign Office instructed Britain's ambassador in Tokyo to request that the Japanese Government immediately send four warships to the Indian Ocean to protect grain ships and troop transports sailing from the west coast of Australia to Colombo. Mindful that the *Wolf* might be heading east towards the Pacific, where commerce ships brought supplies up from New Zealand and the east coast of Australia, the British sent a second cable emphasising that they were 'anxious that [the] Japanese Government should send ships to the vicinity of Hong Kong, in case the raider should appear there, and also that they should send a squadron to the Coast of Queensland to be ready in the event of the raider operating against trade in Australian or New Zealand waters'.

The urgency of these instructions reflected the discomfiting knowledge that Britain's naval strategy had left Australia and New Zealand, the two most distant outposts of the empire, essentially defenceless. Alone among Britain's dominions, Australia had created its own operational navy in the years before the war, spending nearly £4 million on the battle-cruiser *Australia* and three light-cruisers to supplement the flotilla of destroyers, gunboats and torpedo-boats that the British Government had previously provided. To smooth the Admiralty's vehement opposition to this outbreak of independence in the colonies, the Australian Government had offered Britain complete control of its new navy during wartime. That agreement had come into force in August 1914, and by early 1917 every significant warship in the newly formed Royal Australian Navy was far from home. HMAS *Australia* and the light-cruisers *Melbourne*, *Sydney* and *Brisbane* were all in European waters, while three destroyers from the old colonial flotilla were patrolling the East Indies under the command of the China station. That left a continent not a great deal smaller than the United States protected by one antiquated cruiser, the *Encounter* – on loan from Britain – and three puny 700-ton torpedo-boats that the Australian Navy's most senior admiral, William Rooke Creswell, dismissed as 'unspeakably useless'. Even these few ships were periodically seconded to China or detained in harbour for repairs, and the Australian Naval Board had asked the Admiralty in February 1916 to send reinforcements so it could protect key trade routes and troop transports. The request, however, had been declined.

Across the Tasman, New Zealand's defences were even more parlous, for this small nation of barely more than a million people had no warships at all. In 1912, New Zealand had donated £2 million to Britain for the construction of the battle-cruiser *New Zealand*, which was to have been the flagship of the Admiralty's Pacific fleet. Instead, she had been sent to Europe, leaving the country she was named after with only the *Philomel*, a twenty-eight-year-old rust bucket that was moored in Wellington Harbour in an unseaworthy condition.

Even though slavish devotion to empire was at a high-water mark in Australia and New Zealand during the First World War, the situation caused deep resentment in both countries. Between them, they had already sent nearly four hundred thousand men to the front, roughly one-tenth of whom had been killed. Troops were still regularly making the arduous six-week ocean crossing to Britain, along with freighters carrying wheat, food and wool. In theory, these ships were protected by Japan's navy, but Australia and New Zealand derived no great comfort from that arrangement. Isolated and sparsely populated as they were on the rim of the Pacific, both nations shared a deep unease about the 'yellow hordes' to the north, a fear made more acute by Japan's forcible occupation of several German Pacific island colonies at the outbreak of the war. When New Zealand's prime minister, the blunt-talking Irish-born ex-farmer William Massey, visited London for the Imperial War Conference of March 1917, he expressed 'serious grievance' about the inadequacy of his country's defences and rebuked the Admiralty for imperilling the lives of thousands of troops who were shipped to Britain without adequate protection. New Zealand had been promised naval protection, said Massey, 'and I am sorry to say, as a British citizen, and [one] who will die a British citizen, that so far as we are able to judge, there was never the slightest attempt made to keep that promise'.

Australia's Naval Board had sent much the same message to the conference, albeit more judiciously worded, in a report written in early 1917 which detailed the country's extraordinary vulnerability to raider or submarine attack. 'It is sometimes necessary to leave south-western Australia quite unprotected, and at times there have been no vessels available for the protection of southern and eastern Australian waters,' the report warned, before tactfully adding that the situation was being drawn to the attention of the lords of the Admiralty 'not in a spirit of alarm, but in order that they may be sure that the condition of preparedness of Australia is of a degree that has the approval of their Lordships'.

Their lordships, however, did not respond in a manner that Australia and New Zealand had been anticipating, despite the fact that the Imperial War Conference took place just as the *Wolf* appeared in the Indian Ocean. Australia's only battle-cruiser, HMAS *Australia*, was at the time engaged in routine patrol work off Scotland, as she would be for most of the year. (The *Australia* would survive the war without firing a shot in action.) Instead of redeploying her, the Admiralty ordered HMAS *Brisbane* to assist with the search for the *Wolf* in the Indian Ocean and then, over the ensuing weeks, requisitioned every destroyer in the Australian fleet for other duties. The *Encounter* was to escort a troop convoy from New Zealand to the Indian Ocean, and the three remaining small destroyers on the eastern seaboard – the *Warrego*, *Parramatta* and *Yarra* – were directed to sail for Europe, where shipping losses from the U-boat campaign had reached a staggering 800,000 tons per month. London assured Australia that four Japanese warships would be sent to the country's eastern coastline, but only one, the light-cruiser *Hirado*, had arrived by late April. Sydney, Melbourne and all of New Zealand were thus left wide open to attack, even as local navy chiefs braced themselves for the appearance of the raider.

In Aden, meanwhile, a British army major had been paying daily visits to the jail cells of the German crewmen captured from the *Turritella*, offering them morsels of news from the war and listening sympathetically to their complaints of sexual frustration. 'Some of the sailors,' he reported, 'in expressing a desire for women, informed the wardens in charge that they had had no opportunities in this regard for *two months* since leaving Germany.' After less than a fortnight, he had gleaned enough information to compile an eleven-page intelligence report for the Admiralty that profiled each of the captured crewmen and revealed that the *Wolf* had probably left Germany before Christmas, loaded with 6000 tons of coal and enough provisions to remain at sea for a year. By early April, a detailed sketch of the *Wolf* had been cabled to every naval commander in the Pacific and Indian oceans, and Aden was able to provide another key piece of news: 'Prisoners claim that Cape Town harbour was mined.'

It was final confirmation that the minefields off Cape Town, Bombay and Colombo were all the work of one elusive raider. As to where it might be heading, the Germans had remained mute.

* *

In the wake of the reports on the *Wolf*, the Admiralty had suspended all troop transports in the Indian Ocean, ordered minesweepers into the Gulf of Aden and dispatched eight warships to protect future transport convoys approaching east Africa and the Persian Gulf. By now, Britain had more than fifty warships searching for raiders in the oceans off China, South America, the United States, Britain, Africa, India and Australia – a situation that might have been tenable if at least one of them had caught a glimpse of the *Moewe* before she had successfully sailed back into Kiel harbour. As the Admiralty itself subsequently admitted with regards to the *Moewe*, 'One single armed merchantman defied the power of the combined Navies because of the fundamental difficulty of locating ships on the wide expanse of the ocean.'

If there was consolation in the fact that no major loss of life had occurred, that came to an end in the early hours of 26 May as the Spanish mail-steamer *C. de Eizaguirre* approached Cape Town from the west through a storm-churned sea. The 4367-ton ship was making her return journey from Barcelona to Manila carrying a 100-strong crew and nearly sixty passengers, including the Spanish consul of Colombo and several families with small children. With the exception of a skeleton night crew, all were asleep in their cabins when the ship shuddered from a dull explosion around 3 am and was plunged into darkness. One of the *Wolf*'s submerged mines had blown a hole in the starboard hull so large that the steamer began cracking apart almost immediately, leaving most of the suddenly woken passengers and crew no time to even seize their life-vests before they felt her lurch heavily from the water flooding into the holds. The *C. de Eizaguirre* sank with such terrible swiftness that her captain never transmitted a distress signal, and in the night-time chaos of rain and lashing winds only one of the eight lifeboats was launched before she went down. The ship simply vanished in the darkness, leaving in her wake a small lifeboat containing twenty-one crew members and two first-class male passengers, shivering in their nightclothes.

After three hours in the rain and heaving sea, the survivors were rescued by a passing steamer as dawn broke over Table Bay. The only other survivor was a ship's engineer who had thrown himself overboard wearing a life-vest and had clung to a raft for thirty hours before being picked up. The remaining passengers and crew were all killed, the bodies of several washing up on beaches outside Cape Town over succeeding days. A cable reporting the disaster reached defence-intelligence headquarters in London the following day, and the analyst who responded – perhaps inured by then to news of death at sea – merely asked, 'Is this the same old spot?'

Within weeks of the *C. de Eizaguirre* tragedy, two more ships had struck mines near Bombay harbour. On 11 June, the 9373-ton cargo-steamer *City of Exeter* was crippled by an explosion as she approached the city but managed to limp back into harbour without loss of life. Five days later, the much smaller Japanese tramp *Unkai Maru* struck a mine as she sailed towards the port. The ship sank, but her crew of thirty-six was rescued by a passing steamship. Censorship was again enforced, and the *C. de Eizaguirre* sinking was the only incident reported, in a brief dispatch that gave little clue as to the location or magnitude of the incident.

The news blackout meant that passengers and even crews on ships sailing to and from India remained ignorant of the minefields reported in the area over the preceding four months. Thus, when the P&O cargo-liner *Mongolia* approached Bombay a week after the *Unkai Maru* sinking, en route from London to Australia, her crew was entirely unprepared for an emergency and the passengers were so oblivious to the danger that many were playing a pre-lunch game of deck quoits. Among them was Richard Reading, an invalided British war veteran who had just spent two and a half years in a military hospital and was heading to Australia to recuperate.

'We had left Aden on the [preceding] Saturday,' Reading later recalled, 'and all doubts and fears had been thrown aside. The danger zone was behind us, and folk began to ignore lifebelts, the lifeboats were swung in-ship on their davits and few if any thought of danger. Saturday morning dawned beautifully with the cool south-west monsoon blowing almost astern. I had been fixing up some sports and had left this day for winding up the deck quoit championship of the *Mongolia*.' Even for a soldier such as Reading, what followed was terrifying: 'I've heard the roaring, destroying noises from the big shells the Germans rained on the Belgian villages and towns in 1914, but with this one great quivering burst there was a terrible and terrifying accompaniment. I think it was the tremendous yet almost human shiver the ship gave, and the dread silence that followed almost immediately, which intensified the nerve-racking shock.'

The *Mongolia* had struck two mines almost simultaneously, triggering an explosion so fierce that it destroyed her engine room and killed almost everyone in it instantly. Chunks of coal and shrapnel belched from the funnels and showered down on passengers who were rushing to locate their life-vests. The ship was carrying 470 crew and passengers, including Justice John Rooth of the Supreme Court of Western Australia, former Wimbledon tennis champion Norman Brookes, Sydney philanthropist and politician Fred Winchcombe, the recently knighted Australian army general Sir Robert Anderson, his wife Dame Mary, and Doris Downes, the pregnant wife of a senior Australian medical officer stationed in the Middle East. None of the ship's twelve lifeboats was ready for launching, and crew members struggled to unlash them as the *Mongolia* began sinking and blowing steam like a wounded animal. Several engineers, trapped below deck with terrible burns, threw themselves into the ocean through portholes. The ship began sinking slowly by the stern, tilted upwards, but then settled forwards with such eerie calmness that all the lifeboats were successfully launched before water began swilling over the decks.

Norman Brookes later described the scene in a letter to his wife, Mabel, mustering all the dispassionate stoicism of the era:

> This is what occurred. I was playing quoits about midday; my tunic, with official papers, hanging on a deck-chair with my life-belt. At 12.16 pm, the ship ran into a double mine and sank in sixteen minutes, listing somewhat. My cabin was blown to pieces, most of the furniture coming out of the door. My little chiming watch has gone down and the gold cigarette case, also the cuff-links you gave me. The life-boat happened to be on the weather side. We went to it and waited our turn, though most of us thought the ship would go before we could get away, every wave leaving her settling deeper . . . Doris Downes was near me and I helped her with her life jacket. She left me to go to her appointed boat on the other side, very calm and collected.

According to Brookes, the *Mongolia*'s captain, Paddy Llewellyn, waited until the ship was nearly submerged before leaping from the rails and swimming to the nearest lifeboat.

The survivors were fifty miles south of Bombay in a heavy sea, surrounded by debris and the floating bodies of crewmen, each of which had to be hauled up by the hair to check for signs of life. Richard Reading was crippled, having been struck by shrapnel on his war-wounded leg; one passenger had two fingers torn off his hand after getting snarled in a pulley-rope while clambering off the ship; a crewman from the boiler room was hideously burned and delirious with pain. The lifeboats, each containing thirty or forty people, hoisted their sails and headed for the coast but became separated as they rode the peaks and troughs of the ocean. As night descended, one managed to make a safe landing on a rocky beach and set up red flares, which four of the others followed. In the darkness, however, a lifeboat capsized and its occupants – including sixty-two-year-old Fred Winchcombe – were thrown into the ocean. One young Australian drowned while trying to swim to shore; the rest clung to the upturned boat and were washed up on a reef. Other boats managed to land further up the coast and the survivors waited out the night, huddled on the shoreline.

When dawn broke, the boiler-room engineer was dead from his burns, despite the ministrations of two Australian Red Cross nurses, and Winchcombe was perilously ill from pneumonia. Several groups of men set off through the hills in search of help, one of them eventually finding the coastal village of Velas. But by then a rescue party was already on its way, for at midday a lifeboat crowded with forty-two survivors had sailed into Bombay harbour after twenty-four hours at sea. Alerted to the *Mongolia*'s fate, naval authorities sent a ship to pick up the remaining survivors and bring them back to Bombay. Several days later, Fred Winchcombe died in hospital, bringing the death toll from the disaster to twenty-three. Writing from his hotel, Norman Brookes assured his wife he had suffered nothing more serious than cracked lips and blistered hands; his diary for the ensuing two weeks was a fastidious catalogue of tennis games, shopping expeditions and lunches at the Royal Yacht Club that – as Dame Mabel would later observe – studiously avoided any reflection on the traumatic event he had survived.

* *

The *Mongolia* sinking, although delayed by the censor for several days, was a story that could not be suppressed. The minefields outside Bombay thus finally became public knowledge, and a month later the British Government acknowledged in parliament that the *Wolf* was responsible. The raider's whereabouts, however, had become a source of perplexity in London.

Nothing had been heard of her since the *Turritella*'s sinking, no new minefields had been reported and no confirmed ship captures had come to light.

Searching for commerce-raiders was a drain on the military-intelligence system. Every overdue freighter was a possible victim, every unidentified steamship a potential sighting. The telegraph machine became a conduit for hundreds of erroneous sightings and false alarms, which were dutifully logged in naval-intelligence files. From April to June 1917, a stream of possible raider sightings reached the Admiralty from Africa, Australia, the China Station, the islands of the South Pacific, the oceans off India and the mid-Atlantic. Each was logged, investigated and assessed – a process that took weeks and usually ended inconclusively or with a confirmed false lead. A suspected raider seen off Samoa proved to be a local trading-steamer, although not before several Germans living on the island were arrested on suspicion of signalling to her from the shore. A boatload of men wearing helmets and wielding swords was reported to have landed on Australia's northern coastline near Darwin but proved on close inspection to be a group of Javanese fishermen. Another suspected raider sighting off the east coast of Australia prompted a halt to all shipping in Bass Strait and the dispatch of three warships from Melbourne, until the mystery ship was revealed to be a Swedish freighter.

In July came a report from India, where Kapitänleutnant Iwan Brandes and his crewmen from the *Wolf* had been shipped to an internment camp. Two inmates in the camp – German-born residents of India locked up as suspected enemies of the state – reported that they had been talking to the captured sailors and gleaned valuable information. Their report was a testament to the vivid imagination of prisoners. The mystery raider was the *Bee*, they confidently stated, and her course would take her from Germany to South America, Australia and then India. She communicated by wireless with passing submarines and purchased coal for cash from Portuguese ports. Her captain, it was said, obtained shipping information by sending parties of his men ashore in Allied countries, where they set up surveillance equipment to tap the inland telegraph with the help of 'paid native agents'. Alternatively, crew members were known to have landed in boats, changed into civilian clothes and walked into hotels, where they would telephone shipping companies to obtain information. This rich concoction of the fanciful and the half-true was judged by a naval-intelligence analyst to be 'unreliable' and filed away.

The one possible clue to the *Wolf*'s whereabouts lay in the disappearance of three more British ships in the Indian Ocean. One was the *Jumna*, a 4152-ton steamer that had not been heard of since she left Egypt with a cargo of salt bound for Colombo; the second was the *Wordsworth*, a slightly smaller freighter that had sailed from Colombo on 5 March with a load of rice destined for Britain via the Suez Canal; and the third was a three-masted sailing vessel, the *Dee*, which had disappeared while sailing from Mauritius, 1400 miles off Africa's south-eastern coastline, to pick up cargo from Bunbury in south-western Australia. The *Dee*'s course was well below the 20th parallel south; to capture her, the *Wolf* would have needed to travel nearly 3000 miles into the lowest reaches of the Indian Ocean – a scenario that suggested the raider might be attempting to reach the Pacific by sailing beneath Australia.

According to the calculations of naval intelligence, such a course would have taken the *Wolf* to New Zealand as early as late April. Yet no ships had disappeared nor any mines been detected in the oceans east of Australia. The conundrum was laid out in a naval-intelligence briefing in late May that made several prescient observations before reaching a wrong conclusion:

> According to the Chinese crew of the 'TURRITELLA' the 'WOLF' expects to remain out a year and mention was made of a proposed visit to Borneo.
>
> It would be in accordance with German ideas for the 'WOLF' to try to go round the world, as an account of such a cruise in the bombastic German style would be useful for propaganda

purposes. The cruise must, however, also serve a useful purpose and as the German submarine campaign is directed towards starving us out, it seems reasonable to assume that raiders would also make special efforts to sink food ships.

Arguing from this basis, a raider which has arrived in the Indian Ocean via the Cape of Good Hope appears to have two possible objectives:

1. The food traffic from Australia.
2. The food traffic from the Argentine.

No German warship had ever reached Australia – the *Emden* had come closest with her brief, disastrous foray to the Cocos Islands, 1300 miles from the country's north-west coast. Given the depleted state of the Australian and New Zealand naval defences, one German raider could wage a fruitful campaign of havoc along the trade routes that led east from both countries to the Panama Canal and north to Asia. Indeed, the dangers of such an eventuality had been discussed in Australian naval circles for years, and Rear-Admiral William Creswell had been warned only four months earlier that a single U-boat could destroy every warship in Sydney Harbour. But the *Moewe* and *Seeadler* had so far confined their raiding to the Atlantic, and history suggested it more likely that the *Wolf* would bypass Australia and continue east across the Pacific Ocean to South America, with the intention of rounding Cape Horn and attacking ships sailing from Argentina to Britain.

'On the whole, therefore,' concluded the Admiralty's analysis, 'on the basis of the information available, the chances appear to be in favour of the next news of the *Wolf* coming from the SW Atlantic.'

In just a few months, the *Wolf* had shut down the ports of Aden, Cape Town, Bombay and Colombo, laid minefields that had sunk or damaged eight ships, captured at least one freighter and possibly more, dispatched a second raider into the Red Sea and prompted the Admiralty to redeploy its forces across three oceans. Warships around Australia were on alert for the raider's appearance, the Japanese Navy had been dispatched to the South Pacific off Queensland and the British Navy's Pacific commander had cabled from Colón, Panama, to warn that with only three warships at his disposal to patrol the entire western seaboard of South America, he could do little to prevent a raid on the Panama Canal.

Had Stan and Mary Cameron known any of this, they might well have postponed their voyage across the Pacific in the spring of 1917. But the British Government had so successfully stymied reporting of the *Wolf* that any news reaching San Francisco was a distorted echo of the truth, a confusing mishmash of fanciful speculations about U-boat bases in Mexico, miniature one-man submarines off Argentina and mythical Japanese warships being sunk near Hawaii. As May gave way to June and then July, even the rumours started to dry up. No trace had been found of the three ships missing in the Indian Ocean, and the file on the *Wolf* at naval intelligence in Whitehall lay all but dormant. Patrols were called off and raider warnings were suspended. The black raider, it seemed, had simply evaporated.

4

EDGE OF THE WORLD

Albert Wieduwilt, a thirty-four-year-old engineer aboard the *Wolf*, lay in his bunk below decks on 21 May 1917, scribbling desultorily in a diary. 'The crew on board doesn't feel like working; there is a general feeling of irritation,' the veteran seaman wrote. 'For a change we had another bunker fire, but it doesn't worry me for this has become a daily occurrence . . .' For most of his adult life, Wieduwilt had toiled in steamship boiler rooms. As a merchant seaman, he had sailed as far as China; in the navy, he had served aboard the *Iltis*, Karl Nerger's old warship in the Boxer Uprising, and survived the sinking of the *Ariadne* in the Battle of Heligoland. Now, he found himself on a voyage that seemed without end.

The *Wolf* was tracing a zigzagging course around the Pacific Ocean east of New Zealand, having just a few weeks earlier sailed within 1300 miles of the Antarctic ice shelf. Out on the blank blue ocean to the east lay the 180th meridian, the invisible demarcation between eastern and western time zones. Every time the *Wolf* passed that meridian, her clocks were wound back and the day stretched out to thirty-six hours; then she would cross back heading west and the clocks would be wound forward

– a warping of time that seemed to symbolise the suspended animation enveloping the ship. The voyage was an endurance test that Wieduwilt now calculated in increments – 26,159 nautical miles, ten million revolutions of the engine.

Above Wieduwilt in the officers' quarters, gunnery officer Fritz Witschetzky sensed a mutinous anger building inside the *Wolf*. In seven weeks, they had not encountered another ship nor laid a single mine. Rough seas had sluiced water into their food holds, soaking the flour supplies; thirty crates of flour had been thrown overboard, and what remained was baked into bread that turned to a glutinous mulch in the crew's fingers. Tobacco was running so low that men joked about smoking the stuffing from their mattresses, and the ship had insufficient coal to return to Germany. Witschetzky had heard his men muttering that their captain was a coward, that his only plan was to have them all interned on some godforsaken island prison. Radio transmissions brought momentous news from the other side of the world: Russia's armies were collapsing since the abdication of Tsar Nicholas and the rise of the Bolsheviks; the United States had declared war on Germany and was preparing to dispatch troops to Europe. Some of the crewmen proclaimed that they would rather be risking death on the Western Front than mired in this interminable waiting.

'The sailors made gloomy faces and did their shifts resentfully,' Witschetzky recalled. 'They no longer believed in the further success of our venture or even in the possibility of returning home. We were indeed at the edge of the world, so to speak – without coal.'

Isolated in his cabin, Karl Nerger pored over his charts, read his Schopenhauer and tried to divine some plan that would salvage success from what now appeared to be dismal failure. He had brought the *Wolf* here aiming to hijack one of the many coal-ships that crossed the Pacific Ocean from the eastern seaboard of Australia to South America. The country exported six million tons of coal a year, and Nerger needed but a fraction of it to refuel his ship and resume his attacks on troop transports and grain-ships leaving for Europe. Instead, he had expended the *Wolf*'s fuel in fruitless, aimless reconnaissance sorties on this empty ocean, so that the raider sat high on the swell with her propeller partially exposed, lurching in the gale-force winds of the Pacific winter. The ship's hull was encrusted with barnacles and weeds, and her engines were in desperate need of maintenance after six months' continuous operation. An acrid stench of coal smoke permeated every cabin, hold and gangway from the coal fires that had repeatedly ignited deep inside the bunkers, the latest of which was proving impossible to locate and extinguish. On those rare days when the weather cleared and the winds subsided enough for the *Wolfchen* to be launched, the aircraft reported not a single ship within a ninety-mile radius. For weeks on end, Nerger's daily log had ended with the same two-word phrase: '*Nichts gesichtet*.' Nothing sighted.

All of these travails had begun with one miscalculation: his decision to transform the *Turritella* into the raider *Iltis*. Only a week after the *Iltis* sailed off towards the Red Sea, Nerger's wireless operators had picked up the Admiralty's urgent raider warnings with their full description of the *Wolf*, and he knew in an instant that Kapitänleutnant Brandes and his crew had been captured. The *Wolf* was only a few days' sailing east of Aden at the time, and Nerger had hastily ordered the ship south as he once again rewrote his plans. With navy warships already on alert off India and Colombo, his route east to Singapore and the East Indies was a gauntlet of Allied warships. He could return to the Atlantic via the Cape, but that would contravene his orders and interfere with the *Moewe*'s raiding mission in those waters, which he had been following via fragments of news over the airwaves. The *Turritella*'s officers had told him the entire Allied naval force from Cape Town to Singapore was on alert for him, so Nerger had taken a calculated gamble to escape the Indian Ocean and make his way to the Pacific by sailing beneath Australia – a 7000-mile voyage across the notorious Southern Ocean from which there would be no return unless he found coal.

The gamble now seemed to have been a folly, for since that first week of March he had captured and sunk just three ships, all in the Indian Ocean: the *Jumna*, a rusty old 4000-ton tramp carrying salt destined for Colombo; the *Wordsworth*, a similar-sized freighter heading to Britain with a cargo of rice and other food; and the *Dee*, a three-masted barque he had intercepted in late March as she sailed from Mauritius to Western Australia loaded with nothing but ballast. All he had to show for those prizes were eighty-two new prisoners, some food provisions and 300 tons of coal, and even that had come at a heavy cost, for as the *Wolf* closed in on the *Jumna* off the Maldives a starboard gun had discharged while still turned in-board, detonating an oil barrel and an ammunition stockpile that had sprayed hot shrapnel and burning oil across the aft deck. A nearby torpedo crew and another crew preparing the motorboat for launch had taken the brunt of the blast, which killed four of them and wounded twenty-four others, some with shocking lacerations and burns.

The incident still cast a pall over the ship, for many of the injured were not yet fully recovered – one crewman had lost an eye, and another had had his arm amputated by Dr Hauswaldt, whose hospital became so overcrowded that he had been forced to set up an open-air surgery on the foredeck, where the cries of the wounded and burned drifted over the ship until morphine quietened them. No one who had witnessed the carnage would forget it quickly – Fritz Witschetzky's journal recorded the scene he had encountered after running down from the bridge: 'Seamen covered in blood come running towards me. A few of the severely wounded are already helped into the hospital. One is crawling on his hands dragging his useless legs along to get away from that place of horror. He is pale like wax and a trail of blood pours out of his body. That is as far as he gets; he collapses and dies . . . Two seamen support each other, the first holding his hand in front of his bleeding eyes, the second covering a gaping chest wound with an already blood-soaked cloth . . .'

Theodor Plivier, who witnessed the explosion tearing apart

the aft deck, had seen his shipmate Alrich Buskohl almost disembowelled and another seaman, Dierck Butendrift, running from the flames holding his lacerated arm aloft 'like a torch'. Buskohl had endured four days of agony before he eventually died, and Plivier described with bitterness the funerals of the dead, which were brief interregnums in the back-breaking work of transferring coal from the *Jumna*:

> We had a ten-minute pause in our labours and stood in a half-circle on the fore-deck – the bunker and whip parties and the men at the winches and derricks. Backs and legs were bare, black and sticky with sweat . . . In the middle lay the dead man sewn up in sail-cloth, with a piece of iron at his feet. The commander read a prayer. We stared at the yellow glare of the ship's lanterns set out in solemn array, and at the outspread ensign. Two men raised the bier and the dead man slipped overboard. We heard the splash in the water.
>
> Next day we sank the Jumna.

As gunnery officer, Fritz Witschetzky was compelled to accept responsibility for the tragedy, which had been caused when a tiny steel shaving from a lathe lodged itself on the base of one of the shells, triggering the detonation when the gun's breech slammed shut. It was a freakish accident, but one that redoubled the contempt some of the crew felt towards Witschetzky. 'Perhaps it wasn't the gunnery officer's fault,' Plivier reasoned. 'But was it necessary to load the guns while they were still trained inboard our own ship? And against a poor, unarmed merchantman, moreover? Besides, we all knew him, absorbed in his dachshunds, with his paint-box and pencil, or playing at photography.'

Beneath the aft deck, in the prison bunker that had once been the number-four cargo hold, the mood was no less gloomy. There were now nearly ninety men in this windowless iron tank, which measured fifty feet long by thirty feet wide and was accessible only by a single ladder descending from a hatch cover between decks under the poop. The prisoners were mostly British, Irish,

Australian or New Zealand merchant seamen, along with a handful of Europeans and the picaresque addition of the *Dee*'s crew – two Frenchmen and a dozen Mauritians, some as young as thirteen, under the command of a white-bearded sexagenarian named Captain John Rugg.

In the first month of their captivity, the men had been united by a cocky bravado that masked their very real fear of the Germans. Tom Meadows, the burly and sun-burnished thirty-eight-year-old captain of the *Turritella*, had offered one of the German officers a £3-bet that the Royal Navy would capture the *Wolf* within two weeks. The *Jumna*'s captain, a veteran British seaman named Shaw Wickmann, had remarked phlegmatically that the war would be over soon anyway, if Germany's U-boats continued to wreak such immense devastation. The *Jumna*, Wickmann said, had been the only one of six freighters that had left Spain on the same day to survive the Mediterranean crossing. When Captain John Shields and his thirty-strong crew from the *Wordsworth* were brought down into the hold, Wickmann had stepped forward with a sardonic smile and said, 'Hello, John, it's a small world.' The two men, it transpired, were cousins.

That jocularity had ebbed away after the *Wolf*'s course took it below Australia and the men realised that the Germans had eluded their pursuers. Until then, the prisoners had been allowed up to the poop deck every day to wash, exercise and play cards under armed guard, but the vicious weather of these legendary latitudes had forced everyone below for days at a stretch. The currents of the Southern Ocean, which encircle Antarctica unimpeded by any land mass, conjure storm-force westerly gales and mountainous seas. The *Wolf* was fortunate to be crossing in early autumn, when icebergs rarely drift up on the polar currents, but the raider's course cut through a stretch of ocean between southern Australia and the northern shores of Antarctica that was known to all sailors as the 'Roaring Forties'. At night, the prisoners' hammocks had swayed and rocked to the ship's pitching course through the freezing waters; by day, the hammocks were stashed away and the prisoners sat under swaying light bulbs at makeshift card tables or sprawled on the iron floor. Above them, the wind shrieked through the rigging and hurled the ocean across the deck in grey sheets; crewmen on watch clung to their posts enshrouded in wet-weather gear, enduring hours of whipping rain and sea spray. For two weeks, no land had been seen, the sky was perpetually leaden with storm clouds and no wireless transmissions had reached the ship through the blizzards of static. When the weather had briefly cleared south of New Zealand, the sky in the distance had glowed green and red with the optical atmospherics of Antarctica's aurora australis, before another storm front swept in and the sea again turned violent.

In the aftermath of those grinding weeks, life for the prisoners had become a numbing routine. Every morning, they rose at six o'clock to roll up hammocks and climb up on deck for muster and a quick bathe with a dipper of water under the poop. After a breakfast of black bread and bad coffee, they gathered on the poop to play cards and spin yarns until noon, when they would eat a meal of prune soup or preserved meat with rice. After another few hours on the poop, a dinner of more bread and more coffee was served, and at sunset they were sent below. By 9 pm, hammocks were slung and reading lights extinguished.

Boredom inevitably begat frustration, and fissures opened up between the men. The presence of the black crewmen from the *Dee* was now a grievance to some of the British sailors, unaccustomed as they were to sharing close quarters with 'niggers'. The Mauritians themselves were only just recovering from the trauma of their capture; the youngest of them had been so terrified at the sight of the *Wolf* that they had guzzled the *Dee*'s entire rum supply and become so incapacitated they had been winched aboard the raider with rope and tackle. Captain 'Jack' Rugg would normally have defended his young crew against the hostility of the whites, but he had sunk into a deep depression after watching his beloved barque blown to splinters off the coast of Australia – a spectacle that had caused him to weep openly.

Rugg's first mate, a wiry and pockmarked Frenchman named Jean Marton, was meanwhile absorbed in a splenetic feud with his captain. Marton claimed to have received a premonition of the *Dee*'s fate when a dead aunt visited him in a dream shortly after they left Mauritius, warning him that the ship was destined for trouble. But Rugg had brusquely dismissed the omen, and now the Frenchman blamed his dire predicament on his skipper and filled his diary with a scribbled litany of complaints about the food, the cold and the nightmares that woke him in the enveloping darkness of the prison hold. With only an iron wall separating them from the mine and torpedo armoury further forward, Marton was haunted by the knowledge that his hammock swayed a few feet from nearly a hundred tons of high explosives. Rugg, meanwhile, barely spoke except to quote the biblical scripture that had become his refuge.

In the dismal and fractious atmosphere that pervaded the ship, even Fritz Witschetzky had begun pondering the absurdity of the voyage. The gunnery officer could remember sailing into Auckland harbour in Christmas 1912 as a *leutnant* aboard the German warship *Cormoran*. In those happier days when New Zealand and Germany were still wary allies, Witschetzky had stood in full regalia alongside British sailors from the warship *Encounter* at the inauguration of New Zealand's first governor-general, the Earl of Liverpool, known more formally as Sir Arthur William de Brito Savile Foljambe. Now, the *Encounter* and her crewmen were thought to be somewhere on the nearby ocean hunting them, and Sir Arthur was sending telegrams from Auckland – intercepted and decoded by the *Wolf*'s wireless room – that reported the suicides of German immigrants imprisoned in the country's internment camps. The only land masses they had seen in two months were the rocky and uninhabited Antipodes Islands, with their precipitous grey cliffs plunging into icy white foam breakers, and the Bounty Islands further north – an unfortunate augury given that these islands had been named by Captain William Bligh shortly before he suffered the most legendary mutiny in naval history.

The *Wolf*'s crew were so restive that their veteran first officer, Kapitänleutnant Karl Schmehl, had been forced to call them together and dress them down, urging them to remember that internment meant spending the rest of the war in an Allied prison. The numbing monotony of their diet – black bread, bad coffee and stews made from tinned meat and dehydrated vegetables, supplemented by rice seized from the *Wordsworth* and tinned pineapple from the *Turritella* – was exacerbated by the tobacco shortage and the grinding labour caused by the constant coal fires, which had to be located in the darkened smoke-filled bunkers below and doused. Plivier was among the men assigned the onerous job of hauling endless baskets of coal from the vault, where lights hung suspended in wreaths of steam and the smoke was so thick that visibility was reduced to momentary glimpses of a leg, arm or face.

'Our heads buzzed and our bones were like lead,' he wrote. 'It was an effort to lift our shovels. And when we stood below the wind-sail and breathed in the air, not one of us spoke a word. We just stared stupidly at those who stood and vomited . . . They hauled a man up through the hatch and laid him on deck, another, and a third and fourth. Coal-gas poisoning! Beneath the cover of coaldust their faces and skin were ashy grey. The four men were borne lifeless to the sick bay.'

It was now depressingly clear to Nerger that his intelligence had been wrong; this windswept outer zone of the British Empire was a barren field for commerce-raiding. A steady stream of wireless reports was delivered to him in those fruitless days off New Zealand. To his amazement, the local shipping authorities were not bothering to encode their telegrams, despite the Admiralty's earlier warnings of a raider somewhere in the Indian Ocean, so he could eavesdrop freely on these *en clair* (plain English) Morse-code dispatches detailing ship movements all around him. But most were local ships running inconsequential cargo, and the few bulletins intercepted from the Pacific islands to the north complained of dwindling food and fuel supplies caused by the drastic shortage of freighters in the region. Few ships were making the crossing to South America, or even to the South Pacific islands. What Nerger could not have realised was that in the month just passed, Germany's U-boats had sunk an extraordinary 860,334 tons of shipping, prompting the British Government to postpone all troop transports and requisition virtually every freighter it could obtain.

In the last week of May, Nerger finally settled on a plan: he would lay mines off Australia and New Zealand, then head north and weave through the islands of New Guinea and the Dutch East Indies to return to the Indian Ocean, where he would wage his last campaign of sabotage. To accomplish the task, however, the *Wolf* needed a complete engine overhaul, which required a safe and isolated harbour. On 24 May, he issued the order to sail north to a small, crescent-shaped, uninhabited speck known as Sunday Island, more than 600 miles north of New Zealand. It was there, among the islands known as the Kermadecs, that the *Wolf* would drop anchor for the first time.

Sunday Island, also known as Raoul Island, was a rocky-shored and heavily forested volcanic outcrop that reared out of the Pacific twenty-nine degrees below the equator. A succession of foolhardy families had tried to settle on the island over the preceding seven decades, lured by the lush soil and sweeping bay that stretched along its western flank, only to be driven off by howling winds, sub-oceanic earthquakes and the volcanic rumblings that regularly emanated from deep in the island's bowels. The last occupants, Tom Bell and his wife Frederica, had spent thirty-six years on the island and raised a family of ten children, survived a cyclone that destroyed their entire settlement and finally had their tenancy revoked by the New Zealand Government, which evacuated them in 1914 on the prescient grounds that German raiders might head to the Pacific. The *Wolf*'s visit would add another melancholic chapter to the island's benighted history.

On a rain-sodden afternoon under a lowering grey sky, the raider dropped anchor off a north-east point of the island, sheltered from the westerlies by the looming hulk of Mount Moumoukar, whose peak was enshrouded in clouds. It was the day of the Pentecost, and crewmen emerged on deck to find the ship surrounded by rock formations and small islets veiled in rain mist, like ghost sentries. That evening, Witschetzky wrote in his diary, 'Black night without any stars; the rocks around us are black too and the rain continues without a break; the wind howls through the rigging and the stench of the coal gas coming from the cargo hold covers the ship like a blanket. Where and how will this trip end?'

The weather cleared the following morning to reveal Sunday Island's virtues: the Bell family's settlement could be seen on the beach surrounded by eucalypts and orange trees laden with fruit, and the bay in which the *Wolf* was anchored was so crystalline that the tropical fish darting beneath the ship flashed like shards of coloured glass. Nerger permitted his men to launch the rowboats and throw fishing lines overboard, but, after watching their incompetent attempts from the prisoners' deck for several hours, Captain Tom Meadows approached the guards and requested that he be allowed to take a boatload of prisoners out. Nerger acquiesced and the Germans watched with rueful amusement as their British and Australian captives hauled in a catch that almost filled their launch. A landing party, meanwhile, had gone ashore and found wild goats roaming the island, several of which were killed and brought on board, along with baskets of oranges and bananas. The Bells' house, they reported, had been evacuated so hastily that a 1914 calendar was still pinned to the kitchen wall and the family's furniture, cutlery and even a child's rocking horse remained in place as if awaiting their return.

Over the ensuing week, Meadows and the other prisoners watched enviously as boatloads of the *Wolf*'s crew rowed ashore to experience the luxury of setting their feet on land for the first time in six months. These sojourns were, however, short rests in a routine of relentless toil, as Nerger ordered his crew to completely overhaul the *Wolf* in round-the-clock four-hour shifts. Teams of men suspended from ropes scoured and repainted the corroded hull; more than 450 tons of coal was hauled up from the smoke-filled forward storage hold in baskets, then dragged across the deck to be dropped down into the coal bunkers near the engine room. The ship's engineers tested valves and cylinders, and shut down boilers to inspect them for damage and wear; the boiler tanks, whose seams were coming apart, were resealed with hot rivets forged from sawn-off segments of the iron handrails purloined from the *Turritella*. On 30 May, the source of the coal fire in the forward hold was finally located when a wooden partition burst into flames and the area was flooded with seawater.

The *Wolf*'s engines were still partially disabled on the afternoon of 2 June when a lookout in the topmast suddenly announced an approaching ship. Nerger swung his binoculars to the south and saw the outline of a steamship eight miles distant, its wireless aerial clearly visible. With only one boiler operational, Nerger had no hope of chasing the ship but realised he must intercept her or his position would be betrayed by nightfall, when the freighter's wireless signals would reach Samoa. Gambling that he could bluff the steamer's captain into surrendering, Nerger ordered the *Wolfchen* airborne.

The cargo ship *Wairuna* had left Auckland two days previously with a load of wool, hides, copra and flax, bound for San Francisco. The ship was a 3947-ton steamer with a crew of forty-two, several of whom had survived stints as infantrymen in Europe. One of them, Harry Ross, had been wounded at the ill-fated Gallipoli invasion in 1915 and suffered such ill health since his return to New Zealand that his doctor had recommended a sea voyage as a curative. Tom Rees, a hot-tempered Welshman who was the *Wairuna*'s second mate, had already survived one encounter with the German Navy, for he had been serving as second mate aboard the Australian steamship *Ashburton* when she was torpedoed and sunk by a U-boat in the English Channel in early 1915. Rees was first to spot the *Wolf* as the *Wairuna* approached Sunday Island, but his premonitory remark that the ship looked like a German raider was dismissed as 'ridiculous' by his captain, Harold Saunders.

Saunders was not the most likeable skipper employed by the Union Steamship Company – his ill temper was aggravated by an addiction to patent medicine – but he couldn't be entirely blamed for his lack of foresight. Although New Zealand and Australian naval authorities had known about the dangers of a raider in the Pacific since March, and although Japan had been asked to send warships to northern Australia, raider warnings were no longer being issued to merchant ships, and uncoded wireless communication was still permitted. So Saunders was entirely unprepared when, within twenty minutes of his first mate's remark, a biplane lifted off from the sea near the black freighter and headed towards them, droning so low overhead that it nearly clipped their masts as it dropped a weighted bag onto the *Wairuna*'s deck. Retrieved by a crew member, the bag was brought up to the bridge, where Saunders opened it and found the *Wolf*'s customary note of greeting. On a second pass, the *Wolfchen* added emphasis by dropping a bomb, which exploded off the *Wairuna*'s bow, and Saunders hastily brought his ship to a halt. Well out of wireless range of any land, he watched helplessly as the black raider cast off from Sunday Island and approached at slow speed with its guns visible.

Roy Alexander, the *Wairuna*'s twenty-year-old Australian-born wireless operator, was still destroying the ship's documentation on the bridge when the German prize crew walked in, bearing guns and cheerful greetings. By sunset, the two ships were back in the lee of Sunday Island, and Alexander and most of the officers were in the prison hold of the *Wolf* while the ordinary crewmen of the *Wairuna* were kept aboard her to help transfer cargo. It would prove an arduous job, for the *Wairuna* was to have sailed on to London from San Francisco and had been generously provisioned with enough food to last eighteen months, including forty-two live sheep and large stores of butter, frozen meat, cheese and fresh water. She was also carrying 1150 tons of coal – a godsend to Nerger after his months of fruitless searching. In a sign of the familiarity developing between the Germans and their prisoners, several of the British prisoners offered to help with the coaling, until Tom Meadows unleashed a barrage of abuse at them.

By dint of his glowering presence and caustic wit, Meadows had emerged as the de facto leader of the prison hold. Like most New Zealanders of his era, he was an ardent Anglophile, and the Germans honoured his unquenchable patriotism by dubbing him 'John Bull'. After three months of observing Nerger's rigorous approach to his mission, however, Meadows was no longer predicting the *Wolf*'s imminent capture. The speed and efficiency with which the Germans had converted his oil-tanker into a minelayer had earned Meadows's reluctant admiration; even the processing of each new intake of prisoners – the strip-and-search on the poop deck, the inventory of all their belongings, the shower with antiseptic soap, the steam-cleaning of clothes and the distribution of hammocks and instructions – was carried out with systematic rigour. The *Wairuna*'s crewmen were astonished when Meadows told them the raider had been at sea since December, and aghast to hear his assessment of their prospects. The ship's mission, he explained, hinged on absolute secrecy, making it unthinkable that Nerger would let any of his prisoners go free. 'We shall return to Germany with her,' he predicted, 'if she ever gets there.'

It was a prediction that proved too much to contemplate for Meadows's chief engineer, Arthur Steers. A New Zealander like his skipper, Steers lived in Dunedin, less than a week's sailing from where they were now anchored, and reasoned that if he could swim to Sunday Island he could survive on fish and fruit until a passing whaler or steamship spotted him. The main obstacles, apart from the German guards, were the gliding shadows beneath the ship. Sharks were so numerous here that the German crewmen had taken to hauling them from the water with baited fishing lines and slaughtering them on deck to carve out their spinal columns, which they fashioned into pearl-white walking sticks. Nerger had requisitioned one of these creations as a lucky talisman, which was now fastened to the *Wolf*'s prow. Despite the dangers, Steers convinced the *Turritella*'s first officer, Alec Clelland, to attempt an escape before the *Wolf* left the island, and the two men put together a survival kit consisting of knives, fishing line, matches wrapped in oiled silk and makeshift flotation devices made from cork panels torn from two of the *Wolf*'s life-vests.

Nerger's plan, once coaling was complete, was to sink the *Wairuna* and sail west to lay mines off Sydney harbour, Australia's largest port, before the moon became too bright. But bad weather bedevilled him, and the howling westerlies that whipped across Sunday Island sometimes made it impossible to lash the two ships together. For two weeks, Nerger moved the *Wolf* and the *Wairuna* around the island, searching for anchorages calm enough to enable his crew to finish their maintenance and transfer the coal and food supplies. The decks of both ships became caked with coal dust, and the boredom of the prisoners was relieved only by an occasional concert performance by the German brass band, which Roy Alexander judged to be among the very worst he had ever heard.

At some point during those interminable days, Clelland and Steers made their move. At dusk one evening as the Germans ordered everyone below from the aft deck, the other prisoners huddled together to form a shield, enabling the two men to slip over the aft deck rail and shin down a shark rope to the rudder. Their plan was to hang on until nightfall and then swim the mile across to the island. By the next morning, there was no sign of them.

On 16 June, the coal transfer was finally finished, and the *Wairuna* was taken out to sea to meet her fate, only to get a brief reprieve when a sailing ship appeared in the distance. It was the *Winslow*, a 567-ton American barque carrying supplies from Sydney to Samoa and then San Francisco, where her captain, Robert Trudgett, lived with his wife and two children. Trudgett was an old friend of Stan and Mary Cameron's, who were at that moment approaching Fiji from the north-east in the *Beluga*.

Intercepted by the *Wolfchen*, the ship was found to be carrying 350 tons of coal, fifty boxes of benzine fuel and 1500 boiler bricks that could be used to reline the *Wolf*'s overworked boilers. It was a prize too tempting for Nerger to pass up, and he ordered all three ships back to the island.

It would be another five days before the *Wolf* finally left Sunday Island. The *Wairuna* was taken out to sea on 18 June and punctured with holes by the raider's guns until she rolled over and was sucked under the Pacific. The *Winslow* followed her three days later, after an arduous transfer of coal and cargo delayed by gale-force winds. Destroying the barque proved just as difficult – like Jack Rugg, Trudgett wept openly as he watched his ship set afire, bombed and finally ripped apart by a fusillade of shells, all of which failed to sink her, so that the splintered skeleton of the old barque drifted back towards the island in flames. Nerger had now lost the advantage of a new moon and was forced to abandon his plans to mine Sydney Harbour.

Trudgett's crewmen had told him the oceans around Australia were patrolled by a formidable contingent of warships that included the battle-cruiser *Australia* along with five Australian and Japanese destroyers and sundry British cruisers sent to protect troop transports. Whether by design or ignorance, this was as far from the truth as could be imagined: only a few weeks earlier, Australia's remnant flotilla of three destroyers had been requisitioned to the Mediterranean on the Admiralty's orders, leaving the entire eastern seaboard of the country defended by the *Encounter* and two light-cruisers from the Japanese Navy, which had arrived in response to the beseeching requests Australia had sent to London. Nerger might well have fulfilled the Australian Navy's fears about the destruction of Sydney Harbour had he been able to gather more accurate intelligence and secure his coal supply more quickly. Instead, he decided to set course further south towards the coastline of Victoria. It was not until three days into the voyage that his guards finally discovered that Clelland and Steers had disappeared.

In the confusion and chaos of the final days off Sunday Island, the prisoners had covered the absence of the two missing men by answering to their names at roll call. A more rigorous inspection once the ship was under way had revealed their escape, prompting an appearance in the prison hold by the young prison officer Leutnant Arthur von Auerswald, clad in full dress-whites and incandescent with rage. Auerswald berated the prisoners for abusing their privileges as guests of the German Navy, then went up to the bridge to report the escape and endure an equally violent tirade from his captain, who ordered the guards confined to the ship's punishment cells. Nerger's worst fears seemed to be confirmed when a crewman reported evidence that the escapees might have reached Sunday Island: during one of their final visits to collect fruit on the island, a crewman had noticed that the calendar in the Bell cottage was open to 21 June 1914, exactly three years earlier. At the time, it had seemed merely an uncanny coincidence; now it seemed possible that Clelland and Steers had been using the Bell cottage for shelter and gone into hiding when the *Wolf* suddenly reappeared with the *Winslow* in tow.

In the prison hold, the hilarity generated by Auerswald's rant was soon muted by the news that a lockdown was being enforced. The prisoners were to be held below until further notice, with latrine breaks their only respite. The arrival of the *Wairuna* and *Winslow* crews meant there were now more than a hundred and fifty men below, and hammocks were being strung in two tiers to accommodate them. It was over the ensuing weeks, as they endured bitterly cold nights and long days of boredom and overcrowding, that the prisoners devised a new nickname for their claustrophobic iron bunker: the Hell Hole.

* *

On the night of 25 June 1917 – the same day on which the escape of Clelland and Steers was detected – the prisoners heard above them the dull thud of iron rails being laid across the aft deck in preparation for minelaying. The iron wall separating the Hell Hole from the mines had been so shaken by the shuddering discharges of the *Wolf*'s guns that rivets had popped out, leaving holes the prisoners could peer through to observe the deadly iron eggs in their horizontal racks. Now they could see the Germans checking fuses, measuring cable lengths and preparing to winch the mines up to the deck. During their last glimpse of daylight earlier that morning, the prisoners had deduced that they were near Cape Maria van Diemen, on the north-west tip of New Zealand. At ten o'clock that night, the mines began going overboard.

An uneasy silence now settled over the Hell Hole, for the prisoners had sensed the jittery nerves of the crew even before the minelaying began. The shared dread of the prisoners was accentuated by a security measure the Germans had instituted to minimise the visibility of the ship at night. Blue light bulbs had been installed, and these swaying lights now cast a deadened spectral glow over the prisoners that suggested, to Roy Alexander, their death foretold. 'The prisoners, in that ghastly light, looked like moving corpses,' recalled Alexander. 'Each man seemed to see his neighbour in a new aspect; to scrutinise him with a ghoulish curiosity – to suddenly see him as he would appear if, and when, he were drowned.'

The minelaying lasted five hours as the ship methodically moved about the cape, spreading twenty-five mines over several square miles. By the time it was over, the only prisoners still awake were Tom Rees and the Frenchman Jean Marton, both of whom were determinedly counting the mines as they went overboard and recording their estimated location – Marton by tying knots in a length of string (while cursing the Germans) and Rees using a pencil and paper salvaged from the *Wairuna*. Shaw Wickmann from the *Jumna* had miraculously managed to smuggle one of his charts into the prison hold, and Rees had resolved to keep as accurate a record as he could of the minelaying in the unlikely chance he was able to get it to the Allies.

Two nights later, a prisoner returned from the latrine to report that he had just glimpsed the distant snow-capped peak of Mount Egmont, which towers above the northern shore of the strait separating the north and south islands of New Zealand. That night, the *Wolf* ventured within a hundred miles of Wellington, the capital, and laid thirty-five mines just outside the strait before slipping back out to sea. For three days, the *Wolf* made heavy going due west, and the prisoners surmised that Nerger intended to lay more mines off the eastern coast of Australia. On the afternoon of 3 July, the ship reached its destination.

Nerger had set his sights on Gabo Island, a tiny outcrop so close to the south-eastern tip of mainland Australia as to be virtually a promontory. Roughly equidistant between Sydney to the north and Melbourne to the south, it was a kind of crossing point for freighters and passenger-ships operating between the two cities. Nerger had wanted to reach here by 2 June, before the full moon, but the heavy seas of the Tasman had delayed him. As a precaution, he ordered the *Wolf*'s telescopic masts lowered and the funnel extension dismantled; from a distance, such simple changes gave the raider a squat silhouette that was significantly different from the description circulated in March. Nerger had already picked up wireless messages from the Japanese cruisers *Chikuma* and *Hirado*, which were stationed just 160 miles up the coast at Jervis Bay; he had seen no evidence of the flotilla of warships the *Winslow*'s crew spoke of, but venturing within ten miles of the Australian coastline under a nearly full moon was a gamble. As if in warning, the setting sun drenched the sea blood red as land came into sight. The crew were winching mines up to the *Wolf*'s deck in its fading glow when a steamship suddenly appeared and passed within five miles. By nightfall, the raider was starkly framed in the moon's ghost-light, and the minelaying was suspended three times as steamships appeared and sailed past in clear view. At midnight, a fourth steamer suddenly appeared from the south, hugging the coastline, to draw within 1500 yards of the Germans. Alarmed, Nerger ordered a general alert and the crew abandoned the mines to rush to the gun and torpedo placements, preparing to drop the raider's bulwarks and fire on the interloper.

Down in the prison hold, the prisoners heard the commotion above deck and waited in the darkness, feeling the ship lurch as she abruptly changed direction. Roy Alexander recalled that the only sounds were the pounding of the *Wolf*'s engines and the whimpering of a terrified young Mauritian boy from the *Dee*. In that suspended state, they lay in their hammocks, nerves tuned to the pitch and yaw of the ship, ears straining for the first shouted order to fire. The moment lingered, every man aware of the ocean lapping against the sides of the hold, and minutes dragged past until the sound of another mine trundling across the deck broke the tension. One of the prisoners got up to stretch, others followed suit, and wary conversation began again in the darkness. The danger had passed, and an hour later the raider was heading back out into the Tasman.

* *

The *Wolf* had laid thirty mines off Australia and sixty-one in two separate fields off New Zealand, and the crew's rekindled sense of their mission was emboldened still further when the wireless operators picked up a report of the *Mongolia*'s sinking off Bombay. The *Wolf* was barely more than a day's sailing from the Australian coast when the radio brought more immediate news – the minefield off Gabo Island had already claimed its first victim, the 9471-ton British freighter *Cumberland*.

The *Cumberland*'s captain, a tough Scotsman by the name of Alex McGibbon, would later recall that he was just finishing his breakfast porridge on the morning of 6 July when two loud explosions shook the ship and he rushed on deck to see smoke drifting from a forward hatch. The ship had left Sydney barely twenty-four hours earlier, destined for London with a full cargo of frozen meat, wool bales, Red Cross parcels, lead and copper, and the crew immediately launched the lifeboats and stood off to watch her death throes. But the *Cumberland* settled low in the ocean and McGibbon – who only three days earlier had been released from hospital after having his appendix removed – took ten of the crew back on board and managed to nurse the crippled ship onto the beach at Gabo Island, where she lay listing so dangerously to the port side that her decks were awash. After sending out a distress signal reporting that he had struck a mine, McGibbon waited for assistance.

In Melbourne, news of the disaster reached Australian naval headquarters almost immediately, and a telegram was dispatched to the Admiralty in London. An immediate ban was imposed on any press reporting of the matter and the Japanese Navy cruiser *Chikuma* – at the time conducting torpedo practice off the coast only 160 miles to the north – was dispatched to the scene. The commander of the *Chikuma* was Rear-Admiral Kazuyoshi Yamaji, whose impossible task it was to protect the oceans around Australia and New Zealand in 1917. For three days, no information about the *Cumberland* disaster was released, and rumours swept Australia that a German raider or submarine was prowling off the eastern coastline. Finally, on 8 July, the Japanese admiral reported that divers sent down to inspect the freighter had observed a twenty-two-foot gash in her hull, the edges of which curled outwards. This, Yamaji said, 'fully illustrates that her explosion occurred from inside and not from outside, and I dare say that the damage was not caused by striking [a] mine as was first supposed'.

When the news was released, Australia's newspapers erupted with sensational headlines. 'INTERNAL EXPLOSIONS' announced *The Age* on 9 July, quoting official statements from the Australian Navy that suggested, in essence, that two bombs had gone off in the *Cumberland*'s cargo holds. Mirroring the false stories of sabotage that had previously circulated in South Africa and India, it implied that traitors were at work on the Australian docks. It was an alarming claim that would soon blossom into a government-orchestrated panic.

Serious doubts about Rear-Admiral Yamaji's assessment arose almost immediately within the navy, for even as Australia's newspapers carried breathless reports of this act of sabotage on home soil, a navy diver named Henry Maiden arrived on the scene to inspect the *Cumberland*, and his conclusions were diametrically different from those of the Japanese. Maiden reported that the hole in the *Cumberland* turned inwards, suggesting the ship had struck a mine, and he believed it would have been impossible for a small explosive device hidden in the cargo hold to have caused such immense damage to a freighter of the *Cumberland*'s size. Although he was completely correct, Maiden suffered the fate of many who bear unwelcome news to their superiors: he was ignored. By the time his views were circulating in the navy, the state government of New South Wales had already offered a £1000 reward for information leading to the capture of the saboteurs, along with a pardon to any accomplice willing to testify. Police in Sydney were grilling the *Cumberland*'s crew, and an undercover agent was assigned to infiltrate them after their release. The unlucky Swedish freighter *Tasmanic*, which had just docked in Melbourne, was again detained and her crew interrogated. Having already crossed paths with the *Wolf* in South Africa nearly six months earlier, the *Tasmanic* had managed to arrive in port just as another ship fell victim to the raider's mines.

'Everything points to foul play,' said the navy minister, Joseph Cook. 'I hope we may discover the fiends responsible for it and punish them.'

The readiness of navy and government officials to accept the sabotage theory is remarkable considering that Australia had been on alert for more than a year for signs of raider activity. As recently as March, after the *Wolf* was first detected in the Indian Ocean, Brigadier-General Victor Selheim, a senior army officer, had warned the navy that 'the first intimation of the presence of the raider in our waters will probably be the loss of some of our shipping'. Prime Minister Hughes had himself initially acknowledged that the *Cumberland* might have been mined but within two weeks was offering a £2000 reward to anyone who could provide information that unmasked the ship's saboteurs.

To acknowledge the most likely explanation – that a minefield had been laid less than ten miles off the Australian coast – was something no one in Allied officialdom readily welcomed. It would have created acute difficulties for Rear-Admiral Yamaji, who was supposed to be defending the country with two light cruisers that had much the same firepower as the *Wolf* but lacked the *Wolf*'s great advantage of a seaplane. It would be a major embarrassment for the Admiralty, which had been rebuffing Australia's demands for more naval protection for more than a year. And it would strongly suggest that the *Wolf* had reached the South Pacific – a scenario Britain's own naval-intelligence analysts had raised only five weeks earlier but that had never been made public. So Henry Maiden's views were shunted aside, and the hunt for the *Cumberland*'s saboteurs was launched in earnest.

Aboard the *Wolf*, which escaped north as Rear-Admiral Yamaji's ship passed it to the west, Nerger was able to monitor all the communications between the Japanese warship and the Australian Navy, which he recorded verbatim in his war diary. These latest reports of internal explosions caused much mirth aboard the raider. 'I naturally thought of my share in the two "internal explosions",' Nerger remarked. '. . . As it was very painful [for Britain] to think that a German cruiser could continue her wicked course undisturbed, innocent people had to be accused of the crimes.' Albert Wieduwilt was similarly nonplussed. 'For the time being it is thought in Australia that the accident was caused by an internal explosion and not by a mine,' he wrote in his diary. 'Why this is thought in Australia one doesn't know. In any case, it is to be kept from the people . . .'

It had become clear to the Germans, listening in on local naval communications, that the few warships in the area presented little threat to them. 'Proud England no longer has enough warships here for the protection of its local shipping,' Wieduwilt remarked. But Nerger was anxious to put some distance between himself and the minefields he had just laid, reasoning that whatever the Australian Navy was telling the public about the *Cumberland* disaster might bear little relation to its actual knowledge. Putting the ship on full throttle to the north-east, he was heading away from the cool winds of the Pacific's lower latitudes and towards the balmier warmth of the tropics. Two days out from Gabo Island, the prisoners were allowed out on deck for their first time in more than two weeks, and by 9 July the raider was 1100 miles away from Gabo Island, sailing under a brilliant blue Pacific sky. At 2.30 that afternoon, a lookout spotted the white flash of a sail on the horizon and called out a warning.

Nerger raised his binoculars and focused on the ship, leisurely approaching under full sail. He could just make out her three masts and a lanyard flying the Stars and Stripes, and ordered his men to their battle stations. It was only as the *Wolf* drew close that Nerger saw the tiny figure of six-year-old Juanita Cameron emerging from below the aft deck, dressed in her best Sunday frock and cheerfully waving a handkerchief.

2

2

5

JUANITA'S WAR

The morning after her father's sailing ship was destroyed in a pyre of flame, the diminutive figure of Juanita Cameron could be found roaming the deck of the *Wolf*, dressed in a white smock and clutching her favourite doll. When Leutnant Fritz Witschetzky came across the little girl, she was crouched on the poop deck trying vainly to sit her doll astride one of the five hyperactive dachshunds that had the run of the ship. Witschetzky stooped to talk and learned very quickly that this gaggle of stumpy-legged sausage dogs named Gottlieb, Moritz, Lorbass, Flock and Schumm was a terrible disappointment to an American six-year-old. Dachshunds, like all things German, were now shunned and reviled in the United States, and Juanita had absorbed some of that prejudice. But, as the day wore on, her resistance to the dogs' antics gave way, for with her mother lying ill in their cabin and her father keeping a constant bedside vigil, there was little else for her to do.

With a child's happy knack for focusing on the moment, Juanita had quickly discarded her memories of the disturbing few days just passed; even her mother's illness, mystifying as it was, granted her unfettered freedom to explore the strange new environment of this enormous ship. Already on that first morning she had watched in wonderment as the *Wolfchen* was lowered by crane onto the water like some ungainly bird, then cranked into life and sent scudding across the waves, finally roaring up into the blue Pacific sky at impossible speed to disappear like a speck of dust.

The ship's decks were a jumbled obstacle course that demanded exploration, with their spools and webs of rigging, their mysterious canvas-shrouded mounds and towering ventilation funnels. Winches loomed overhead and hatches led down to darkness. Venturing to the back of the ship, Juanita discovered a wooden pen where the surviving sheep from the *Wairuna* were kept. Men appeared in hatchways from below, their faces and arms caked black from coal dust, their smiles a comical flash of white. From the upper reaches of the ship, near the cabins where her parents were confined, came men like Witschetzky, dressed in tropical whites. Crewmen and officers alike stopped to talk to her in their hesitant, amusing English, asking her name and her age. By the end of that first day, she was already accustomed to a newly Germanicised nickname: 'Anita'.

Stan Cameron was discomfited by his daughter's solitary roamings around the ship, but for the moment he had far greater worries. Since their capture three days ago, neither he nor Mary had slept. Fear and anxiety had kept them awake aboard the *Beluga*, and unrelenting noise had prevented sleep here on the *Wolf*, for the small cabin they had first been assigned amidships was located directly above a pump room that emitted a continual din of ice machines and air pistons. Mary had refused to watch the *Beluga*'s destruction, knowing that its sinking would take with it any hope of her long-anticipated reunion with her parents. To have almost reached Australia made the cruelty of their imprisonment even keener, and in desperation Mary had asked Nerger to transmit a wireless message confirming their capture, so that her parents would at least know she was alive. The German captain, however, had apologetically explained that such a favour would endanger his mission and was thus impossible. Exhausted and fearful, distressed by the knowledge that they would soon be reported lost at sea, Mary's stoicism had cracked. Within days of coming aboard the *Wolf*, she was bedridden with a severe fever.

Stan had consulted the ship's physician, Dr Hermann Hauswaldt, who prescribed a sleeping powder and arranged for the Camerons to be moved to a quieter room further back in the deckhouse. But the new quarters, while quieter, were situated above the engine boilers, and intense heat radiated from the iron bulkhead next to the bunk. With the ship baking under the tropical sun all day, the temperature in the room regularly reached forty degrees Celsius even with the door propped open, and for Stan the claustrophobia was exacerbated by the security precautions on the *Wolf*, because an automatic switch in each cabin extinguished the lights when the door opened, rendering it impossible for him to read after dark. After two nights in this room, Mary still had not slept, and her condition deteriorated so drastically that Stan was finally forced to call on Hauswaldt to come and see her. When the doctor arrived, he found her in a delirious state, her face burning from a ferocious fever.

Stan would later say that the ensuing two weeks were his most awful experience aboard the *Wolf*, which gives some measure of the gravity of his wife's condition given all that was to follow. Consumed by fever and her fear of the Germans, Mary began suffering horrendous hallucinations, thrashing around in her bunk, saturated in sweat for hours on end. 'Owing to the experience I had undergone during the past few days my own nerves were all ragged and upset,' Stan recalled, 'and the continual raving and shrieking of my wife, who imagined herself undergoing the most awful torture, drove me nearly crazy. Some days and nights seemed never to come to an end.'

Brushing Mary's hair one day to try to calm her, Stan was shocked to feel it come away in his hands; soon, her luxuriant brown mane had almost entirely fallen out. Hauswaldt ordered her to be packed in ice, but her temperature continued to soar and her condition deteriorated so badly that Stan became convinced she was 'gradually sinking until she had come to the place where she either had to make a turn for the better or pass into the Great Beyond'. Like many men of his generation, Cameron was wont to blame women's ailments on the mysteries of the female nervous system; he described Mary, somewhat contradictorily, as 'highly strung and courageous' and believed she was having a breakdown. Hauswaldt's journal offers another clue – on 20 July, she was admitted to the ship's hospital after a streptococcal sore erupted on her left arm, and the severity of her illness suggests an infection exacerbated by her psychological distress. After three weeks aboard the raider, she was still bedridden and delirious.

Loath to let Juanita witness her mother's disintegration, Stan resigned himself to letting his daughter roam the ship, and her absences grew longer. Strictly forbidden from approaching the prisoners on the aft deck, Juanita turned to the German crewmen for company and quickly acquired a retinue of her favourite sailors and a grasp of their strange language. Among them was Leutnant Ernst Szielasko, who had been thoroughly disarmed by the little girl's unfettered friendliness towards her new companions after enduring two months of solitude on the *Beluga*. Szielasko was sitting on the deck of the *Wolf* with her one afternoon, as she scribbled in a colouring book and chatted nonsensically about horses, when Juanita suddenly exclaimed, 'Oh, how nice it is to be here with you – I'm so glad I don't have to stay on Papa's old tub.'

'She was a very smart and bright little girl,' he recalled. 'It took me some trouble to convince her family that the English tales about our treatment of prisoners were completely false and they had nothing to fear from us.'

To sailors whose days were spent in a cycle of toil, tedium and uncertainty, the innocent delight that this moon-faced urchin took in her new surrounds was a balm. Crewmen hoisted her on their shoulders or chased her around the deck, and the two doctors and three of the ship's officers dressed up in their tropical whites to pose for a photograph with her seated along the barrel of one of the ship's guns. As the *Wolf* approached the Solomon Islands, work on the deck was occasionally interrupted by the incongruous sight of four German sailors linking hands with her to dance around the deck. In those moments, the war and its hatreds were briefly forgotten, and the barriers that separated the Germans from their prisoners dissolved.

In the officers' wardroom, the crew's mess and even the stokers' mess under the forecastle deck, where grime-caked men from the engine rooms congregated for their meals, Juanita whiled away the hours enjoying, as her father recalled, 'the time of her life'. The ship's tailor mended her clothes; the cooks gave her treats; the crew devised a nickname that she wore with pride: '*bordplage*' ('ship's pest'). In the tropical heat, crewmen working night shifts often slept on deck during daylight, and Juanita would creep among them armed with a feather, tickling their noses. Occasionally, she lay between two of them feigning sleep – an innocent game that cannot have assuaged her father's worries. Her presence was even tolerated up on the bridge, where she would appear with the dachshunds in tow and idly flick through logbooks and wireless transcripts. Her hair became so entangled that her ailing mother instructed Stan to cut it into a bob, and her dresses became so grimy that they were packed away and she wore pants and shirts.

Even the reclusive Karl Nerger succumbed to her charms, and she became a daily intruder into the sanctity of his cabin. Nerger's youngest child, Bruno, was roughly the same age as Juanita, and in his account of the voyage he devoted several pages of affectionate reminiscence to the antics of 'Anita': 'A "*Dreikäsehoch*" she was – a bit of a boy, with her blonde hair cropped short, khaki shirt and trousers. She had bright blue eyes. Only on Sundays did she present herself as a lady, in a white dress. She had a strong affection for the pilot of the *Wolfchen*. Not surprising, as he had a daughter of about the same age back home.'

Juanita had good reason to notice Paul Fabeck, for she had witnessed a great drama involving the pilot on her very first afternoon aboard the raider, when the *Wolfchen* came in to land on a heavy swell and suddenly crashed nose-first into the ocean. The impact flipped the plane vertically onto its propeller, splintering its pontoons, tearing gashes in its threadbare fabric and forcing Fabeck and his flight officer to climb the inverted tail as sharks began circling. For Fabeck, it meant two weeks aboard the ship with nothing to do while the *Wolfchen* was repaired, and the airman quickly became Juanita's favourite among the crew. 'He was her "dear Paul",' recalled Nerger, 'her "darling", and was offered all the pet names and endearments the little devil could think of.'

For Stan Cameron, the fears of those first weeks aboard the *Wolf* were exacerbated by isolation, because Nerger at first insisted on his conditions that he remain amidships and not attempt to approach any of the prisoners or crew. But the American quickly became friendly with the German officers, in particular Leutnant Szielasko, who stopped by almost every evening to discuss the war or share tales of his sailing days in San Francisco. Like most old-school seamen, Szielasko had an almost inexhaustible fund of adventure stories, and he had survived a semi-legendary shipwreck in these very waters twelve years earlier while working on the American barque *Susquehanna*. When the ship went down near the Solomon Islands, the German and several fellow-crewmen had washed up on a nearby island, where they lived for two months and narrowly escaped a tribe of headhunters before being rescued by a passing freighter – or so the story went.

Cameron also began frequenting Karl Nerger's quarters, for the two skippers had developed a grudging mutual admiration that overrode their language barrier. Stan was profoundly grateful for the care his wife had received from Dr Hauswaldt, a tall and unflappable young surgeon who had trained in obstetrics; he was surprised, too, by the civility that Nerger displayed towards his family. The clothes they had retrieved from the *Beluga* had been steam-cleaned and returned to them neatly folded, and his camera had even been given back to him with its roll of film developed. The meals brought to their cabin were identical to those eaten by Nerger and his officers – bread and coffee for breakfast, then soup, vegetables and meat or rice for midday dinner, followed by a supper of bread with corned beef or sardines, and every second day a dessert of stewed fruit. In consideration of Mary Cameron's fragile health, Nerger had ordered his crew to avoid the passageway outside her cabin and instructed the *Wolf*'s purser to supply the family with milk from the *Beluga*'s food supply, along with wine for Stan and some of the delicacies taken from their ship. Nerger had even appointed a crewman to act as their orderly. When Cameron noticed a German sailor wearing a pair of his deck shoes from the *Beluga*, he asked the orderly whether they could be returned to him; twenty-four hours later, the shoes were sitting outside his cabin door, freshly polished.

In their halting conversations, Stan was surprised to find the German captain 'a very agreeable man to talk to; a thorough gentleman and apparently anxious to do anything he could to make our lot bearable'. When Cameron complained of his isolation, Nerger replied with a sardonic smile, 'One can get used to it.' The German captain was, indeed, a man alone. As far as Stan could tell, he confided his plans to no one, spent long hours confined in his cabin and exercised his ironclad control of the ship through sheer force of personality. His uniform was so immaculate that he seemed to have 'just stepped out of a bandbox'. Loneliness may well have led Nerger to respond to the company of this American skipper, whose family surely reminded him of his own wife and children in Hamburg. In Nerger's estimation, Cameron was 'a splendid chap with honest, straight opinions'.

It was not until the end of July that Dr Hauswaldt advised Stan that his wife appeared to be over the worst of her illness, although he warned her recovery would be slow and prolonged. The trauma of Mary's illness was so great that Stan had paid little heed when, on 14 July, the *Wolf* overtook another sailing ship 250 miles west of Nouméa. It was the third San Francisco ship the *Wolf* had intercepted in the past month – the *Encore*, a 650-ton barque much like the *Beluga* and *Winslow*, carrying a cargo of Oregon timber to Sydney. Her captain, Anton Olsen, and his crew of ten were well known to Stan but had come aboard without seeing him and were taken straight down to the prison hold.

The mood in the prison hold had become even more fractious as the overcrowding worsened. A strong camaraderie had united the prisoners when most of them were from Britain and its dominions, but that was splintering now that the dim hold was congested with 175 men from many different backgrounds.

Roy Alexander had sensed the growing tensions during the lockdown, a month after he arrived aboard the *Wolf* with the rest of the *Wairuna*'s fifty-strong crew. The resentment that Alexander's crewmates felt towards their imperious captain, Harold Saunders, had deepened since they discovered that the *Wolf* had been running on only one boiler when she intercepted them. Saunders had tried to salvage his dignity by insisting that his personal armchair be brought aboard the raider and installed in a corner of the prison hold. To Alexander's disbelief, he then issued strict instructions that no one but himself and a select retinue of officers could enjoy the comfort of the chair, which became a territorial marker in the dingy confines of the bunker. 'It was more than a chair,' Alexander recalled, 'it was a symbol, a seat of state, even as is a judge's bench or an Episcopal throne.'

Inevitably, an interloper sat in the throne one afternoon while the *Wairuna*'s skipper was up on deck – an impudent red-headed steward, who was in the process of lighting a cigarette when Saunders returned. The youth not only refused to vacate the chair but blew smoke in the captain's face, sparking a melee in which he was hurled to the floor by one of the *Wairuna*'s officers. Called to the scene, Leutnant von Auerswald solved the dispute by applying the hierarchical logic of the German Navy: after berating the young steward for insulting a superior officer, Auerswald ordered his men to bring packing cases down into the hold and construct separate quarters for officers according to their rank. Chief engineers, chief officers and masters were assigned a designated area on the port side at the rear of the hold. Junior officers were corralled into quarters directly forward of their superiors. Ordinary seamen congregated on the starboard side. The packing cases served not only as walls between these territories but also as makeshift lockers. It was the beginning of a segregated caste system that would become more pronounced as the voyage wore on.

Racial divisions, too, were worsening. A Portuguese crewman from the *Jumna*, insulted as a 'dago' by one of the British prisoners, had brandished his British naturalisation papers in the Englishman's face before pulling out a knife and trying to stab him. The Scandinavian and Swedish sailors had discovered that because they were 'neutrals', Nerger was prepared to hire them on seaman's pay rates to work alongside his crew. Several of the *Beluga*'s crew had taken up the offer, and Robert Trudgett of the *Winslow* was apoplectic when most of his men helped the Germans plunder his ship before it was sunk. To a young man like Roy Alexander, the 'Swedes' were simply making a pragmatic choice. To officers like Trudgett, they were confirming all the Allies' worst suspicions about the loyalties of neutrals. Watching from the *Wolf*'s deck as his former crewmen helped strip the *Winslow*, Trudgett had erupted with a stream of the rawest insults he could muster.

As the ship continued north, the muggy heat of the tropics closed in and the air inside the prison hold turned to a swampy fug. The smell of so many men trapped inside this iron room was, according to Roy Alexander, 'ripe'. The *Wolf*'s crew were now dressed in their light tropical gear; the men in the prison hold simply began discarding clothes until many of them wore only shorts, fearing that the constant sweating would rot their shirts. Nerger once again permitted them to congregate on the poop deck during the day, where they played cards and swapped tales under the blistering sun, but at sunset when they returned to the hold the temperature outside had barely dropped and the humidity was still overpowering. Alexander had noticed, as he lay in his sweat-soaked hammock under the blue lights, that some of the men who had been aboard since February were showing signs of ill health, their skin erupting in sores. Already there had been an outbreak of headlice, which had necessitated the men having their heads shaved.

What haunted these sailors, however, was the spectre of an illness that every one of them knew by its fearsome mythology. Scurvy had been the scourge of the tall ships, and its terrifying effects – rotting gums, gangrenous sores and a slow-creeping, lethargic death – had once claimed more lives at sea than all other dangers combined. In the days since Horatio Nelson nearly died of the illness, medical science had deduced that lack of vitamin C caused the body's connective tissues to begin disintegrating – hence the frightening phenomenon of teeth becoming loose and old mended fractures reopening. Citrus juice, fresh fruit and vegetables were the curative, but when Alexander reviewed the diet in the prison hold over the previous month it gave him pause. The fresh fruit obtained from Sunday Island had been eaten, and while the food supplies purloined from the *Wairuna* and the three American schooners had provided a supply of prunes and other sources of vitamin C, Alexander wondered how the Germans planned to stretch those supplies among more than five hundred people.

The crew had already experienced another seaman's malady during their crossing of the Southern Ocean, when many of them developed an anaemic pallor and swollen joints. Plivier recalled the shortness of breath and physical weakness he had experienced during that period, when rice had been their staple and fresh food was scarce. He recognised the symptoms as the early signs of beriberi, the wasting disease caused when the body is starved of vitamin B.

The disabling of the *Wolfchen* had forced Nerger to turn away from the main trade routes, where he feared navy warships were searching for him. His fuel supply was still meagre and the only wireless signals he could hear were local island steamers or distant freighters whose positions were unclear. In the final days of July, however, his luck finally turned. After nearly three weeks of toiling over the *Wolfchen*'s broken frame, Nerger's engineers reported that the aircraft was ready to fly again. New wooden wing-struts had been fashioned from tea chests, spare canvas had been stretched over the fuselage and the saltwater-flooded motor had finally kicked back into life. A day after the plane was relaunched, Nerger's wireless operators picked up an uncoded message that offered him salvation: 'Burns Philp Rabaul. Donaldson left Sydney twenty-seventh via Newcastle. Three forty tons general cargo, five hundred tons Westport coal Rabaul . . .'

The meaning was clear even if the details were vague: Burns Philp was an Australian shipping line, Donaldson was presumably the name of one of its skippers, and the wireless message suggested his ship had just left Sydney carrying 500 tons of coal to Rabaul in New Guinea. Nerger immediately shifted course to the west and waited for further details to drift in on the air.

* *

Captain Alec Donaldson had been shipping freight and passengers between Australia and the South Pacific islands for most of the war, and in mid-1917 his regular commission was commanding the Burns Philp steamship *Matunga* on her regular six-week round trip from Sydney to Rabaul, the easternmost port of what had once been German New Guinea. The *Matunga*, a somewhat ancient and cantankerous 1618-ton passenger-freighter, was nominally a civilian ship but her principal job was to carry military personnel and supplies to the army garrison that had been established at Rabaul after the Australian Navy seized control of German New Guinea in the opening month of the war. On the return voyage, she brought back copra and a retinue of soldiers and sailors lucky enough to be taking furlough from the relentless heat and nightmarish ailments of the tropics.

On her 27 July departure from Sydney, the *Matunga*'s passenger list included sixteen army and navy personnel from the garrison, most notably Colonel Cecil Lucius Strangman, a fifty-year-old doctor who had enrolled in the Australian Army at the outbreak of war and was posted to Rabaul because of his expertise in tropical diseases. Strangman was returning to New

Guinea to take up the blighted post of acting-administrator from the incumbent brigadier-general, who had succumbed to malaria and would soon be dead at age fifty-five. Also among the military passengers were two other Australian medical staff – Sergeant Alcon Webb and Major John Flood, who was returning to Rabaul with his thirty-three-year-old wife, Rose. Three businessmen from Melbourne – William McEnnally, George Green and Edward Noble, brother of the well-known Test cricketer 'Monty' Noble – were making the trip to survey their copra plantations, and the ship's forty-three crewmen included a stewardess, Agnes Mackenzie, and two fourteen-year-old cabin boys, Eric Minns and Keith Harris. With a freight load that included three horses, a shipment of bicycles, a piano and Rabaul's entire monthly liquor supply, the old *Matunga* was heavily laden.

Strangman and Flood would later say that they were warned before they stepped aboard the *Matunga* that a German raider was lurking somewhere in the Pacific. Strangman was told by his military superiors in Sydney; Flood heard the warning from a private source. Australian military officials certainly had ample reasons for such suspicions, despite their public statements that the *Cumberland* had been sabotaged. In the weeks since the *Cumberland* incident, the *Wairuna* and the *Winslow* had both been reported lost and the wreck of *Encore* – burnt beyond recognition – had been spotted off Fiji. In London, a naval-intelligence brief had already surmised that the *Wairuna* 'could have been captured by the *Wolf*'.

Alec Donaldson was concerned enough to raise the issue with local officials on the morning of his departure, for the *Cumberland* incident had been in the newspapers every day he was in Sydney. But no one at the Burns Philp office or navy headquarters offered the *Matunga*'s skipper any intimation of danger when he visited them on the way to the Sydney wharf. 'They brightly told me that there was nothing to worry about in the Pacific,' he said of the navy officials, 'and that the sinking of the *Cumberland* was not caused by a mine, but by internal explosion, so I departed from Sydney quite cheerfully.' The navy, furthermore, was still permitting shipping information to be sent in uncoded wireless transmissions.

Oblivious to the danger, Donaldson sealed his own fate only a day later when he wirelessed a brief message to Brisbane announcing his impending arrival there: 'VHV to VHB. Burns Philp Brisbane. Cape Moreton Monday. Donaldson.' The Australian captain apparently believed that by using his ship's call-sign, VHV, he was complying with instructions not to identify her in any wireless messages. But more than twelve hundred miles to his north, the message was picked up by the *Wolf*'s radio operators and sent immediately to their captain, who looked up VHV in his pre-war wireless register and quickly deduced that the ship he was hunting was the *Matunga*. To reach Rabaul, the freighter would pass through the narrow strait separating the Solomon Islands from the east coast of New Guinea; on 30 July, Nerger positioned the *Wolf* directly in its centre, sent the *Wolfchen* into the sky and lay in wait.

Alec Donaldson was still feeling uneasy as he approached New Guinea nearly a week later, for when an unidentifiable black freighter appeared off the *Matunga*'s starboard bow on the morning of 6 August, he wondered aloud to one of his passengers whether this German-looking ship might be a raider. Any doubt was erased fifteen minutes later, when the *Wolfchen* droned low overhead to deliver a warning message and the *Wolf* dropped her bulwarks and fired a warning shot. Donaldson killed the engines and ordered everyone to prepare to abandon ship, for even on a good day the *Matunga* could barely reach 7.5 knots, and reversing the engines sometimes took up to five minutes. Even ruder than the shock of capture, however, was the greeting he received from the German officer who stepped aboard his ship five minutes later. 'Good morning, Captain Donaldson!' said Leutnant Karl Rose with a dazzling smile and snap salute. 'You are late – we expected you two days ago. Now, where can I find your five hundred tons of Westport coal?'

Small as she was, the *Matunga* was indeed a rich prize for the *Wolf*. Her coal would keep the raider going for at least another month, and she was almost as generously provisioned as the *Wairuna*, for the supplies she was taking to Rabaul included three and a half tons of frozen meat, crates of canned fish, several tons of flour, rice, cigarettes, clothing, toiletries and three live horses. The 753 pounds of fresh fruit in her cooler, along with twelve tons of canned vegetables and jam, would keep scurvy at bay for some time. And, not inconsequentially, the cargo holds also contained more than thirty tons of beer, wine and spirits – enough to last the *Wolf*'s crew all the way back to Germany. Captain Donaldson himself directed the Germans towards this treasure, reasoning that if he were to be held captive on a raider, he would need stronger solace than weak tea. The booty was so large, in fact, that Nerger realised it would take up to a week to transfer it, requiring a safe harbour out of sight of any warships looking for the *Matunga*. After Donaldson, his officers and all the military passengers apart from the two doctors were brought across to the *Wolf* and taken down to the Hell Hole, the two ships set off north in tandem.

Volcanic islands dot the Bismarck Sea in a wide arc north-east of New Guinea, and as the *Wolf* threaded its way through them in the first days of August the wireless came alive with increasingly frantic messages from the naval base at Rabaul to the missing *Matunga*. Still uncertain of the strength of enemy forces he faced in the Pacific, Nerger was happy to learn from his new prisoners that the only Allied warship in harbour at Rabaul was HMAS *Una*, a motorised yacht of only 977 tons that had formerly been the German governor's sloop until the Australian Navy seized it. Even more reassuring, albeit perplexing, was the news that the Australian Government was still steadfastly blaming its shipping losses on sabotage, for the Australian newspapers aboard the *Matunga* were full of reports on the topic, along with the seemingly contradictory news that the Australian Navy was recruiting men for minesweepers.

Guarded by the *Wolfchen*'s reconnaissance patrols, the *Wolf* and the *Matunga* sailed north, passing within a hundred miles of Rabaul before turning west to follow the northern coastline of what had once been Germany's largest New Guinea colony, Kaiser Wilhelm's Land. Unknown to Nerger, HMAS *Una* was at that moment sailing towards him from Madang to begin searching for the *Matunga*. The little Australian yacht would have encountered a startling sight had the ships met, for Nerger had ordered his crew to use the *Matunga* as a dummy target in firing and boarding drills as they made their way west, so that for two days it appeared the Australian ship was under attack from heavily armed pirates. But the *Una* passed without sighting the Germans, on her way to a fruitless search to the south.

It was the dry season in the tropics and the sky was brilliantly clear, with not a trace of breeze to relieve the burning glare of the sun. Many of the German crewmen had torn the legs off their ragged pants below the knee and now wore their shirts open; the faces and torsos of crew and prisoners alike were burnished to a deep brown. Down in the Hell Hole, the sour smell of nearly two hundred sweat-drenched men mingled with a heavy haze of tobacco smoke. Although the hold was cleaned out with brushes and sand three times a week, the iron walls and floor radiated such intense heat that perspiration dripping from the men gathered in pools on the floor. Stan Cameron was horrified by the conditions he saw there when he talked himself past the guards one evening and descended the ladder to meet his fellow prisoners for the first time:

> It was probably 8:30 pm when I was there, and I would judge the temperature to have been between 118 and 120 degrees Fahrenheit, and the reek of feet, breath and bodies was something awful. On this particular night, I should judge from one-quarter to three-eighths of an inch of sweat was on the floor, and when the vessel rolled there would be a thin scum of liquid running from side to side. The walls and ceiling were literally running water, which was caused by moisture drawn from the bodies of

> the men by the hot iron sides of the ship and the deck overhead. Combine stale tobacco smoke with this atmosphere, and it was a wonder to me that a human being could exist in it.

From his own dealings with Karl Nerger, Cameron was certain the German captain had no idea of the abject conditions his prisoners were enduring below – indeed, when Nerger discovered what was going on he confined Leutnant Auerswald to his quarters for five days. Only twenty-three years old, Arthur von Auerswald was a constant butt of jokes and jibes from the prisoners, who had nicknamed him 'Little Willie' in honour of his resemblance to the Kaiser. Roy Alexander could replicate his outraged broken English word for word ('It is ungentlemanly, most! You are impolite . . . you blighters!') and Alec Donaldson had rendered him speechless by saying, with a deadpan straight face, that he would require an iced bottle of champagne brought to him every morning. Auerswald had responded by treating the men with brusque contempt, even whistling 'Rule Britannia' as they watched ships being sunk. His relations with the men in the Hell Hole became so hostile that he would eventually be replaced. For now, Nerger ordered the prisoners moved to the poop deck while their quarters were cleaned and painted, and for two nights they slept under the stars as guards patrolled around them. When they returned below, the iron walls were painted white and new ventilation tubes had been installed. But the suffocating heat remained, and the chemical fumes of fresh paint lingered for days.

Aboard the *Matunga*, an entirely different mood held sway, for the prize crew on the captured ship had been fortunate to find themselves placed under the command of Leutnant Karl Rose, who had risen to become Nerger's prize officer since the loss of Iwan Brandes. Young and brash, with a swaggering self-confidence that rivalled Fritz Witschetzky's, Rose was in every respect the antithesis of his reserved and self-disciplined commander. Before the war, he had lived for four years in Britain, where he joined the Richmond Tennis Club and acquired a perfect mastery of English. Rose was tall, good-looking and spoke four languages, and he enjoyed nothing more than showing off his worldly charm to the fairer sex. Now, he found himself temporarily in charge of a ship that carried enough liquor for an entire military garrison and numbered among its passengers a fetching woman of his age who immediately caught his eye.

Dark-haired and porcelain-skinned, Rose Flood was destined to become the focus of every carnal longing shared by the sexually deprived crew of the *Wolf*. Along with the *Matunga*'s stewardess, Agnes Mackenzie, she was the first woman any of the Germans had been in close proximity to for ten months, Mary Cameron having been confined to her cabin. Her presence had already created a stir.

The daughter of a British merchant-navy captain, Rose had married her husband when he was a medical student studying in Dublin, and had accompanied him back to his native Australia, then on to Rabaul after he enlisted in the medical corps. It was a childless marriage that had experienced its share of trials, for despite John Flood's prowess as a sportsman – he had been a first-class batsman and bowler in Ireland's 1909 cricket team – he had inherited the weak constitution of his father, and Rabaul was in the throes of a malaria and amoebic-dysentery outbreak when he arrived in 1915. Nearly a dozen men had since died, and when he wasn't forcing his reluctant patients to drink quinine mixed with hydrochloric acid, Dr Flood spent his days treating soldiers and natives alike for a plague of tropical illnesses that ranged from ringworm to pneumonia, prickly heart, dhobi itch, ulcerated sores and elephantiasis.

Rose Flood's physical charms are not immediately evident from the one photograph taken of her aboard the *Wolf*, where she stands amid a group of her fellow prisoners in rather matronly pose, dressed in an immaculately white, lace-frilled ankle-length dress, her hands behind her back, her hair tied back somewhat severely, her stockings and patent-leather shoes just visible below the hem. But Karl Rose, despite his wife and son back home in

Hamburg, was the first of many among the *Wolf*'s crew to become fixated on her. One of his earliest actions as prize commander of the *Matunga* was to summon Agnes Mackenzie and instruct her to cater to whatever needs the doctor's wife might have. The New Zealand-born stewardess took this as a personal affront, for she had already developed a dislike for this young British wife and did not fancy herself an unpaid employee of the German Navy.

Although she was a widow, Mackenzie was only thirty-nine years old herself and had already attracted admiring glances from the German crewmen, one of whom had surreptitiously handed her a love letter so ardent it left her severely flustered and embarrassed. 'Miss Agnes was not the least interested in this attempt at "German-English friendship",' recalled Ernst Szielasko jocularly, 'and the love proposal got lost on the ocean floor.' Mackenzie point-blank refused to work as Rose Flood's maid, until Karl Rose threatened to put her on the crew's rations. It was a harbinger of the difficulties that the presence of women, and Mrs Flood in particular, would kindle as the voyage continued.

Karl Rose's other early initiative as commander of the *Matunga* was to take personal inventory of the ship's vast below-deck stores of beer, champagne and whisky, securing the best of it for his private bar. Safely distant from the authoritarian gaze of his commander, the *leutnant* allowed his small prize crew to freely indulge their long-denied thirst over successive nights at the freighter's saloon bar in the company of their small retinue of prisoners. The revelries got so out of hand that one crewman suffered a severe laceration to the face from the jagged edge of a flying bottleneck, and Dr Hauswaldt had to surgically remove the sailor's eye. As Roy Alexander wryly noted, the last voyage of the *Matunga* was such a wild party that some were hoping it would never end.

Nerger was heading for neutral territory – the Dutch-occupied western half of New Guinea – and on 14 August he found the anchorage he was seeking on the remote island of Waigeo, off the very north-west tip of the colony. Sailing through a narrow passage between steep headlands, the *Wolf* and *Matunga* entered a lush tropical bay surrounded on all sides by heavily forested hills – a vine-entangled jungle of coconut palms, breadfruit and rubber trees, bamboo and banana bushes alive with the electric screech of parrots and cockatoos.

This was Offak Bay, a secluded haven that Roy Alexander would come to describe as 'evilly beautiful'. Only ten miles north of the equator, its bowl-like contours formed a natural heat trap in which the tropical humidity seemed suspended like warm soup. As the two ships dropped anchor, a stink of rotting fleshy vegetation gradually enveloped them from the surrounding hills. Staring down into the pale green waters, the crew saw the serrated backs of crocodiles drifting silently past the ship; deeper still were the coiled black shapes of enormous eels. From the jungle, several near-naked tribesmen appeared and rowed across in canoes bearing woven mats and coconuts for trading; only as they got nearer did it become clear that several had festering sores across their bodies from some nameless affliction.

On their first night in this airless harbour, several prisoners inside the Hell Hole came close to collapse as they lay gasping on the iron floor or huddled desperately around the ventilation pipes in 120-degree heat. Convinced that the older and less robust men were in danger of suffocation, Tom Meadows began shouting for the ship's doctor and prison officer. It was Leutnant Karl Dietrich, the officer in charge of minelaying, who eventually responded to Meadows's haranguing, summoning Dr Hauswaldt, who endured only a few seconds in the fetid hold before recommending that the main cover be pulled back at one end to increase ventilation.

This was to be the only concession to the prisoners' comfort, however, for among the guards there was now a real fear of a breakout. The sheer number of prisoners, the presence of more than a dozen Australian troops who were familiar with this region, and the tantalising proximity of land and native canoes all made a repeat of the Sunday Island escapes seem entirely possible, even though the decks of both the *Wolf* and the *Matunga* were swarming day and night with extra guards and crewmen transferring coal and stores. On their first morning above deck, the prisoners were herded into a roped-off area four feet inside the poop-deck rail and instructed not to step outside it. When the *Matunga*'s forty-strong crew were brought across a day later, the number of men in the hold reached more than two hundred.

In truth, the prisoners had already calculated that the guards, the crocodiles and the patrolling German motorboats gave them an infinitesimal chance of reaching the shore. But the Australians – freshly arrived and with their irreverent spirit still intact – could not resist tweaking the paranoia of the Germans. Huddling mock-conspiratorially on the poop deck one morning, several of them began pointing to the nearby shoreline and whispering imaginary escape plans for their own entertainment. The guards anxiously reported this possible insurrection to Leutnant Auerswald, who passed it on to his captain, and extra spotlights and machine-gun placements were soon being installed on the raider's decks.

The joke was ill timed, however, for later that afternoon several of the German sentries began imbibing from the liquor supplies that had made their way across from the *Matunga* during the day. As darkness descended, a mood of boozy uncertainty settled over the aft deck, and just before midnight the nerve of the Hell Hole's only guard snapped when a prisoner slid out of his hammock in the darkness and began crawling across the floor under his slumbering mates to reach the latrine bucket. Unable to see clearly in the dim glow of the light bulbs, the panicked guard fired his pistol into the floor and began shouting for help, sparking a melee among the suddenly woken prisoners and a general alert above deck. Inebriated guards stumbled into one another, spotlights arced wildly across the water surrounding the ship and the ruckus quickly spread to the *Matunga*, which was lashed alongside the raider, interrupting the drunken revelry that Leutnant Karl Rose was conducting with his superior officer, Karl Schmehl, in the saloon.

By the time Schmehl reached the deck, the *Wolf*'s sentries were shouting that several prisoners had gone overboard, pointing excitedly to a disturbance in the water just beyond the reach of the spotlight beams. Shots were fired into the darkness and Schmehl and several men clambered into one of the *Matunga*'s launches to investigate, but as they rowed out from the ship the starburst of a signal rocket lit the sky overhead and a machine gunner on the *Wolf*'s aft deck sprayed the bay with a burst of fire that very nearly took Schmehl's head off. Nerger emerged on deck to a scene of complete chaos as another signal rocket was launched, more wild shooting erupted and Schmehl began screaming abuse at the guards from his wobbling perch in the bullet-riddled launch.

It was not until the prisoners were mustered on the poop deck and counted that Auerswald realised no one was missing. The enraged Schmehl, meanwhile, had appeared on the *Wolf*'s deck to report that the suspected escapees in the water were in fact crocodiles feeding. In the long and painful recriminations that followed, only Leutnant Rose seemed to find humour in the situation. As Schmehl berated his men in front of the prisoners, Rose leaned woozily towards Alec Donaldson, breathing beer fumes and offering the Australian skipper a cigar from his own cabin aboard the *Matunga*. 'Damn funny, captain, nobody missing,' Rose murmured, sotto voce. 'Have a cigar.'

The transfer of coal and stores from the *Matunga* was as grinding a labour as the German crew had experienced since the voyage began. Some of the prisoners took delight in watching the neutral crewmen of the *Beluga*, *Encore* and *Winslow* bathed in sweat and coal grit, toiling to the point of collapse. Nerger needed as many of the ship's provisions as he could store on the *Wolf* – not just food but hardware supplies, medicines, rope, firebricks, cutlery, crockery, kerosene, glassware, tarpaulins and anything else remotely useful. The two horses and pony were winched over, slaughtered, butchered and frozen for future meals. Wall panels and fittings from the *Matunga*'s passenger cabins were removed and brought across to the boat deck behind the *Wolf*'s bridge; here, they were reassembled with wire netting and canvas sheets to create makeshift prisoners' quarters among the deck's congested jumble of lifeboats, searchlights, machine-gun placements and range finders. After some beseeching from the three plantation owners and the three most senior Australian military officers, Nerger permitted all six of them to be transferred from the Hell Hole up to these temporary quarters, and on 24 August he brought across the Floods, Major Strangman and Agnes Mackenzie, accommodating them in quarters near the Camerons.

Emerging from the seclusion of her cabin for the first time, an emaciated and gaunt Mary Cameron greeted the two women, wearing a bonnet to disguise her lost hair. The prospect of company after six weeks of isolation rejuvenated Stan's spirits, although Mary was still so disorientated from her illness that she confided to her husband, later in their cabin, that she suspected these newcomers to be Germans cleverly disguised. As it turned out, relations between the Camerons and some of these fellow prisoners would quickly become strained.

The possibility that Kapitän Nerger would be compelled to find some safe harbour in which to set free his upper-deck passengers burned bright in Stan Cameron's mind. The *Wolf* now had two military doctors among her prisoners, and the Geneva Convention specified that medical officers enjoyed the status of neutrals and should be allowed to rejoin their units if captured. It was arguable whether such rules applied under prize law at sea but, at the very least, Cameron believed Nerger had a moral obligation to release the women and children he had captured. The two men had become familiar with each other, and Stan was now permitted to roam further from his cabin. He had visited the bridge, talked to the wireless operators, even scanned their bulletins for news from the outside world. It seemed logical that Nerger would live up to his promise to free his most vulnerable prisoners.

On 26 August, Cameron's hopes soared when the German crew began preparing the two ships to leave Offak Bay and hoisted one of the *Matunga*'s lifeboats and a small gasoline launch over to the raider, dropping them on the foredeck near the gun emplacements. A crewman asked Cameron whether he knew how to operate the engine of the smaller boat, and when Stan's affirmative answer was relayed to Kapitänleutnant Schmehl, the above-deck prisoners became convinced they were to be set free after the *Matunga* was sunk. Whether Nerger seriously contemplated such a plan, he never revealed, but the pitfalls for him were obvious: he still had 110 mines to lay before his mission was complete, and it made no sense to release his prisoners now and risk alerting every Allied port in Asia to his presence. A small boatload of prisoners might find their way to a local New Guinea mission and raise the alarm within days, leaving the *Wolf* barely enough time to reach the open seas to the south.

When the two ships raised anchor and headed out into the Halmahera Sea, Cameron was devastated to see the crew hoist the two small boats off the *Wolf*'s deck, lower them onto the waves and row them across to the *Matunga*, where they were fastened to her sides. After all the promises Nerger had made, it was a particularly bitter betrayal.

'I claim this to have been the acme of inhumanity,' he said. 'He might just as well have condemned the women and children to death right there, because at that time there were ninety-nine-and-a-half chances to a hundred that they would be either killed in action or drowned. I don't believe there were five men in all the crew of the *Wolf*, officers included, who ever expected the *Wolf* to win safely back to Germany.'

Just after 1 pm, ten miles north of Waigeo, the Camerons' orderly appeared to hand out ear-batting, and the prisoners gathered on the poop deck to watch the ritual destruction of the *Matunga*. Bombs had been planted fore and aft inside the old steamer, and at 1.30 the first one exploded in the stern. The ship's bow tilted upwards and she listed to port. The second bomb followed two minutes later, and the *Matunga*'s deck was soon awash as she slowly submerged. When the ship finally went under, stern first and with a gush of black smoke, Alec Donaldson remarked that he had never seen the old steamer turn so quickly. Standing beside him, his chief engineer, Ross Ainsworth, muttered, 'She's a bloody good riddance.'

As the prisoners were led back below, the *Wolf* turned south towards the fabled Moluccas Islands, where the British and Dutch had fought for control of the spice trade in the seventeenth century. Among the prisoners and crew alike, there was now intense speculation about the raider's likely course and next destination. The *Wolf* had apparently evaded the Australian Navy, and her most direct run to the open seas was due south to the Timor Sea, which separated the Dutch East Indies from Australia's northern coastline. From there, the Indian Ocean beckoned to the west. As always, however, the only person aboard who knew their destination was in his cabin beneath the bridge, saying nothing.

6

THE ENEMY WITHIN

In the same week that the *Wolf* was steaming away from New Guinea in late August, Australia's most senior spy, George Steward, was at his desk inside Government House in Melbourne, puzzling over the growing number of ships that had recently disappeared or come to grief on his side of the Pacific Ocean. A former boxer and sculler, son of a London labourer, Steward had undergone a colonial reinvention since arriving in the island state of Tasmania as a young man in the early 1890s; from a lowly public servant's job in Hobart, he had risen to become official secretary to the governor-general, the king's representative in Australia, while simultaneously attaining the rank of major in the army's Intelligence Corps. At fifty-two, Steward carried off his dual roles with a suitably domineering air: his posture was ramrod straight, his eyes burned like black orbs and he cultivated a moustache that *Punch* magazine described as 'rampant'.

To all outward appearances, Steward was a minor functionary whose job it was to manage the correspondence and budget of his ostensible boss, Sir Ronald Munro-Ferguson, a white-haired Scotsman who had been dispatched from England to take up the governor-general's post in 1914. In reality, however,

Steward was the head of the first secret service in Australia's history – a clandestine organisation that had been formed in 1916 at the direction of the British Government. Originally called the Counter-Espionage Bureau, now named the Special Intelligence Bureau, the agency's existence was such a tightly guarded secret that few knew of it beyond Steward's own small network of spies and a handful of key political and military figures, including Prime Minister Billy Hughes and Sir Ronald, whose white Italianate mansion overlooking Melbourne had become the bureau's de facto headquarters.

The governor-general was not entirely sanguine about his secretary's long absences on clandestine assignments; nor was he happy that Government House was now frequented at all hours by detectives, informers and other disreputables. Somewhat witheringly, Sir Ronald referred to Steward behind his back as 'Pickle the Spy' – a reference to the eighteenth-century Scottish agent who had spied on Bonnie Prince Charlie for the British Government. But the governor-general was keenly interested in Steward's latest investigation, for it centred on the alarming possibility that a German commerce-raider might be operating off Australia's eastern coastline. Two weeks earlier, the Navy Office in Melbourne had confirmed that the steamship *Matunga* had disappeared without trace while carrying military personnel from Sydney to New Guinea. That news had come hard on the heels of the mysterious explosion aboard the *Cumberland* in June and the disappearance of the New Zealand ship *Wairuna* en route to San Francisco. Now, the industrious Steward had amassed convincing evidence that the *Cumberland* incident was not caused by an 'internal explosion', as the navy had announced, but by a submerged mine.

A maritime inquiry into the *Cumberland* disaster had just concluded behind closed doors in Sydney, and five navy divers had testified that the hole in the ship's hull curled inwards, not outwards as Rear-Admiral Kazuyoshi Yamaji had originally reported. No one from the Japanese Navy had given evidence to the inquiry, which had been hampered by the fact that the *Cumberland* herself sank on 11 August while the navy was trying to refloat her. But Steward's deputy, the military-intelligence officer Major Harold Jones, had attended the closed hearings and obtained the opinions of two explosives experts who were adamant that the *Cumberland* had struck a mine. Perplexingly, however, Australian navy officials appeared equally adamant that the ship had been the victim of an 'infernal device' planted in its cargo, and the Federal and New South Wales governments persisted in offering a combined reward of £3000 to anyone who could help unmask the supposed saboteurs.

At Government House, Major Steward was now in the process of writing a secret report to the prime minister, which would strongly suggest that a German commerce-raider had been active off Australia. But the sabotage story had assumed a life of its own since the navy announced it in July. The public was outraged that bombs were being smuggled onto the Australian docks. The press was baying for the government to lock up all German immigrants. The British Board of Trade and the Queensland Government had each offered £1000 rewards to capture the traitors responsible, bringing the total bounty to £5000 – ten times the annual salary of a senior public servant. The government was now suggesting that the *Matunga* may also have been sabotaged. To Sir Ronald – whose job it was to send London regular reports on the situation in the Antipodes – it was all rather confounding.

Australia was a country peculiarly susceptible to conspiracy fever as the First World War entered its fourth year, for an hysterical form of anti-German paranoia had taken root there since hostilities began. It was a mood influenced partly by British propaganda and United States news reports and partly by this isolated island nation's own home-grown fears of a German invasion. The country's enormous sacrifice – more than 100,000 of its soldiers had so far been killed or wounded, in a nation of only five million people – meant that few people remained untouched by the war. Yet the battlefields of Gallipoli and Messines were so distant, and the news from them was so heavily censored, that many Australians felt a paradoxical disconnection from events. As if longing for some proximate evidence of the conflict that had cost them so dearly, the country's citizens had been reporting signs of German invasion with increasing frequency as the war dragged on. German aircraft were said to have been spotted in the skies over Melbourne, German submarines glimpsed off the coast and even uniformed German soldiers sighted in the streets of country towns – all of them phantoms sprung from the collective anxieties of the community.

Inevitably, German immigrants became the focus of these fears. Australia's German community was roughly 100,000-strong, a third of whom were born in Germany and the rest their children or grandchildren. Among their number were the brewer Edmund Resch and the steel-industry executive Franz Wallach, both of whom would be interned for suspected disloyalty. 'On casual inspection, they seemed to look like us and behave like us; but now we found that they were savage and inhuman,' recalled one Australian who lived through that time. 'The Sydney *Bulletin* full-page cartoons were no longer of rat-faced Chinese but ape-faced Germans marching through Belgium with babies stuck to their bayonets.'

Newspapers such as the *Mirror* claimed to have evidence that Germans working in the government, the defence forces, the media and the unions were actively plotting to bring down the empire. The *Mirror*'s Hun-hating editor, Jack Myers, had taken to publicly naming German-born businessmen and government officials who constituted, in his words, 'Australia's grave danger from within'. The animosity ran so hot that even a group of actors dressed up as German soldiers found themselves encircled by an angry mob while making an anti-Hun propaganda film in the streets of Melbourne in early 1917.

It was a hatred actively encouraged by Australia's combative and shrewd prime minister, William Morris Hughes. Frail, tiny, partially deaf and plagued by chronic dyspepsia, Billy Hughes was 'cold as sea-ice, vain as a peacock, cruel as a butcher bird, sly as a weasel and mean as cat shit', according to Tom Hungerford, his private secretary later in life. But Hughes was also a gifted orator who strode the world stage as few Australian statesmen have done before or since. Born in London and raised in Wales, he was a former unionist and founding member of the Australian Labor Party, but also an impassioned Anglophile who described Australians as 'more British than the people of Great Britain'. His anti-Hun rhetoric and warmongering, which earned him the nickname the 'Little Digger', even caused a minor sensation in Britain, where he had been offered a seat in the British Parliament by several Labour figures during a six-month speaking tour shortly after he became prime minister in October 1915.

In the Little Digger's speeches, the Germans were rapacious monsters who would subject the English-speaking world to mass slaughter should they achieve victory. The First World War was thus a 'racial war' that necessitated draconian measures against all Germans, even those who had emigrated to Commonwealth countries and become naturalised British citizens. Claiming the Germans were planning a takeover of Australia, the Hughes government introduced some of the most repressive war-time restrictions in the entire Commonwealth: blacklists of individuals and companies were compiled in order to expunge the 'cancer' of German commercial interests; the enemy-alien laws were widened to permit the internment of German-born women and children, and of Australians with even one grandparent born in Germany; censorship laws forbade the press from publishing any unauthorised information about military plans or movements, any illustration of warships or soldiers' camps, any item that might be useful to the enemy, any cartoon likely to give offence to Allied nations and any illustration of the 'gruesome effects of warfare'. Newspapers could be searched at any time and forced to hand over their files, while their editors were constrained from publishing anything likely to impair the 'essential unity' of the people of the British Empire.

The fact that newspapers of the day were unbridled in their patriotism did not stop the censors from engaging in endless interference. Words and phrases were excised from cablegrams; page proofs submitted for approval were held up late into the night. Tom Heney, editor of the *Sydney Morning Herald*, described the confusion and disruption created by censors who knew nothing of the way newspapers operated: 'Delays abounded and increased, and it came to appear as if, the more a man laboured for a completely accurate exposition of some effort on behalf of the war, the more likely he was to bring his toil to naught through an oversight in respect of some practically obsolete or obsolescent war-regulation, censor's order, or pedantry which some new censor regarded as still of formidable importance.'

In the entire course of the First World War, not a single case of German espionage within Australia would be substantiated, yet the pursuit of such plots became a national obsession driven by the prime minister. Thousands of Australians of German extraction were fired from their jobs and spied on by neighbours, and more than four thousand of them were imprisoned in rural concentration camps, often on mere suspicion of disloyalty. More than two and a half thousand companies were identified as suspicious or shut down completely, and up to ten thousand letters a week were intercepted by the censor. The names of dozens of Australian towns – Bismarck, Blumberg, Heidelberg, Germanton – were changed to remove all traces of their origins as German immigrant communities. Even the Australian army general John Monash – later hailed as one of the most brilliant military tacticians of the First World War – was subject to hostility and rumour because his parents were German-speaking Poles.

Australians, being simultaneously devoted to empire and yet innately suspicious of authority, fervently supported the anti-German crackdown even as their enthusiasm for the war itself began to wane. It was a fissure in the national psyche that Hughes opened up when he tried to introduce conscription in 1916. Compulsory military service may have come to Britain, the United States and Canada, but Australians strongly resisted it, and in his attempts to roll back that resistance, Hughes's fear-mongering reached a fearsome intensity.

Conscription's most outspoken opponents were unionists, Irish nationalists and pacifists – or, as Hughes saw them, an 'unholy alliance' of Syndicalists, Sinn Feiners and shirkers. In speech after speech, he accused them of being the dupes or agents of Germany, enmeshed in a conspiracy orchestrated by the Kaiser's 'cunning men'. Union leaders who spoke out against military recruitment were raided by plain-clothes army-intelligence agents and charged under the War Precautions Act. The prime minister personally instructed the censor to ban any press reports that were hostile to him or prejudicial to conscription, and directed the Special Intelligence Bureau to hunt out subversives. In the process, Hughes forged such a close relationship with the bureau's Major George Steward that, in the eyes of the governor-general, the prime minister came to trust Pickle the Spy above all others.

High on Billy Hughes's hate list was the Industrial Workers of the World (IWW), the Chicago-based radical union that advocated sabotage as a means of disrupting the capitalist system. Vehemently opposed to the war, IWW leaders in the United States had been run out of several towns at gunpoint and embroiled in violent incidents. Their headquarters in Seattle had been attacked by off-duty soldiers, a shoot-out between their members and several law-enforcement officials in Washington had left two sheriffs and five unionists dead, and on August 1917 one of their organisers in Montana, Frank Little, was lynched. In Australia, the IWW – colloquially known as the Wobblies – could barely muster a membership of 2000 men, but in Hughes's speeches they loomed as an ominous threat to the nation, perpetrating murder, arson, forgery and sabotage on behalf of Germany. In the midst of the conscription campaign, Steward had told police the IWW was plotting to blow up Government House; Hughes publicly accused the union of disabling the warship HMAS *Brisbane* and claimed a government agent investigating the affair had been shot. No evidence of these conspiracies was ever produced (the 'sabotage' of the *Brisbane* was caused by cotton waste inside an oil filter) but in their wake the government passed a new law – the Unlawful Associations Act – that made membership of the IWW illegal.

Australians voted against conscription in December 1916, during a rancorous referendum campaign that divided the nation and turned many of Hughes's Labor government colleagues against him. The prime minister had then performed a dramatic political volte-face, packing up his ear trumpet and walking out on his own Cabinet to form a new government in alliance with his former opponents, the men of the conservative Liberal Party he had once scorned. Re-elected in May 1917, the once-ardent socialist was now engaged in a vehement campaign of reprisals against the 'junta' of radicals he believed to be undermining the nation. His public appearances became so divisive and confrontational that he would soon take to carrying a pistol in his jacket pocket. When 100,000 workers went on strike in August 1917 to protest against wages and prices, he developed an irrational belief that his enemies on the Left had called the strike in retribution for his defection from the Labor Party.

Publicly, he blamed the Germans. 'I firmly believe that there is a directing hand,' he said of the strike, 'and that if we could discover it we would see that that hand was a hand of Teutonic origin.'

* *

It was against this backdrop that ships began sinking and disappearing near Australia in the latter half of 1917. The government, of course, had known since March that the *Wolf* was at large and possibly heading towards Australia – Hughes himself had made the inflammatory suggestion that the raider was only a few hundred miles from the nation's coastline. Now, he used every means possible to generate a scare story that was entirely different but equally erroneous – that the missing ships had fallen victim to the very 'Teutonic hand' he had been warning about. Hughes had already ordered the Special Intelligence Bureau to investigate the *Cumberland* explosion, but his spy agency had failed to find any evidence of Wobbly sabotage; its interim report in July strongly suggested that the freighter had struck a mine. That theory was buttressed by the evidence of the five navy divers at the closed maritime inquiry into the sinking, which concluded in Sydney on 18 August. The prime minister, however, continued to offer a substantial reward for information about the supposed saboteurs, and when the *Matunga* was reported missing, he publicly suggested that she had also been sabotaged.

The press, not surprisingly, immediately fell in line. 'It is now surmised,' reported the *Age* newspaper in Melbourne on 15 August, 'that the *Matunga* has been lost due to an internal explosion.' Navy minister Joseph Cook told the *Mirror* that the ship's disappearance had prompted the government to increase surveillance on the wharves to detect German agents.

The public was conditioned to accept such sinister inferences, for they were common currency in all Allied nations. Around the time the Australian Government made its fallacious claims about the *Matunga*, wire stories were published claiming that five ships in the Pacific had been destroyed by German time bombs, that 'Hun agents' were being placed aboard merchant ships to signal to U-boats, and that neutral Norwegian merchant skippers were on the payroll of the Kaiser's spy network. The *New York Times* reported that the sinking of two coal-steamers on the Great Lakes was believed to be a plot 'engineered by Germans, assisted by sympathising American citizens'. (In fact, the two ships had simply collided.)

In Cape Town, meanwhile, suspicions about local Germans were being reignited by a tragedy that created headlines around the world. On 10 August, the 5900-ton steamship *City of Athens*, en route from New York to Bombay with ninety-seven passengers and a crew of 112, struck one of the *Wolf*'s mines off Dassen Island

and sank at 3.30 in the afternoon. Among the passengers rushing to escape the crippled ship were fifty-nine Methodist missionaries from the United States, including Reverend Arthur Duckworth, his wife and their six children, the youngest a five-month-old infant. When their lifeboat took on water and capsized, the entire family drowned, along with another Methodist couple, two young missionary women and nine others. An inquest concluded that a mine was responsible, and newspaper stories soon appeared that blamed the minelaying on German immigrants living in Cape Town. The *New York Times* reported that 'no German mine layers or submarines have been reported in that section of the Indian Ocean since the war began'. A British mining engineer told the newspaper that military officials in South Africa believed the mines were being manufactured locally and taken out into the harbour at night. Anonymous letter writers in the *Cape Times* suggested similar conspiracies. 'The authorities ought to keep a close eye on persons of German parentage, who speak and write German, and have been very closely associated with officials of the German Government . . .' warned one.

Australians would quickly come to believe that similar dark treacheries were afoot on their own shores. Privately, the Hughes government and its navy had by late August come to the view that a German commerce-raider had, in fact, been active off Australia. A search for the *Matunga* in the oceans near New Guinea had failed to find any floating debris of the kind usually left by a ship that has sunk without warning; not even a slick of her benzine consignment had been detected. The Union Steamship Company of New Zealand likewise reported that, although its ships had searched for the *Wairuna* across all the usual Pacific trade routes, no clue as to her fate had been found. The burnt-out wrecks of three unidentifiable sailing ships had been sighted in the waters south of Fiji, at a time when the *Encore*, *Winslow* and *Beluga* were all posted as missing. All these incidents, combined with the evidence presented at the *Cumberland* inquiry, prompted the Australian Naval Board to inform Hughes on 30 August that a raider was probably at large and that three Australian warships – the *Encounter*, the *Psyche* and the *Fantome* (the latter two about to return to Australia from Singapore) – were being sent to investigate.

One theory in Australian navy circles was that the raider might be the *Seeadler*, which had been reported off Argentina and heading towards the Pacific several months earlier. In London, however, a naval-intelligence analyst noted that 'it was presumed raider *Wolf* was in these waters'. The dormant Admiralty intelligence file on the *Wolf* was reactivated, and it was speculated that the raider might have reached New Zealand by late April, capturing the *Wairuna* in early June and the *Matunga* in the first week of August. All available information, it concluded, 'point[s] to the presence of the Raider working off the S.E. of New Guinea during the month of August'.

Whether London informed Melbourne of its suspicions is unclear, but when Prime Minister Hughes received the Special Intelligence Bureau's final report on the *Cumberland* sinking in the second week of September, evidence of a raider became compelling. Two eminent explosives experts – an engineering professor from Sydney University, William Warren, and a physics professor from Melbourne, Dr Thomas Lyle – informed the prime minister that after attending the maritime inquiry and inspecting sections of the sunken ship's hull they could find no evidence to support the theory of a bomb. Professor Warren expressed some bafflement at the navy's insistent promotion of the sabotage theory, finding that all evidence pointed to the ship having struck a mine.

The bureau's deputy, Major Harold Jones, was even more emphatic. 'The results of the investigations show conclusively that a mine was responsible for the damage,' Jones concluded in his own secret report, adding that it was difficult to conceive how German spies could have laid a minefield in a location as remote and inaccessible as Gabo Island. Instead, he strongly suggested that the mine or mines were planted by a German ship, either before or since the outbreak of war.

But these findings put the government in a difficult position, because Australia's navy had no minesweepers and virtually no warships of any substance to deal with a rogue German raider. Since the British Government had seconded Australia's three remaining destroyers to Europe in July, the country's only significant warship was the *Encounter*, a twelve-year-old cruiser armed with eleven six-inch guns, which was on loan from Britain and by no means certain to survive an encounter with a raider. The *Psyche* and the *Fantome*, which were on their way to assist from Singapore, were much smaller ships that were both overdue for the scrapping yard, and the rest of Australia's available fleet consisted of torpedo-boats and gunboats that were wholly inadequate for the task.

The navy was thus heavily dependent on the assistance of Rear-Admiral Yamaji, who now proved so stubbornly uncooperative that he refused to send either the *Chikuma* or the *Hirado* to help. In a long missive to the Australian Naval Board, Yamaji explained that he thought it unlikely a raider was in the Pacific, theorising that it was 'highly probable' the *Wairuna* had struck a submerged rock on the way to San Francisco and that the *Matunga* had been the victim of another bomb plot. 'So far as I can summarise from the recent progress of the German warfare,' he concluded, 'they seem to have given up their idea of sending raiders to all the oceans and their present idea seems to put more emphasis to the tricky plot as they have done to SS *Cumberland*.' Anyway, the Japanese admiral added, searching vast stretches of the Pacific with a handful of ships would be almost pointless.

Yamaji's reluctance to go hunting for German raiders may well have been motivated by self-preservation: his two warships were light-cruisers of only 5000 tons, and if the Germans had captured other ships and converted them to raiders he could be facing more than one enemy vessel. But his snub was guaranteed to rile the Australians, for behind their profusely polite official exchanges the two allies shared a virulent mistrust and antipathy. When Sir Ronald Munro-Ferguson lunched with Rear-Admiral

Yamaji and his officers aboard the *Hirado* some months later, he heard the Japanese openly voicing their 'dislike and distrust' of the Australians. The Australian Navy, for its part, later bitterly complained to London about Yamaji's recalcitrance. Embarrassingly for the Japanese admiral, however, his assessment of the raider threat was quickly rendered redundant by a series of dramatic developments.

Shortly after 1 am on 18 September, the steamship *Port Kembla* was approaching New Zealand from Melbourne with a load of frozen meat, wool, lead and general cargo bound for London when it struck the *Wolf*'s minefield off Cape Farewell. An explosion tore a hole in the freighter's starboard hull, sucking the ocean into the number-one hold, and within half an hour the ship had listed, rolled heavily and disappeared in the darkness – remarkably, without the loss of any of its crew, who took to the lifeboats and were picked up off Wellington. The sinking confirmed the Australian Navy's belief that a German minelayer had been active in local waters. Upon hearing the news, the Naval Board in Melbourne cabled its New Zealand counterpart to urge that minesweepers be dispatched to Cape Farewell, pointing out that 'expert opinion' suggested a mine had sunk the *Cumberland*. Unfortunately, New Zealand also possessed no minesweepers, and the country's only working warship, the *New Zealand*, was 15,000 miles away under Royal Navy command.

By then, anyway, the country's Minister for Marine, G. W. Russell, had already offered a familiar but misleading explanation for the sinking. 'The cause of the disaster, I regret to say, was an internal explosion,' Russell told parliament less than twenty-four hours after the ship went down. 'I regret to have to make this announcement, but as rumours may get about, I think it is advisable to give members all the facts.'

The *Port Kembla*'s captain, John Jack, was reportedly convinced that an 'infernal machine' had gone off in his ship's number-one hold. If true, the skipper may well have succumbed to the sabotage fever that had been gripping Melbourne before he left, for his own description of security aboard the *Port Kembla* suggested that a bomb big enough to sink a 4700-ton freighter would have been exceedingly difficult to secrete among the freight. The ship had been guarded by twenty-four armed troops while in harbour; every bag brought aboard her had been searched and no one had been allowed to board or disembark without producing a security pass; guards had been posted on the gangway, bridge and aft deck, and wire mesh had been placed over ventilators to prevent anyone from dropping any object into the hold. The Australian Navy considered the bomb theory 'improbable' and cabled New Zealand's head of naval intelligence, Captain Percival Hall-Thompson, to tell him.

From his floating office aboard the unseaworthy warship *Philomel*, docked in Wellington Harbour, Hall-Thompson had been closely following the events of the past several weeks. He knew that Australian warships were secretly steaming towards New Guinea looking for a suspected German raider; he knew that the *Cumberland* was thought to have hit a mine; only two weeks earlier, he had himself warned the New Zealand Government that a commerce-raider could be at large in the Pacific. Despite this, Hall-Thompson now dismissed the need for any minesweepers to be dispatched to Cape Farewell, telling Melbourne that he was 'certain' the *Port Kembla* had been sunk by a bomb.

When mercantile marine authorities in Wellington got wind of the raider rumours, he assured them there was not even the 'smallest likelihood' that the *Port Kembla* had struck a mine. 'It is just possible that [a raider] . . . may be involved,' Hall-Thompson told the Secretary of Marine, 'but it is very undesirable at present, in the Public Interest, that any details as to the amount and description of the knowledge in the possession of the Naval Authority should be revealed.'

* *

The task of keeping the public uninformed, however, was about to become even more difficult, because even as Hall-Thompson was sending off this dispatch, news of a remarkable discovery arrived from Fijian authorities. In mid-September, a police boat patrolling the islands east of Suva had spotted the red-painted hull of a thirty-foot launch near Wakaya, and upon investigating encountered six German sailors from the raider *Seeadler*, led by their captain, Count Felix von Luckner. Confronted by a Fijian police officer waving a pistol loaded only with blanks, Luckner surrendered immediately, even though his boat was found to contain an arsenal of rifles, automatic pistols, detonators and bombs.

For Luckner, it was the end of an unlikely nine-month raiding mission, which had begun with great flourish and ended in ignominy when his sailing ship was wrecked on a reef in the middle of the Pacific Ocean. Having sailed from Kiel a few weeks after the *Wolf* with a crew of sixty-three aboard the *Seeadler*, Luckner had headed south-west down the Atlantic towards the trade routes off Argentina, where he had captured and sunk eleven ships in short order. After his now-famous gesture of chivalry towards his prisoners – releasing all 300 of them to a passing French freighter that he permitted to sail to Rio de Janeiro – Luckner had escaped south and evaded several British warships to round Cape Horn and head up into the Pacific during a fierce storm in April.

Like Karl Nerger, however, he had encountered a chronic shortage of shipping in the Pacific. For six weeks in June and July, he had roamed above the equator north-east of Tahiti, capturing just three San Francisco barques and in all likelihood narrowly missing an encounter with the Cameron family, who passed through the same waters aboard the *Beluga* during late June. Food shortages and scurvy eventually forced him to seek shelter on the tiny island of Mopelia, south of Tahiti; there, the *Seeadler* smashed into a reef, in circumstances that would later be the subject of much mythology and dispute, leaving the Germans and their twenty-nine prisoners stranded. Among them was Gladys Taylor, an adventurous young woman from Washington State who had been a stowaway on one of the American ships, and who later testified to the gentlemanly conduct of all her companions.

The indefatigable Luckner had subsequently taken five of his men in one of the *Seeadler*'s two surviving lifeboats and embarked on an epic voyage nearly 2000 miles west, stopping for supplies at the Cook Islands, where they posed as Norwegian castaways. Pressing onwards with his exhausted and half-starved men, Luckner dropped in on the Lau Islands to purloin some stores from a depot (leaving behind two pounds sterling and a note of thanks signed 'Max Pemberton'), before finally reaching Wakaya, where he was still hatching plans to capture another ship when intercepted by the Fijian police.

The full story of these adventures would take some weeks to emerge, after Luckner was taken back to Suva and then to an island prison off the New Zealand coast. Interrogated by Rear-Admiral Yamaji in his Suva jail cell, the wily count spun many fabulous stories of his exploits, not the least being that a giant tidal wave had capsized the *Seeadler* onto the Mopelia reef. Later, it would be revealed that he had anchored the ship too close to the reef, so that it foundered while he was eating lunch on the island with his prisoners. But Luckner admitted enough in his first two weeks of captivity to make it clear that he knew nothing of the *Wairuna* or *Matunga*, had never laid mines and had not sailed within 4000 miles of New Guinea. In short, he had nothing to do with the shipping losses reported around Fiji, New Zealand and Australia, which suggested the unpleasant possibility that two German raiders had reached the Pacific and that the *Matunga* may have been converted to a third.

Keeping details of Luckner's capture secret, the Admiralty dispatched the *Encounter* to Mopelia to locate the rest of the *Seeadler*'s shipwrecked survivors, while Australian Navy officials wired Rear-Admiral Yamaji – no doubt with some relish – to suggest his two warships might care to help search for the *Matunga*.

The British Government was now coming under increasing pressure to reveal what it knew of the raider situation. In July and early August, the secretary to the Admiralty, Thomas Macnamara, had refused to answer questions in parliament concerning the whereabouts of the *Wolf* and other raiders, arguing it was not in the public interest. In Australia, the government's secretiveness was also under attack. The *Sun* newspaper had published leaked material from the *Cumberland* inquiry suggesting that the ship had struck a mine, and the *Argus* newspaper wanted to know whether there was anyone intelligent in naval intelligence. Opposition MPs decried the censorship of the press and demanded the release of the *Cumberland* inquiry's findings. Rumour again outpaced reality. At the *Brisbane Courier* newspaper, a report was prepared suggesting that the *Matunga* had been captured by a German raider, or perhaps by 'a gang of spies and German sympathisers with headquarters in Brisbane'. The censor quashed the story.

In the midst of it all, maritime officials in Wellington hastily convened an inquiry to investigate the *Port Kembla* sinking. Lasting only one day, the hearing was conducted by a magistrate who was told nothing about the capture of the *Seeadler*, the Admiralty's suspicions about the *Wolf* or the Australian Navy's belief that mines had been laid in nearby waters. The *Port Kembla*'s captain and crew were virtually the only witnesses, and all were now convinced a bomb had gone off in the cargo hold. Inevitably, the inquiry ruled that the ship had been destroyed by 'a quantity of high explosive substance' in the fore hold, an official finding that created an instant sensation on both sides of the Tasman Sea.

'INTERN THE GERMANS' demanded the *Sun* in Sydney, speculating that a Teutonic conspiracy lay behind the losses of the *Cumberland*, *Matunga*, *Wairuna* and *Port Kembla*. The *Argus* echoed the claim but also pointed its finger at the Wobblies. 'There are, it is evident, enemies within our gates,' the paper editorialised. 'It is apparent that mingling with loyal citizens are men either in the pay of Germany or associated with an unlawful organisation, doing all they can to injure the industrial and commercial interests of the empire . . .' In New Zealand, the Merchant Service Guild demanded that all Germans be imprisoned, and the *New Zealand Herald* chimed in with an editorial arguing that 'the freedom given to enemy aliens has been a source of public complaint throughout the war . . . Consideration for the feelings of Germans of reputed good character should give way to consideration for the lives of our seamen.' In response, the New Zealand Government banned all 'aliens and undesirable characters' from working on the country's wharves. Suspicions swirled around the crew of the *Port Kembla*, who had been detained and interrogated after their rescue. A Dutchman among them was arrested and charged with sedition after getting drunk in a New Zealand hotel and shouting that he loved the Kaiser – an offence for which he received two months in jail.

In Melbourne, Prime Minister Hughes leapt on the *Port Kembla* inquiry's finding as further evidence of the German espionage system, offering a £5000 reward for information on the *Port Kembla*'s sinking. Although he knew that navy minesweepers were being hastily fitted out in Sydney to trawl the coastline near Gabo Island, Hughes chose this moment to release an entirely misleading statement about the *Cumberland* disaster. The official maritime inquiry into the disaster, he announced, had been unable to find a cause of the ship's sinking. Conducted by a maritime bureaucrat named Fergus Cumming, the inquiry had come to the remarkably vague conclusion that no definitive finding could be justified, even though the trend of the evidence pointed to an external explosion.

Like a dog unleashed, the press now pursued every report of an overdue freighter or unexplained ship fire as evidence of the dark conspiracies the prime minister had been warning about. Ramping up its 'Intern the Hun' campaign, the *Sun* announced its own £1000 bounty for information about the criminals responsible for the destruction of the *Port Kembla*. Within days, a number of prominent business and shipping figures had contributed to the fund, although the newspaper confronted a dilemma when it discovered that two of the donors – Henry Markwald and Henry Abel – were German-born naturalised Australians. Adroitly turning embarrassment to its own advantage, the *Sun* announced it was refusing Markwald's and Abel's money because 'we prefer, as a newspaper of a British community, to exclude from such a list [of donors] the names of any persons born in any enemy countries . . .' Below this announcement, under the headline 'HOW THE DANGER SPREADS', was a table of statistics displaying the number of German-born men still at large in the community ('The Menace'), next to a tally of all ship losses during the war. 'In a year, if drastic steps are not taken to grapple with the menace, our shipping losses may almost equal our war expenditure,' the newspaper warned.

Unexpectedly, however, the elaborate veil of secrecy that the Admiralty had drawn over the Pacific-raider threat was now pulled aside by one of its own allies. In the last week of September, a small launch appeared in the harbour of Pago Pago – the main port in the United States territory of Samoa – bearing the sunburnt and dehydrated figures of four of the *Seeadler*'s former prisoners. Led by a San Franciscan merchant captain named Hador Smith, the four men had just made a perilous 1300-mile crossing from Mopelia Island and told United States Navy officials in Samoa their bewildering tale of being captured by the *Seeadler* and shipwrecked with their German captors. After Luckner's departure with his five men, their circumstances had become even grimmer, for the French schooner *Lutèce* had pulled into Mopelia's harbour and the Germans had seized the ship, evicted her sixteen-man crew, loaded her with their remaining weapons and sailed east into the Pacific, leaving nearly fifty people stranded on Mopelia. Desperate for food and water, Smith, his second mate and two other seamen from San Francisco had decided to risk death by taking the *Seeadler*'s one remaining lifeboat out to sea to seek help.

The United States Navy in Washington released news of the castaways on 4 October, thus revealing for the first time the *Seeadler*'s Pacific raiding sorties and her demise off Tahiti. The story was published around the world, embellished with details from several civilians recently arrived in San Francisco and Sydney from Samoa. Angry at this breach of secrecy, the British Government complained to the United States administration.

In Melbourne, it was left to the minister for the navy, Joseph Cook, to explain what the Australian Government knew of the *Seeadler*, his prime minister having just repaired to a secluded holiday resort on Port Phillip Bay, near Melbourne. Assuring the nation that the raider threat was receiving the government's 'undivided attention', Cook then dismissed its significance. Australians should be much more concerned, he said, 'in the disasters to our shipping by means of explosions and fires and such-like incendiary and devilish agencies. They seemed to point unerringly to enemy agency within our own gates.' The public, he urged, should bend all its energies and will to the task of hunting down traitors and spies.

Even as he made this announcement, however, Cook knew that even more discomfiting developments would have to be revealed, for two days earlier the navy's newly formed minesweeping squadron had exploded one of the *Wolf*'s submerged mines off Gabo Island. On 12 October, when a second mine was discovered, Cook was finally forced to release the news, stirring a furore in the tabloids that was this time directed at the government. The *Sun*'s editors immediately grasped the extent to which Hughes and Cook had misled them, and published a major editorial that fulminated against official secrecy and censorship. 'The censor-germ which has possessed ministers has been very deadly to public news,' the editorial complained. 'The theory that people must not know of dangers which threaten them is today triumphant . . . It has been revealed that for weeks German raiders were in our southern waters. Did the Government know? Presumably it knew . . .'

But the *Sun*, like most newspapers, was loath to admit that its campaign against German immigrants had been misguided. Somewhat vaguely, it suggested that neutral ships containing Dutch, Swedish and German sailors might have deposited secret agents of the Kaiser into the country. 'Why not take the sure course and intern all aliens?' the newspaper demanded. 'Especially the rich ones.' Other newspapers took up the cry, mirroring events in South Africa. The *Sydney Morning Herald* surmised that the minefield 'is part of a scheme . . . carried on by Germans settled in Allied countries, and in which they have employed every neutral agent who would listen to persuasions or bribes'. The Federated Seaman's Union supported that view, while Australia's newly formed Anti-German League called for all German-Australians to be prohibited from approaching within twenty-five miles of the coastline. More alarmist than any of them was the *Mirror*, which speculated that German settlers in Australia might be preparing for 'an army of invasion'.

'We have already, in the loss of the *Cumberland* and the *Matunga*, [had] a taste of what is going on in other parts of the world,' the newspaper warned darkly, 'and it behoves the authorities to be suspiciously on the alert. Nothing short of wholesale internment will allay public anxiety.'

The discovery of the *Wolf*'s minefield off Australia was thus woven into the War Office fear campaign directed at German immigrants and other suspected subversives. In London, *The Times* reported Australia's ship losses as examples of sabotage, and the Admiralty's beliefs about the *Wolf* remained secret. To the War Office, these deceptions were doubtless seen as necessary, for they prevented politically unpalatable news reaching the public and increased the chances of hunting down the *Wolf*. But the secrecy had unavoidable consequences, not the least of which was that merchant captains sailing between major ports in the Pacific and Indian oceans were unaware of the extent of the dangers they faced, both from minefields and raiders. In New Zealand, where no minesweeping was conducted until well into 1918, the consequences would be tragic.

The secrecy also meant that thousands of people whose relatives or friends had gone missing aboard the nine ships captured by the *Wolf* became convinced, by late 1917, that their loved ones had perished. In San Francisco, the *Chronicle* had reported that the burning wreck of a barque similar to the *Beluga* had been sighted east of Fiji, and with the Cameron family nearly two months overdue in Sydney, the newspaper said that little hope was entertained for their survival. In Berkeley, just outside San Francisco, the couple caring for Stan and Mary's youngest daughter, Edris, would soon begin proceedings to formally adopt the little girl; in Newcastle, Mary's grief-stricken parents assumed the worst. In New Guinea, too, it was surmised that everyone aboard the *Matunga* had died, for some Australian newspapers had reported that the ship had been sunk by an undersea earthquake. An *in memoriam* to the crew and passengers was published in the *Rabaul Record*, listing the ship as 'lost at sea' and lamenting the deaths of all on board. In Britain, the crew of the *Wordsworth* had been listed by the ship's owner as drowned. Despairing parents would soon begin writing to government officials seeking information about the hundreds of missing passengers and crews. Typical of them was Elizabeth Pearce, an Australian mother whose only remaining child, Rupert, was a twenty-one-year-old army private who had sailed aboard the *Matunga* two months after he enlisted. In a letter to the Australian Navy, two months after the ship disappeared, she made a desperate plea:

> Could you not tell one now if it was a raider that took the 'Matunga' & if they are safe. Oh how I wish you would tell one something definite, there are so many rumours about, even some have said they are on an island, & some that they are at a port. I have been expecting to hear from you every day since the reports in the papers about raiders. If you only knew the awful suspense I am passing through, I am sure you would give me just one ray of hope, seeing I only had the two sons and the other was killed in France last May 12.

The navy replied that, regrettably, nothing further could be added. Like many others, the grieving Mrs Pearce would endure months more of 'awful suspense' before the truth could be revealed.

7

MESSAGE IN A BOTTLE

The Halmahera Sea lay as flat as a plane of blue glass, an incongruously beautiful sight to the prisoners clustered along the deck rails of the *Wolf*. It was almost possible, here under the burning glare of the equatorial sun, to forget the armed German guards patrolling the ship and simply bask in the distant vista of Ceram Island, with its yellow sands and slender coconut palms passing by on the raider's port side. A tantalising scent blew in on the breeze from that land, like a balm for the intense heat, and close to its shores could be glimpsed the white woven sails and wooden hulls of native canoes, which occasionally drifted past the ship piloted by turbaned fishermen. The white flash of a pelican or heron would periodically streak across the sky to land on a drifting tree trunk, or the sea's surface would be disturbed by a geyser of white spray, as a whale breached the surface and languidly lifted its tail.

The 'spice islands' of the Dutch East Indies were a place of such natural beauty that even hardened merchant seamen were known to lapse into lyrical reverie at their mention. To young Roy Alexander, they rivalled the South Pacific islands as an idyll. Alexander was in the ship's hospital, directly under the bridge on the starboard side, when the *Wolf* steamed south through the South Moluccas islands and into the Ceram and Banda seas in the final days of August. He had succumbed to appendicitis during the two weeks in Offak Bay, but even his illness could not cloud the pleasure of breathing uncontaminated air as the scenery drifted past his porthole. In these neutral waters, with the nearest Allied naval bases thousands of miles to the south and west, the jittery nerves of the Germans also eased and the prisoners were once more allowed to congregate on the poop deck during the day. Fritz Witschetzky had encountered Rose Flood one evening up on the boat deck behind the bridge, wearing 'a light blue chiffon dress that went hand in hand with the matt yellow of the evening sky'; she was chatting to the three Australian military captains who had been granted above-deck quarters with the plantation owners from Melbourne.

The presence of 'good-looking Frau Flood', as Witschetzky liked to call her, had altered the chemistry aboard the *Wolf*. Even the men in the Hell Hole, shaven-headed and clothed in grimy rags as they were, had been jolted by this feminine apparition in their midst. When the *Matunga* had first pulled alongside the *Wolf* in Offak Bay, with Rose standing at the rails, many of the prisoners congregating on the raider's poop deck had rushed downstairs to don shirts and smarten themselves up. Her effect on the Germans, deprived of female company for nine months, was even more electric. Witschetzky provided a colourful account of the stir the thirty-two-year-old created on her first night aboard the *Wolf*.

'After dinner, we were all treated to quite a sight. A very elegantly dressed lady promenaded with the British officers on deck – it was Frau Flood. According to British custom she was always dressed impeccably. Today, for example, she was dressed in pink satin, glossy patent leather shoes and fine satin stockings. Her gown train kicked up the coaldust.'

Rose herself seemed to enjoy her effect on the men, despite the presence of her husband. Witschetzky recalled her openly flirting with the young officers, who vied for the honour of escorting her on her post-dinner walk along the deck. Even in the cramped and dirty conditions aboard the *Wolf*, she kept her wardrobe of satin and chiffon gowns in perfect order, and these evening strolls became the focus of the German crew's pent-up longings, the merest rustle of her silk stockings and petticoats conjuring a hundred sexual fantasies. 'Every night the question was: What is Frau Flood wearing tonight?' recalled Witschetzky. '"*The pale green dress*" murmured through the ship.'

Karl Nerger had always anticipated that he might capture women prisoners, but now that it had happened he was far from sanguine. 'My God,' he complained to Szielasko, 'where do I accommodate them?' But the German captain extended the same courtesies towards John and Rose Flood that the Camerons enjoyed: a junior officer vacated his cabin to provide accommodation for them, and a crew member was appointed to act as their orderly.

Agnes Mackenzie, too, had been provided her own private cabin. But the close confines of the raider raised a tangle of potential problems for these women, and for Nerger. On any given morning, a good proportion of the 550 men aboard the ship bathed naked under saltwater showers in the open air of the aft deck; a heavy rainstorm during the day would be the signal for crew and prisoners alike to strip off their clothes, haul out canvas baths and indulge in the bacchanalian luxury of a communal freshwater wash – a scene that Stan Cameron likened to 'the Garden of Eden before Eve showed on the job'. The women not only had to be shielded from such sights, they also had to be provided with their own private and tightly policed bathing area on the aft deck. An unseemly encounter of any kind between Nerger's crew and one of these women could wreck the rigidly maintained discipline of the ship and cause an uprising among the prisoners. To Roy Alexander, it was clear that Nerger felt a warship was no place for women, 'particularly good-looking ones who were likely to cause trouble'.

The German captain got an early taste of the problems he would experience when Agnes Mackenzie demanded to see him shortly after her arrival on board and again indignantly objected to her new role as Rose Flood's maid. The diminutive stewardess disliked the young Mrs Flood so intensely that not even Leutnant Karl Rose's offer of a modest weekly wage had placated her. Nerger listened patiently to her tirade and replied that unless she cooperated, she would be forced to eat dinner with his crew. 'That changed her mind,' he recalled. Mackenzie hastily backed down but began taking her meals in her cabin.

Despite his dismay at the sinking of the *Matunga*, Stan Cameron still nurtured a hope that, with several women and a child on board, Nerger would seek a safe harbour in which to free some of his prisoners. There were, surely, some remote mission islands along their route that would allow Nerger to rid himself of some of his human cargo and make his escape. But when the ship's course began to bear west away from the Moluccas, that hope again evaporated, for it was clear that Nerger was not heading back out to the open sea. Captain Tom Meadows had sailed these waters many times and was tracking the *Wolf*'s course, past the cloud-encircled mountains of Boeroe on the left, skirting the southern coastline of Celebes on the right and entering the Flores Sea to thread through the archipelago of the Dutch East Indies. Far ahead of them lay the tiny island that Meadows feared was their ultimate destination, and when the lighthouse of Den Bril came into view, he turned to one of the German officers.

'I see your Commandant is heading for Singapore,' Meadows remarked gruffly. 'Do you really expect to get through? It's impossible! All approaches to Singapore are heavily guarded. Down here in the south, in the Karimata and Malacca Straits, British and Japanese cruisers are on constant patrol. In the north, the French are operating out of Saigon and the Americans out of Manila. You'll never make it close to Singapore. And even if you managed to get close to the port, you'll never get yourselves out of that trap again.'

Singapore was the headquarters of the Admiralty's China Squadron, the port from which its warships patrolled all of eastern Asia in a sweeping radius that extended west towards India and Ceylon, north towards China and east as far as New Guinea. A rotating contingent of Australian and Japanese warships was stationed there, but what made the port such a forbidding target for a minelayer was its hemmed-in location. To get there, Nerger was entering a bottleneck formed by the islands on either side of him. To his north were Celebes and then Borneo; to the south were the elongated coastlines of Java and Sumatra, which together stretched for more than one thousand six hundred miles and were broken only by the Sunda Strait, a congested channel between the two islands that led south to the Indian Ocean. Nine hundred miles ahead of him, the Asian mainland reached down almost to touch Sumatra's northern coastline, and wedged between them was the narrow Malacca Strait, which continued west towards India. Singapore lay at the entrance to that strait, and once he laid his mines there – assuming that could be done undetected – Nerger would be trapped. The westward course through the Malacca Strait was so congested that he had no chance of passing through there undetected, and the seas north of Singapore led nowhere but up to China and Japan, and ultimately back to the Pacific. His only escape was to turn around and go back the way he had come, due east until he reached the Sunda Strait or one of the other southerly passages to the Indian Ocean. He was effectively putting his head in a noose.

Nerger had weighed up other options. He could have sailed directly south from New Guinea into the Timor Sea, heading from there to India to complete the minelaying he had been forced to cut short seven months earlier. But it was still the monsoon season in India, and with the *Wolf* mustering a maximum speed of only ten knots, it was unlikely the ship could reach Calcutta in time for a new moon. The Indian ports would be more vigilant because of his earlier minelaying, and Karachi as a secondary target was not a major Allied port. Singapore, by contrast, was reachable while the weather and moon were still favourable, and was a major transit point for shipping. With some irritation, Nerger noted in his log that he was under strict orders not to lay mines outside the three-mile zone of a port that lay directly opposite neutral territory, in compliance with the Hague rules. Given that Singapore was directly across the strait from Dutch Sumatra, he would be forced to lay his mines 150 miles north-east of the port, off the Anambas Islands.

In the hospital, Roy Alexander watched the ship's course and felt the same apprehension as Tom Meadows. From the milky-green colour of the sea outside his hospital porthole, he knew they were sailing past Java and Borneo; in this busy stretch of the Java Sea, the vast majority of ships passing them were Dutch-owned mail-boats and inter-island steamers of the Royal Packet line, all absolutely distinctive with their white superstructures and yellow funnels. Only occasionally did an Australian or Asian steamship pass, and Alexander knew most of them as regulars on the three trade lanes that converged on Singapore. With her hulking black appearance and battered condition, her distinctly German lines and her curious lack of identifying insignia, the *Wolf* could not have been more conspicuous.

On the bridge, Nerger audaciously signalled passing ships by hoisting an assortment of different flags – the Union Jack, the Stars and Stripes, the Norwegian blue cross – while steadfastly ignoring any request to identify himself. The atmosphere aboard the ship became tenser as her destination approached and the traffic around them became heavier. Prisoners were locked down in the Hell Hole, and rotating shifts of gun crews lay on the deck beside their concealed weapons, constantly on alert. Below deck, preparations were made to winch the final 110 mines from the armoury. The dangers of the undertaking soon became manifest.

Four hundred miles from Singapore, just before midnight on 2 September, the ship's alarm jolted everyone awake. Stan and Mary Cameron stumbled out of bed and opened their cabin door to see the two doctors rushing past with first-aid kits strapped to their waists; in the darkness of the Hell Hole, the prisoners heard the reverberating thud of boots on the wooden deck above and the familiar metallic clang of the hinged bulwarks dropping against the hull; in the hospital, Roy Alexander's slumber was shattered by an intercom message from the bridge announcing that an armed cruiser was approaching. Stan Cameron reached the deck rail to see the Karimata Strait stretched out before him under a full moon that burnished its surface to a silver sheen. It was a cloudless and brilliantly clear night, and below him on the port side of the ship Cameron saw all three guns and two torpedo tubes swung out ready to fire. Straining his eyes into the distance, he could just make out the distant profile of a grey cruiser approaching with its lights out, perhaps four miles ahead of them but starkly outlined in the moonlight. Cameron paused just long enough to take in its details – two masts, two funnels, a low and flat grey hull – before rushing back into the cabin to urge Mary and Juanita to pull on the clothes they kept ready for such emergencies.

Fritz Witschetzky rushed to his gunnery command post still buttoning his shirt, passing a partially undressed John and Rose Flood as they scurried back to their cabin from the deck where they had been sleeping to escape the night-time heat. Through his binoculars, Witschetzky saw, unmistakably, that the ship was an Allied cruiser of approximately 2000 tons, approaching from almost directly ahead but now shifting course to pass them on the port bow. A weak light leaking from the cruiser's open portholes allowed Witschetzky's range finder to calibrate her distance, which was closing to 13,000 feet, while from below him the gunnery crews announced they were loaded and ready. Torpedo crewmen were frantically shouting that they had a direct bearing on the approaching ship and could fire at any time, but Nerger's voice barked over the intercom that they were to open fire only on his orders.

The Australian light-cruiser HMAS *Psyche* was a nineteenth-century relic, nearly twenty years old in 1917 and, at 2135 tons, less than half the size of the *Wolf*. Her crew of 200 mostly young and untrained ratings had spent the past two years slogging between China, India, Malaya and Singapore on numbingly routine patrols, succumbing to a variety of tropical illnesses en route. At one point in 1916, more than a third of the men had been hospitalised, and a rebellion among them had precipitated the ship's return to Singapore, where several of the crew were court-martialled. Her commander, Henry Feakes, was a British-born former Royal Navy officer who resented his posting, for the *Psyche*'s four-inch guns had nowhere near the range or firepower necessary to tackle even a moderately well-equipped raider. And on the night of 2 September, Feakes was steaming away from Asia to help look for the very raider that was now closing in on his starboard bow.

Witschetzky could barely suppress his excitement at seeing an Allied warship in his sights at last. From the bridge, his captain authorised him to open fire if the cruiser showed any sign of stopping them or attempting Morse-code contact. As the *Psyche* drew level, even Nerger felt a powerful impulse to fire his torpedoes, so clear was the target. But such an attack would have derailed his minelaying plans for Singapore and could well have ended in catastrophe for both ships, for despite the *Psyche*'s inferior firepower, the *Wolf* was still carrying a considerable load of explosives in her aft hold.

Nerger held firm and ordered the *Wolf* to shift course away to starboard. The cruiser had a clear vision of them, and in the bright moonlight it seemed inconceivable that her captain could not see that this nameless black freighter appeared to be bristling with weapons. Witschetzky described the two ships closing to within 6000 feet as they passed one another; watching from his hospital bed, Roy Alexander saw a glimmer of light on the bridge when a cabin door opened. The *Wolf*'s torpedo crew beseeched Nerger for permission to fire, but the captain shouted back, 'Permission not granted! I repeat – do not open fire.' In their cabin, the Camerons desperately threw on their clothes while steeling themselves for the first discharge of the guns, while down in the Hell Hole the prisoners waited uncomprehendingly in the inky blackness.

Alec Donaldson would later remember the silence stretching out for an hour, when in fact it was mere minutes. In that suspended moment, the grey cruiser almost imperceptibly began shifting course, turning away from the *Wolf* towards Sumatra and picking up speed as she headed in the direction of an approaching passenger-ship. Witschetzky cursed as he ordered his crews to disarm.

Why the *Psyche* failed to challenge the *Wolf*, or even report her appearance, was a question more than one person aboard the raider later asked. Nerger found it incomprehensible and quipped that perhaps everyone aboard the cruiser was asleep. Captain Feakes's subsequent memoirs omitted any mention of his close brush with the Pacific Ocean's most notorious raider, although Alexander had his own sardonic explanation: 'He may have been tired; or, it being a Sunday night, he was against examining ships on the day of rest. Still, this writer would be the last to censure any slackness on the part of the commander of the cruiser, for one round from that cruiser placed among the mines just aft of the engine room would have sent *Wolf*, crew and prisoners all sky high together.'

The tension aboard the *Wolf* was palpable long after the *Psyche* slipped from view, for the crew were now only twenty-four hours from their final and most dangerous minelaying mission. Hugging the southern coastline of Borneo, the ship turned north towards the lower reaches of the South China Sea as a monsoonal storm swept in, draping the mountains to their right in a veil of rain and turning the sea slate-grey. North of them, the largest ocean in eastern Asia opened out, encircling the ship with enemies: 500 miles north-west was the French navy base at Saigon; 1200 miles north-east was the United States Navy force at Manila; all around them, unseen, were the warships of the Japanese Navy, with its formidable new 27,500-ton battle-cruisers patrolling off China and its lighter cruisers roaming these more southerly waters from Singapore, just 150 miles south-west.

Japan had four destroyers on regular patrol in the Malacca Strait and several larger cruisers operating out of Singapore; as the *Wolf* passed between Borneo and the Anambas Islands, Nerger picked up wireless messages from one of them, the *Yahagi*, to a nearby Dutch warship. A constant procession of oil-tankers, passenger-steamers, mail-boats and Chinese junks passed the raider, for the Anambas Islands marked a transit point where trade routes from Singapore fanned out north. But in this more open stretch of sea, surrounded by other battered freighters and tankers, the raider was at least less conspicuous. And although Nerger did not realise it, his luck had held once more, for the Admiralty had recalled several of its China Squadron ships to Europe in the preceding months, leaving Singapore's naval forces depleted.

Fixing his position by the stars, Nerger took the *Wolf* in a shallow north-west arc above the Anambas Islands on the night of 4 September, circling back so that the ship could lay mines in the trajectory of her escape route. In the muggy night air, the crew were already winching the first of the mines to the aft deck, where they lay on their tracks shrouded in canvas. Just before midnight, the order came to begin dropping them overboard.

In the darkness of their cabin, Stan and Mary Cameron lay awake for several hours listening to the rumble of the mines trundling repeatedly along the rails before they were jettisoned. That dull reverberation was now so familiar to the prisoners in the Hell Hole that it had lost its power to instil dread; many of the men dozed off to its rhythm. Among the few to stay awake were Jean Marton and Tom Rees, still doggedly counting the mines as they went overboard. Rees was gaunt and ailing from the combined effects of bad air, poor diet and diabetes, but he determinedly scribbled his calculations of the mine placements with his purloined pencil and paper.

At 3.51 am, three muffled cheers sounded from the German

crew on the rear deck and the *Wolf* suddenly picked up speed. The last of the mines had finally been swallowed by the waves.

* *

Roy Alexander had been moved back to the Hell Hole from his hospital bed just before the minelaying began, and the shock of descending once again into that fetid tomb was re-doubled by the sight of the prisoners. In the two weeks he had been absent, he had forgotten how rank the air was, and how emaciated and pale the prisoners looked despite the improved diet of fruit and horse-meat stews that had been served since Offak Bay. Alexander wondered how long it could be before a serious outbreak of illness swept through the hold. Even the indomitable Tom Meadows was panting and drenched in sweat as he ate his bowl of meaty gruel one evening, solemnly vowing that if he escaped this nightmare he would never again complain about anything.

Depleted as he was, Meadows remained a defiant presence. Since the capture of the *Matunga*, he had become determined to alert local navy authorities to the *Wolf*'s raiding and was willing to gamble his life to do so. The Germans had made it clear that any prisoner caught trying to communicate with the shore would be shot, but Meadows had persuaded one of the Scandinavian neutrals who frequented the crew's mess to steal several empty pickle jars for him. The New Zealand captain had scrawled several handwritten notes about the *Wolf*'s raiding mission, along with roughly rendered maps and sketches of the ship, and stuffed them into the jars, which he had managed to toss overboard on several occasions while other prisoners distracted the guards. It was the oldest SOS device in the sailor's trick-bag, but Meadows knew that the straits around New Guinea and the East Indies – dotted with islands and frequented by all manner of small fishing boats and native canoes – were the most likely place for such a message to be either washed ashore or found at sea. The same thought had occurred to the *Matunga*'s crew during Leutnant Karl Rose's lax command of the ship north of New Guinea. The ship's purser,

Norman Pyne, had been carrying a case of deflated footballs in his luggage – a present for the Australian troops at Rabaul – and managed to throw overboard several messages in bottles attached to inflated balls.

More than one prisoner would later take credit for the message that was dropped into the Java Sea near Celebes in the first week of September, and the story of it grew in the telling. The most elaborate account came from Norman Pyne, who claimed he had sneaked one last football from the *Matunga* aboard the *Wolf* and conspired with Meadows and the other prisoners to hide it on the poop deck just after the raider left Offak Bay. As they steamed south through the Moluccas in that last week of August, Meadows had sketched a pencil drawing of the *Wolf* detailing her armaments and proportions, and written a six-line message giving a succinct account of the raider's minelaying off South Africa, Colombo, India, New Zealand and Australia, along with the names of all the ships she had captured and a warning that she appeared to be headed for Singapore.

Meadows had been nursing the note ever since, unable to send it overboard because of the lockdown. A day after the minelaying off Singapore, he finally got his chance when Leutnant Auerswald appeared in the Hell Hole and told the prisoners they would be permitted a brief respite on deck. Stuffing the note in a jar and wrapping the jar in a ragged towel, which he tucked under his arm, Meadows climbed the ladder with the other prisoners up to the poop deck. The *Wolf* was making ten knots against a southerly swell and the surrounding sea was empty of other ships; off the port bow, the prisoners could see the forested mountains of Borneo close by. Whether Meadows really did take advantage of Norman Pyne's inflated Australian football is not known, but at dusk, as the prisoners were being herded below, he hung back from the group and slipped towards the rail in the dim light, clutching his rolled-up towel. As he began removing the jar from the towel, however, a German sentry who had seen his furtive movement called out and walked rapidly towards him. Barely breaking stride, Meadows turned and slammed his hefty shoulder into the German, knocking him to the deck and hastily throwing the bottle overboard. The guard scrambled to his feet, shouting, and had just cocked his pistol in Meadows's face when a German officer rushed on the scene and ordered him not to shoot.

In the confusion and fading light, it was impossible for the guard to give a clear account of what had happened, and Meadows brazened it out, claiming he had knocked the German over accidentally. Furious, Auerswald took Meadows to the ship's tiny airless prison cell on the portside upper deck and locked him away before reporting the incident to their captain. Nerger was convinced a bottle had gone overboard, but perhaps mindful that executing the most respected man in the Hell Hole would very likely cause an uprising among his prisoners, he decided to give the bullish New Zealander the benefit of the doubt. For the next five days, Meadows would remain imprisoned, while his bottle bobbed away on the tides of the Java Sea.

The *Wolf*'s profile had changed since she had first passed between Borneo and Sumatra a week ago; the crew had lowered the *Wolf*'s false funnel and dropped the telescopic masts by six feet, so that she again looked squat. The raider's keel was still encrusted with weeds, which the divers had been unable to reach in Offak Bay, so she struggled to make ten knots as Nerger tried to put a maximum distance between himself and Singapore. They were approaching the location of their encounter with the *Psyche* several nights earlier, and the jittery nerves of the crew became evident when the distant wingspan of a stork in the sky was mistaken for an aircraft, prompting a false alarm and lockdown.

Nerger's quickest escape route to the Indian Ocean was south through the Sunda Strait, between Sumatra and Java, but that was a notoriously shallow passage, often patrolled by warships, and they passed it on 7 September. Nerger picked up messages that a British freighter was sinking off Singapore and thought his minefield might have claimed its first victim. Passing Java on the starboard side, the ship's alarm sirens erupted several times when freighters approached, but Nerger was able to avoid them and the mood among the crew and prisoners began to lift. Despite Tom Meadows's infraction, the prisoners were allowed on deck again, and on the morning of 9 September Alec Donaldson saw the conical peak of Mount Agung, the volcano that bestrides Bali, appear in the red dawn haze to the south-east. Donaldson realised that during the night the *Wolf* had passed between the small rocky islands that lead into the Bali Sea.

The crew and prisoners alike were now debating Nerger's next move. Donaldson surmised that Nerger was heading for the strait between the islands of Bali and Lombok, a common route for larger ships, but the *Wolf* again shifted course during the morning and Bali slid away to the right. The towering hulk of Mount Rinjani, Lombok's 12,500-foot active volcano, now loomed ahead. Nerger was approaching the Alas Strait, a passage between Lombok and Sumbawa that spanned a mere six miles at its narrowest point. He slowed the ship to five knots as they drew closer and turned due south, timing his entry for dusk so they would reach the open sea before the moon had risen. From his gunnery post, Fritz Witschetzky saw the village huts of Sumbawa ahead, set among yellow and green fields and coconut plantations; fishing boats drifted past, their sails blindingly white, small fires burning in them.

When the sun set behind Mount Rinjani, the hills of Lombok turned blue and purple against a sulphurous yellow sky, and the *Wolf* moved into the strait. It was fifty miles to the open sea; in the darkness they passed the village of Lombok itself on the right and the tiny island of Belang on the left. That night, the lockdown in the Hell Hole was so strictly enforced that even the blue lights were extinguished and the prisoners lay in total blackness, listening to the dull thunder of the engines reverberating inside the iron walls. An almost imperceptible roll of the hull told them, in the early hours of 10 September, that the *Wolf* had slipped the noose and escaped into the Indian Ocean.

* *

Roy Alexander would later recall that the *Wolf*'s band struck up a particularly vigorous rendition of '*Holdrio, Es Geht Zur Heimat!*' ('Holdrio, We're Going Home!') on the foredeck during the first morning out in the open seas. Hearing the blare of trumpets and tubas, Nerger appeared at the bridge rail above his men and bowed to a rousing cheer. It was as if the ship, divested of its mines, was relieved of a psychological burden. They were sailing west, with the unpatrolled northern coastline of Australia 650 miles below them and the neutral East Indies to their north. Ahead was a 5000-mile-wide expanse of ocean. The sun still burned fiercely, but the breeze coming off these blue waters was a balm after the fecund mugginess of the Java Sea. With her mines jettisoned, the *Wolf*'s mission was effectively completed, and crew and prisoners alike were imbued with a sense of having survived against the odds.

When the band's celebratory blast faded, however, Alexander detected a lingering note of discord. During his two-week sojourn in the ship's hospital, he had befriended many of the crew members who dropped in to visit sick comrades or consult Dr Hauswaldt. They had proved to be 'cheery, good-hearted chaps' in his estimation; the novelty of conversing with a young Australian seaman had lured them to his bedside, and they had brought him food from their mess and taught him some German, including a rich repertoire of expletives. It had become clear to Alexander that some of these men were convinced their captain would seek internment in a neutral port once the last of the *Wolf*'s mines were laid. The ship was now carrying nearly 560 people, and fresh food was in drastically short supply. The coal stolen from the *Matunga* and *Wairuna* was clearly inadequate to get the *Wolf* back to Germany. And once ships started hitting the minefield off Singapore, the entire Allied naval forces of Asia would be sent out to hunt them down.

Feigning sickness in order to escape the Hell Hole, Alexander talked his way back into the care of Dr Hauswaldt in that second week of September, and from his vantage point in a hospital cot amidships he sensed a sullen and restive mood among some of the crew. Several days after leaving behind the Java Sea, these men had begun to realise that internment might not be part of their captain's plans. The nearest neutral port was Dutch Batavia, but the *Wolf* had just laid a minefield on its very doorstep, and every day the East Indies fell further behind them. The ocean ahead was vast, but ringed by enemy naval bases – Cape Town, Aden, Bombay, Singapore, Fremantle. Even if the raider could return to the Atlantic Ocean via the Cape of Good Hope, few neutral havens awaited them there, for the United States was now at war with Germany and Argentina was reported to be on the brink of joining the Allies because of her shipping losses from U-boat attacks.

The prisoners, too, were plagued by a paradoxical sense of hope and uncertainty. The *Wolf*'s westward course was taking it close to the Cocos Islands, where the charred wreck of the *Emden* still lay beached. That tiny cluster of atolls and coral islands, halfway between Colombo and Australia, symbolised a last hope of freedom to the Camerons and the other prisoners, who had periodically been promised release from captivity. It was a privately held territory, owned by the descendants of the Scottish adventurer John Clunies-Ross, and so isolated that it seemed an ideal place for the *Wolf* to disgorge its prisoners and make good its escape.

Up on the bridge, however, Karl Nerger had already fixed on a very different plan. After the minelaying off Singapore, he had asked for a report on the coal supply and learned that he had enough fuel for another six weeks at sea. Nerger calculated that if he could intercept one last coal ship in the Indian Ocean, he could reach the Denmark Strait within three months, before ice floes made a passage through its northerly reaches impossible. His wireless operators were picking up Allied raider warnings for the Indian Ocean, but none of them suggested his mines had yet been detected off Singapore. Curious as that was, it increased his chances of getting a clean run to the Cape. With luck, the *Wolf* could be home in Germany before Christmas, and Nerger could receive his hero's welcome almost exactly a year after they had departed.

Releasing the prisoners on the Cocos Islands, however, was not an option. Those islands, he well knew, had a wireless station and transmission tower in direct contact with London, Singapore and Australia – the very reason the *Emden* had attacked them in 1914. Five days out from the Alas Strait, the *Wolf* passed north of the Cocos and kept on course due west, heading directly towards a trade route that every merchant sailor knew as the '1½ Channel' – the principal shipping route between Colombo and southern Africa. Tom Meadows, just released from his prison cell, knew it better than most – he had been captured there aboard the *Turritella* nearly seven months earlier.

The dawning realisation of what Nerger might be attempting divided the crew. Some were jubilant, others aghast. It would be a 20,000-mile voyage back to Kiel, crossing the Atlantic as winter set in. It would mean another death run through the British naval blockade and the mine-infested North Sea, this time facing the added menace of their own U-boats, which would be unlikely to recognise the *Wolf* as a German ship. The men had been nearly ten months at sea and had already felt the cold touch of beriberi. In the engine room, Albert Wieduwilt had recalibrated his calculations and concluded that they had travelled 43,000 miles since leaving Kiel. The ship's engines had been through eighteen million revolutions. The weather seemed to reflect back their fears, for a violent monsoonal storm welled up from the south-west, darkening the sky and lashing the ship with sheets of rain. It seemed barely possible that they could make it back to Germany intact.

Theodor Plivier was among the dissidents down in the crew's mess who gathered every afternoon to bemoan the grinding routine of the voyage: four hours down in the coal hold, their heads buzzing from carbon-monoxide fumes, then up on deck if the weather cleared to scrub the boards and clean the guns, followed by another shift in the coal bunkers. In the mess, the men played the same repetitive card games, listened to the same handful of records on a wind-up phonograph or carved yet another sailing ship from another block of wood. For the first time, there was talk of outright rebellion.

Until now, Nerger had quelled any ill discipline with well-timed displays of his fearsome wrath, directed at ordinary seamen and officers alike. When someone had stolen a case of canned pineapple from the *Turritella*, he had assembled the entire crew on deck and harangued them from the bridge, warning that the next man caught looting would be strung from the yardarm. The organiser of the theft was court-martialled and locked in the brig for several weeks. Later, when he discovered that a shipment of eggs seized from another ship had ended up in the officers' mess, he berated his officers with equal ferocity, reminding them that depriving the crew of food was a wartime offence punishable by death. Despite his slender build, Nerger's habit of quoting the Military Criminal Code chapter and verse gave these threats of execution added gravitas. Even minor infractions triggered a near-hysterical rage in him. Roy Alexander was on deck one afternoon when a crewman turned up for coaling duty dressed in a top hat, frock coat and walking stick pilfered from a captured ship, just as Nerger looked down over the rail of the bridge.

'The flood of language that flowed down on the unlucky sailor was staggering,' Alexander recalled. 'The captain worked himself into a screaming frenzy which lasted for minutes.'

But a dangerous mood of cynicism had taken root in men such as Plivier. Like the radicalised unionists and disillusioned servicemen of Australia, they had come to see this war as a brutal folly in which millions were being slaughtered while profiteering businessmen grew rich. Even their own successes as a raiding crew seemed tainted: reading English-language newspapers seized from the ships they had captured, they spotted articles about the sinking of the *Mongolia* and the *Cumberland* alongside reports of rising freight rates in the shipping industry. 'We're slaving for the insurance companies and the shipowners,' one crewman complained bitterly. 'It's them that profits; and the dockyards, that have to build more ships. In fact, everybody that trades in iron and steel and sells projectiles and guns.'

Nerger's iron grip on his men was loosening. When an order came from the bridge to winch the *Wolfchen* up on deck and assemble her on the morning of 26 September, the sullen demeanour of the crew was palpable. But Nerger was about to get one of his lucky reprieves, for the *Wolfchen* had not even been lowered into the water when smoke appeared on the horizon to the north-east. All dissent was stifled by the piercing shriek of the alarm signalling lockdown.

8

SCANDAL AND MUTINY

The *Hitachi Maru*, a 6557-ton mail-ship of the Nippon Yusen Kaisha line, left Yokohama on the morning of 29 August destined for London, with a large crew of 117 for the eight-week voyage. En route, the ship stopped in Shanghai, Hong Kong and Singapore, passing the Anambas Islands only a few days after the *Wolf* laid her mines there, and arriving in Ceylon in late September. By the time she sailed out of Colombo harbour on 24 September, negotiating a channel cleared by minesweepers six months earlier, her cabins were almost fully booked with a typically disparate retinue of more than forty Far East travellers.

An executive of the Nippon Yusen company, Kiyoshi Konagei, was making his way to Britain from Tokyo, as was a young lieutenant-commander in the Imperial Japanese Navy, Kenkichi Shiraishi, who had married only three weeks earlier. Dr Frederick Trayes, the recently retired principal of Royal Normal College in Bangkok, was returning to London with his wife, Jessie. Several British expatriates were heading back home to enlist, among them the twenty-nine-year-old Singapore solicitor Courtenay Dickinson and his large and forthright fiancée, Mabel Whittaker. In a neighbouring first-class cabin was Gerald Haxton, a dashing and moustachioed twenty-four-year-old who had just toured the South Pacific islands with his lover, the novelist and playwright William Somerset Maugham, and whose presence aboard the ship would sow the seeds of one of Maugham's most famous plays. Also in first class were an Australian mining engineer, Barker Benson, and his wife, Mary, and a corpulent grey-bearded Englishman, William Cross, who worked for the Chinese Imperial Customs office in Shanghai and bore a passing resemblance to King Edward VII. Among the intermediate-class passengers were five uniformed Portuguese soldiers, a Mauritian man with his Chinese wife and a wizened fifty-two-year-old Chinese woman travelling with her six-year-old granddaughter to Mauritius, where she now lived.

After thirty-six hours of rough sailing through a heavy monsoonal sea, the ship's passengers woke on the morning of 26 September to the first clear skies they had seen since leaving Colombo. Frederick Trayes, like most of the first-class passengers, was enjoying a post-prandial doze in a deckchair when he awoke at 1.45 to see a black freighter in the distance off the port bow. When the ship approached them on a diagonal course, Trayes felt a sudden apprehension and wondered aloud to Courtenay Dickinson whether she might be German. But the *Hitachi Maru* held her speed, and both men relaxed.

Lieutenant-Commander Shiraishi had also noticed the ship and went to his cabin to retrieve his binoculars; training them on the mystery freighter, he realised almost immediately what was about to happen, but said nothing. By now, a ripple of concern had spread through the passengers who had been drawn to the rail. 'Five bells had just gone,' recalled Trayes, 'when the vessel, then about 700 yards away from us, took a sudden turn to port and ran up signals and the German Imperial Navy flag. There was no longer any doubt – the worst had happened.' As the *Wolfchen* roared overhead, the raider's guns appeared and a shell streaked over the *Hitachi Maru*'s bow to land in the water several hundred yards from the frightened passengers.

From the *Wolf*'s bridge, Nerger signalled the Japanese captain to stop and cease wireless transmission. The *Hitachi Maru* was maintaining her course, but with the raider's guns and torpedo tubes trained on her port side and the *Wolfchen* droning threateningly overhead, she appeared helpless. To Nerger's astonishment, however, the ship suddenly began accelerating and shifting course away from the raider, as several of her crewmen rushed to the stern and hauled a tarpaulin away from a gun mounted on the aft deck. Through his binoculars, Nerger saw the Japanese sailors frantically loading a shell into the breach and swinging the barrel in the *Wolf*'s direction – an act of suicidal futility. Nerger ordered his gunners to open fire, and the broadside that erupted – the first time four of the *Wolf*'s guns had fired simultaneously – caused the raider to lurch sideways as if she herself had been hit.

In the darkened Hell Hole, men careened into each other and wooden partitions crashed to the floor as the deafening boom of the guns reverberated inside the iron hull. To Roy Alexander, it was like being inside a steel tank that was being beaten with crowbars, and many of the men believed the *Wolf* had herself been hit and steeled themselves for the first inrush of water. Up on the berth deck, concussion from the discharge blew in the stateroom doors and portholes, and the shiver that ran through the raider's superstructure cracked a washbasin and burst several plumbing pipes. The shells tore through the aft deck of the *Hitachi Maru*, obliterating the gun crew in a hail of shrapnel and splintered timber. When the smoke cleared, Nerger saw the gun still intact and three new crewmen rushing to load it; two more salvos from the *Wolf* blew them over the rails, leaving the gun still standing amid the smoke and twisted metal.

Amidships on the *Hitachi Maru*, passengers scattered in disbelief as smoke rose from the ship's aft. Alfred Clarke, an expatriate British engineer from Ceylon, was aghast that the Japanese captain had attempted to counter-attack such a heavily armed raider – an act of 'sheer madness', in his estimation. Clarke joined the throng rushing to the cabins to retrieve life-vests and valuables. In the first-class section, Frederick Trayes rummaged through his belongings to locate his spare set of spectacles as his wife grabbed her jewellery box; in a neighbouring cabin, Courtenay Dickinson and Mabel Whittaker searched frantically for Mabel's automatic pistol and ammunition, having both agreed that a swift death was preferable to drowning or Hunnish barbarity.

A new round of shells slammed into an upper area of the bridge, showering the companionway below with fragments and sparking a rumour that the Germans were destroying the lifeboats. In fact, Nerger had detected an SOS signal coming from the *Hitachi Maru* and ordered his gunners to destroy the wireless room. In their life-vests, the passengers rushed to seek shelter in an anteroom off the saloon, where they huddled and waited in vain for instructions from the Japanese crew.

There had been no emergency drills on the *Hitachi Maru*, and the crew were clearly in chaos. One of the *Wolf*'s shells had crashed through the wireless room and exploded on the deck, wounding half a dozen seamen who were trying to launch a lifeboat. The captain had finally slowed the ship and raised a flag signalling his surrender, but when Clarke ventured out to the deck he was appalled to see Japanese crewmen clambering into a crowded lifeboat, heedless of the women and little girl still aboard. The *Hitachi Maru* was still moving when the lifeboat suddenly capsized as its suspension ropes unspooled, spilling its screaming occupants into the ocean thirty feet below. Several crewmen who witnessed the debacle took off their shoes and jumped overboard. The passengers hurried to the starboard deck, where they were shepherded into lifeboats by a Japanese steward. The first boat – containing the Trayes, the Bensons, Dickinson, Mabel Whittaker and about a dozen others – was ten feet above the water when it slipped from its ropes and nosedived, leaving its occupants clinging to seats and stanchions before someone cut the ropes and it straightened and crashed onto the ocean swell. In the still afternoon air, the desperate cries of those who had fallen into the sea mingled with the rich obscenities of an Irishman shouting abuse at the Japanese crewmen.

Nerger ordered his launches lowered to rescue those who were floundering in the ocean around the *Hitachi Maru*. Two of the passengers from the capsized lifeboat had drowned, and through a macabre effect of light on the crystal-clear ocean, the sinking corpse of one appeared to be drifting just below the surface, face-up and eyes wide open. Four of the six surviving lifeboats were now joined together in a line by ropes, and the passengers and crew formed a floating procession, waiting in dread for the Germans' next move. Watching the *Wolf* shift course towards them, many expected they would be shelled as they floated helplessly on the water. 'Most of us thought the end had come,' recalled Frederick Trayes, who only two days earlier had read lurid reports in the Ceylon newspapers of German outrages at sea. Sitting in the lead boat, the portly William Cross courteously offered around a packet of his bromide sedatives.

Within an hour, the terrified passengers were hauled aboard the raider, where they were further bewildered by Leutnant Schmehl's customary salute and solicitous enquiry as to their health, whereupon he directed them either to Dr Hauswaldt's surgery or to the well deck aft, where they were served coffee in tin cans. Frederick Trayes was flummoxed when a young German officer procured several wicker chairs for his wife and the other women passengers, then offered them lemonade and ordered his men to construct a canvas sun-shelter. To Trayes, this was 'a new type of Hun. The young Lieutenant was most polite, and courteous and attentive. He apologised profusely for the discomfort which the ladies and ourselves would have to put up with – "But it is war, you know, and your Government is to blame for allowing you to travel when they know a raider is out . . ."' Alfred Clarke was gratified when one of the Germans distributed cigarettes to all the prisoners.

The carnage aboard the *Hitachi Maru* – the first gunfight in the *Wolf*'s ten-month voyage – cast a pall over the prisoners and their captors. Eleven Japanese crewmen and an Indian passenger had been killed during the shelling, and several of the wounded Japanese were suffering ghastly shrapnel injuries. Alfred Clarke was surprised when Schmehl and the other officers expressed regret over the deaths and offered elaborate explanations of what had happened. Aboard the Japanese ship, her shattered captain, Seizu Tominaga, was refusing to leave the bridge and insisted that if the Germans were going to sink his vessel he would exercise his right to drown with her. Tominaga was eventually removed by force and brought to Nerger, who expressed perplexity at what had just transpired. Tominaga explained that he had been following the procedure for evading U-boat attack, which had been part of his official orders – an account Nerger later confirmed when he examined the *Hitachi Maru*'s logbook and papers. It was, evidently, a variation on Churchill's instructions to armed merchantmen in the North Sea. As a mark of respect, Nerger offered Tominaga a cabin amidships, but the Japanese captain was so deeply shamed by the deaths of his crewmen that he chose to pay penance by joining his men in the stifling hold below.

With customary formality, Nerger conducted funeral ceremonies for all of the dead, appearing with his officers in full uniform as the remains were interred in the sea. Aboard the *Hitachi Maru*, Leutnant Karl Rose and his prize crew had taken control and checked the manifest, signalling back news that the ship was loaded with food and coal, along with unspecified cargo. But Nerger now faced the task of accommodating nearly 150 new prisoners, many of whom clearly could not be held below.

The Japanese crew included a forty-eight-year-old stewardess, Kameno Kuziraoka; the thirty-six passengers included five women and a child. It was a massive addition to the *Wolf*'s already crowded holds, and among the new arrivals were some picaresque characters. William Cross, who had lost his trousers while ascending the rope ladder to the *Wolf*'s deck, was an alcoholic who immediately demanded whisky to stave off his delirium tremens. Mabel Whittaker proved almost equally fond of a stiff drink: after being relieved of her pistol, she refused the offered lemonade and requested a whisky and soda. Karl Nerger later claimed that when he first looked closely at the *Hitachi Maru* through binoculars, he was astounded to see several effete young British men standing on the deck wearing kimonos that split open at the thigh to reveal 'pink silk petticoats bordered with lace, silk stockings and patent leather boots with most elegant rosettes' – a sight so incongruous that he asked one of his crewmen whether he was seeing things.

The story sounds like one of Nerger's few lapses into anti-British propaganda, but there is no doubt that among the *Hitachi Maru*'s passengers was one of the most extravagantly unashamed homosexuals of his era. Gerald Haxton was born in San Francisco and raised in Britain – a country he had been forced to leave in 1915 after police burst into his London hotel room and caught him in flagrante with another man. A prodigious drinker and gambler, Haxton was a young man having an eventful war: in 1914, while working as an orderly in a military hospital near the Western Front, he had met and seduced an interpreter working at the hospital, William Somerset Maugham, who was eighteen years older than him. After returning to Britain and running foul of the vice police, Haxton had been tried and acquitted of gross indecency, then reunited with Maugham in San Francisco before the two of them embarked on a long and licentious cruise through the South Pacific islands, where the novelist researched his famous book *The Moon and Sixpence*. When Maugham returned to London – to marry the divorcee Syrie Wellcome and become a spy in Russia for the British Secret Intelligence Service – Haxton had gone back to the United States, where he avoided the military draft by pleading a physical disability. He was on his way to further adventures in South Africa as an employee of the International Directory Company of Chicago when hijacked by the *Wolf*.

Some later suspected that Haxton was a spy, for his Home Office file in Britain was destroyed and he was registered as an undesirable alien. It was also rumoured that his arrest and black-banning had been orchestrated by Maugham's family, who were appalled by the writer's infatuation with such an incorrigible character. Haxton was 'full of charm and full of liquor, in almost equal parts', recalled one of the writer's close friends; others used adjectives like reckless, feckless and wayward. Whether he was one of the fetchingly attired young *faux femmes* Nerger claims to have seen through his binoculars is impossible to determine, but Roy Alexander certainly remembered him vividly, for the young Australian seaman had passed through Tahiti only seven months earlier when Somerset Maugham and his 'secretary' were at the tail end of their travels. On that occasion, Haxton had entertained the patrons of the Hotel Tiare by consuming half a pint of crème de menthe and staging a naked hula dance in the bar. When Alexander saw Haxton being led down into the prison hold, 'he looked as if he could have done with that Tahiti cocktail'.

* *

Although the *Hitachi Maru*'s SOS signal had been scrambled by the *Wolf*'s transmitters, Nerger needed a safe haven to plot out his next move, and the nearest land was the southern rim of the Maldives, a half-day's sailing away. It was British territory, but it was also extremely isolated and he knew the *Emden* had sheltered there three years earlier. Nerger ordered the Japanese crew and the unmarried male prisoners sent down to the former mine-hold between-decks, immediately forward of the Hell Hole, where hammocks and makeshift beds made from hessian bags were rigged up for them. The married couples and female prisoners slept the night on deck chairs under the stars and the gaze of armed guards. They were approaching the southern rim of the Maldives when one of the injured Japanese crewmen died in the *Wolf*'s hospital, prompting another burial at sea. An hour later, the two ships entered Suvadiva Atoll from the east, passing between low-lying islands before dropping anchor to the south of the main island, Devadu.

The Maldives are transfixingly beautiful, and the two ships

had dropped anchor in one of their most remote southerly archipelagos, in a lagoon whose pale green waters shimmered against a sweep of deep blue sky. Encircling the ships was an elongated loop of twenty islands that formed a distant perimeter of white-sand beaches and palms, the rich green undergrowth of the nearest island yielding glimpses of red and yellow from the decorated huts of local villagers. Roy Alexander likened the atoll to a string of jade beads on a white cord; Fritz Witschetzky later visited one of the villages and was entranced as he walked down a natural promenade formed by parallel rows of palm trees, their silver-grey trunks and dark green canopy extending half a kilometre to form 'the most beautiful track or road I have ever seen'.

From a distance, the *Hitachi Maru* may have resembled a cruise ship anchored in some equatorial paradise, but the curious Muslim villagers who paddled up in canoes later that day – dressed almost formally in a colourful array of sarongs, kaftans and kufi caps – confronted an altogether more incongruous sight. As German coolies swabbed the Japanese ship's poop deck, blood and chunks of human flesh flowed over the ship's sides, drawing sharks into the lagoon's shallow waters. The promenade deck was littered with capsized deckchairs, splayed books and scattered chess sets, while shoes lying here and there marked the spots where panicked crewmen had thrown themselves overboard. Repair crews wielding oxyacetylene torches and buckets of cement filled gaping shell-holes in the ship's hull and funnel. Behind the *Hitachi Maru* lurked the hulking black shape of the *Wolf*, whose brass band was practising woozy renditions of its favourite patriotic German songs. When another Japanese crewman died in the hospital, a funeral ceremony was held and his body interred at the entrance to the lagoon. The islanders quickly retreated, and it would be another day before they returned.

The German prize crew aboard the *Hitachi Maru*, led by Leutnant Karl Rose, had investigated the ship's storage holds and discovered a rich cargo: hundreds of bales of fine Japanese silk and a large shipment of furs, copper ingots, rubber and tinned food destined for Britain. By Nerger's estimation, the cargo was worth at least £1 million, and the propaganda coup of delivering such a prize to his superiors in Kiel was irresistible. If the *Hitachi Maru* could be made seaworthy, he would also have an auxiliary vessel to relieve the dire overcrowding aboard the *Wolf*, because her cabins could accommodate all the upper-deck prisoners from the raider. At the end of the first day in the Maldives, Nerger ordered the two ships lashed together so that coal and cargo transferring could begin, and a gangplank was laid between them to permit the first-class passengers and families to return to the ship. Fifteen people made the crossing, arriving aboard the blood-spattered ship to find their cabins unchanged and their belongings intact.

While the *Wolfchen* flew regular reconnaissance patrols over the surrounding ocean and the raider's crew toiled in the blistering heat – repairing the *Hitachi Maru*'s superstructure, hauling coal and cargo into the *Wolf*'s bunkers – Nerger took stock. The *Hitachi Maru* was due in Delagoa Bay, east Africa, in a little over a week, and he knew that local Allied navy patrols were already on alert for the *Wolf*, for his wireless operators had picked up raider warnings from both Mauritius and Bombay as they had steamed through the Timor Sea. The Japanese Navy would be alerted immediately, because the *Hitachi Maru*'s cargo included a parcel of mail for the cruiser *Tsushima*, docked in Cape Town. Nerger's engineers were confident that the *Hitachi Maru* could be made seaworthy, but by the time the *Wolf*'s fuel supply was replenished, the Japanese ship would be left with little more than 700 tons of coal – enough to get no further than Mauritius. The only solution was to take the *Wolf* out on another raiding mission.

On the last day of September, Nerger called in Leutnant Rose and formally appointed him commander of the *Hitachi Maru*, handing him a packet of official orders that included a proposed route back to Germany, several predetermined meeting points with the *Wolf* and identification signals. Rose's crew would consist of twenty-three Germans, twenty neutral prisoners on coolies' pay rates and twenty-eight Japanese; he would be equipped with a wireless transmitter and enough explosives to scuttle the ship, but no guns.

On 1 October, most of the *Wolf*'s top-deck prisoners – the Cameron family, the Floods, Cecil Strangman, Agnes Mackenzie and the three Australian plantation-owners from the *Matunga* – were told to pack their belongings and make their way across the gangplank to the *Hitachi Maru* along with the newly formed crew. They were joined by old Jack Rugg, the God-fearing skipper of the *Dee*, four of his Mauritian boys, an elderly Scottish seaman from the *Wordsworth* and the *Matunga*'s two fourteen-year-old cabin boys, Eric Minns and Keith Harris, for Nerger had decided to move the Hell Hole's oldest and youngest prisoners onto the prize ship.

Escaping the raider was a profound relief for all of them, not least Mary Cameron, who was finally beginning to recuperate from her illness. Leutnant Ernst Szielasko was surprised when Mary approached him as she was leaving, offering him a bundle of folded cloth. When he opened it, he saw it was an elaborately embroidered tablecloth that Mary had hand-stitched during her long weeks of convalescence in her cabin, and that she now insisted he take as a gift. The flustered German explained that he was under orders not to accept gifts from the prisoners, but Mary, with a flash of her old wit, told him she would have to throw it overboard if he did not take it.

Szielasko felt a pang as he watched Juanita Cameron depart the *Wolf*, for her 'precocious, merry chit-chat' had lightened the load of their unending voyage. Alone among the prisoners, the little girl was reluctant to leave the raider, for she had thoroughly inveigled her way into the affections of the crew. She not only took her meals in the officers' mess, she had developed a passable grasp of German and ended her evening prayer with a heartfelt '*Lieber Gott, mach mich fromm, dass ich in den Himmel komm*' ('Dear Lord, make me gentle and pious, so I will go to heaven'). To ease her departure, the German pilot Paul Fabeck helped Juanita pack her things and took her to the gangplank, where she sorrowfully waved to him and said she hoped she would be back soon. Just after dawn on 3 October, the *Wolf* pulled anchor and headed out into the Indian Ocean, leaving her prize moored alone off Suvadiva Atoll.

In these idyllic surrounds, life aboard the *Hitachi Maru* briefly acquired the somnolent atmosphere of some strangely hallucinatory holiday cruise. Over the preceding days, winches and derricks had worked ceaselessly and noisily through the night; now, quiet descended on the atoll. Stan and Mary Cameron were astonished to find themselves accommodated in a tastefully appointed bridal suite, and prisoners who had endured months in the Hell Hole were given passenger cabins or crews' quarters. Meals were served in a fully appointed wood-panelled dining room, staffed by white-uniformed Japanese stewards and furnished with carved oak chairs and a forty-foot-long dining table. The saloon was open and a bartender dispensed beer, spirits and champagne. After months of isolation, the Camerons could mix freely with other prisoners, and the after-dinner conversations often turned on renewed talk of freedom, for Leutnant Rose had told some of the *Hitachi Maru* prisoners that they might be dropped on a local island. Only Alfred Clarke remained sceptical: he was crestfallen to hear from Stan and Mary that the Germans had offered such promises before, and even more dejected to learn that Jack Rugg had been held prisoner since March.

With the black raider out of sight, it quickly became clear that life on the *Hitachi Maru* would be governed by an entirely different regimen to the rigid discipline imposed aboard the *Wolf*. During his brief tenure in charge of the *Matunga* and its substantial liquor supply, Karl Rose had shown a strong liking for the fringe benefits of wartime plundering. Newly promoted and placed in command of a well-stocked ocean liner and a contingent of female prisoners, Rose's sense of entitlement became even more pronounced. Courtenay Dickinson, the lawyer from Singapore, was surprised to see that Rose was drunk on his first night in command of the prize ship. Having commandeered the *Hitachi Maru*'s extensive stocks of booze and food, Rose initiated a nightly champagne supper for himself in Captain Tominaga's old quarters. Soon, he formed a private bridge club and invited select prisoners to take part.

Still only thirty-three, Rose treated his prisoners with a paradoxical mixture of arrogance and deference. Like many German naval officers, he projected an air of supreme self-regard that never failed to aggravate. Courtenay Dickinson took an instant dislike to him, and Stan Cameron grew weary of the German's constant anti-American gibes, in which he mocked the capacities of American troops and referred to their flag as the 'Star Spangled Banana'. In Cameron's estimation, Karl Rose was 'a snob and man who did not know the meaning of the word gentleman'.

Yet Rose, who had lived in London and saw himself as a well-travelled cosmopolitan, took pains to establish himself as a man of civility and honour, as if to confute the openly racist contempt his British prisoners felt towards all things German. Frederick Trayes's wife, upon seeing Juanita Cameron for the first time, had remarked airily, 'I wonder that the Germans didn't cut off the little girl's ears and nose. It is normally their custom, isn't it?' However, when Rose heard that Mrs Trayes had lost a box of jewellery in the *Hitachi Maru*'s lifeboat, he made a great show of locating the missing item and returning it to her with a chivalrous flourish. 'The Germans are not thieves,' he said proudly.

During the first dinner aboard the *Hitachi Maru*, Rose joined his prisoners at the head of the table, proposing a toast to the Kaiser and expounding with great enthusiasm on the *Wolf*'s exploits and his own role in them. Alfred Clarke was struck by the young *leutnant*'s egocentric anxiety to please. Rose arranged for the smoking room and bar to be opened at designated hours in the morning, afternoon and evening, and gave his prisoners freedom to roam the promenade deck.

But as the ship's food and liquor supplies dwindled, he cut the bar supply back to beer (two shillings a bottle) and gin, and was seen increasingly rarely at the communal dinner table. Arriving in the dining room for a meal one evening, the Camerons sat with some anticipation at a table formally laid out with cutlery and a white cloth. A Japanese steward duly appeared in crisp white uniform and placed before each of them a plate containing two crackers topped with a sardine. Cameron was furious, aware that Rose was at the time enjoying privately cooked meals in his cabin. When confronted, however, the German commander smiled superciliously. 'What do you expect?' he responded. 'You're not first-class passengers, you know.'

Rose had posted up a set of rules that forbade the prisoners from talking to the crew, but in practice it was impossible to prevent such socialising as their sojourn in the tropics entered its second week. The German officers ate their meals with the prisoners, and in the boozy post-dinner gatherings around the saloon piano the war became a subject of mockery. Even Frederick Trayes, a staunch British colonialist, laughed when Rose threatened to have him shot at dawn if he didn't join the communal singing one night. Everyone on board shared the same enforced intimacy, endured the same tedium and harboured the same fear of death from Allied-warship attack – a fear made tangible by their near-disastrous encounter with the *Psyche* several weeks earlier. Even the pervasive tropical heat worked to loosen social constraints. The sight of muscular young sailors stripped nearly naked as they worked was a titillating novelty to women raised in the rigid sexual mores of Edwardian Britain, and one English lady remarked to Trayes on the 'rather unusual exhibition of the European male torso' on constant display. The German sailors were equally distracted by the presence of the women, and it was inevitable that a certain amount of fraternising went on in the highly charged confines of the ship.

In this atmosphere, the conduct of Rose Flood, wife of the Australian medical officer Major John Flood, caused outrage among her fellow passengers. Mrs Flood had excited the men on the *Wolf* from the moment they first saw her standing at the rails of the *Matunga* in early August. In the intervening weeks, rumours had coursed through the ship of some untoward contact between her and the German officers, for even Albert Wieduwilt down in the engine room took time to record a withering comment about her virtue in his journal. The ship had been joined, he noted, by 'a madame, the wife of a doctor who was taken prisoner of war with the *Matunga* (if it is a wife that is). The gentlemen officers "called on her".'

Among the German officers, none paid Mrs Flood more attention than Karl Rose. For as objectionable as he could be with men, the *leutnant* was the epitome of charm when dealing with the opposite sex. Roy Alexander had noticed his unerring talent for 'soothing the fears' of his women captives. And despite his wife and young son back in Hamburg, nine months at sea had made him – in Stan Cameron's words – 'very partial' to Rose Flood's charms. Having already ingratiated himself with her by appointing Agnes Mackenzie to be her personal maid, the *leutnant* did everything he could to make her life aboard the *Hitachi Maru* pleasant. He established a special morning tea for ladies, presented them with gifts, such as boxes of biscuits, and organised a laundry detail whereby Jack Rugg's crew of Mauritian boys was enlisted to help wash and hang clothing. On his strolls around the deck, Karl Rose often stopped to speak to the women gathered on the games deck, joining in their games of quoits or discussing his days in London.

As the indolent days at anchor in the Maldives stretched into their second week while the *Wolf* continued to search for coal, there was little else for the passengers to do but entertain themselves with endless deck games, singalongs around the piano or evening rounds of bridge and poker. The ship became a hermetic refuge from the dangers of the open sea, and the freewheeling socialising reached a giddy peak one evening when the Japanese stewards unlocked a closet to reveal all the theatrical props necessary for an amateur musical: masks, wigs, wooden swords, false beards and piles of fancy-dress costumes. The ensuing revelry, in which the passengers staged a variety show that included clog-dancing, sword-dancing and multiple renditions of an improvised piano rag named after the ship, attracted sailors from the German crew, who began dancing with their prisoners. Within minutes, most of the crew had joined with the Japanese stewards and the thirty-odd prisoners in their rowdy celebrating, which became so noisy that an officer appeared to order his men back to their stations and put an end to the vaudevillian antics.

Something transpired during the *Hitachi Maru*'s interlude in the tropics that grievously shocked the women but that none of the passengers was indiscreet enough to detail. On 6 October, the *Wolfchen* suddenly appeared in the sky and dropped written orders from Nerger, and the Japanese ship hastily raised anchor and set off on a south-west course towards the distant shores of Africa. Even out on the open sea, the days were a succession of deck games, naps and evening drinking sessions. But when the *Hitachi Maru* pulled alongside the *Wolf* two weeks later, near a small island 600 miles west of Mauritius, relations among the women passengers had deteriorated drastically. As the two ships were lashed together, Agnes Mackenzie rushed to the rails of the *Hitachi Maru* to 'shriek scandal' across the gap to one of her former shipmates from the *Matunga* standing on the poop deck of the *Wolf*. Roy Alexander was standing nearby, watching the scene in disbelief: 'It had been my lot to hear much scandal retailed in my time, but this was unique: to hear a woman stand at the rail of a ship under way and (in the manner of Mrs 'Arris over the back fence) scream aspersions on a sister prisoner, her spellbound listener being on another ship some thirty yards away. Still in the style of Mrs 'Arris, the lady unconsciously made it funnier by dropping her voice to a confidential yell at the more spicy revelations.'

Mary Cameron, a woman not easily shocked after spending her whole life around seamen, later gave her own scalding assessment of Rose Flood. 'This woman,' she wrote, 'was a beast of the lowest' – a phrase redolent of sexual impropriety. A woman's honour was easily stained by rumour and innuendo in those times, and if Rose Flood did commit the unforgivable sin of consorting with the enemy, no official documents record the fact. But with the voyage now entering a dangerous phase in which death was an increasingly imminent possibility, contact between the men and women thrown together in the close confines of the ship inevitably became charged. For all her indignation, even Agnes Mackenzie would soon find solace in the company of the German crewmen.

* *

The mood aboard the *Wolf* had turned grim in the three weeks since the raider had left the Maldives. Nerger's attempts to hijack more coal had come to nothing, despite a fruitless chase with the Danish steamship *Peru* on the night of 6 October and an encounter soon afterwards with a large and heavily armed British passenger-freighter steaming towards Colombo. Although the *Peru* was a neutral vessel, Nerger had pursued her just south of the Maldives in the hope that she was carrying British freight to Australia, but the *Wolf* was slowed by her encrusted hull and buoyant draught, and the Danish ship escaped. In the middle of the chase, the British ship had appeared out of the darkness, and when Nerger shifted course to follow, his quarry had made a sudden feint at the *Wolf*. Movement on her deck suggested that the crew were readying her guns for a confrontation, and Nerger had dropped his bulwarks and sounded a general alarm, only to watch the steamer pick up speed and slip away to the north-east.

Having given away his position, Nerger had been forced to send the *Wolfchen* back to the Maldives to warn the *Hitachi Maru* to head south. Since then, he had roamed the Indian Ocean without sighting another ship, and his wireless operators brought him only bad news: from Karachi, Mauritius and Singapore came continued warnings that a raider from the Pacific was suspected to be in the Indian Ocean; the evening news from Colombo broadcast the revelation that his old colleague Count

Kapitän Karl Nerger, 'the loneliest man on board'.
(© Australian War Memorial: H13504)

Karl Nerger in tropical whites aboard the *Wolf*.
(© Australian War Memorial: P05338.005)

SMS *Wolf* in Kiel harbour.
(Courtesy of Dr Christian Hauswaldt)

The *Wolf* was armed with sixteen torpedoes for commerce-raiding.
(© Australian War Memorial: P05338.003)

Wolf gun crew.
(© Australian War Memorial: P05338.011)

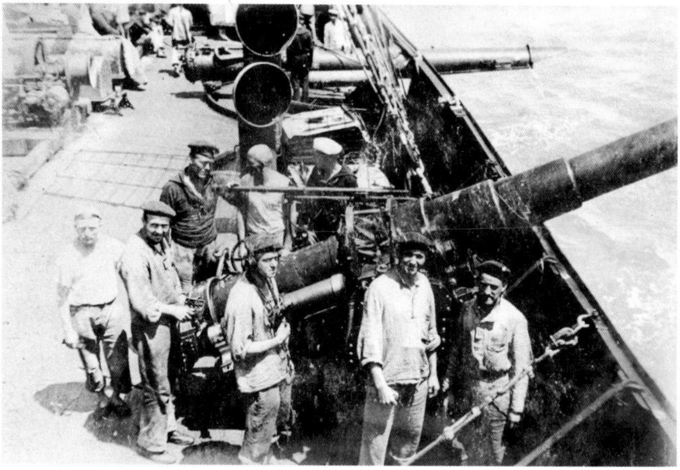

A mine is launched from the hatch door under the poop deck.
(© Australian War Memorial: P05338.010)

Karl Nerger and his officers dining aboard the *Wolf*. Leutnant Fritz Witschetzky is seated at far left. Dr Hermann Hauswaldt is sitting under the porthole on the right.
(© Australian War Memorial: P05338.091)

'The Kaiser's coolies': coal-stokers aboard the *Wolf*, who at one point mutinied.
(© Australian War Memorial: P05338.081)

Theodor Plivier, who later became a celebrated novelist and outspoken communist.
(© Ullstein Bild agency)

Stan Cameron and his nineteen-year-old wife, Mary, shipwrecked in Alaska in 1909.
(Courtesy of Walt Coburn)

The Camerons and their ship, the *Beluga*, are captured by the *Wolf* in July 1917.
(© Australian War Memorial: P05338.058)

Juanita Cameron on board the *Wolf*, with dachshund.
(Courtesy of Dr Christian Hauswaldt)

Juanita Cameron with Leutnant Vissering and Leutnant Adolf Wulff.
(Courtesy of Walt Coburn)

Captain Alec Donaldson (turning to face camera) and Captain Tom Meadows, leader of the Hell Hole.
(© Australian War Memorial: P05338.151)

The *Dee* sinks while her ageing captain, Jack Rugg, looks on and weeps.
(Courtesy of Dr Christian Hauswaldt)

The Australian steamship *Cumberland*, whose wrecking off Australia's southern coast was falsely attributed to sabotage by 'Hun agents'.
(© Australian War Memorial: A00711)

SENSATIONAL SHIPPING DISASTER

WRECK OFF VICTORIAN COAST

INTERNAL EXPLOSIONS

NO LIVES LOST.

THE VESSEL BEACHED.

The Navy Office announces that the ... rived on Sunday morning, and will ...

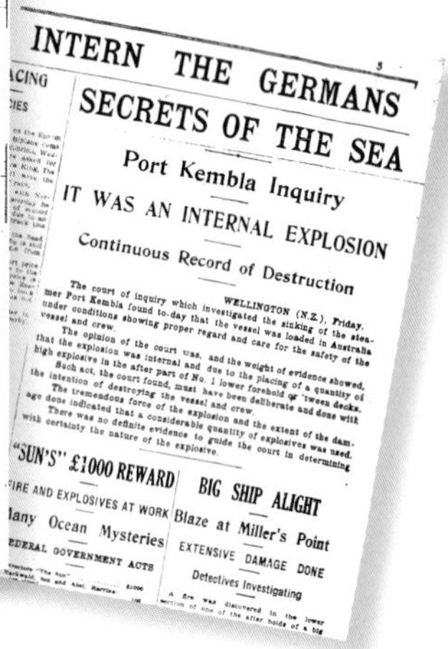

INTERN THE GERMANS

SECRETS OF THE SEA

Port Kembla Inquiry

IT WAS AN INTERNAL EXPLOSION

Continuous Record of Destruction

WELLINGTON (N.Z.), Friday.

The court of inquiry which investigated the sinking of the steamer Port Kembla found to-day that the vessel was loaded in Australia under conditions showing proper regard and care for the safety of the vessel and crew.

The opinion of the court was, and the weight of evidence showed, that the explosion was internal and due to the placing of a quantity of high explosive in the after part of No. 1 lower forehold or 'tween decks.

Such act, the court found, must have been deliberate and done with the intention of destroying the vessel and crew.

The tremendous force of the explosion and the extent of the damage done indicated that a considerable quantity of explosives was used.

There was no definite evidence to guide the court in determining with certainty the nature of the explosive.

"SUN'S" £1000 REWARD

FIRE AND EXPLOSIVES AT WORK

Many Ocean Mysteries

FEDERAL GOVERNMENT ACTS

BIG SHIP ALIGHT

Blaze at Miller's Point

EXTENSIVE DAMAGE DONE

Detectives Investigating

A fire was discovered in the lower section of one of the after holds of a big

Scare headlines from the *Sun* and the *Age* newspapers in Australia in 1917. The Australian Government claimed ships that had been captured and mined by the *Wolf* had been destroyed by bombs planted by German immigrants and traitors.

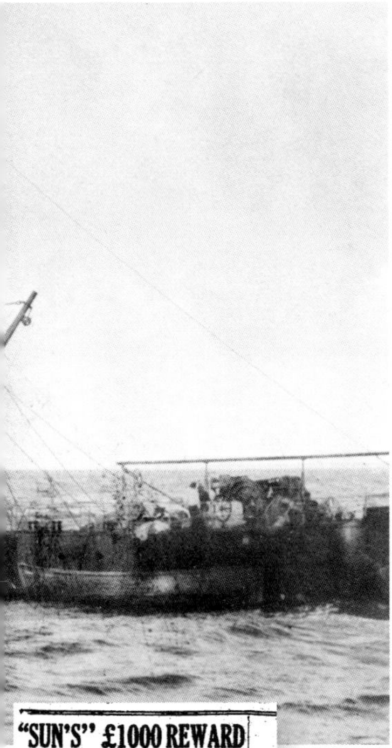

"SUN'S" £1000 REWARD

GERMAN AGENTS EVERYWHERE

SHIP SINKING SCHEMES

How Factory Fires Are Started

Directors "The Sun"	£1000
Sydney Harbor Small Tug and Lighter Owners' Association	100
Marsh Bros., Ltd., tanners, Granville	100
R. Eastway (Eastway Bros.)	26/5/
A. N. White, 316 George-street	25
A. M. Loewenthal, Perpetual Trustee Building	25
R. Dundas Smith, 49 Clarence-st.	10/10/
H. L. Tweedie, Katoomba	10/10/
Commonwealth Government	5000

Every day produces fresh evidence of the urgent necessity of dealing with the enemy

'Vain as a peacock, cruel as a butcher bird': Australia's wartime prime minister, William Morris Hughes, *c.*1925

(© National Library of Australia: VN3307731)

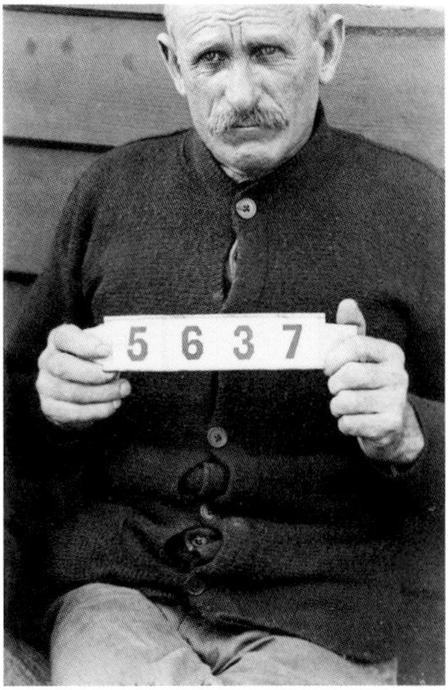

German fisherman Carl Newman, wrongly blamed for the *Cumberland* disaster and imprisoned by the Hughes government.

(© National Archives of Australia: D3597/4, item 5627)

The *Wolfchen* is winched on to the water for take-off.
(Courtesy of Dr Christian Hauswaldt)

The *Wolfchen*'s pilot, Paul Fabeck, and flight officer, Matthaus Stein, climb up the plane's tail to escape sharks after a crash-landing in the Pacific.
(© Australian War Memorial: P05338.113)

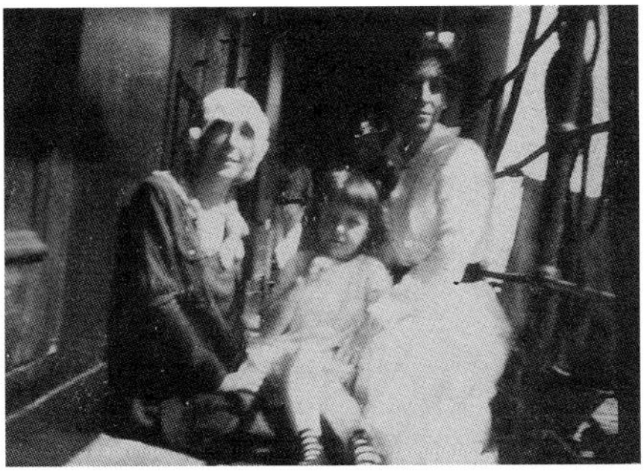

Mary Cameron, her daughter Juanita and Agnes Mackenzie aboard the *Hitachi Maru*.
(Courtesy of Walt Coburn)

Roy Alexander (right, standing), chronicler of life in the Hell Hole, was best man at the 1919 wedding of Norman Pyne (seated), his fellow prisoner.
(Courtesy of Michael Pyne)

The Singapore lawyer Courtenay Dickinson and his gun-toting, whisky-loving fiancée, Mabel Whittaker.
(Courtesy of Walt Coburn)

Eric Minns shortly before he departed Sydney on his first voyage to sea. He became the youngest Australian prisoner of the First World War.
(Courtesy of Gregg Minns)

Rose Flood as a young woman, before she caused a scandal aboard the *Wolf*.
(Courtesy of Richard Bell)

Alexander Ross Ainsworth, who was chief engineer of the *Matunga* when she was captured, in his early twenties before the war.

The *Wolf*'s 'top-deck' prisoners. Standing, L to R: Colonel Cecil Lucius Strangman – 'the quintessence of egotistical selfishness'; Rose Flood – 'a beast of the lowest'; Captain P. H. Macintosh and Major John Flood of the Australian expeditionary forces, Rabaul; Agnes Mackenzie, over whom the German crewmen swooned and fought; Captain F. Laycock and Captain A. W. Cains of the Australian expeditionary forces. Seated, L to R: Mary Cameron, gaunt and still recovering from her 'brain fever'; Australian businessman George Green.
(Courtesy of Walt Coburn)

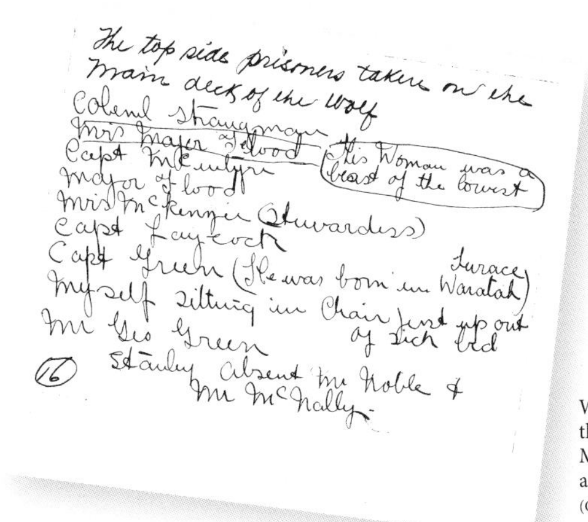
The top side prisoners taken on the
main deck of the Wolf
Colonel Strangman
Mrs Major Flood (This Woman was a beast of the lowest)
Capt McIntyre
Major Flood
Mrs McKenzie (Stewardess)
Capt Laycock
Capt Green (He was born in Waratah Furnace)
Myself sitting in Chair just up out of sick bed
Mr Geo Green
(16) Standing absent Mr Noble & Mr McNally

Written on the back of the above photograph is Mary Cameron's scathing assessment of Rose Flood.
(Courtesy of Walt Coburn)

Passengers from the *Hitachi Maru* in lifeboats after the ship was fired on by the *Wolf*.
(© Australian War Memorial: P05338.068)

Passengers on the *Hitachi Maru*. The notorious Gerald Haxton, secret lover of novelist W. Somerset Maugham, is believed to be the young man seated at the front.
(© Australian War Memorial: P05338.158)

Prisoners from the *Hitachi Maru*. Back row, L to R: Mary Benson, Barker Benson, Jess Trayes, Professor Frederick Trayes. Front row: Captain Seizu Tominaga (centre), others unknown.
(© Australian War Memorial: P05338.156)

The Japanese mail steamer *Hitachi Maru* is sunk by bombs in the Indian Ocean.
(Courtesy of Dr Christian Hauswaldt)

The *Wolf*'s crew in costume for a ceremony as their ship crosses the equator.
(© Australian War Memorial: P05338.041)

The Atlantic storm that terrified even the raider's crew on the last leg of her voyage.
(© Australian War Memorial: P05338.028)

Danish lifesavers rescue prisoners from the *Igotz Mendi.*
(Courtesy of Walt Coburn)

Stan Cameron, gaunt and grey-haired after his ordeal as a prisoner. He had recently turned thirty-three.
(Courtesy of Walt Coburn)

German crew members under arrest in Skagen, Denmark.
(Courtesy of the Skagen Museum)

The raider *Wolf* being welcomed home to Kiel on 24 February 1918.
(Courtesy of the Nerger family)

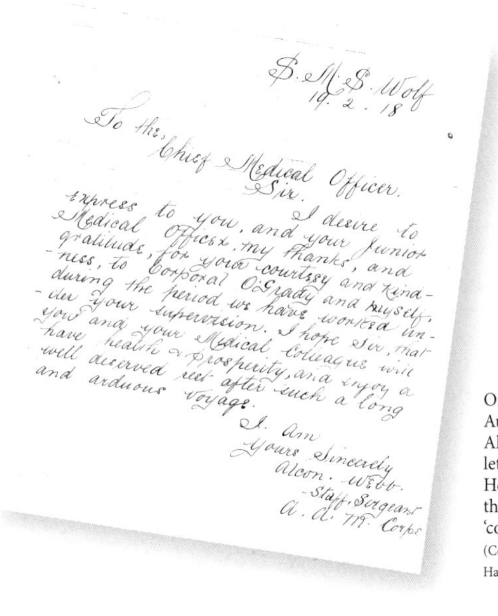

S.M.S. Wolf
19. 2. 18

To the,
Chief Medical Officer.
Sir.

I desire to express to you, and your Junior Medical Officer, my thanks, and gratitude, for your courtesy and kindness, to Corporal O'Grady and myself, during the period we have worked under your supervision. I hope Sir, that you and your Medical Colleague will have health & prosperity, and enjoy a well deserved rest after such a long and arduous voyage.

I am
Yours Sincerely
Alcon. Webb.
Staff, Sergeant
A. A. M. Corps

One of the *Wolf*'s prisoners, Australian Army sergeant Alcon Webb, wrote a letter to the *Wolf*'s doctor, Hermann Hauswaldt, thanking him for his 'courtesy and kindness'.
(Courtesy of Dr Christian Hauswaldt)

Felix von Luckner had been shipwrecked aboard the *Seeadler* off Tahiti; then a brief coded transmission from the Japanese cruiser *Tsushima* suggested that the *Hitachi Maru* was officially listed as missing and the Allied navies were already on the hunt.

On the morning of 12 October, Nerger presided over another funeral aboard the raider, this time for the *Beluga*'s second mate, Axel Johnson. The San Francisco seaman had been the last crew member to join Stan Cameron's ship, cajoled aboard with an offer of generous pay; he had died suddenly in the Hell Hole during the night, from a heart attack induced by the continual stress and toll of imprisonment. Another San Franciscan, Captain Anton Olsen of the *Encore*, gruffly recited the funeral rites under the shadow of the *Wolf*'s starboard guns. The German crew stood in full tropical whites with heads bowed as Johnson's body, enshrouded in the American flag and weighted down at the feet, was dispatched into the ocean.

The gloom brought on by Johnson's death exacerbated an already tense situation in the *Wolf*'s prison hold. In the weeks at sea after the *Hitachi Maru*'s capture, Nerger had allowed his prisoners a daily ration of one bottle of beer and one nip of whisky – a luxury that ameliorated their misery and helped reduce the *Wolf*'s large liquor supply. The alcohol had been distributed using a ticketing system, but one of the prisoners somehow rorted his allowance and the alcohol ration was withdrawn. Already disgruntled, the prisoners promptly succumbed to an outbreak of dhobi itch, an aggravating inflammation of the armpits and groin that was immediately blamed on the new clothing they had acquired from the crew of the *Hitachi Maru*.

The mood was little better among the crew, for the raider had less than three weeks' coal supply left, and the officers were again beginning to doubt their captain. With his lofty ambition of taking the *Hitachi Maru* back to Germany now slipping away, Nerger retired to his cabin in the third week of October to brood over his options, and in his absence an atmosphere of dissension and impatience pervaded the ship. Officers began arguing among themselves about the best way out of their imbroglio; succumbing to the stress and boredom, Witschetzky sacked his orderly after a blazing row over some petty lapse and got into a dispute with the unflappable Dr Hauswaldt. With strange synchronicity, the wireless brought disturbing news of mutinies in the German Navy back home. A news dispatch picked up from the Seychelles transmitter reported that the German Navy minister, Vice-Admiral Eduard von Capelle, had stood down after crews refused to serve aboard ships docked in Wilhelmshaven.

Over several days, the *Wolf*'s crew clustered around the noticeboard reading news bulletins about these mutinies, for the story was an international sensation: a mass uprising was said to have spread from the warships *Prinz Regent Luitpold* and *Kaiser* to the *Friedrich der Gross*, flagship of the Kaiser's fleet; the captain of the *Westfalen* had supposedly been thrown overboard and drowned; another warship was said to have been hijacked by her crew while at sea; the mutineers were reported to have been executed. No one quite knew whether to believe such reports – with good reason, for much of it was pure propaganda. The truth was that sailors in Wilhelmshaven and Kiel had staged a series of hunger strikes and stoppages to protest their abject working conditions, a rebellion that culminated on 2 August with 600 men walking off the *Prinz Regent Luitpold* and refusing to return for several hours. It was more a strike than a mutiny – the culmination of years of pent-up anger – but the navy was so fearful of a general uprising that the two principal ringleaders had been shot by firing squad.

Theodore Plivier was among the crewmen who gathered around these new bulletins, heatedly arguing about them. 'There was a perpetual crowd around the bit of paper,' Plivier recalled. 'They came down from the deck and out from the bunkers and stoke-hold. Everyone was discussing the telegram.' Plivier surmised that their captain had posted up the reports as examples of British propaganda; perhaps Nerger also intended them as a warning. If so, he miscalculated, for news of the mutinies struck a deep chord with many of the *Wolf*'s men. The deprivations of the voyage, the overcrowding of the ship and the seemingly suicidal plan to run the blockade back to Germany were pushing many of them to breaking point.

The reunion of the *Wolf* and the *Hitachi Maru* took place off Coco Island, south of the Seychelles and 1200 miles east of the African coast, an uninhabited and unvegetated fingernail of land that no one aboard either ship would remember fondly. Soon after the ships pulled alongside one another, the *Wolf*'s crew came aboard the Japanese ship and began systematically stripping her of everything remotely useful or valuable. The steam-heating pipes were dismantled and carried across to the *Wolf*; cabins were plundered for their berths, washstands, carpets, bookshelves, linen and curtains, which were transferred to the raider's boat deck, where they were installed in jerry-rigged new quarters; even the cutlery, crockery and clocks were carted across. Winches swung between the ships bearing sagging baskets of coal, cargo and provisions. The Japanese ship, it was clear, was to be sunk and her prisoners moved on to the raider. For Nerger, it was a bitter defeat. For Karl Rose, it meant an effective demotion. For everyone else, the overcrowding was about to become intolerable.

The ships would lie off Coco Island for two weeks with their hulls grinding against each other and men swarming over their decks, lugging coal and cargo around the clock. A week into the sojourn, a squalling storm blew in from the south-east, throwing white foam breakers across the nearby coral reefs. In the midst of the storm, one of the Japanese prisoners on the *Wolf* was taken to the hospital in a state of physical collapse, barely able to rise from his hammock. It was the first acute case of beriberi. Aboard the *Wolf*, the shortage of fresh food and unrefined cereals meant that those already prone to the illness could spiral rapidly into its end stages. Roy Alexander was appalled by the state of the Japanese crewman when he saw him on one of his periodic trips to Dr Hauswaldt. 'The patient, normally a big man, appeared too bloated to fit the hospital cot,' Alexander recalled. 'He became paralysed. And when he was touched, the impressions of the orderlies' fingers were left in the swollen flesh, like fingermarks on a bladder of lard.' On 27 October, the crewman died from heart failure, and work above deck was briefly halted to observe his burial at sea.

Three days later, even more alarming news swept the two ships when it was announced that Dr Hauswaldt would immunise everyone aboard for typhoid. Two Japanese crewmen had been removed from the *Wolf*'s number-three hold with severe fever. In 1917, typhoid was no longer the virulent killer it had been in centuries past; treated with serums, it was usually not fatal. But nearly everyone aboard knew it as a contagion spread by poor hygiene, or had heard about the recent sensation of 'Typhoid' Mary Mallon, the Irish-born cook who inadvertently killed three people and infected forty-four others while working in hospitals and homes in New York. And typhoid raised the spectre of an unrelated but even more forbidding disease: typhus, the 'ship fever' epidemic spread by infected lice, for which no serum yet existed. The disease was as old as warfare itself and had most recently swept through Serbia in 1915, killing more than 150,000 people. An outbreak aboard the crowded confines of the *Wolf* could potentially kill everyone.

Aboard the *Hitachi Maru*, Stan Cameron was still desperately trying to convince the Germans to let him take a contingent of prisoners to freedom, presenting Karl Rose with a petition signed by all the married couples on the ship. Its tone of courteous pleading, addressed to Karl Nerger, was directed at his German pride:

> We, the undersigned detained enemy subjects travelling with our wives, some of whom have already been exposed to shell-fire, and the remainder to the risk thereof, and have suffered many weeks' detention on board, respectfully beg that no women be transferred to the auxiliary cruiser, thereby exposing them to a repetition of the grave danger they have already run. We earnestly trust that some means may be found by which consideration

> may be shown to all the women on board by landing them safely without their incurring further peril. We take this opportunity of expressing our gratitude for the treatment we have received since our capture, and our sincere appreciation of the courtesy and consideration shown us by every officer and man from your ship with whom we have been brought in contact.

No word came back from the captain, however, and on 5 November the prisoners were told that they were being relocated to the *Wolf* – final confirmation that Cameron's appeal had fallen on deaf ears. In his cabin, Frederick Trayes made out his last will and testament on the back of a letter he was carrying from the Hong Kong and Shanghai Bank. Trayes and his wife were to have been reunited in England with their fifteen-year-old daughter, Dorothy, who they had sent off to boarding school as a small girl; now, they grappled with the thought that they would never see her again. In the saloon, already stripped of all its fittings, they shared one last lunch with the Camerons and their fellow passengers.

A pall hung over everyone as they trudged back across the gangway to the *Wolf*. 'The people on the whole were about as merry as mutes at a funeral,' recalled Courtenay Dickinson. Alfred Clarke was taken below with the rest of the *Hitachi Maru*'s single male passengers to the number-three hold under the aft deck, where the hundred-strong Japanese crew were kept. Using bunk beds and wooden packing cases, the Germans had constructed a partitioned area of about twenty square feet for Clarke and his group, who were joined by Jack Rugg and some of the more senior British officers from the *Jumna*, *Wordsworth* and *Turritella*. The hold had been painted white, fumigated and fitted with heating pipes for the approaching winter; the *Hitachi Maru*'s piano had even been lowered into it and lashed into a corner. But the outbreaks of disease and illness among the Japanese left a residual air of discord. For an Englishman like Clarke, it was simply intolerable to live and sleep in such close proximity to the 'all-pervading, loathsome smell of sweating Eastern humanity'.

Such open racism would soon spark outright violence.

Above deck, the Camerons and Floods had been resettled in their old cabins, displacing the German officers who had been sleeping there. Around them, the other first-class prisoners from the *Hitachi Maru* and the *Matunga* were accommodated in cabins and storerooms, or in a jumble of makeshift quarters made from painted canvas strung up in the galleyways and fitted out with electric fans and lights. Even Frederick Trayes was impressed by the deferential treatment that the Germans extended towards his wife and the other ladies aboard, but with nine women and nearly seven hundred men now sharing the ship, the problems of maintaining discipline were obvious.

The most vulnerable woman aboard the *Wolf* was the *Hitachi Maru*'s stewardess, Kameno Kuziraoka, who was sharing quarters above-deck with the Chinese-Mauritian woman Marie Long and her granddaughter. With all her former shipmates imprisoned below and Lieutenant-Commander Shiraishi the only Japanese-speaker above deck, the diminutive forty-eight-year-old spent much of her time in solitude and carried herself with a posture of self-abasing meekness. In later years, she would reveal that on one of her solitary wanders around the *Wolf* she was accosted by a German officer who dragged her into a vacant cabin, produced a gun and demanded sex, threatening to kill her if she screamed for help. Kuziraoka had feared such an encounter from the first time she came aboard the *Wolf*, and by her own account – which emerged decades later – she stared down her attacker by gazing up at him reproachfully and placing her hand over her heart. At that point, the young officer broke down and fell to the floor, begging her not to report his crime to Kapitän Nerger.

The incident, which passed entirely unnoticed by Kuziraoka's fellow prisoners, betrayed the fracturing state of many aboard the raider. Down in the Hell Hole, the reappearance of the Swedish and Scandinavian sailors who had worked alongside the Germans aboard the *Hitachi Maru* sparked such animosity that Nerger was forced to move them into his own crew's quarters under the foredeck. The Japanese and English prisoners in the neighbouring number-four hold, meanwhile, were so hostile to one another that Nerger noted in his log that 'an outbreak of war' between them seemed imminent.

At 8.30 on the morning of 7 November, both ships weighed anchor and sailed several miles west of Coco Island, where they stopped in a becalmed sea. Even to the prisoners who had been aboard the raider for nine months, the sight of the 6700-ton *Hitachi Maru* being led to her grave was sobering. Just before 1.30 pm, they saw the ant-like figure of Karl Rose climb down from the Japanese ship to join the last of his men in a waiting launch that brought them across to the *Wolf*. The first bomb erupted in the *Hitachi Maru*'s keel ten minutes later, followed in quick succession by two other explosions amidships and forward. The ship sank reluctantly, listing for more than twenty minutes before water began enveloping the superstructure and her bow tilted down, taking her under in a swirl of floating detritus, from the centre of which a spar shot skywards like an arrow. Alone among the prisoners, Captain Seizu Tominaga could not bring himself to watch the spectacle; he was down in the prison hold, so filled with shame that he was physically ill.

* *

The *Wolf* was barely two days out from Coco Island, approaching the south-east coastline of Madagascar on a squally night, when Nerger was graced with another of his miraculous strokes of luck. In the early hours of 10 November, the lights of a steamer appeared through the moonlit mist to the south-west, approaching them on the trade route from Mozambique up to Colombo. Nerger shifted course to follow the ship and, five hours later, with the *Wolf* just barely mustering the speed needed to gain on the ship, the dawn light revealed the distinctive white and yellow smokestack of the Spanish Seta Y Aznar line.

Nerger dropped his bulwarks and hoisted his German flag, and the ship surrendered immediately, her captain perhaps assuming that as a neutral freighter he would be left unmolested. But as Nerger was soon to discover from the prize crew he sent aboard, the ship was carrying British cargo, which made her fair game for seizure. And the cargo in question was 5580 tons of coal destined for the Royal Navy's depot in Colombo harbour.

Nerger had captured the *Igotz Mendi*, a 4648-ton coal-freighter. It was in some ways a bittersweet piece of luck, for had he known of the ship's proximity a few days earlier he could have saved the *Hitachi Maru* and persisted with his original plan. But the Spanish ship's coal cargo, combined with her own fuel supply of around 1600 tons, would be more than enough to get both ships back to Germany, and Nerger would once again be able to relieve the chronic overburdening by shifting many of his top-deck prisoners off the *Wolf*. At gunpoint, the Spanish crew were ordered to follow the raider on a north-east course. They were heading back to Coco Island.

Nerger knew he had to move quickly, for the *Wolf*'s receivers were picking up stronger signals from the *Tsushima*, suggesting that the Japanese cruiser was closing in on them. It was now more than a month since the *Hitachi Maru* had been due in Delagoa Bay, and Nerger feared that a search of the Maldives might already have turned up evidence of the *Wolf*'s visit. Adding to his concerns, the *Wolfchen* was once again disabled, for the canvas stretched across her wing-frames had shredded and there were no more replacement supplies. Within hours of putting down anchor at the reef off Coco Island, Nerger's wireless operators picked up an alarmingly clear signal from the *Tsushima*, which they estimated to be within a forty-mile radius.

Nerger ordered the immediate transfer of seventeen of his top-deck prisoners to the *Igotz Mendi*, forcing the Spanish officers to vacate their cabins and take up quarters with the crew. The Camerons, the Bensons, the Trayes, the Floods, Courtenay Dickinson and Mabel Whittaker, the Mauritian Kiam Joseph and his wife, Marie Long and her granddaughter, William Cross and Cecil Strangman were all hustled across so hurriedly that their belongings were simply thrown into sacks and dumped on the *Igotz Mendi*'s deck. Three ailing prisoners from the Hell Hole were also nominated by Dr Hauswaldt to be moved across. One was Tom Rees, the second mate of the *Wairuna*, a diabetic whose health had deteriorated drastically during the months of poor food. His old shipmate Richard Donovan, a diminutive former jockey, was also transferred, as was Denis Patterson, a British passenger from the *Hitachi Maru* who suffered epileptic fits.

Leutnant Ernst Szielasko once again bid farewell to the Camerons, this time with a feeling that he would not see them again. Szielasko had been touched by Mary Cameron's gift, and he was not the only crewman who felt a sense of loss as he watched Juanita walking reluctantly across the gangway, waving sadly at them. 'She was a real ray of sunshine,' he recalled, 'and she had brought us some feeling of hope in the neverending toil of our mission.'

The *Wolf*'s crew now faced the onerous prospect of transshipping several thousand tons of coal from the *Igotz Mendi* to the *Wolf*, only a week after their labours aboard the *Hitachi Maru* had ceased. Adding to their exhaustion, fires had ignited in the raider's coal bunkers on the return to Coco Island, spreading so quickly that iron bulkheads glowed red through the wreaths of smoke. The fires recurred repetitively over the ensuing days, and men collapsed in the frantic haste to empty the bunkers, extinguish the smouldering coals and refill the holds. Working in dense clouds of smoke, the crew choked and vomited as they hauled hoses down into the ship's depths to douse the coal with water and carbonic acid. One afternoon, as the exhausted men gathered above deck, Theodor Plivier overheard Dierck Butendrift – the sailor whose arm had been shockingly burned in the gun misfire in March – cursing Nerger and threatening to string him up. It was as if reading of the mutinies back in Germany had emboldened the men to their own fantasies of overthrowing their captain.

On 17 November, after picking up a clear signal from the *Tsushima* to the missing *Hitachi Maru*, Nerger called off the coaling and readied the ships for a hasty departure. Leutnant Karl Rose was again promoted to prize captain, and he went across to the *Igotz Mendi* with just one officer, seven of the *Wolf*'s crew and ten neutral prisoners to supervise the Spanish ship's thirty-two crewmen. The disabled *Wolfchen* was stored below and the two ships set sail at 5.30 pm, turning south-west with an agreed meeting point for just under a week's time.

The *Wolf* had been at sea less than twenty-four hours when outright rebellion erupted among the crew. An able seaman named Wenzel broke into the store and stole enough liquor to fuel a drunken free-for-all in the crew's mess, and a sullen mob of twenty to thirty sailors gathered there. Kapitänleutnant Karl Schmehl, summoning the men for coal-lugging duty, was flummoxed to find them adamantly refusing to move. The men announced they'd had enough, that life in an internment camp would be better than this interminable voyage, that Nerger should find a neutral port and surrender. A uniformed sub lieutenant was summoned, but his shouted commands failed to stir the men from their benches. Finally, the master-at-arms arrived with five armed officers. Confronted with the task of arresting an entire division, he focused on the most formidable of them, a hulking seaman named Kuddl Bülow, who sat glowering drunkenly behind a mess table. The master-at-arms stood over Bülow and screamed at him to get up, and Plivier described the scene that ensued:

> Bülow's ponderous face assumed a rigid expression. You could hear his voice in the remotest corners of the deck: 'If Bülow won't, then he won't.' With these words he seized his seaman's knife and plunged the blade through his hand. With his left hand thus pinned to the table, he stood leaning over and glared at the master-at-arms.

News of the rebellion swept the ship. Alfred Clarke, who had been moved into a cabin above deck with Lieutenant-Commander

Shiraishi, heard the commotion as Bülow and Wenzel were thrown into the prison cell, and saw their captain appear shortly afterwards, in full uniform and a towering rage. Nerger seemed close to outright violence as he strode back and forth in front of Bülow and Wenzel's cell, brandishing a pistol and screaming abuse at them. Their insurrection was as close to mutiny as his crew had come, and there was a certain theatre in Nerger's tirade, which was witnessed by many officers gathered in the background.

Later in life, however, Nerger professed he would have shot any man who tried to wrest control of his ship. Even after he finished abusing the two men, he stayed on deck for half an hour, striding back and forth with the ribbons of his service medals flapping in the breeze, looking to Clarke like 'an infuriated and outraged turkey-cock'. The two would-be mutineers were ordered to remain imprisoned for the remainder of the voyage, pending their trial in Germany should the raider ever reach home.

On 24 November, the *Wolf* and the *Igotz Mendi* met briefly, well to the south of Madagascar, and exchanged signals before separating again. Five days later, the *Wolf* was approaching the Cape of Good Hope, 300 miles east of the South African coastline, with thunderheads gathering like a dark portent on the horizon. The raider had been at sea for exactly one year.

3

9

A SPECK ON THE OCEAN

Earl Curzon of Kedleston, the British Government's leader in the House of Lords, rose in the chamber on 29 October 1917 to deliver a long and impassioned tribute to the valour of the nation's troops as the First World War approached its fourth winter. A culminating point in the conflict was near, declared the hawk-nosed fifty-eight-year-old peer, and although there had been no glorious naval victory to rival Trafalgar, he was happy to report that the Royal Navy had swept the oceans clean of German warships. 'At the present moment, there only remains one small German merchant boat, converted into an armed raider, which is not accounted for,' Lord Curzon declared, 'and for three months it has not been heard of. It is a solitary speck on the boundless ocean, and for all we know, and hope, it is probably at this moment at the bottom of the sea.'

It was the government's only public acknowledgement that a raider might still be at large, but the optimistic suggestion that the *Wolf* had been destroyed would quickly be dispelled by events already unfolding as Lord Curzon made his speech. Across the other side of the world, near western New Guinea, a ship's wooden galley chest bearing the inscription 'Rabaul Sydney' had washed up on the beach at Gebi Island, and the Admiralty's commander in Singapore had wired London to report that it was presumed to be wreckage from the *Matunga*. In the Indian Ocean, meanwhile, the *Hitachi Maru* had been officially reported missing on 11 October, four days after her scheduled arrival in Delagoa Bay, and a search was under way by the Japanese Navy and the Nippon Yusen Kaisha line.

The Admiralty would little realise how close it came to capturing the *Wolf* in late 1917, for when the Nippon Yusen mail-ship *Kashima Maru* scoured the seas around Madagascar and the Seychelles in the third week of October, the raider was only a few hundred miles away, stripping the *Hitachi Maru* clean at Coco Island and monitoring the *Kashima Maru*'s wireless signals. The *Wolf* was still there a week later when the Japanese cruiser *Tsushima* ventured even closer, after joining the search from her base at Simon's Town, South Africa. But the *Tsushima* did not reach Coco Island, and the *Kashima Maru*, although she visited the Maldives, did not call in at Suvadiva. By then, another opportunity to catch the raider had already been lost, for in mid-October a boatload of Suvadiva villagers had arrived by canoe in the island nation's capital, Malé, bearing silk handkerchiefs from the *Hitachi Maru* and a strange story of being visited by two large steamships and an aircraft. Their account had reached the ears of King Shamsudeen II, who passed the information on to his representative in Colombo. But the sultan regarded the Suvadiva natives as 'ignorant' and his Colombo officials failed to inform the British Navy of the unusual report.

So it was not until the third week of November, when the small French navy cruiser *D'Estrees* was sent from Colombo to the Maldives, that the fate of the *Hitachi Maru* – and the *Wolf* – became clear. The captain of the *D'Estrees*, having arrived in Malé and met King Shamsudeen, wired Colombo details of the Suvadiva villagers' sighting. The mystery ships, he reported, were said to have flown no flags but carried passengers who spoke English. On 27 November, the Admiralty released details to its Indian Ocean commanders and advised, 'It is considered probable that ships reported were *WOLF* and *HITACHI MARU*.' A day later, it alerted the commanders of the Grand Fleet in the North Sea that the raider and the Japanese ship might attempt to reach Germany. After nearly nine months in which the *Wolf* had been a shadowy presence across three oceans, the British Navy finally had an opportunity to hunt down the elusive raider.

But the Admiralty faced a familiar problem: the logistical nightmare of trying to find one lone ship in thirty-two-million square miles of ocean. On paper, the combined Allied naval forces available to search for the *Wolf* were formidable: some thirty British, Japanese and French warships operated in the Indian Ocean in late 1917, with another twenty stationed in West Africa, Australia and Singapore. In practice, however, only a few of them were adequate to take on a heavily armed 5800-ton raider. By November 1917, the Admiralty had withdrawn nearly all of its significant warships to the North Sea and the Mediterranean, for Germany's U-boats had proved so devastatingly effective that Britain's admirals had been forced to introduce a system of naval convoys to protect freighter traffic sailing to and from Britain. It was a measure the admirals had previously dismissed as futile, until they were overruled by Prime Minister Lloyd George. The convoys, supplemented by newly available United States warships, were so remarkably successful that by September shipping losses had more than halved from their April peak of 860,334 tons.

Of the warships that remained in Aden, Ceylon and South Africa, only eight had the speed and firepower necessary to take on the raider. The *Juno* and the *Venus*, two 5600-ton cruisers, were immediately dispatched from Ceylon to search the Maldives and the more southerly Chagos Archipelago; others were assigned to escort troop transports sailing in and out of Aden, while smaller cruisers were sent out to patrol the entrance to the Red Sea, the south-west coast of Africa and the western coastline of India. In Japan, the Nippon Yusen line refitted one of its largest passenger-ships, the *Chikuzen Maru*, with defensive guns and two navy seaplanes and dispatched it from Kobe with two Japanese Navy destroyers as escorts. But the dilemma of how best to intercept the raider was highlighted by a defence-intelligence briefing pointing out that if the *Wolf* and *Hitachi Maru* had left the Maldives in the second week of October, they might already be close to Germany.

In Australia, the navy informed the Burns Philp shipping company on 29 October that wreckage from the *Matunga* may have washed up near New Guinea, but confusion now reigned among maritime and navy officials in the wake of the government's campaign to blame all its shipping losses on time bombs or other sabotage.

The discovery of the *Wolf*'s minefield off Gabo Island had been an acute embarrassment to the Australian Navy, ameliorated only by the fact that most newspapers were happy to promote the government's new theory that the mines had been planted by German immigrants or possibly a neutral freighter. 'The chances are altogether against a minelayer paying a visit to Australian waters without being seen,' the *Argus* assured its readers. Another story in the press suggested that the *Matunga* had been sunk by a sub-oceanic earthquake – a theory that originated from navy headquarters in Melbourne after the captain of HMAS *Una* reported a seismic disturbance off New Guinea around the time of the *Matunga*'s disappearance. In New Zealand, a newspaper report appeared in October falsely claiming that the *Wairuna* had been captured by the *Seeadler* and her crew killed by the Germans. The report was so widely believed that enraged crowds had greeted the arrival of Count Felix von Luckner in Wellington, demanding his execution.

In New Zealand, too, there was widespread embarrassment and confusion in the wake of the *Port Kembla* 'sabotage'. The government had ordered Captain Percival Hall-Thompson to establish a fleet of minesweepers, yet publicly it continued to promote fallacious notions of bomb plots on the docks. At a maritime inquiry into the disappearance of the *Wairuna*, Crown lawyers accused the ship's owner, the Union Steamship Company, of 'extraordinary laxity' in failing to perform character checks on stevedores loading cargo, before requesting that the inquiry be held in closed session to discuss evidence of 'enemy action' within New Zealand. Hall-Thompson, meanwhile, informed the Admiralty on 12 November that minesweeping off the country's coast 'hardly appears necessary' – an assessment that proved ill timed, for a floating mine was reported off Wellington Harbour three days later.

By mid-December, the *Igotz Mendi* was a month overdue in Colombo and HMS *Juno* had confirmed that the *Hitachi Maru* was one of the two ships that visited the Maldive Islands in September. While searching the south-east coastline of Suvadiva Atoll, the *Juno*'s lookout spotted a pile of washed-up flotsam that proved to be twenty pairs of Japanese sandals, three futon mattresses, a case of coconuts from the *Hitachi Maru*'s cargo and a copy of the Nippon Yusen Kaisha cabin regulations. The Japanese ship, it seemed clear, had been attacked and captured by the *Wolf*, which had then intercepted the *Igotz Mendi* and in the process acquired enough coal to get herself back to Germany. 'Raider may be anywhere in the Indian Ocean,' advised the Admiralty's Cape Town commander, 'but presumably not in any need of coal.'

The sudden reappearance of the *Wolf* in the Indian Ocean, a full ten months since she first captured the *Turritella* there, was bewildering to the Admiralty. The raider was known to have mined Colombo and Bombay early in 1917 and strongly believed to have prowled the South Pacific from June to August. Now, she seemed to have rematerialised in the same locale where her raiding began. Her minelaying raid on Singapore was not yet known, for not a single ship had been lost there. (After the war, it would be explained that Nerger's crew had taken a false reading of the ocean bottom off the Anambas Islands, and the mines had been anchored too deeply. All 110 of them were floating beneath the surface, just below the keels of hundreds of passing ships.) Adding to the confusion, several of the *Wolf*'s mines had just been found floating near Bombay, leading to the erroneous belief that the raider might recently have revisited the harbour and sown a second minefield.

Uncertain of the *Wolf*'s whereabouts and alert to the possibility that the *Igotz Mendi* or *Hitachi Maru* might themselves have been converted into raiders, the Admiralty increased patrols and escorts around its Indian Ocean ports. There were thus no ships it could spare for the task of searching the open seas. And if the *Wolf* had already slipped below South Africa and up into the Atlantic Ocean, there was little the Admiralty could do in the immediate term, for in the vast stretches of the south-eastern Atlantic the Royal Navy had just three warships. The 5600-ton cruiser *Hyacinth* was stationed at Cape Town, and a converted 7000-ton P&O liner, the *Himalaya*, was in the harbour at St Helena, a remote British island roughly equidistant between south-west Africa and Brazil. Further north, the 9800-ton cruiser *Kent* was at Sierra Leone in west Africa. The job of hunting for the *Wolf* therefore devolved to the Nippon Yusen liner *Chikuzen Maru* and her two naval destroyer escorts.

Secrecy, of course, was to be rigidly maintained. In Japan, the disappearance of the *Hitachi Maru* had caused anguish and intense debate in the newspapers, but even the ship's owners remained unaware that a raider was believed responsible, and newspaper stories continued to suggest that the ship had been sunk by a bomb or lost in bad weather. (A professor of maritime studies also noted that there were rumours of a giant octopus in the vicinity of the Maldives.)

Britain's political and military leaders were, to be sure, burdened by weightier issues as the dismal Christmas of 1917 approached. In late October, a massive offensive by the combined troops of Germany, Austria and Hungary had pushed seventy miles into northern Italy and crushed the Italian Army's divisions there, leaving more than three hundred thousand of its men killed, wounded or captured. In October and December, the German Navy had launched surprise attacks on Allied freighter convoys in the North Sea, sinking three British destroyers and fifteen merchant ships and bringing enormous pressure on Admiral Jellicoe to resign. And on 7 November, the Bolsheviks had seized power in Russia, leading five weeks later to a Russian armistice with Germany. Thousands of German troops could soon be transferred from the Eastern Front towards France, at a time when American soldiers were yet to arrive in significant numbers. Even Lord Lansdowne, the former foreign secretary, was advocating a negotiated peace.

Two days before Christmas, the head of the Royal Navy's 9th Cruiser Squadron in the northern Atlantic offered to detach his 12,000-ton warship *Bacchante* to hunt for the elusive *Wolf* but first requested further information about the raider's likely position and course. The Admiralty simply replied, 'No further information regarding *Wolf*.'

* *

Australia, too, was gripped by larger dramas in late 1917, for Prime Minister Hughes had suddenly announced that he would again attempt to introduce military conscription by referendum, setting in motion a five-week political campaign that had propelled the country to the brink of mob bloodshed. Hughes's public speeches became tirades in which he denounced 'reckless extremists, peace cranks, disloyalists and pro-Germans', accusing the anti-conscriptionist Catholic archbishop Daniel Mannix of being an ally of Germany. In turn, Hughes was jeered and jostled by conscription opponents, splattered with eggs and assaulted. Facing a hostile crowd in Queensland, the diminutive prime minister became so enraged that he leapt into the audience to join one melee and was reported by an onlooker to have reached for his revolver (which fortuitously was in his other trousers). The violence reached its apogee at a massive rally of 100,000 people inside the Melbourne Cricket Ground, where eggs, shards of glass and rocks were thrown at the speakers and a police officer only just prevented one man from hurling a knife at the prime minister.

When the voters again rejected conscription – this time more emphatically – Hughes was forced to resign and seek a vote from his own party to form a newly constituted government. The political tumult completely overshadowed all other issues, even the recent discovery of the minefield off Gabo Island. The government had quietly dropped its campaign to find the 'saboteurs' behind the *Port Kembla* and *Cumberland* sinkings, and the *Sun*'s reward fund had disappeared from its pages. In maritime circles, there was now a growing realisation that the governments of Australia and New Zealand had been far from candid about the ship losses in local waters. The Sydney manager of Burns Philp complained to the Australian Navy about the meagre information he was being given about the *Matunga*, and many shipping officials now believed her to have been captured by a raider.

An inquiry had been held in Sydney, once again headed by Fergus Cumming, the government bureaucrat who had been unable to decide why the *Cumberland* sank. But Cumming this time emphatically rejected the prime minister's suggestion that a bomb had been planted aboard the ship and also dismissed the theory of an oceanic earthquake. Noting that the 'prevailing theory' in shipping circles was that the *Matunga* had been captured by a raider, Cumming pointedly remarked that he had found it impossible to obtain information from the navy regarding this issue, and suspended his inquiry pending further information.

But the suspicions unleashed by the prime minister and the anti-Hun newspapers had created a witch-hunt that was not easily quelled. In the coastal towns of south-east Victoria, close to the site of the *Cumberland* sinking, there was now fervid speculation about which of the local Germans might have been responsible for planting the minefield off Gabo Island, a rumour mill encouraged by the £10,000 in government rewards that were still on offer. The navy and police were receiving a steady stream of reports about suspicious lights seen flashing along the coast, and about one particular German fisherman who lived in a notably wild and remote outpost of the coastline. By late October, the man's name had reached the highest levels of Australia's military intelligence.

Christoph Johann Niemann was a stocky, moustachioed fifty-four-year-old who lived with his Australian-born wife Louisa and their many children in Bool Pool, an isolated peninsula at the very south-east tip of Australia. Born in Germany in 1863, Niemann had arrived in Melbourne aboard a sailing ship as a sixteen-year-old merchant seaman, stayed on to find work with a local fishing family and anglicised his name to Carl Newman (or Charles, as his family sometimes called him). After settling on the coast 200 miles east of Melbourne, Newman had married his boss's sixteen-year-old daughter, built a rough-hewn house and thrown his considerable energies into the task of raising and supporting a family. By the outbreak of war, he boasted twelve children aged between two and twenty-eight, operated several fishing boats with his oldest sons and owned a half-share in a thirty-acre farm outside the town of Inverloch.

Newman had sworn allegiance to Australia when he was naturalised in 1908. His wife was Australian and his oldest son, Charles, had tried to enlist in the army. Despite all this, he had become the subject of a vicious rumour campaign among rival fishermen in the Gippsland region, many of whom were convinced he had somehow planted the mines discovered off Gabo Island. Such speculation should have been easy to dismiss, for the idea that a lone German agent could have strewn an entire minefield off that wild coastline had already been rejected by the Special Intelligence Bureau three months earlier, and the navy had suspected for months that a commerce-raider had visited Australian waters. Despite this, the navy's intelligence department decided to launch a major investigation into Newman.

This was, in fact, the third such investigation that Carl Newman had been subjected to, for by late 1917 he had already been exonerated twice by military intelligence. The rumour campaign against Newman had started early in 1917, when a pro-conscriptionist who lived near him sent a two-page letter to the Defence Department advising them that 'if submarines ever worked on the coast of Australia, this would be a dangerous man'. The destruction of the *Cumberland* only 100 miles east of Newman's house had predictably inspired a frenzy of renewed speculation about this swarthy and suspect German. Rival fishermen sent letters to the Defence Department claiming, among other things, that he lived in a huge five-room residence at Bool Pool and ventured out at night in a boat so large it 'could lay enough mines in the night to blow up half the shipping around our coast . . .'.

As a result, two undercover army-intelligence agents had been dispatched to investigate in August. Posing as hunters, they had rented a boat and landed in Bool Pool, trudging through a mile of swamp and scrub to Newman's house, where the absent fisherman's wife and daughters – delighted at seeing their first visitors for more than a year – provided afternoon tea. To their disappointment, the agents discovered nothing, even after returning at night to search the property and eavesdrop on conversations inside the house. Newman's residence proved to be a modest one-room corrugated tin structure. His boat was large but no grander than several other fishing vessels on the coast, and local townsfolk who knew him spoke highly of him. Not a single complaint, in fact, had been substantiated against any Germans in the area, who were described as 'loyal and law-abiding, it being extremely dangerous for them to be otherwise . . .'.

When the minefield off Gabo Island was discovered in early October, however, a new swirl of rumours had been activated, and fresh letters arrived at the Defence Department reporting suspicious lights blinking off headlands near his home and warning that German agents were believed to be hiding in caves along the coast. A new investigation was launched, this time headed by the naval officer Captain John Richardson. (Richardson had already played a decisive but unheralded role in the Allied war effort, for it was he who had discovered the third of the German codebooks that had ended up in the hands of British naval intelligence. In August 1914, the intrepid Richardson had donned a bowler hat and overcoat to pose as a quarantine official and boarded the

German freighter *Hobart* while it was docked in Melbourne's Port Phillip Bay. After arresting the freighter's skipper at gunpoint, he had located the hidden panel in his cabin where the codebooks were stored.) A proven undercover operative, the fifty-seven-year-old navy veteran was dispatched to Gippsland shortly after the first of the Gabo Island mines was discovered. There, he interviewed locals, inspected Carl Newman's boat, surveyed his house and came to exactly the same conclusion as the previous investigators.

'My personal opinion of Newman is that he is not involved in any improper practices,' Richardson wrote. Rather, the allegations against him came from rival fishermen who appeared resentful of his success and were engaging in a vicious feud typical of those which erupt in small and isolated communities. 'The reports all emanated from tainted sources,' Richardson reported, 'and their origin lay in Newman's superior capacity for work and consequent prosperity.'

Newman himself had not yet been interviewed and may well have been oblivious to the avid interest his fishing activities had attracted in the upper reaches of Australia's military intelligence. But the rumours about him were so persistent that even his local police began to believe, by the end of 1917, that he must have had a hand in the *Cumberland* disaster. Rival fishermen claimed he had been buying large stores of wire and petrol. A grocer heard from a farmer that Newman regularly stocked up his boat and sailed out at night to issue signals at sea. A local judge advised naval intelligence to keep an eye on him, as 'gossip is plentiful'. Inevitably, the rumours found their way into the *Age* newspaper, and the navy – already the subject of derisive newspaper editorials for its handling of the *Cumberland* affair – felt compelled to act. Its response was to send out a third investigator, Lieutenant D. W. Drysdale.

Drysdale was a man with a keen eye for 'foreigners' and 'Huns', for he believed that he could spot them by their facial features. In his view, 'the naturalised German is more dangerous than the unnaturalised man, as his movements are not known in the same way as the man on parole'. His investigation would turn Carl Newman into the victim of a flagrant misuse of the government's powers over 'enemy aliens'.

* *

Karl Nerger's dream of a triumphant homecoming in Kiel just before Christmas had evaporated during the long and arduous days the *Wolf* was anchored off Coco Island. The raider was still in the lower reaches of the Indian Ocean in early December, labouring through heavy seas towards the Cape of Good Hope with the *Igotz Mendi* sailing alongside her. Now that her coal bunkers were depleted, the Spanish freighter rolled with sickening buoyancy across the heavy swell, while the *Wolf*'s engines were so fatigued and her keel so encrusted with weeds that her maximum speed had dropped to below ten knots. When Nerger was woken on the night of 26 November and told that a large darkened freighter was approaching from Cape Town, he could do nothing but watch it pass, for it was travelling at fifteen knots and would easily outrun the *Wolf*.

Captain John Blom was therefore particularly unlucky when, only four days later, he ran straight into the raider's path while sailing his three-masted 1395-ton barque, the *John H. Kirby*, from Port Elizabeth up to Durban. Blom had set sail from his home town of New York in August carrying 270 T-Model cars fresh off the Ford production line in Detroit, and he was only a day's sailing from his final destination when a broken chronometer took him several hundred miles off course during a particularly vicious storm along the east African coast. The *Wolf* overhauled him just after breakfast. By lunchtime the next day, the American barque and its load of Fords was at the bottom of the ocean, and Blom and his thirteen-man crew were down in the Hell Hole.

Conditions were now so crowded in the two prison holds that new hammocks had to be strung in the narrow gap formed by the ends of adjoining hammocks, 'like sardines packed in a tin', as

Roy Alexander put it. The congestion and boredom had taken a particular toll in the number-three hold, where relations between the Japanese and British prisoners had deteriorated to a level of outright violence. To maintain their spirits, the Japanese had developed a program of entertainment, which they staged every day with ritualised formality. Central to it was the traditional storytelling known as *rakugo*, in which a lone performer kneels before his audience and constructs a long comedic monologue using the voices of multiple characters, often building to a punchline. The sound of a hundred Japanese men laughing riotously as the day's *rakugo* unfolded would thus drift over the wooden packing cases separating them from the other eighty-odd prisoners who now crowded the hold – British officers, ex-passengers from the *Hitachi Maru* and crewmen from the *John H. Kirby*.

To Alfred Clarke, who made no effort to disguise his repugnance for all things oriental, this 'maddening din' was made even worse by the musical program that followed, often involving a succession of singers and harmonica players, along with the repetitive spinning of the same handful of 78 rpm gramophone records on a wind-up Victrola. 'The mad riot of music was accompanied by irritating shrieks of laughter, fatuous chattering and murmuring, and the hum of conversation in the vernacular,' said Clarke, whose sour bigotry was doubtless worsened by illness, for he had been taken prisoner while on an ill-advised sea cruise to improve his health.

Nerger had become aware of the animosity between the Japanese and the British some weeks earlier when he spoke to Major John Flood, who stated unequivocally that he regarded Asia's most powerful military power as a treacherous enemy rather than an ally. Flood was incredulous that the Royal Navy would rely on Japan to protect Australia, saying the Japanese 'couldn't have cared less about the security of British trade, and came to Australia only for espionage'.

Such animosities were exacerbated in the prison holds by the widespread belief that Asians were inherently dirty and disease ridden, and a rumour soon swept the hold that some of the Japanese were suffering from syphilis, as well as typhoid and beriberi. 'The hatred of some of these people, even among the more educated, was palpable,' Nerger said. He recalled one incident in which a Japanese steward was swabbing the deck when an English prisoner sauntered up and spat directly near his hand. For emphasis, the Englishman spat a second time, sparking a fight in which a group of Japanese picked him up and slammed him into the deck railing.

The tensions of the voyage were also manifest aboard the *Igotz Mendi*, where Leutnant Karl Rose and his handful of men were settling into an uneasy accommodation with their twenty-one prisoners and the thirty-two Spanish crewmen. The *Igotz Mendi* was not a ship designed for passenger comfort, and it was carrying twice its normal occupancy. Rose had assigned himself the Spanish captain's cabin, amidships under the bridge; adjacent to it, along a narrow corridor, was a small saloon, and then a second officer's quarters that he nominated for John and Rose Flood. The Camerons, the Trayes and the Bensons occupied neighbouring cabins that had once housed the Spanish officers and stewards; each was about eight feet square and contained one narrow bunk and a sofa-bench. Further back in the deckhouse, Courtenay Dickinson and Mabel Whittaker were given a more spacious engineer's cabin, across the corridor from a larger room that now housed six people: Kameno Kuziraoka from the *Hitachi Maru*, Kiam Joseph and his wife, Marie Long and her granddaughter, and Agnes Mackenzie. The single men – Cecil Strangman, William Cross, Richard Donovan, Tom Rees and Denis Patterson – were sharing a converted storeroom under the poop deck, adjacent to a pigsty that housed three fully grown occupants.

With his typical flair for trampling on the sensitivities of the English, Leutnant Rose had caused outrage by housing Agnes Mackenzie in the same quarters as a coloured man. 'Many of us were highly incensed because of this treatment of a white woman, but were powerless to do anything with Rose in the matter,' recalled Stan Cameron. Mackenzie had, in fact, refused to submit to the indignity when first brought aboard the *Igotz Mendi* at Coco Island, demanding to see Karl Nerger. Insisting that she would rather remain aboard the *Wolf* than share quarters with Kiam Joseph, Mackenzie had made such a scene that the German captain had acquiesced and allowed her to remain in her cabin aboard the raider. But two days later, as the two ships were preparing to cast off, Nerger had been forced to remove Mackenzie from his ship after what he described as 'a somewhat embarrassing incident'.

The incident in question was a knife fight between two of the *Wolf*'s crewmen who had been vying one night for the widow's affections. The love-starved men of the *Wolf*, it emerged, had continued to feel a burning ardour for Mackenzie, despite her indignant response to the love letter she had received from one of them. And notwithstanding her outrage at Rose Flood's behaviour, the stewardess had apparently succumbed to the advances of at least one crewman during the long and lonely nights in the Indian Ocean. Roy Alexander – who seems to have believed Mackenzie was nearer to fifty than forty – was certainly convinced this was the case and found the whole episode vastly amusing.

'After all,' he commented, 'it is not given to every woman to have hefty young men fighting over her in the autumn of her days. The lady's willingness to risk being blown sky-high aboard the raider was now explained. It was a clear case of: "O Death! Where is thy sting?"'

As a result of the knife fight, Mackenzie had been lowered into a launch shortly before the *Wolf* left Coco Island and transshipped to the *Igotz Mendi*, wearing an expression of dignified piety as she made her way across on a choppy sea. It was, Alexander noted, possibly the only recorded case in modern times of a woman's love affairs interrupting the operations of a warship.

The feud between Karl Rose and the New Zealand stewardess had thus been resumed with renewed animosity. Leutnant Rose eventually acquiesced to the complaints of Cameron and several other prisoners, and moved Agnes Mackenzie into the same cabin as Courtenay Dickinson and his fiancée. This caused its own troubles, however, for Dickinson and Mabel Whittaker found that sharing quarters with Agnes Mackenzie was no peaceful affair. 'Her presence,' he confided to a friend later, 'entailed the constant ingress, egress and regress of German sailors, who came at all hours of the day and night to see her.' Thankfully, Dickinson was a broad-minded fellow: his own relationship with Mabel was somewhat unconventional, as she was ten years older than him and a widow. Her fondness for liquor had inspired the German crewmen to nickname her 'The Whisky Madame' – Fritz Witschetzky even claimed to have seen her standing on the deck of the *Igotz Mendi* waving a bottle of Scotch.

Rose Flood's sour relations with the other women – in particular Mary Cameron – had also not improved. The Camerons and the Floods shared neighbouring cabins on the *Igotz Mendi* but appear hardly to have spoken, and Stan Cameron's opinion of John Flood was evidently not much higher than Mary's opinion of Rose. Although Flood was an army major and only thirty-three years old, Cameron later described himself as the only able-bodied man among the ship's prisoners. For his part, Courtenay Dickinson ascribed the bickering among the women to the cramped and uncomfortable quarters.

Although only a year old, the Spanish ship was cheaply built, infested with bugs and caked in coal dust, and her tiny cabins leaked in high seas. With more than sixty people crowded aboard her, the water supply to the toilets and bathrooms had to be cut off in order to conserve the ship's limited reserves, and everyone was issued with a small supply of water twice a day for drinking and washing. Meals were taken in a saloon that measured eighteen feet across and accommodated only ten people – eight during high seas, for the chairs at either end of the table were not fixed and would topple over as the ship lurched.

Stan Cameron was amazed that some of the British prisoners at these cramped gatherings continued to disport themselves as though they were 'first class passengers on a modern liner with servants to supply their every whim'. Among the worst offenders was Frederick Trayes, nicknamed 'Herr Professor' by the Germans, who took to lodging official complaints with Leutnant Rose about the appalling service he and his wife endured. Tablecloths in the saloon, he grumbled, were splattered with food and drink from the ship's pitching and rolling, tea was served in cups without saucers and the Trayes were forced to share teaspoons with other passengers. Trayes clung so steadfastly to his British sense of propriety that he still ironed his handkerchiefs in his tiny cabin. When he complained to one 'boorish, loutish' German crewman about the quality of the waiters, the crewman retorted that he was a soldier, not a steward. Trayes promptly reported him to Leutnant Rose for insolence.

But the retired headmaster's bête noire was a young Spanish steward named Manuel who seemed constitutionally incapable of bearing a tray of coffee, tea or soup across the saloon without sloshing half the contents over the table and its diners. Stan Cameron observed these accidents with some amusement, for he had deduced that Manuel harboured such a violent dislike towards some of the prisoners that he was spilling food on them deliberately.

Although the ship was carrying three pigs, two cows, two calves and several chickens, food was tightly rationed and meals were small and repetitious. Rice from the *Jumna*'s endless supply and tinned crab from the *Hitachi Maru* – which had been carrying several thousand cases of the delicacy – were served with such numbing repetition that everyone aboard developed a lifelong revulsion for crab. Richard Donovan was permitted to work in the kitchen, primarily baking bread to accompany the soups and bully-beef stews that were the other staple meals, but the prisoners were becoming visibly thinner. Mabel Whittaker's ample girth had shrunk considerably, and Stan Cameron's trousers hung so loosely that he now cinched his belts halfway around his waist.

Hunger turned mealtimes into displays of naked self-interest, which Karl Rose aggravated by seating himself at the head of the table and dispensing food from a communal tray. The German *leutnant* always sat next to a 'friend', recalled Stan Cameron, whom he passed the tray to first. (The description suggests it may have been Rose Flood.) The tray would then pass back to the German *leutnant* and on to another prisoner who was, in Cameron's words, 'a glutton, and without shame'. After giving much of his meagre meal to Mary and Juanita, Stan would frequently leave the table ravenous. It was an awful sensation, he remarked, 'suddenly to realise that you actually covet the food another person is eating'.

Rose had maintained his bridge circle, which included Colonel Cecil Strangman, the white-haired Australian-army medical officer. Although he was born in Ireland and had spent most of his professional life in remote northern Australia, the Cambridge-educated doctor carried himself with an imperious air and was fond of quoting the Geneva Convention's myriad clauses and subclauses to enumerate the reasons he should receive various forms of preferential treatment. 'All throughout the trip this man had behaved like a dog in a manger,' recalled Stan Cameron, 'being the quintessence of egotistical selfishness and despised by us, one and all.' That scathing assessment was corroborated by other passengers, who reported that Strangman's demeanour towards the Germans was 'servile' and unworthy of a British officer.

Stan Cameron had a fiery side that he had forcefully contained in the face of Karl Rose's provocations, fearing the repercussions for Mary and Juanita. He was young enough – his thirty-third birthday was approaching – and strong enough to have contemplated organising an uprising by the prisoners while aboard the *Wolf*, but given the size of the raider's German crew, such thoughts had been in the realm of pure fantasy. Here on the *Igotz Mendi*, Cameron began to think seriously that a handful of determined men could wrest control of the ship. Leutnant Rose and his eight men were heavily reliant on the Spanish crew and the ten neutral prisoners from the *Wolf* who had agreed to work for them. Cameron knew that the neutrals – Scandinavian, Chilean and Greek crewmen from the *Winslow*, *Wairuna* and *Beluga* – felt no great allegiance to the Germans beyond self-preservation. The Spanish were more difficult to read: their captain, Quintín Ugalde, and first officer, Gervasio Susasta, were jovial fellows who made a great show of drinking with Rose and his men, toasting Germany's military victories in Italy and lustily singing around the saloon table. One of them had even written a poem in tribute to the *Wolf*'s heroic voyage. How much of it was genuine was difficult to tell; Courtenay Dickinson, for one, thought the Spanish were duping the Germans with 'a very artful piece of shamming'.

Cameron had canvassed the other prisoners about overpowering the Germans and found his strongest ally in Tom Rees, whose animosity towards the enemy burned fiercely despite his fragile health. But Rees, Richard Donovan and Denis Patterson were all too ill to help, and the others expressed no great enthusiasm for the plan. When Cameron surreptitiously approached the Spanish first officer to mutter an outline of his mutiny proposal, Susasta demurred and Cameron hurriedly dropped the discussion. The reason for his reluctance soon became clear: Leutnant Rose had told the Spanish crew that they would soon be permitted to take the *Igotz Mendi* back home to Bilbao with her prisoners.

The idea had emerged in the first week of December, after the *Igotz Mendi* and the *Wolf* came to a brief rest 200 miles south of Cape Town. The two ships had cruised in tandem for several days and, after Rose took a dinghy across to visit his commander, he returned with supplies and news that caused great excitement when the Camerons got wind of it from members of the Spanish crew. The Germans intended taking the raider and the prize ship to Trinidade Island, a small and remote Brazilian territory in the southern Atlantic roughly eight hundred miles east of Rio de Janeiro, where an isolated harbour would be found for a final transfer of coal across to the *Wolf*. After spending Christmas at

Trinidade, the ships would set off north into the chillier climes of the North Atlantic – a course that would take them west of Spain. At some point – information was vague and different versions of the plan passed among the prisoners – Leutnant Rose and his crew would transfer across to the *Wolf*, leaving the Spanish captain and his crew free to sail back home. The Camerons and their fellow prisoners could theoretically be on land in either Cádiz, in southern Spain, or the northern port of Bilbao by mid-January.

Such a plan contained one glaringly obvious pitfall for the Germans: the *Igotz Mendi* would arrive in Spain just as the *Wolf* was approaching the British blockade in the North Sea, and the Royal Navy's warships would inevitably be alerted to the raider's attempted run home to Kiel. But when Rose confirmed to the prisoners that they might be free within six weeks, all scepticism was swept aside. Someone produced a Spanish phrase book and the Camerons, the Trayes, Courtenay Dickinson, Mabel Whittaker and several others began enthusiastically learning the language in anticipation of their arrival. Mary Cameron, who by now had recovered sufficiently to take walks around the deck with Stan in the evening, was particularly elated.

Although he had never said this to Mary, Stan Cameron had always harboured the gravest fears about their chances of surviving that final passage to Germany. If Nerger intended returning to Kiel along the same route by which he had left, they would be forced to carve their way through the ice floes of the Denmark Strait and the southern Arctic Ocean in the depths of winter – a task for which the unstable and poorly built *Igotz Mendi* was wholly ill equipped.

Assuming they could survive that leg of the voyage, the ships would then sail down through the North Sea east of Scotland, within 250 miles of the British Grand Fleet's main base at Scapa Flow on the Orkney Islands, and straight into the naval blockade that had kept Germany's High Seas Fleet landlocked for most of the war. The *Igotz Mendi*'s crew had told Cameron that the British Navy kept a fleet of warships and armed merchantmen on constant patrol between Scotland and the shores of Norway, stopping and searching every freighter they encountered. Despite her new coat of battleship grey, the *Igotz Mendi* was clearly an unarmed freighter and thus unlikely to be attacked by a British dreadnought. But Leutnant Rose had made it clear that in the event of encountering an Allied warship, he would order all hands to abandon ship and would plant timer bombs to destroy the Spanish collier – a terrifying ordeal that Stan had no wish for his wife and child to endure. Mary lived in a perpetual dread of being rushed into the lifeboats; the women who had survived the horrors of the *Hitachi Maru* evacuation feared it even more.

Most threatening to Stan, however, were the minefields that both the British and the Germans had strewn throughout the seas off Denmark over the past three years, and the U-boats that had wrought such immense destruction on freighter traffic in the North Sea. How Nerger and Rose proposed to negotiate a safe passage through those perils was difficult for Cameron to conceive. The Spanish crew were emphatic that it was an impossibility.

So freedom in Spain was a notion that even Stan clung to, despite his distrust of Karl Rose. Buoyed by the prospect, he requested Rose's permission to take Mary and Juanita fishing in a dinghy at Trinidade Island, where the abundant sea bass were legendary. As the Camerons and their fellow prisoners contemplated an island Christmas followed by a quick voyage to Spain, the nightmare of captivity lifted with every passing day. The fine weather of the southern Atlantic seemed to match their spirits, which not even persistent hunger pangs could dampen. 'When we got up from the table hungry,' recalled Cameron, 'we would think of Spain and freedom in a few short weeks, and forget all about how empty we were.'

It was only on 19 December, shortly after the *Wolf* appeared off the starboard bow, that reality intruded. The raider and her prize met at a prearranged location 100 miles north-east of Trinidade Island. The *Igotz Mendi* had made the two-week,

3000-mile voyage without incident, crossing the Tropic of Capricorn the previous day in fine weather. The *Wolf*'s voyage had been more eventful, for Stan Cameron learned from Leutnant Rose that the raider had captured and sunk another sailing vessel, the French barque *Maréchal Davout*, four days earlier. The barque had been taking 36,000 sacks of wheat from Australia to France, and although she was armed with two six-inch guns, her captain had wisely surrendered to the raider without attempting to resist, adding another thirty-five prisoners to the crowded prison holds.

The *Wolf* and the *Igotz Mendi* now sailed together on a south-west course towards their Christmas destination, a small volcanic outpost of Brazil that had been romanticised in several nineteenth-century seafaring novels as a place of shipwrecks and buried treasure. But as Stan and Mary took a night-time stroll on the deck of the collier after dinner, they saw the *Wolf* suddenly shift course due north and send urgent flashlight signals across the darkened water, and the *Igotz Mendi* diverted away from Trinidade Island at full speed. Within an hour, the two ships had traced a broad 180-degree turn and were sailing south.

What had precipitated the sudden shift was a message in Portuguese that the *Wolf*'s wireless operators had picked up shortly after 8 pm, then translated into German and rushed in to Karl Nerger on the bridge. It was an uncoded transmission sent from Vice-Admiral Adelino Martins, in the Brazilian Navy's Rio de Janeiro headquarters, announcing his promotion to chief of staff of naval operations. Among the listed recipients was '*Commandante militar Ilha Trinidad*'. Nerger was less than fifty miles from Trinidade Island when the message came through, alerting him to the fact that Brazil – which had declared war on Germany some seven weeks earlier – had a naval command post, and presumably warships, now stationed on the island. It was a miracle of good fortune, even by the German captain's standards, which enabled him to change course only hours before sailing straight into the arms of the enemy.

The Camerons went to bed mystified by the sudden change of course; they awoke the next morning to learn that their Christmas would now be spent aboard the bug-infested collier on the open sea. A bitter mood descended on the prisoners as they ate their bread and forced down their coffee that morning in the saloon. For the next four days, the ships sailed south, with the weather turning against them, as a strong easterly wind and a massive swell caused the *Igotz Mendi* to lurch like a drunk. On 23 December, they came to rest 500 miles south-east of Trinidade Island, in the middle of the South Atlantic.

The winds had eased but the Germans now had to contend with the *Igotz Mendi*'s most perverse quirk: the collier seemed to roll more violently in a light swell than she did in heavy seas. Both ships desperately needed supplies from each other, for Leutnant Rose was running low on fresh food and water, while the *Wolf* had exhausted most of her coal from the *Igotz Mendi*; the raider's stokers reported that it burned seventy per cent faster than the fuel they had brought from Germany, and Karl Nerger was determined to save his reserves of German coal for the North Sea to avoid excessive smoke. But when the two ships drew alongside each other, the collier rolled so heavily that they crashed together with sickening force, staving in bulwarks and deck rails, and making transfer of coal and supplies impossible.

On 25 December, Nerger suspended the coaling attempts, and the war itself was briefly adjourned so that everyone aboard the two ships could observe a pan-national Christmas celebration on the open seas. On the *Wolf*, crewmen constructed Christmas trees out of brooms and ropes, draped the ship's gangways and iron walls with hand-painted banners and hung festive flags from masts. Red lanterns and paper chains, taken from the *Hitachi Maru*'s cargo holds, bedecked the raider's black superstructure. The band assembled on the poop deck and struck up a seasonal repertoire, which was followed by communal hymns sung by the crew and prisoners. In the mess, a Christmas dinner for nearly seven hundred and eighty people was prepared: three pigs and a cow from the *Igotz Mendi* had been slaughtered, and Nerger authorised the last of the frozen meat to be thawed; a precious supply of fresh potatoes taken from the *Maréchal Davout* supplemented the usual reconstituted dehydrated vegetables, and barrels of wine from the French barque were also tapped. It was the German crew's second Christmas aboard the raider, and Fritz Witschetzky claimed that the carols 'never sounded merrier or more blissful'.

The gunnery officer's memory was not corroborated by others. 'Our thoughts were of home,' Albert Wieduwilt wrote in his diary. 'There were tears in some eyes, because none of us knew with certainty what would happen to us.' Aboard the *Igotz Mendi*, Courtenay Dickinson sensed that some of the women were also tearful. To Frederick Trayes, it was 'a dismal farce', and Stan Cameron confessed that he had the blues for the entire day. When Leutnant Karl Rose appeared in the saloon to cheerfully wish everyone a happy Christmas and many happy returns, the crueller meaning of that last phrase hung in the air. Mary Cameron fumed afterwards that she felt like stabbing Rose with a hatpin. Plagued by memories of far happier gatherings, and by the knowledge that their loved ones would be grieving for them, few of the prisoners were able to lift their spirits.

The only bright moment was provided by Juanita Cameron, who had expressed unwavering faith to her parents that Father Christmas would not forget her despite their circumstances. Confirming her conviction, the *Wolfchen*'s pilot, Paul Fabeck, appeared suddenly on the *Igotz Mendi* on Christmas morning, having come across from the *Wolf* in a launch carrying gift-wrapped boxes. The boxes contained toys that Fabeck had taken from the *Hitachi Maru*'s extensive cargo, and as he presented them to the Camerons' daughter, the pilot cheerfully concocted a story about having flown up in the *Wolfchen* early that morning and encountered Santa Claus making one of his final cross-Atlantic sleigh journeys. Juanita, the only person aboard the *Igotz Mendi* who had been pleased to see the *Wolf* again, responded with a perfectly pronounced '*Danke schön*'.

The festivities, such as they were, did not last long. On Boxing Day, Nerger ordered the two ships lashed together despite the swell, for he desperately needed coal to continue the homeward voyage. Heavy rope fenders were slung between the ships, but the *Igotz Mendi* slammed into the *Wolf* with such violence that crewmen slinging coal baskets from one ship to another were knocked off their feet. Coaling began at 5 pm and continued through the night under spotlights, but the *Wolf* sat so high on the ocean that the smaller Spanish ship, weighed down by her cargo, continually collided with the underside of the raider's hull, creating a cacophony of iron grinding against iron that made sleep impossible.

Dawn broke to reveal that the entire starboard side of the *Igotz Mendi*'s bridge was misshapen and twisted, while several of the *Wolf*'s hull plates were staved in at the waterline and the sea was pouring into the raider's port bunker at a rate of ten tons an hour. Nerger ordered his ship to be reweighted to starboard so that the crew could repair the plates with iron wedges and rivets. But when the easterly winds increased on the afternoon of 27 December, it became impossible to tie the ships together, and coal transfers were stopped. It had taken nearly thirty-six hours to move 545 tons of coal – not enough to get the raider back to Germany.

For two days, the ships lay alongside each other, waiting for the weather to ease. Crewmen cleaned out the boilers, patched leaks in the hull, pumped water from the *Wolf*'s holds and repaired some of the damage to the *Igotz Mendi*'s bridge. Finally, Nerger could wait no longer, and at dusk on 30 December he ordered the ships to sail north in search of calmer weather. The two battered freighters moved off at a torturously slow speed of seven knots, for only two boilers were operating on the *Wolf*. Reviewing his engineer's report, Nerger discovered that his coal consumption had more than doubled to thirty-two tons a day. The coal just loaded would last him little more than a fortnight.

The two ships were on an empty sea 700 miles off north-west Africa when the year drew to a close. Aboard the *Igotz Mendi*, a rowdy celebration continued through the night, and at 2 am Stan Cameron was woken by a drunken German sailor thrusting a bottle of wine through his cabin porthole. But on the *Wolf*, a more subdued mood prevailed. Roy Alexander, who had been making regular visits to Dr Hauswaldt's surgery suffering appendicitis, had finally been granted a permanent bed in the hospital just before Christmas, and he was surprised by the quiet that prevailed amidships on New Year's Eve.

Alexander suspected that he knew why the celebrations were so muted, for one of the German crewmen in a neighbouring bed was being treated for beriberi. Even more disturbing signs had appeared among the prisoners just before he had left the Hell Hole for the last time. The men who had been down there longest – those from the *Turritella*, the *Jumna* and the *Wordsworth* – were looking listless and sallow. Some complained of rheumatic pains and loose teeth. 'Others were covered with skin eruptions: purple, red and even green spots appearing over their bodies,' recalled Alexander. 'This diseased flesh would be maddeningly irritating; and when the sufferers scratched their puffy sores the irritated areas broke into huge ulcers.'

The first cases of scurvy had appeared just as 1918 began.

10

END RUN

In the first weeks of 1918, two arresting pieces of information crossed the desk of Rear-Admiral William Lowther Grant, commander of the Royal Navy's China Station in Singapore. The first was a report from an employee of the Burns Philp shipping company who had travelled to northern New Guinea in search of the missing steamship *Matunga* and learned from local missionaries and natives that two ships had been seen in the area some months earlier, one of them a German freighter resembling the raider *Moewe*, the other a steamer that was rumoured to have been sunk. The second, and far more startling, news came in a letter from the British consul-general in Batavia, capital of the Dutch East Indies; it contained two scraps of paper that had been found inside a glass jar bobbing on the Celebes Sea.

When Rear-Admiral Grant opened the scraps of paper, he found a crude pencil illustration of an armed merchant ship, with hidden guns and torpedo tubes marked in black pen. Accompanying it was a note, scrawled in the handwriting of Captain Tom Meadows:

> Prisoners on board German raider. Will finder please notify British authorities that German raider passed Celebes this day

> 29th August on her way we presume to mine Singapore, Pedra Blanca, having previously mined Cape Town, Bombay, Colombo, North Cape, New Zealand, Cook Strait, Gabo Island. Crews of following vessels are on board: *Turritella*, *Jumna*, *Wordsworth*, *Dee*, *Wairuna*, *Winslow*, *Beluga*, *Encore*, *Matunga*. She has on board 110 mines, to mine we think, Rangoon, Calcutta. She was formerly *Wachenfels* [*sic*] of German service.

The note had travelled a long and circuitous route to reach the hands of Rear-Admiral Grant in Singapore. After Tom Meadows had risked his life to fling it in a sealed jar over the *Wolf*'s deck rail, it had floated on the tides of the East Indies straits for three months, bobbing 500 miles eastwards until it passed Java, then 700 miles north between Celebes and Borneo towards the open seas leading to the Philippines. On 9 December, it had been picked up by two fishermen paddling their canoe near Toli Toli, a coastal village in the mountainous and remote northern arm of Celebes. Unable to decipher the note's contents, they had passed it to a local missionary, who had passed it to a local government official, who had put it on a boat to Batavia, more than a thousand miles away. There, the Dutch authorities had handed the note to the British consul-general, who read it and – displaying commendable lack of panic – mailed it to Rear-Admiral Grant.

It was not until 15 January, therefore, that the contents of the note finally reached London in an urgent wireless message from Singapore. To the Admiralty's intelligence analysts, it offered an answer to the riddle of the *Wolf*'s movements. The course of the raider's epic and unlikely voyage could now be plotted: she had apparently traversed three major oceans in a little over twelve months and sunk at least twenty-three ships through minelaying and raiding. The mysterious minefields and ship disappearances in the South Pacific were explained, if not the raider's periodic disappearances.

That the *Wolf* was still at large became clear only a few days later, when the Japanese Navy wired confirmation from Colombo that the *Hitachi Maru* had been captured by a German raider. The warships *Suma* and *Hatsuyuki*, and the converted liner *Chikuzen Maru* and its seaplanes, had searched the waters off Suvadiva Atoll and retrieved sections of the missing ship's wooden toilet doors, embedded with metal shards that appeared to be shell fragments. Local natives had provided detailed descriptions of sailors repairing a damaged steamship in the lagoon. The logical conclusion was that the *Hitachi Maru* had been attacked and captured, and the missing *Igotz Mendi* had fallen victim to the raider weeks later.

The news placed the Admiralty in a quandary: if either the *Igotz Mendi* or the *Hitachi Maru* had been converted into raiders, and if the *Wolf* was still carrying mines, all ports on the Indian Ocean were potentially vulnerable. Further clouding the picture, ships arriving at Aden and Colombo had recently sighted unidentified steamers near those ports that could be any one of the three missing ships. After notifying its Indian Ocean stations to be vigilant for raiders and minefields, and alerting Rangoon that the *Wolf* might be heading its way to lay mines off the port, the Admiralty wired Australia and New Zealand with details of Tom Meadows's note.

To navy officials in Melbourne and Wellington, the news was bittersweet. Heartening as it was to learn that the *Matunga* and *Wairuna* had not been sunk by seaquakes, capsized by submerged rocks or sabotaged by immigrants, the scenario detailed by the Meadows note presented yet another acute embarrassment. New Zealand's navy chief, Captain Percival Hall-Thompson, had only two months earlier confidently stated that sweeping New Zealand waters for mines seemed unnecessary; now he was forced to issue a new warning to merchant ships that minefields might have been laid off North Cape and somewhere in the Cook Strait approaches to Wellington. Having admitted his own error, however, Hall-Thompson was still helpless to take action, for after three months of searching he had been unable to find any commercial fishing trawlers in New Zealand suitable for conversion to minesweeping. Putting the best possible light on the situation, he reassured shipping officials that danger from the mines was 'slight' – a judgement that sadly proved far from accurate.

In Australia, the government faced a different embarrassment, for only two weeks earlier it had begun informing relatives of those aboard the *Matunga* that their loved ones were dead. On 31 December, Joseph Cook had received a plaintive handwritten letter from Elizabeth Pearce, the grief-stricken mother of Private Rupert Pearce, again pleading for information about the fate of her only remaining son and his shipmates. 'I have a right to know if Rupert is alive or dead after all these weary months of waiting,' Mrs Pearce wrote, adding that she would be 'grateful to you all the days of my life' for any information. Cook had passed the letter to his naval secretary, George Macandie, who wrote to Mrs Pearce on 2 January and informed her that 'the Minister, whilst sympathising deeply with you in the loss of your brave sons on active service, does not think it would be fair to you to hold out any hope of those on board being prisoners of war. There is no information which is being kept back from those concerned and it is very much regretted that there is no clue whatever as to the ship's disappearance.'

Given that the government had known for five months of the compelling evidence pointing to the *Matunga*'s capture by a raider, it is difficult to fathom how Macandie came to write such a letter. But by January, Elizabeth Pearce was far from the only grieving relative demanding answers about the fate of the ship. When the *Matunga* had disappeared, her owner, Burns Philp Company, had cut off payment of wages to the missing crew's families, leaving some of their wives and children destitute. They were now demanding payment from the Commonwealth, arguing that their husbands – whom they believed to be dead – had been helping the war effort by transporting troops and supplies to New Guinea. Laura McBride, whose husband, William, was first officer of the *Matunga*, spent six months writing imploring letters to politicians in New Zealand and Australia, until she finally became so desperate that she borrowed money to catch a boat from her home in New Zealand to Australia to put her case directly to the Hughes government.

'The vessel was doing war work and should have been insured against all risks,' she told Australian newspapers after her arrival. 'I believe that the Navy Department will get the insurance money, and so lose nothing, but what of all those like myself who have lost everything?' With four children and no income, she described herself as 'right up against it'. Under pressure from the Australian Government, Burns Philp agreed to help Mrs McBride – they sent her a cheque for £34 and nine shillings, the equivalent of a month and a half of her husband's wage.

The appearance of Meadows's note presented a quandary to navy officials, torn as they were between their fixation with secrecy and their obligation to inform relatives of the missing men. Four weeks after he had informed Mrs Pearce to give up all hope of her son, Naval Secretary Macandie dispatched a hasty letter to her admitting that Rupert might well be alive aboard a German raider. But, Macandie emphasised, the information was strictly secret and on no account to be shared with the press, 'as we do not want the Germans to find out we know anything about their movements or doings'. At the same time, Macandie wrote to Burns Philp and the Union Steamship Company, authorising them to inform relatives of those aboard the *Matunga* and *Wairuna* that it appeared the ships had been captured by a raider. The companies were similarly admonished to inform no one else.

The affair was an embarrassment that exposed both the inadequacy of the naval defences in Australia and New Zealand and the hollowness of the government scare campaign about sabotage. Determined to suppress the matter, the Admiralty instructed its naval officials not to inform the press about the Meadows note. But the Australian deputy censor bungled the instruction by sending a letter to the nation's newspaper editors admitting that the *Wairuna* and *Matunga* were now believed to have been captured by a German raider, yet strictly forbidding them from publishing the news. The result, predictably, was uproar within the nation's newspaper offices, which had spent the past several months dutifully publishing the Australian Government's false stories about saboteurs, infernal devices and undersea earthquakes. The censor's letter appeared to confirm what had long been rumoured – that a German raider had captured ships near Australia and planted the minefields that had claimed the *Cumberland* and the *Port Kembla*. Editors demanded the right to publish this news, and within a fortnight the censor's office was forced to admit to the Hughes government that the truth was 'practically public all over Australia'.

Furious, Naval Secretary Macandie insisted that the suppression be maintained and refused to countenance the idea of asking the Admiralty to relax its censorship strictures. Macandie couldn't have known that, in just a few short weeks, all these efforts at suppressing the truth would be rendered redundant by a startling news dispatch from Europe.

* *

Karl Nerger also received unwelcome news in the first days of the New Year, for as the *Wolf* and *Igotz Mendi* sailed in tandem 970 miles north-east of Rio de Janeiro, the German captain learned beyond doubt that the British Navy knew about his ship and its mission. Shortly after breakfast on 4 January, the *Wolf*'s lookout spotted the sails of a large four-masted barque on the eastern horizon, and Nerger hurriedly hoisted the Union Jack on his mainmast and signalled the *Igotz Mendi* to fall back out of sight. Through his binoculars, Nerger saw the barque's white hull riding high above the waterline, showing the name clearly on her side, *Storebror*, and the neutrality badges of Norway. When the two ships passed, the barque's captain signalled that he was on his way from Mozambique to Uruguay and Nerger wished him a good voyage.

When the German captain consulted his Lloyd's register, however, he discovered that the ship was English-built and had been owned by the County Shipping Company of Liverpool until 1915. It was a flimsy pretext on which to pursue a neutral ship sailing without cargo, but Nerger turned the *Wolf* around and followed the *Storebror* towards Uruguay. The raider was running on only two boilers and could barely muster a top speed of seven knots, but after nearly eight hours Nerger ran the barque down, and – once his prize crew were aboard her – found the justification he needed for claiming her as a prize. The ship's papers showed that her new Norwegian owner was a commercial affiliate of a major British shipping company, and the *Storebror* had spent the past several years shipping war supplies between Allied ports. Nerger judged that the barque's neutral status was a sham and ordered the crew – twenty-four Norwegians and one Englishman – sent down to the prison hold. The bombing and sinking of this thirty-four-year-old windjammer was by now such a routine event that Nerger did not even bother recording it in his log.

The Norwegian crew told Nerger that minesweepers were still operating off Cape Agulhas and that the *City of Exeter* had struck his minefield off Bombay in June. (Those mines had actually claimed a more recent victim, for the 5580-ton British freighter *Croxteth Hall* had sunk off Bombay only seven weeks earlier, with the loss of nine crewmen, but that story had gone unreported.) Perusing old newspapers found on the *Storebror*, Nerger was amused to see that the Australian Government was claiming the *Port Kembla* had been sabotaged. More sobering, however, was a small news item from August revealing that the British Government had acknowledged in parliament that the *Mongolia*'s destruction off Bombay had been caused by 'a minefield laid by the German raider *Wolf*. It was the first time that Nerger had seen his ship's name in an enemy press report – stark confirmation that despite the phoney reports of 'internal explosions', the *Wolf* was well known to the Allied navies hunting her.

Lord Curzon's claim in October that the *Wolf* was the last German warship still at large had been only slightly hyperbolic, for although Admiral Scheer's destroyers occasionally ventured out to attack Allied shipping convoys in the North Sea, the *Wolf* was certainly the last of the Kaiser's surface warships still loose outside the British blockade. The destruction of the *Storebror* – Nerger's only deviation from the strict rules of commerce war – betrayed his awareness of the dangers ahead. Neutral or not, the *Storebror* had been heading towards an enemy South American port, and her captain's sighting of a strangely battered-looking black freighter flying the Union Jack would very probably have been passed on to London. Nerger was within a few weeks of reaching Germany and absolutely determined that the British Navy learn nothing of his course.

The *Wolf* and the *Igotz Mendi* were now in the humid climes just below the equator; ahead of them lay the world's busiest shipping lanes and the frigid North Atlantic winter. Since passing the Cape six weeks earlier, the crew had been revelling in the balmy weather, staying up on deck to carve shark bones into assorted ornaments or simply watch pods of whales, lone albatrosses and schools of flying fish escorting them north. But the fine weather could not mask an underlying mood of uncertainty; the proximity of Germany may have washed away any vestige of mutinous talk, but every man aboard was weighing up the odds of surviving the homeward leg. In the hospital, Roy Alexander sensed the feeling of subdued expectation shared by every crew member he spoke to. It had become a ritual among some of the Germans to walk to the bow of the ship and make sure the lucky shark spine was still in place.

Alexander himself, after spending so much time in the hospital talking only to the crew, had lost any sense of the Germans as a hated enemy. 'I seemed to have become almost German,' he confessed. 'Not such a bad fate; it would have been impossible to have found a finer crowd of men to live among than the crew of the *Wolf*.' In the long conversations with crewmen in hospital,

Alexander had come to see them as seamen no different from himself, forced by their political leaders to participate in a 'senseless war of extermination'. He could not help admiring their skill and the courage of their captain – even the sinking of the neutral *Storebror* was 'quite right' in his estimation, for how else was Nerger to get his ship back to Germany?

Alexander was far from the only prisoner to bond with his captors, for a strange inversion had slowly taken place in the prison holds: while putative allies such as the Japanese and British could now barely stand one another, friendships had formed with the once-feared Germans. Robert Trudgett, captain of the *Winslow*, discovered that one of the German officers, Leutnant Adolf Wulff, had spent years visiting San Francisco while working as a merchant seaman on the Kosmos line, and in their conversations Wulff revealed that he had a greater knowledge of Trudgett's home town than the American himself. Other prisoners were surprised to learn that Fritz Witschetzky knew some of their friends in Sydney, and Eric Minns, the diminutive fourteen-year-old cabin boy from the *Matunga*, was startled when a German crewman approached him one day and asked, 'Are the trams still running in George Street, mate?' Warily, the youngster struck up a conversation and discovered that the German had not only lived in Sydney before the war but had worked in a business run by Minns's family.

Prisoners now had far more latitude to move around the ship; several of them, including the American steward from the *John H. Kirby* and the cooks from the *Hitachi Maru*, worked in the *Wolf*'s kitchens preparing meals alongside the Germans. Eric Minns and Keith Harris, his teenage sidekick from the *Matunga*, managed to creep past the guards posted near a storeroom one afternoon and pilfer an armful each of winter clothes – a theft carried off with such ease that Minns was convinced that the Germans simply turned a blind eye.

Relations between prisoners and crew had warmed further when Nerger replaced the despised young prison officer Arthur von Auerswald with Leutnant Karl Dietrich, who had previously been in charge of minelaying. Dietrich, a dark-haired and moustachioed officer with an easy manner, was ten years older than Auerswald and shared none of his callow hatred of the British. He began visiting the prison holds every evening to talk at length to the men crowded below, fostering a mutual respect that was remarkable, considering that Dietrich's mines had killed dozens of merchant seamen and civilians. 'We all liked "Mines", as we called him,' recalled Alec Donaldson. 'No complaint was too trivial for his attention, and our comfort was well looked after when he took charge.'

Dietrich authorised the removal of the main hatches over the prison holds when the air became bad and provided an extra ration of water in the evening. He also permitted the men to write letters to their loved ones, which he promised would be transferred to the *Igotz Mendi* at the next available opportunity. It was a gesture that suggested the Germans were still planning to send the Spanish ship home, rather than to Germany, although many of the men struggled to write a message that did not have some ominous tone of finality. Robert Trudgett wrote one simple sentence to his wife in San Francisco: 'I am well and on the *Wolf*: take care of yourself and whatever I may have at home.'

The prisoners and crew were united, too, by their fear of a death far more terrifying than drowning. Albert Wieduwilt had noticed among his fellow crewmen in the engine room that 'tooth diseases' were now common after weeks of canned crab, rehydrated vegetables and rice. Dr Hauswaldt had noticed the first signs of scurvy among the prisoners just before Christmas, and had been attempting to contain the illness by distributing lime juice and diluted acetic acid to everyone aboard, along with a daily ration of wine from the *Maréchal Davout*. But Dr Hauswaldt's supplies of anti-scorbutics were now running perilously low, and he was forced to reserve what little remained for the crew. More than twenty men in the Hell Hole began reporting gum disease and extreme lethargy, and one man – a British stoker in his fifties who had been aboard since February – deteriorated so drastically that he was taken to the hospital.

Only Roy Alexander, lying in a hospital cot with appendicitis, witnessed the horrifying advanced stages of the man's illness. 'His flesh had gone puffy and rotten; his hair had fallen out; his gums had swollen to a mass of bluish fungus; and the poor wretch stank – stank like a corpse,' Alexander recalled. 'Most of the time he lay in a stupor, but sometimes he sat up in his bunk singing. He liked to pull out his loose teeth, play with them, throw them on the decking and sing snatches of foc'sle songs.' Neither Dr Hauswaldt's medical journal nor Karl Nerger's log record any case of death by scurvy, so this helpless sailor's illness may well have been contained in its chronic phase. The sight so terrified Alexander that he begged the German doctor to ensure that he did not come down with the disease, and Hauswaldt began administering an anti-scorbutic to the Australian seaman.

Unable to accommodate all the scurvy cases in his ward, Dr Hauswaldt organised a makeshift infirmary in the number-three prison hold. A group of more than twenty prisoners from one corner of the hold were moved into the Hell Hole, and the area was partitioned off with canvas screens and fitted out with mattresses for the sickest of the sufferers. Two Australian medical staff from the *Matunga*, Sergeant Alcon Webb and Corporal James O'Grady, were assigned to care for the sick under Dr Hauswaldt's supervision – a task that would require heroic efforts from both men.

Theodor Plivier, too, had started showing symptoms: 'At first it was only little pockets around my teeth. Other men's teeth were falling out and their flesh was turning flabby. And a few Portuguese from the prisoners' deck lay in the sickbay with swollen legs. When the doctor pressed his finger against their thighs, he poked holes.'

According to Plivier, Dr Hauswaldt donned his full-dress uniform to deliver an ultimatum to Nerger in his cabin, warning him that thirty of the crew were unable to stand on their feet and many faced death unless the voyage ended soon. Nerger's log certainly reflects his realisation that he had to accelerate his homeward voyage. His stores of frozen meat were almost gone, there was no fresh fruit and his water condensers were breaking down. One crew member had already been hospitalised with acute beriberi.

But Nerger needed coal – at least 500 tons – to get back to Germany. On 10 January, the wind dropped and he ordered the *Wolf* and the *Igotz Mendi* to be lashed together on the open sea ninety miles below the equator. Despite the barely perceptible swell, the *Igotz Mendi* again rolled alarmingly, slamming herself into the *Wolf*'s rope buffers. Alfred Clarke went to the rail to say hello to his former shipmates aboard the collier but found that the conversation could only be conducted in snatches as they flashed past each other on the *Igotz Mendi*'s vertiginous upward and downward swings. The *Wolf* was still leaking from the dented plates and bent ribs that had opened up in her hull during the last coaling, and Stan Cameron was alarmed to see Nerger attempt another trans-shipment on the open seas, even in apparently calm weather. The crew worked so frantically that coal was simply winched over and capsized from baskets directly onto the *Wolf*'s deck, spreading in glittering black mounds that partially buried the aft guns.

The coaling continued all night and into the next morning, when the wind picked up and the swell began to build, smashing the *Igotz Mendi* repeatedly into the *Wolf*'s hull. Cracks reopened in the raider's iron plates at the waterline and the ocean began pouring into her bunkers at a rate of twenty tons an hour. The ship's already strained bilge pumps could barely cope with the inflow and anxious crewmen began leaning over the side, watching the escalating damage. On the bridge, Nerger stubbornly ordered the coaling to continue until, at 4.30 pm, he was told that 521 tons had been transferred and the two ships were hastily decoupled. Roy Alexander was among the many who were aghast at the damage he saw as they pulled away from one another.

'*Igotz Mendi*'s plates had been scraped bare of paint right along the hull,' he recalled. 'Boats and davits had been further damaged;

rails were twisted or had disappeared; and her smashed-in bridge now appeared to have a list to starboard. The *Wolf* was in worse shape. The leaks caused by the earlier coaling had opened up and she was now making forty tons an hour; like the collier, her badly dented hull showed bare patches of steel where the paint had gone.'

As the two ships separated, Alexander saw the women aboard the *Igotz Mendi* standing at the collier's twisted deck rails, waving tearfully. It occurred to him that they were crying because they believed everyone aboard the *Wolf* was doomed.

* *

The storms that swept the North Atlantic in the winter of early 1918 were among the worst even veteran seamen could remember. Hurricane-force winds smashed towns along the eastern coastline of the United States, flattening houses and leaving scores of people homeless. A record ten inches of snow fell on Washington DC in one day and eastern Canada was paralysed by one of the worst blizzards on record. Freighter convoys from the United States were so badly hit that one ship, the *Hatteras*, wrecked her steering system on two successive attempted crossings and was forced back to Boston until a third crossing finally succeeded.

The *Wolf* and the *Igotz Mendi*, already battered and leaking, inched their way north towards the storm fronts in the last two weeks of January, sailing at less than eight knots as the easterly winds picked up, sweeping away the balmy warmth of the equator. The air cooled and the sun disappeared behind mountainous formations of black cloud, which darkened the sea to a leaden grey and brought gusting rain. Nerger had ordered the *Wolf* repainted from hull to bridge immediately after the last coaling, but even this new coating of black could not hide her dents and warps, or the crusted patches of corrosion scabbed to her hull.

On 18 January, the *Wolf*'s wireless operators picked up the Telefunken transmission tower at Nauen for the first time in months, bringing news that U-boats had now extended their unrestricted warfare zone but unhappily giving no details of the new parameters. Nerger once again had the acute feeling of being a ghost in the machinery of war; the *Admiralstab*, it seemed, was no longer bothering to get helpful information to him.

'It would have been extremely favourable,' he noted sourly in his log, '. . . if the opportunity had been used by Nauen to indicate the total borders of the restricted areas, particularly in consideration of *Wolf*.'

Nerger's primary aim now was to reach the North Sea before the full moon of late February, and when a Norwegian barque passed him under full sail on 22 January, heading to the West Indies, he let it pass. The following day, the raider arrived at a prearranged rendezvous point nearly two thousand miles due west of Morocco. The Atlantic now rolled with a mountainous swell, and while waiting for the collier to appear, Nerger picked up an SOS signal from a nearby freighter – a portent of the wild storm that was bearing down on them. For a while, he feared that the *Igotz Mendi* had been lost, but in the early afternoon she finally appeared, lurching and labouring across the face of the waves.

The sight of the *Wolf* never failed to make Stan Cameron's heart sink. 'It seemed that she could appear at will,' he remarked, 'like some gigantic evil spirit.' The morale of the *Igotz Mendi* prisoners had never really recovered from the aborted Christmas landing at Trinidade Island, which clouded all their hopes of reaching Spain and freedom. Cameron felt certain that Nerger now needed the *Igotz Mendi* to follow him all the way to Germany, for the *Wolf* was damaged and had only just enough coal to make the distance. Some of the prisoners had nursed a slender hope of being landed in Mexico or Guyana, two of the last neutral countries on the western Atlantic, but that prospect had died once the ships had continued north past the equator.

There was a bitter feeling that Leutnant Karl Rose's promises were merely elaborate deceptions piled one on the other. Over dinner one night, Rose had advised Stan to look north-east, in the direction of Spain, when he was gazing across the Atlantic;

to Frederick Trayes, he had suggested that the prisoners would be landed on the island of Las Palmas, off Morocco. Later still, he aired a plan to drop them on the coast of Norway, just before the ships turned into the Skagerrak channel to Germany.

If Karl Nerger ever seriously entertained any of these ideas, he made no mention of them in his log, and Fritz Witschetzky believed it was always his captain's intention to take both ships back to Germany. Rose's lies may well have been contrived to placate his prisoners and maintain the cooperation of the Spanish crew, for within hours of meeting the *Wolf* on 23 January, he certainly knew their true destination. When he took a launch across to the raider, he found Nerger waiting for him with new supplies: there were stores of whisky for the winter crossing ahead and rolls of heavy cloth for the prisoners to make additional blankets and clothing. Far more importantly, Nerger also handed over several charts of the North Sea and the key to the official Germany navy codes, so that Rose could decipher wireless messages from the Nauen transmitter as he approached Germany. When the two ships parted on the drizzly and overcast morning of 24 January, they were heading due north towards Iceland.

Only hours after setting sail, the desultory mood aboard the *Igotz Mendi* was shattered. Stan Cameron was reading a disintegrating copy of a South African newspaper when Mary appeared in their cabin doorway and said, 'Stan, there's a cruiser with four funnels just ahead of us.' Assuming she was joking, Cameron kept reading and replied, 'All right, Mamie, tell them to reserve an outside room for me.' Then he took one look at his wife's ashen face and jumped up to grab his binoculars, just as Frederick Trayes appeared in the door and said, 'My God, captain, a cruiser at last.'

In the rain haze outside, Cameron peered through his glasses and made out the lines of what appeared to be a massive four-masted warship approaching from the distance in the north-east. Gradually, it emerged from the mist to reveal itself as two ships sailing in tandem. As they drew closer, Cameron saw with a mixture of elation and alarm that they appeared to be troop transports, each easily of 12,000–15,000 tons, evidently sailing back to the east coast of the United States from Britain, and each heavily armed with large deck guns.

Around him, he could hear the *Igotz Mendi*'s crewmen shouting and running along the gangways, and within a minute two armed Germans had bundled him and his family back into the galley and slammed the door shut. Through the porthole, Cameron saw the two ships approaching to within three-quarters of a mile and heard panicked shouting among the German crew.

Like all the prisoners, Cameron had been praying for this moment for months; now that it had arrived, he was filled with a dread uncertainty, for it had never been clear what the Germans would do in a confrontation with an Allied warship. The *Igotz Mendi* was unarmed, but there were bombs on board, and the Germans might well order everyone into the lifeboats so they could scuttle the ship rather than allow her to fall into enemy hands. Did the Germans care enough about this banged-up collier to imperil everyone's lives and risk a diplomatic incident with neutral Spain? The two auxiliary cruisers, which he now recognised clearly as American ships, were carving their way south-west across the Atlantic and were about to cross the *Igotz Mendi*'s bow and pass on the port side.

The Trayes, the Bensons and the Floods were clustering in the cramped corridor outside their cabins, some already clutching valuables in anticipation of being rescued. Frederick Trayes recalled a feeling of elation coursing through the group as they crammed against the available porthole to get a view. The ships were passing so close that the camouflage pattern along the hull of the nearest was clearly visible through the mist.

And then, in an awful repetition of the *Psyche* encounter in the Java Sea, the two cruisers appeared off the *Igotz Mendi*'s port side, steamed diagonally past at a distance of less than a mile and simply kept going, disappearing into the squall without raising a flag in acknowledgement.

* *

At dinner that evening, Karl Rose was exultant at his lucky escape – a mood that proved short-lived when he discovered, later that night, that the timer bombs stored under the bridge had disappeared during the panic of the encounter. Furious, Rose ordered all prisoners on deck the next morning while cabins were searched and the Spanish crew and neutrals were interrogated.

Stan Cameron, whose relationship with the German commander had become increasingly strained, sensed that he was the chief suspect, for some of the other prisoners were avoiding him. Finding a vantage point outside the galley room where Leutnant Rose was questioning the crew, Cameron overheard the Spanish first officer, Gervasio Susasta, dramatically confess to throwing the bombs overboard. It appeared that Susasta's enthusiasm for all things German had been a sham after all, for Cameron claims to have overheard him defiantly declare, 'It was not for me, Captain Rose, but for the women and little children. I am not afraid of you. You can shoot me if you want to, but you can't drown the little children.'

How Cameron deciphered this conversation is not recorded, and the official German records of the voyage suggest that Karl Rose discovered Susasta was the culprit not because he confessed but because Susasta told Cecil Strangman what he had done. The Spaniard's heroism is not in doubt, however, for he risked his life to protect those aboard his ship, and the prisoners regarded him as a hero.

Karl Rose was baffled by Susasta's actions, wondering whether he had temporarily lost his mind. The German commander could do little in the immediate term but order the first officer and his captain confined to their cabins under armed guard, vowing that Susasta would be tried and punished by a court in Germany. Then other priorities quickly took over, for a vicious storm now bore down on the *Igotz Mendi* from the west.

The winds began building only a few hours after the American troop transports disappeared from view, and the temperature plummeted. Rain whipped across the deck and bridge, seeping through cracks that had opened up in the damaged superstructure, so that water trickled over beds and pooled on floors. Cabin walls sweated moisture, leaving clothes limp with damp. Courtenay Dickinson took to plugging the leaks above his bed with dough from the kitchen; the Camerons began sleeping fully clothed. The cabins were unheated and many of the prisoners spent the days huddled in the cramped saloon, gripping the table as the ship lurched across a swell that rose to thirty feet. The gale reached its peak on 27 January – the Kaiser's birthday, many dourly noted – when the shrieking of the wind and the din of the ocean pounding the ship made conversation all but impossible. Each wave was a looming wall of water that the *Igotz Mendi* struggled to climb, sliding across its face and threatening to turn broadside and capsize before she finally crested, rolling over the peak with such a violent lurch that her propeller flipped clear of the sea. Then the ship plunged down into the next trough and was enveloped in darkness. Waves detonated on the deck, sweeping away rigging and smashing down wireless aerials.

'The wind was raging for hours at a hurricane force between eleven and twelve,' recalled Frederick Trayes, 'the seas were between thirty and forty feet high, and it seemed impossible that the ship could live in such a sea. It seemed that she must inevitably founder.' Courtenay Dickinson said that he had not seen the like of it before or since, and Mary Cameron reached such a point of desperation that she no longer cared for her own survival. 'We were so cold and hungry,' she later admitted, 'that we prayed for death.'

When the storm briefly subsided, it was merely the prelude to an intense hailstorm that drilled against the collier's iron walls like shrapnel, then gave way to a blinding snowstorm. Stan Cameron surmised from the intense cold that they were now entering the frigid waters of the North Atlantic, bearing due north towards Greenland so as to avoid the U-boats and Allied warships that roamed the ocean near Britain and Ireland to their east. It was a course that Cameron had feared, for it suggested that Rose and Nerger were proposing to return to Germany the way they had left – in a 2000-mile arc up through the Denmark Strait between Greenland and Iceland, then across the lower rim of the Arctic Ocean and down through the Norwegian Sea until they found their way into the Skagerrak channel. How Rose proposed to get his unstable and leaking collier through the midwinter ice floes of those Arctic waters was hard to envisage. But by 4 February, the ship was only 420 miles south-west of Iceland and Cameron began to realise that his family could not survive the passage in their freezing and sodden cabin. The barometer had dropped to 720 millimetres and snow blanketed the ship's deck. At 4.30 pm that day, the *Wolf* appeared out of the grey swirl.

As frightening as the storm had been to those aboard the *Igotz Mendi*, its wrath had descended on the raider with far greater ferocity, for she had passed through its very centre two days earlier. Even a lifelong seaman like Fritz Witschetzky confessed that he had never experienced anything like it: standing on the bridge with the *Wolf* plunging down the face of the waves, the gunnery officer had felt himself lying flat against the rails as if the ship were in a vertical free fall.

The force of the ocean slamming into the ship had again dislodged her cracked hull plates, and the water sluicing heavily back and forth inside the holds added a crazy angle to the ship's pitching. Coal chunks had been swept into the bilge pumps, choking them off, and teams of men were sent down into the freezing black water to unblock the pumps. Stokers were forced to tie themselves to upright supports to maintain their footing as they shovelled coal in the engine room.

Roy Alexander was in the hospital when the crewmen appeared from below, blue with cold, and one look at their grave faces and the water saturating them up to the waist told him how imperilled the ship was. Yet Alexander recalled feeling strangely calm, as if the prospect of drowning were of minor consequence compared to the deaths he had already imagined. It was a sign, he realised later, that he was no longer 'quite right in the head'.

The peak of the storm had lasted ten hours and three men had been hospitalised with pneumonia, but the *Wolf* had survived in time to emerge, like some wraith swathed in ice crystals and snow, at her designated meeting point with the *Igotz Mendi.* Hail and sleet still drilled down so thickly that the ships were periodically invisible to each other even at close range, and a collision seemed imminent. It was not until the next morning that Karl Rose was able to take a launch across to the raider, and report both the encounter with the American transports and Gervasio Susasta's insurrection. Nerger decided immediately to send another sixteen men across, including Leutnant Adolf Wulff and six more neutrals, along with a fresh supply of guns and bombs.

In the midst of the storm, Nerger had picked up the wireless signal of an unidentifiable U-boat and the distress call of a distant torpedoed freighter; it was imperative that both the *Wolf* and the *Igotz Mendi* get out of the submarine zone, and there was time to carry out only the most cursory maintenance before they pressed northwards. Despite the weather, Nerger had resolved to risk pushing the ships through the ice floes of the Denmark Strait to reach Germany. The two ships were barely making eight knots in calm seas, and it would take them at least four days to complete the most perilous arc of the voyage and reach Norway's northern coastline. But wireless reports suggested to Nerger that the weather to the north was relatively good, and he judged it to be a safer option than running through the blockade and the U-boat zone between Iceland and Scotland. Shortly after night descended on 5 February, they set sail.

At first, Nerger's hope of calmer weather seemed vindicated, for the wind and swell eased, but during the following night another snowstorm swept in. Dawn broke the next morning to reveal a dense fog enshrouding the ship; the air temperature outside was approaching two degrees Celsius, colder than the ocean's Gulf Stream currents, so that vapour rising off the sea thickened to a white mist. When the fog cleared, the lookout saw the first glint of white on the horizon ahead of them, and by midday ice floes were scraping against the hulls of the two ships as they sailed north in tandem. That afternoon, another snowstorm swept in and the *Igotz Mendi* disappeared from Nerger's view.

Roy Alexander was in the hospital when the *Wolf* first approached Iceland, but in the first week of February he was told he must return to the Hell Hole with several of the other top-deck prisoners. When Alexander emerged on deck, the frigid air hit him like a shock; it was minus ten degrees Celsius outside and pack ice stretched away to the west as far as the horizon. Icicles hung from the ship's rails and rigging, the guns were enshrouded in a sheath of glittering white frost and the raider was inching its way through narrow inky black gaps between the ice floes where the ocean was still visible. Somewhere off to the right, less than eighty miles distant but out of sight, was the north-west coastline of Iceland.

As Alexander made his way gingerly across the icy deck, he passed a ventilation tube from the Hell Hole, which wafted a foul smell of putrescent flesh into his face. He descended the ladder under the poop to confront a scene that stopped him in his tracks. Emaciated prisoners were slumped before him on makeshift benches wearing bizarre combinations of clothes – ragged pieces of mismatched uniform, disintegrating pants, caps roughly hewn from bath mats and towels. Warm air from the Hell Hole's steam pipes made the usual smells – stale sweat, tobacco smoke, latrine buckets – hang even heavier in the air, and mingling with them now was an unmistakable odour of disease. It was coming from the forward hold that had previously been separated from the rest of the Hell Hole by a bulkhead. Now, the partition had been removed and Alexander peered in to see Sergeant Alcon Webb stooping over the mattresses in his makeshift medical ward, clad in a ragged dressing gown.

'It was a shock to see Webb's condition,' he said. 'He was a man a couple of inches over six feet tall, but all the flesh had now gone from his bones; his eyes were like two burnt-out coals, and he was shaking with malaria.' Despite his ill health, the Australian medic stayed on his feet night and day, administering what few medications and anti-scorbutics he had to his scurvy patients, the worst of whom were now toothless and hairless, lolling on mattresses in incoherent apathy.

Almost as disturbing to Alexander, however, was the 'feverish cheerfulness' of many of his fellow prisoners. The piano lashed into the corner of number-three hold was being used for recitals and musical productions – endless renditions of 'Gunga Din', 'Mother Machree' and 'It's a Long Way to Tipperary'. The concertina owned by one of the Japanese sailors was commandeered for some of these productions; at other times, Edward Noble, the Melbourne businessman from the *Matunga*, played solo recitals of Schubert and Chopin, their graceful melodies floating incongruously above the sound of men swearing, spitting and groaning. In one corner, an English sergeant recited passages from the Old Testament; in another, one of Jack Rugg's young Mauritians sat hugging all his possessions in a sewn-up bag, crooning to himself. Others who had succumbed to the isolation weaved pieces of string together with obsessive repetition. Their madness was ignored by everyone else.

The thud and scrape of pack ice against the ship's hull was now a constant background noise, an unnerving reminder of the ship's leaky and fragile state. The prisoners could feel the raider weaving to avoid collisions with large icebergs, but it was clear from the labouring of the engines that she was struggling to plough her way through. Several times, the engines reversed and the ship pulled back and shifted course, only to grind to a halt against another wall of ice. A gale blew in from the east, and the prisoners could hear banging above them as blocks of ice hurled by the wind crashed across the deck, smashing rigging and ventilation pipes. Teams of German crewmen, sent on deck with grappling hooks, shouted as they slid around trying to dislodge iceblocks and hurl them overboard. On the afternoon of

8 February, the prisoners felt the ship shift course completely and surmised that Nerger might have abandoned his attempt to find a passage north. Several hours later, the guards told them that Captain Seizu Tominaga from the *Hitachi Maru* was missing.

The Japanese captain had been sharing quarters above deck with Lieutenant-Commander Shiraishi, who had woken at 2 am on 8 February to find his cabin-mate missing. Witschetzky was called in and organised a search party to scour the ship, fearing that Tominaga was planning some act of sabotage, but the search proved fruitless. It was not until daylight that Shiraishi found a note in the cabin, which he translated for the Germans.

'The loss of my ship to the enemy, and the misery I brought through my actions upon the crew, the passengers and their families, demands that I take my own life,' Tominaga had written. 'I made this decision a long time ago, but decided to wait until I was assured of the safety of the passengers and my crew. I know that nothing will relieve my guilt or undo my actions.'

The Japanese captain had left his wristwatch and his few possessions to his crew, but no farewell to his wife and three children in Yokohama. He had thrown himself overboard into the freezing ocean less than a week's sailing from the shores of Europe.

Much to Roy Alexander's horror, Tominaga's death invoked laughter among some of the prisoners in the Hell Hole. It was a measure, he thought, of the madness that had crept into the prison hold. But the tragedy of the suicide was quickly forgotten when the prison guards confirmed that the *Wolf* had changed direction. Nerger had abandoned his attempts to plough through the ice of the Denmark Strait, and they were now heading south, to sail between Iceland and Scotland on an easterly path to the coast of Norway. Any relief at leaving behind the risk of an iceberg collision was tempered by the knowledge that they would be passing directly through the English blockade and the German U-boat zone.

Nerger had wanted above all to avoid this course, for he knew that the raider *Greif* had been destroyed by the British Navy in these waters in March 1916. When he had left Kiel fourteen months earlier, the Admiralty's 10th Cruiser Squadron had been enforcing the blockade in the Norwegian Sea and North Sea with twenty-four armed merchant ships, the largest of them the 18,000-ton liner *Alsatian*, commanded by Rear-Admiral Dudley de Chair. (It was de Chair's ships that had sunk the German raider *Leopard* only eleven months earlier – a disaster of which Nerger was as yet unaware.) Now, the expanded U-boat zone meant shipping would be pushed into an even narrower channel, and he had no up-to-date intelligence on the location of British or German minefields close to the Norwegian coastline. Nerger was absolutely determined to maintain radio silence, calculating that the risks of sending a wireless transmission to Kiel were too great. But typing out his log one evening, he made no attempt to hide the trepidation he felt.

'There is only a small chance of getting through without being seen,' he noted, 'and encountering even a fishing vessel equipped with wireless would be extremely critical for the *Wolf*, since our low speed makes it impossible to disappear in clear weather.'

The same calculations were running through the minds of the men in the Hell Hole, many of whom had sewn their most valuable possessions into towels or torn-off trouser legs in anticipation of the scramble to abandon ship if she was mined, torpedoed or fired on by a British warship. In their cockier moments, the British prisoners had taunted the Germans about their slim chances of evading the Royal Navy in the North Sea, and many still boasted that they would welcome the sight of an Allied battleship bearing down on the raider. But Roy Alexander judged all of that to be bravado, for everyone knew the consequences of the *Wolf* being attacked, and few doubted that Nerger would prefer an honourable death to abject surrender. 'It was better to be a live prisoner-of-war in Germany,' Alexander believed, 'than a dead seaman locked in the riddled hold of a raider at the bottom of the North Sea. Infinitely better.'

When the *Wolf* turned east, just below the southern coastline of Iceland, extra lookouts equipped with telephone headsets were posted across the deck, one at every gun placement. But nature favoured the raider, for snow flurries hid her from view and a gusting wind surged in from the south-west, pushing her forward. Days were short in these northern latitudes, and nights were made darker by a new moon. When the weather cleared on 11 February and Nerger scanned the ocean through his binoculars, he saw with relief that not a single ship was visible. His wireless operators reported no significant enemy transmissions as the raider veered north-east to maintain maximum distance from the Royal Navy base at Scapa Flow. Of the blockade, there was not a sign.

On 13 February, the *Wolf* reached the location of a prearranged rendezvous with the *Igotz Mendi*, 470 miles north of the Scottish coast, and waited for several hours. But the Spanish collier failed to appear, and Nerger resolved to push on, turning south-south-east now towards mainland Europe. Despite the cloud and the winter chill, the sea was calm and the wind had died. An almost preternatural quiet settled over the ship as she approached the final run home under an overcast winter sky. Just after lunch the following day, a lookout spotted a dark line on the horizon off the port beam and, as it drew closer, Nerger recognised with elation the craggy blue and green coastline of Norway. They had entered the North Sea and were only thirty-five miles off Bremanger, a day away from the entrance to the Baltic Sea.

Prisoners below saw the land, too, craning for a view through the narrow gap in the hatch cover over the aft deck. Relief mixed with fear and furious anger. Could the *Wolf* have crossed into the North Sea with any less incident? Some cursed Rear-Admiral de Chair; others bemoaned the British blockade as a farce. Tom Meadows, who had made his final bet with the Germans about the unassailable superiority of the Royal Navy, looked thunderstruck. The New Zealand captain's defiant gaze now stared from a face hollowed out by months of deprivation, for he and his crew had been aboard the *Wolf* longer than anyone else in the Hell Hole. Theodor Plivier had spotted Meadows standing alone on the aft deck one bone chilling and windswept day off Iceland, 'swathed in rags to keep out the cold, an emaciated wreck, with his gnawed pipe in his mouth'. Plivier didn't realise it, but Meadows had a reason for his lonely vigil: he was still throwing SOS messages overboard.

The massed forces of the world's greatest navy lay less than three hundred miles due west of the *Wolf* – more than a hundred and fifty dreadnoughts, cruisers and destroyers from the Grand Fleet of the Royal Navy, strengthened in recent months by the arrival of five United States battleships. Every three to five days, a squadron of up to thirty of these formidable warships would sail out from Scapa Flow to escort a convoy of freighters across the North Sea to Norway, returning several days later with another flotilla of cargo ships destined for Britain from Scandinavian ports. Had the *Wolf* attempted this southerly passage only four days earlier, she would have run straight into the Sixth and Second Battle-Cruiser Squadrons, led by HMAS *Australia*, which had patrolled these waters ceaselessly since 1915. Four days later, she might have encountered another convoy incorporating the Second Light-Cruiser Squadron, which numbered HMAS *Melbourne* and HMAS *Sydney* among its ships. Only two weeks earlier, the entire Grand Fleet had sailed out to the North Sea near Heligoland in one of its periodic displays of strength, designed to goad Germany's navy out of hiding.

But the Grand Fleet was in harbour on 14 February as the *Wolf* crept south on a course parallel to Norway's coastline. The sea was so clear of ships that Nerger allowed those prisoners who were still well enough a brief respite on deck that afternoon, and in their hour of fresh air they glimpsed the lights of Bergen only five miles off the port bow. Then they were shepherded below, along with the last of the top-deck prisoners, Kenkichi Shiraishi and Alfred Clarke, who was aghast when he ventured down into the fetid prison hold for the first time in months.

Twenty-seven men were now bedridden with severe scurvy in Alcon Webb's makeshift medical ward, and a further hundred were suffering serious symptoms. One man with acute appendicitis was in danger of septicaemia and another was suffering agonising joint pain. Roy Alexander could not comprehend how Webb had remained on his feet over the last ten days as he cared for the ill; it seemed that every time Alexander woke up at night and peered into the neighbouring hold through the layers of strung hammocks, he saw the hunched and ragged figure of the Australian sergeant silently moving behind the canvas screens.

Dr Hauswaldt had been down into the hold to see how Webb was coping and offer assistance – an act of compassion that had forged a genuine friendship between the two men. The German doctor's surgery amidships was itself crowded, for dozens of crewmen were trooping in and out of his rooms with scurvy or beriberi, and two of them were already bedridden with advanced illness. The injured Japanese crewman from the *Hitachi Maru* was still alive but desperately in need of hospital treatment, and Hauswaldt's staff were too busy to fill in the medical log; its entries had stopped six weeks earlier.

Nerger now instituted a lockdown in the prison quarters, only allowing the hatch covers to be left slightly open for these final crucial days. The German captain no longer slept in his cabin – as he had done on the outward voyage through this danger zone, he stayed on the bridge around the clock, sleeping only in brief respites on a cot set up behind his command post. As they passed Stavanger on Norway's southern coastline, Nerger saw the wreck of a torpedoed freighter lying crippled on the distant beach, a reminder of the U-boats that patrolled beneath them, unseen.

Freighters and fishing boats passed them, all keeping well within the three-mile limit of the coast; Nerger counted ten steamers passing him on the left as he rounded the southern tip of Norway on the afternoon of 15 February. They were entering the mouth of the Skagerrak, the wide strait that separates Norway from Denmark and leads into the Baltic Sea. Ten weeks earlier, a squadron of British cruisers and destroyers had swept through here to attack and destroy a contingent of German auxiliary warships in the middle of the Danish Sound. But in the cold and clear dawn of 16 February, Nerger saw only freighters and the coast of Sweden in the distance directly ahead.

Sweden marked the point where the strait snaked to the right, leading behind the Jutland Peninsula and into the Kattegat. As they moved into that wide swathe of water, pilot boats approached to guide them through the islands that littered the sound, but Nerger ignored their entreaties to identify himself and pressed on through the steamer traffic heading out to sea. He passed the islands of Sejerø on the right and Samsø on the left, keeping the Danish coastline in view on his starboard side as he approached the Little Belt, the narrow strait between the Jutland Peninsula and the island of Funen.

At 4 pm on the afternoon of 17 February, Nerger saw the town of Fredericia off the starboard bow and knew that Germany was only hours away. It was a Sunday, and not a single freighter appeared before them; Kiel lay only 100 miles further on, beyond the end of the Little Belt. Nerger hoisted the German naval ensign on the mainmast as dusk descended, and the *Wolf* emerged from the Little Belt in darkness, leaving Denmark in her wake. Suddenly, Nerger saw the German patrol ship *Panther* approaching out of the dark – the very ship that had escorted him out of this port in November 1916. The *Panther*'s captain signalled him to stop, and Nerger flashed back with his spotlight: 'Nerger with auxiliary cruiser *Wolf*. Top secret even for senior authorities. Request harbour pilot through barrage.' The patrol boat circled the raider, apparently reluctant to let her pass, but after ten minutes her captain signalled the *Wolf* to follow him and guided them to a location just south of Ærø Island to await further instructions.

Nerger dropped anchor just after 8 pm, staring at the lights of Germany thirty miles off in the distance. Hours later, he sat in his cabin alone, thinking of his wife and children in Hamburg, and pulled out his personal diary. It was 2 am and the ship was silent; Nerger reflected that it was the first time his crew had been able to sleep with complete security since their mission had begun. On that momentous early morning, as he wondered whether Marie even knew he was alive and what awaited him on shore, Nerger transcribed his hopes and fears directly onto the page of his diary:

> When does the first letter from you come? How are things at home? Fifteen months is a long time. Much can happen. Hopefully there is nothing to fear. Have you already given up on us or not? You should have thought that we don't let things get us down.
>
> By God, what joy when we see each other again.
>
> Home oh home.
>
> We are at home.

11

STRANDED

A despondent mood had descended over the *Igotz Mendi* after the *Wolf* disappeared into a snowstorm just south of Iceland on the afternoon of 6 February. As much as the prisoners had come to loathe the sight of the black raider, the voyage ahead of them seemed infinitely more perilous alone. Leaking and unstable, the *Igotz Mendi* had barely survived the Atlantic storm of two weeks ago, and even Leutnant Karl Rose could not mask his apprehension at the prospect of taking her into the lower reaches of the Arctic Circle. Courtenay Dickinson sensed that Rose was at a loss about which course to follow without Karl Nerger's guidance, and when a heavy fog descended the following day, the collier was brought to a halt. Enveloped in mist, the *Igotz Mendi* issued a plaintive siren call to the *Wolf* for several hours, but it died away unanswered.

The snow squalls and sub-zero temperatures outside forced the prisoners to huddle in the saloon or their sodden cabins, where the curtains were now frozen to the portholes. Frederick and Jessie Trayes had spent the last two decades in the tropics and had never endured such agonising cold; so much water leaked into their cabin and saturated their feet that they asked the Germans to drill drainage holes at the base of its exterior wall, for they were siphoning off several bucketfuls a day.

By the time the first ice floes began drifting towards the ship from the north, Stan Cameron realised it would be impossible for Mary and Juanita to remain in their cabin and asked Rose to clear out a coal bunker for them below decks. Here, the Camerons lived behind canvas screens on makeshift beds, kept dry and warm by the heat of the ship's furnaces but breathing air filled with fine coal dust and suffused with a pervading smell of gas. Mary kept up her sewing under lights rigged up by the Germans, working on another elaborately embroidered tablecloth, which was ingrained with grime long before it was finished. Juanita played with her toys from the *Hitachi Maru* while her father sat re-reading months-old newspapers, or brooding about the internment camp that awaited him if they survived the week ahead. It was in this dismal bunker that Juanita turned seven on 7 February, an event that seems to have passed unacknowledged.

A violent crash woke Courtenay Dickinson in his bed at three o'clock the following morning, and he realised from the ship's shuddering that her hull had slammed into an iceberg. The scrape and bang of ice against iron continued throughout the night, making sleep impossible, and the impact of one collision threw Frederick Trayes from his sofa onto the wet cabin floor. Sodden, sleepless and chilled to the bone, Trayes and his wife were reaching the limits of their endurance. 'The cold fog, the great bergs of ice floating by the ship and sometimes crashing into her, the dreary sea, the cold, filthy, miserable ship, our hopeless condition, all helped to lower our spirits,' he recalled, 'and we felt we had plumbed the very depths of misery.'

For several days, the *Igotz Mendi* staggered through this wilderness of white without any purposeful course, grinding to a halt against submerged ice walls and retreating south, then turning north again as Rose vainly tried to weave a path through the bergs that bore down in slow procession on the ship. Like the *Wolf*, however, the *Igotz Mendi* could not penetrate the floes, and on 11 February Rose turned south for the last time and set a course towards the blockade zone. The ship was three days behind the *Wolf* and one of its boilers had broken, bringing its maximum speed down to between six and ten knots, depending on conditions. Standing on the frigid deck one morning, Trayes saw in the distance to the north the masts of several fishing boats, thin as toothpicks, marking a stretch of Iceland's southern coastline. It was the first land any of them had seen since the Maldives four months earlier.

Fresh water was running low, and washing clothes was now prohibited. The meals, too, were more meagre than ever now that the fresh food had gone: cold canned crab, rice with a dollop of gravy, or Richard Donovan's bread served with sugar and watered-down condensed milk. Stan Cameron's strapping six-foot frame was alarmingly lean; he had lost more than fifty pounds and his face had become drawn and grey. Juanita's hunger pains became so terrible one afternoon that she began weeping, and after her father confronted Karl Rose, the food ration was increased slightly. Agnes Mackenzie, who was an asthmatic, had become seriously ill and rarely left the cabin she shared with Courtenay Dickinson and Mabel Whittaker.

Outwardly, Rose professed to be unconcerned about running the blockade, telling Dickinson it would be 'dead easy'. To Trayes, he offered the bewildering assurance that British warships didn't work on weekends, so he was timing their run towards the Baltic Sea for a Saturday. But the professor sensed Rose's anxiety as the ship slogged its way due east towards the Norwegian coast. Every day, the *leutnant* predicted that he would hear from the *Wolf*, but the anticipated wireless message never arrived. It was during their conversations on this passage across the North Sea that Rose admitted the obvious to Trayes: he would be taking every one of his prisoners back to Kiel, not dropping them on a neutral Scandinavian shore as he had most recently promised.

The news was hardly a shock to Trayes, who like the others had long ago judged Rose to be an unblushing liar. At fifty-six, the grey-bearded professor stood a chance of being set free with his wife once they reached Germany. But the other prisoners were facing certain internment in one of Germany's prisoner-of-war camps, at a time when Allied newspapers suggested that the entire country was reduced to starvation rations. For Tom Rees, Denis Patterson and Richard Donovan, all of whom were ill, it was a particularly dark prospect. The prison camps had already been the subject of alarming reports: an outbreak of typhus in one had killed fifty British soldiers, and inmates who had been released and returned to Britain due to ill health told stories of severe food shortages.

The thought had been weighing on Mary Cameron's mind and, as the ship approached northern Norway, she took her husband aside, out of earshot of Juanita. Stan was a strong swimmer, Mary pointed out, and the ship would soon be hugging the neutral Norwegian coastline to keep clear of U-boats and British warships. It was obvious what he should do: jump overboard and swim for it at the first opportunity. Cameron tried to brush the suggestion aside, for he could not countenance the idea of leaving his family in the hands of the Germans, but Mary was insistent. 'I'm not afraid,' she told him. 'They won't hurt us. And what's more, they don't want us. We're no use to them, just a burden; two more mouths to feed in a country where I'm sure there's not enough right now. We wouldn't be good for exchange purposes even. But they do want you, and they'll keep you and send us out. Better to be separated now and united later than leave you there in a prison camp.'

Cameron could only admire Mary's courage, for even after he told her to forget the idea she pressed him so doggedly that he began to give it serious thought. But on 17 February, the dangers still facing his wife and daughter were brought home again, for the *Igotz Mendi* struck another storm that day that sent the ship lurching through the steep swell, and her propeller shaft emitted a banging noise so alarming that Karl Rose rushed from the bridge, thinking they had struck a mine. The number of people aboard the ship had swelled to eighty-four since the extra German and neutral crewmen had joined them, but the lifeboats would accommodate only sixty at best. If they encountered a British destroyer and Rose decided to scuttle the ship, the fight to get off her would be brutal. The *Igotz Mendi*'s dilapidated state, the terrible possibility of being mined or torpedoed and the uncertainties that Mary and Juanita faced even if the ship did reach Germany made Stan push any thought of jumping overboard out of his mind.

The prisoners' one last hope of freedom rested with the apparently impregnable British naval blockade. The British and Australians had spoken so often about the Royal Navy's domination of the North Sea that Stan had come to believe that the *Igotz Mendi*'s only chance of getting back to Germany was to slip past the British warships in a blanketing fog. But while Cameron dreaded what might happen if a British warship appeared, Frederick Trayes clung to that hope as a bulwark against the depression that periodically engulfed him. 'We had cheered ourselves up for a long time past that the *Wolf* would never get through the British blockade,' he recalled, 'and that some friendly vessel would surely be the means of our salvation. The Spanish officers who had had experience of the blockade also assured us that no vessel could possibly get through unchallenged; and we, in our turn, had assured the American captives among us of the same thing. There was no fog to help the enemy, the condition of the moon was favourable to us, and we had pointed out to each other on maps various places where there must be British ships on the watch.'

But on 19 February, Karl Rose came to the prisoners with news that plunged them into uncertainty. His wireless operators, he said, had just picked up a coded transmission from the *Admiralstab* informing him that the *Wolf* had arrived back in Germany. It seemed so unlikely that most of the prisoners took it as another of Rose's artful fabrications and refused to believe him. It was impossible, they argued, for it was well known that the Royal Navy was enforcing a dragnet across the North Sea that had choked Germany's maritime trade virtually to a standstill.

Overhearing the prisoners discussing the news, one of the crew remarked – more presciently than he realised – that perhaps the blockade had been lifted now that so many countries had stopped trading with Germany.

The arguments were still going on the following day when the coastline of Norway appeared in the distance, as another violent storm bore down from the west.

* *

Karl Nerger was still in his cabin aboard the *Wolf* when the news of his return to Germany was transmitted to the *Igotz Mendi.* In the two days since his ship came to rest in the Ærø Sound, Nerger had been forced to remain aboard her with his prisoners and crew while the *Admiralstab* digested the startling news of the raider's sudden reappearance after 444 days at sea. The *Wolf* had long ago been given up as lost within the upper reaches of the navy, which had begun notifying the families of the crew in late January that their loved ones were believed to be dead. By eerie coincidence, Nerger had dropped anchor off Kiel on the very day that the last of those letters was dispatched, so the captain of the patrol ship *Panther* had every reason to feel disbelief as he circled the raider before guiding her into the harbour. Vice-Admiral Gustav Bachmann, head of the Kiel naval station, had recovered sufficiently from the shock to send Kapitän Wolfram von Knorr in a patrol boat to greet Nerger and issue instructions for the *Wolf* to proceed south and drop anchor off Flensburg, a German port hidden away at the end of a winding thirty-mile inlet off the Baltic. There, Nerger was to await the arrival of the *Igotz Mendi*, for the return of SMS *Wolf* to Kiel was to be an extravagant celebration designed to lift the spirits of the German people.

The prisoners had emerged from the aft holds on the morning of 18 February, blinking in perplexity at the sight of Germany's green hills and the fishing boats of Flensburg bobbing at the end of the inlet. Hospital ships pulled alongside and the sickest of the scurvy sufferers were taken aboard for treatment, while medical examinations of the 750 crew and prisoners began. Nerger had sent a brief, urgent report to Admiral Bachmann giving the bare details of his mission's achievements and requesting supplies of fruit and fresh vegetables, which had been sent aboard. Patrol boats periodically passed the raider, their crews appearing on deck to cheer; a U-boat pulled alongside and its men clambered out and stood gaping at the corroded and dented raider. By the following day, however, there was still no word of the *Igotz Mendi.*

Nerger, his crew and captives were still aboard the ship on 20 February when Admiral Bachmann himself arrived on a destroyer from Kiel, bearing a personal note from the Kaiser. Its message of congratulations was read out to Nerger as his crewmen gathered on the forward deck under the bridge: 'I cordially welcome you and your courageous crew back to your homeland after a long and successful cruise across all the oceans. I award you the *Pour le Mérite*, and for the rest of the crew of the auxiliary cruiser we will award numerous Iron Cross medals, Class One and Two. I wish you a happy reunion with your loved ones and a good recovery after your long deprivations and efforts.'

The only other raider captain to have been awarded the *Pour le Mérite* – a blue Maltese cross bearing the royal cipher and four eagles – was the *Moewe*'s Nikolaus Dohna-Schlodien. But immediately after the medals had been pinned to the chests of Nerger and his crew, Bachmann's men hastily collected them and packed them away again. The crew would get them back, it was explained, in a second presentation to be held after the raider's ceremonial arrival in Kiel, which was scheduled for the morning of 24 February and would be filmed for posterity.

The *Wolf* remained in Flensburg Sound for another three days, undergoing extensive maintenance as she waited for the *Igotz Mendi* to appear. The raider's bow and keel were stripped of their encrusted weeds, and the staved-in plates and cracked joints of her hull were repaired and repainted. Boilers were cleaned, her superstructure was repainted white and the *Wolfchen* was hauled up from below in sections, clothed in a new skin of canvas, reassembled and painted a gleaming silver. A white ceremonial pendant, nearly three-hundred feet long and with a brass ball at its end, was hung from the raider's mainmast and a massive German naval ensign was run up the aft mast. Throughout it all, the crew were forbidden from leaving the ship or even sending letters to their families, for the *Admiralstab* was enforcing a blanket ban on any news of the raider's return, anxious not to jeopardise the *Igotz Mendi*'s homeward voyage. When 24 February dawned, however, there was still no sign of the prize ship, nor any word of her fate.

Roy Alexander remembered that morning as shrouded in haze; Fritz Witschetzky described it as blazingly sunny, suggesting that for the prisoners and crew gathered on the raider's deck, memory was filtered through a prism of very different emotions. A flotilla of navy cruisers arrived to escort the *Wolf* out of Flensburg Sound, and as the ships made their way out into the Baltic, several biplanes appeared in the sky and circled low to follow. Kiel lay to the south at the end of another long inlet, a city of brown-brick villas built on wooded hills that descended to the water's edge. Its massive industrial naval yard lay ten miles inside the channel at the town centre.

Even the prisoners – many of them still dazed and ailing from the effects of scurvy – were stirred by the extraordinary spectacle that greeted the *Wolf* after she entered that channel, for an honour guard of destroyers, battle-cruisers and submarines stretched for several miles into the distance on either side of them. Witschetzky recognised the 29,000-ton dreadnoughts *König*, *Großer Kurfürst*, *Markgraf* and *Kronprinz*, lined up like steel-grey behemoths in the cold morning light, and behind them a long row of black U-boats and several flotillas of cruisers and destroyers. Sergeant Alcon Webb counted at least ninety warships arrayed in procession, their crews massed at the rails and the smoke from their funnels hanging suspended in the air. Hundreds of small sailing boats and launches cut across the *Wolf*'s bow and stern as she made her way past them with her white pendant stretched to full length in the breeze. Snow was banked on the hills and the crowds clustered at jetty railings were rugged up against the cold, waving hats and handkerchiefs as they cheered.

The raider came to rest outside the Maritime Academy, which was bedecked with flags and pendants and surrounded by a noisy throng. A brass band struck up 'Deutschland Über Alles' and grey-bearded Admiral Bachmann walked up the gangway to board the ship dressed in a dark winter uniform and peaked cap, a sword in its scabbard slapping his thigh. He was accompanied by a phalanx of navy officers, a film crew from the military propaganda department and several ordinary seamen carrying a wooden chest full of medals. The cameras captured the theatrical charade as Admiral Bachmann descended the ladder from the *Wolf*'s bridge to her forward deck, where Nerger and his crew were gathered, all of them sporting new uniforms and caps bearing the SMS *Wolf* insignia, which had been distributed a few hours earlier. Bachmann read the telegram from the Kaiser, which everyone on board had already heard, pinned on the medals that had already been awarded and led the orchestrated 'hurrahs' for the benefit of the cameras. Even Nerger, with the ribbon on his *Pour le Mérite* flapping in the winter wind, could not suppress a smirk.

Beneath his smile, Nerger knew that all was not well on shore. Sailors who had come aboard the *Wolf* from Flensburg had told him of food shortages, strikes and unrest; some of them had been as desperate to get to the raider's stores of canned food as his own crew had been for fresh tobacco. The thoughts he had recorded in his diary were pensive and uncertain, addressed in part to his loved ones, in part to Germany itself: 'It seems that things are not looking good with you. Strikes, etc. Food plight miserable. Coffee, tea, cocoa, sugar, etc. are unattainable . . . We also hear that not a bit has become known of us and our successes in Germany.' Nerger had been longing to contact Marie and his children, knowing they might well believe he was dead. In his head, he had composed a wry cable message to them: 'Good wares keep. Weed doesn't die.' But he had been prevented from sending it, and the hundreds of questions he wanted to ask her ran through his head unanswered. His crew, too, were restive after being detained on the ship for a week and prevented from seeing their loved ones.

Watching from amid the crowd of prisoners, Alfred Clarke also sensed the darker undercurrents beneath the contrived gaiety. Some of the crew, Clarke noticed, handled their Iron Crosses with a flippancy that bordered on contempt, for even the awarding of medals had conformed to the Germany navy's rigid conventions: while many of the officers had received the Iron Cross First Class, the regular crewmen had been awarded the more lowly Second Class medal, which the Kaiser handed out by the millions in the course of the war. Clarke overheard one crewman commenting bitterly that the men who had done the hardest work received the least recognition. 'Something had caused considerable dissatisfaction among the crew,' Clarke noted. 'Their demeanour had greatly altered since the *Wolf* had arrived in Germany, and they were plainly nursing a grievance, or grievances.'

Like their captain, the crew were uncertain what awaited them when they left the ship, for they had heard the same stories of food shortages and knew this port had been the scene of mutinies during their absence. Their frustration at being kept aboard the ship was mixed with the bitter knowledge that the very admirals who were now celebrating their return had ordered the jailing and execution of their fellow seamen only a few months earlier. Theodor Plivier watched with a jaundiced eye when society women from Kiel dressed in ankle-length gowns were brought aboard the *Wolf* to meet the officers. As the propaganda unit rolled their cameras, the women curtsied before Nerger, officers raised megaphones to their lips to issue mock orders and a gun crew pretended to load and fire. When the brass band struck up a tune, a few of the prisoners were filmed dancing a spontaneous two-step.

To Plivier, it was all a farce. 'The highest military order that the nation had to bestow had been turned into a theatrical property. The captain . . . was himself forced to play the part of an actor with the rest of the officers, including the Admiral and commander of the Baltic station, as extras.'

The night before, the German Government had finally wired an official press announcement of the *Wolf*'s return. Admiral Henning von Holtzendorff, the *Admiralstab* chief who had doubted Nerger's plans to stay at sea for more than a year, was effusive in his praise, if not entirely accurate in his account. 'For the last year, mysterious news from the Cape of Good Hope, South Africa, Ceylon and Bombay has been published in the English press,' Holtzendorrf declared. 'Mines were heard of, and in the Pacific ten ships vanished in a short time. Then all was still. In the meantime, however, the *Wolf* was at work: for fifteen months the *Wolf* has been on her own resources, without a base, cruising the seas of the world.' Karl Nerger, the admiral said, had carried off 'a war achievement which has had no equal and perhaps never will.'

In London, Holtzendorff's cable was intercepted and translated almost immediately by Britain's War Office, then briefly withheld from the newspapers as the Admiralty weighed up its response. Despite the vagueness of the dispatch, Holtzendorff's remarks contained enough detail for naval intelligence to determine that its own suppositions about the *Wolf* had been confirmed. A swift totting-up suggested that the raider had sunk at least twenty ships, perhaps more. It was a propaganda coup for the Germans, to be sure. The only remaining mystery was the fate of the *Igotz Mendi*.

* *

On the same morning that Karl Nerger was navigating the *Wolf* through her celebratory pageant in Kiel harbour, Leutnant Karl Rose was steering the *Igotz Mendi* away from the North Sea and into the mouth of the Skagerrak channel between Norway and Denmark. Rose was in ebullient spirits, for the British Navy had failed to materialise as the collier had laboured down the Norwegian coast over the preceding several days, and he was now less than twenty-four hours from Germany.

The *Igotz Mendi*'s speed had slowed to six knots, and during the violent storm that had rolled in on 19 February, she had floundered for more than two days without making any appreciable progress. Waves had crashed over the bridge and saturated several cabins, forcing the prisoners once again into the saloon, where they crammed into benches, unable to sleep through the wind's screaming and the seawater sluicing underfoot. But when the weather had finally cleared on 23 February to reveal the lights of Bergen off the port bow, there were still no ships in sight, British or otherwise. The *Igotz Mendi* had been even luckier than the *Wolf*: the storm had delayed the ship just long enough to help her evade a British naval convoy that had passed there two days earlier.

'There is no hope left,' Frederick Trayes had written in his journal later that day, 'no boat of ours to save us.' After investing so much hope in a last-minute rescue by a British destroyer, the prisoners were now sour and angry. Stan Cameron could barely speak as he grappled with the seeming inevitability of being separated from Mary and Juanita, perhaps for years. With the neutral coast of Norway in sight, thoughts of jumping overboard once again intruded on his mind. The blazing sunshine, which made visibility clear for miles, only accentuated the bitter feeling of abandonment. As good as his word, Leutnant Rose had timed the last leg of the voyage for a weekend; 24 February was a Sunday, and only a lone fishing boat and a single Danish passenger steamer passed them as they cut diagonally across the Skagerrak channel towards the Danish tip of the Jutland Peninsula.

Standing at the rails, Frederick Trayes and Courtenay Dickinson were alarmed to see a floating mine drift past the ship, but Rose was certain the Skagerrak had not been mined and surmised that it must have drifted in from the North Sea. They would be clear of the danger zone within hours, he predicted. When a fog rolled in just after lunch, the German commander was positively beaming as he walked rapidly back and forth across the bridge, rubbing his hands together. 'Just the weather I want,' he told Cameron and Courtenay Dickinson. 'Made to order.' The *Igotz Mendi* was soon enveloped, and by three o'clock visibility was reduced to a few hundred yards. When a fog whistle sounded ahead of them just after 3.30 pm, Rose joked to Cecil Strangman that he should go inside and tell the other prisoners that their German torpedo-boat escort had arrived.

Stan Cameron was intrigued by the unfamiliar tone of the whistle and asked Rose what it really was. The German replied that it was a lightship marking the Danish side of the channel. Cameron peered into the opaque haze, unable to see anything but trying to guess their position. The Skagerrak was roughly a hundred miles long and he surmised that they were nearing its north-east corner and would soon bear right, around the back of the Jutland Peninsula and into the Kattegat. From there, it was little more than two hundred miles to German waters. The fog whistle sounded again, closer this time, and he wondered about its peculiar tone, which was unlike any boat signal he had ever heard.

As he made his way back to his cabin, he sensed the *Igotz Mendi* was shifting course and realised that Rose was steering the boat further to starboard in order to pass close to the lightship, presumably to avoid mines. And then, as he stood peering out of the cabin porthole, Cameron felt a familiar featherweight vibration travel up through the floor, a sensation that might have been imperceptible to anyone other than an experienced seaman. He looked at his wife in shock and said, 'I think I just felt her smell the bottom.' Seconds later, an audible thump shook the ship, followed by two more, and the *Igotz Mendi* lurched to a halt with her engines still rumbling.

Cameron rushed out onto the deck, hearing the propellers shift into reverse torque. Through the fog, he could just make out a line of white foam breakers off the starboard side of the ship, and beyond them a dark strip of land. With a feeling of elation, he realised he was looking at the shores of neutral Denmark, 400 yards away. The ship had run aground on the sandy north-western tip of the peninsula, and off in the distance was the opalescent glow of a lighthouse that was emitting the fog siren Karl Rose had mistaken for a lightship.

The other prisoners were all now gathering at the ship's rails, talking excitedly. The shore was temptingly close, but a formidable surf was pounding against it. Stan felt confident he could jump overboard and make it to land, but Mary, Juanita and the other women prisoners would never survive such a swim. One of the neutral seamen, Jens Jensen from the *Matunga*, was a Dane who knew this stretch of coastline; he told Cameron they were two miles from Skagen, a remote seaside resort that was home to one of the best lifesaving crews in Europe.

On the bridge, Karl Rose's attempts to dislodge the ship from the sandbank were proving fruitless, and he ordered the water tanks emptied to lighten her load. When Rose appeared in the saloon, where the prisoners had crowded to discuss a plan of action, he nonchalantly said they would be back on course to Kiel in a couple of hours. But Tom Rees and Stan Cameron believed he was bluffing, for experience told them the tide was ebbing, and by nightfall the *Igotz Mendi* would be even more firmly fixed on Danish sand.

Rees suggested that the prisoners pool their money and pay one of the neutrals to jump overboard and swim to shore, then walk to the lighthouse to call the British consul in Copenhagen. Stan Cameron had already resolved that he would jump the rails himself at the first sign of the ship being refloated. Mary had been urging him to do as much for more than a week, and with the North Sea behind them he told himself the danger for his family might well have passed. Once ashore, there was even a slim chance that he could get a message through to the British authorities before the *Igotz Mendi* reached German waters. Before either of these plans could be put into action, however, a long wooden lifeboat from Skagen appeared out of the mist, and the Germans bustled their prisoners into the saloon and its neighbouring cabins as the boat pulled alongside.

Karl Rose invited the Danish lifeboat captain into the chart room on the bridge, having already contrived a credible cover story for his benefit: the ship, he explained, was a German merchant steamer bound from Bergen to Kiel, and would be off the sand as soon as he could contact a salvage company to bring tugs to their aid. While Rose was speaking, however, a muffled sound of women shrieking with laughter and a small girl crying seeped up through the floor. The chart room was directly above the saloon, where Mary Cameron, Mary Benson and Jess Trayes were conducting a parlour game at extravagant volume while Stan Cameron encouraged his six-year-old daughter to unleash her most theatrical wailing. Fifteen minutes later, Karl Rose appeared in the saloon and said with a scowl, 'You people can cut the noise now, the stranger has gone ashore.'

Rose was loath to use his wireless to summon help, so he instructed Leutnant Adolf Wulff to take a launch to the nearby Højen lighthouse, where he was to contact a salvage company in Skagen and telegraph a message to Karl Nerger in Kiel. After months of terror and uncertainty, the prisoners now found themselves discussing an absurdly arcane legal point of warfare: was the Danish Government obligated to help them? Denmark was a major trading partner of Germany; its southern border abutted northern Germany and its capital, Copenhagen, lay only 135 miles across the Baltic Sea from Kiel. When the war began, its navy had mined the Great Belt – the main strait leading into the Baltic Sea – at the German Government's request. But the Danish Government had steadfastly maintained its neutrality, and its regard for Germany had cooled considerably since it had learned during 1915 that the Kaiser – in his private letters to Tsar Nicholas of Russia some years earlier – had discussed the idea of invading Denmark. Stan Cameron consulted Major Cecil Strangman, the most senior military officer among the prisoners, to see if he could shed any light on the legal status of a neutral Spanish freighter under German command stranded on Danish shores. The white-haired Australian promptly launched into his familiar plaint – that a medical officer such as himself was entitled to be set free under the Geneva Convention – until Cameron told him to go to hell and stalked off.

Some time before 10 pm, Karl Rose appeared in the saloon to announce that a tug would be arriving at midnight to take the *Igotz Mendi* off the sand. Leutnant Wulff had returned, having called the Svitzer salvage company in Skagen and sent a telegram to Karl Nerger in Kiel, who at that moment was preparing for bed after his first full day on land. Rose's announcement caused agitation among the prisoners, who resumed a heated debate about what to do. Some argued that an attempt should be made to get a message to the tug captain. Stan Cameron was already steeling himself to say goodbye to his family and jump overboard. The frustration of being so close to neutral land was unendurable, and when the horn of an approaching ship sounded, a silence descended over the saloon.

But the ship that emerged out of the foggy darkness was not a tug; it was the diminutive 300-ton Danish navy inspection boat *Diana*, stationed at Skagen. When her captain, Otto Lagoni, came aboard with his first officer, he adroitly resisted Karl Rose's attempt to steer them upstairs to the chart room, suggesting instead that they talk in the saloon, where it was customary to entertain a fellow officer. When Rose and Lagoni stepped through the door from the deck, the Camerons and Floods were still being hustled into the adjacent cabins, and it was clear that the Danish captain had seen the prisoners. For the next half-hour, as the two officers talked in the saloon, Mary Cameron, Jess Trayes and Mary Benson staged another elaborate pantomime, opening the doors of their neighbouring cabins to call out various meaningless messages to one another.

In the saloon, Karl Rose was attempting to maintain his ruse of being a hapless German merchant skipper, despite the noise of women calling out in the background. But Lagoni already knew there was something amiss about this stranded freighter, because the lifesaver who had come aboard six hours earlier had informed the Skagen lighthouse that there were women and children aboard, and the lighthouse keeper had consulted his Lloyd's register and told Lagoni that the *Igotz*

Mendi was registered in Spain, not Germany. The Danish Navy had thus instructed the salvage tug *Viking* not to approach the ship until the *Diana* had assessed the situation. While Lagoni dawdled amiably in the saloon, his first officer was descending into the coal bunkers, where he found the Camerons' old makeshift quarters and one of Juanita Cameron's abandoned Kewpie dolls lying on the grimy floor. Climbing back up to the deck, he suddenly ran into the redoubtable Mabel Whittaker, who had barged past the guard outside her cabin on the pretext of obtaining water for Agnes Mackenzie. The gun-toting 'Whisky Madame' of Singapore gave him a breathless two-minute summary of their capture by the *Wolf*, their nightmarish crossing of the Atlantic and the presence of twenty-one captive men, women and children aboard the ship.

By the time Captain Lagoni returned to the *Diana* just before midnight on 24 February, Karl Rose had admitted the truth and the Danish Government was confronting a tricky political dilemma. As a neutral nation, Denmark was obliged to protect any ship inside its territorial waters, and the navy had already dispatched the torpedo boat *Spækhuggeren* to the scene. Fearing that the British Navy would attempt to seize the *Igotz Mendi* if it heard of the beaching, the Danish Government sent the small cruiser *Heimdal* along as well, with instructions to resist the British with force, if necessary. Yet the government clearly could not abandon the women and children aboard the *Igotz Mendi*. Lagoni was thus instructed to reboard the ship and inform Rose that Denmark was treating the *Igotz Mendi* as a German auxiliary warship, and as such would protect him from the British but would not permit him to make wireless contact with his consulate or use the services of the salvage tug. After delivering this unwelcome news, Lagoni ordered his men to disable the *Igotz Mendi*'s wireless transmitter, leaving Rose able only to receive signals.

Oblivious to all of this, the prisoners had gone to their cabins in the early hours of 25 February uncertain of what the morning held for them. German guards still patrolled the corridors, and it appeared that the Danish Navy was making little attempt to rescue them. Back in his old cabin near the saloon, Stan Cameron lay in his bunk beneath the chart room listening to the shrieking gale outside and the dull rumble of the collier's engines below. Like many of the prisoners, Cameron had not changed his clothes for several days. Mary clung tightly to Stan in the bunk, showing every sign of suffering another nervous collapse from the uncertainty of their predicament and the strain of knowing she might be separated from her husband the following day. It had been more than a week since any of them had slept properly – wild weather and anxiety had made that impossible – and the shuddering of the ship as Rose tried to dislodge her kept them awake again for many hours. Some time after 4 am, the engines finally stopped and the Camerons drifted into a restless semi-slumber. They were startled awake two hours later by a German crewman standing in the doorway of their cabin. It took Stan several seconds to realise that he was saying, 'Kapitän, Kapitän, wake up and get ready to go ashore in the boats.'

The Camerons hurried out to the rails, where other prisoners were gathering in the dawn light. The weather had turned ugly and a Force 8 westerly was hurling such a heavy swell against the sides of the grounded ship that she had turned ninety degrees overnight. Stan Cameron peered out to sea through the whipping rain and ocean spray but saw no sign of the salvage tug. Then Karl Rose came down from the bridge and brusquely confirmed that he had signalled the Danish Navy to send for the lifeboats from Skagen.

Cameron realised that Rose must be setting his prisoners free as a last desperate attempt to secure assistance from the Danish tug, and the pain of this capitulation was etched so deeply into Rose's face that even Cameron couldn't help pitying the German at that moment, despite all his provocations and lies. His glorious return to Germany was being ruined in increments, and his naval career would end in humiliation unless he could get this ugly

Spanish collier off the sand. The prisoners were in a state of giddy excitement, and Frederick Trayes, too, was struck by the contrast between their voluble chatter and Rose's stricken air. He looked, thought the professor, like 'a fallen enemy'.

The Camerons returned to their cabin to wake Juanita and throw whatever valuables they could fit into their pockets, for they had been told that no one would be permitted to take bags into the lifeboats. Stan collected his notes and his bundle of photographs, wrapping them as securely as he could and stuffing them into his jacket pocket. At 8 am, two wooden longboats pulled alongside, manned by half a dozen weathered, oilskinned and bearded Danish lifesavers who might have stepped out of an illustrated children's book, and a rope ladder was thrown over the side of the *Igotz Mendi*. The wild swell was lifting the lifeboats up within six feet of the collier's deck rails and then dropping them away into a trough twenty feet below, making it impossible for Kameno Kuziraoka, Marie Long and several of the other women to climb down into the boats. In the end, they simply leapt from the ladder into the arms of the waiting Danes or were grabbed and dragged aboard. Alone among them, Mary Cameron expertly judged the jump, while Juanita clung with practised ease to her father's back as he descended the ladder.

The boat pitched so alarmingly that Stan wondered how they would make the shore without overturning. There were more than twenty people aboard, including the lifesavers, and as the oarsmen fought the waves to get them towards the beach, the ocean became a churning expanse of white foam that washed across the boat and drenched everyone aboard. Huge breakers were thundering against the shore and, when the longboat was lifted by one of them, Cameron felt himself pitched forward as if they were about to be ploughed nose-first into the ocean bed. But just then one of the Danes at the stern threw a small anchor and rope overboard and as the anchor touched bottom it hauled the longboat back to an even keel and their trajectory straightened and slowed as they scudded towards the beach. Two more surging breakers pitched them headlong into the shallows and the lifesavers leapt into the wild surf, hauled the women out of the boat, slung them over their shoulders and carried them up onto the sand.

A handful of locals who lived in cottages along the coast had come down on horseback to witness the rescue, and they watched in bemusement as the fourteen sodden and bedraggled escapees from the *Igotz Mendi* hooted, danced and hugged one another, laughing hysterically in the icy wind. Frederick Trayes walked around gingerly on the sand like a man who had never before felt the sensation of land underfoot; others stared around them in a dazed wonder at the green hills behind the beach and the horses standing nearby in the misty air, as if the whole scene might evaporate. Locals who tentatively asked where the ship had come from heard a bewildering story, told in breathless gulps, of capture, imprisonment and now – miraculously – escape just hours from Germany. Within half an hour, the second lifeboat shot through the surf carrying the last of the prisoners and the neutral seamen.

The escapees were quickly broken into groups and taken to the lighthouse and the nearby cottages, where locals gave them blankets, hot coffee and the luxury of jam on toast while their clothes were dried in front of fires. At 1 pm, all of them set off on the two-mile walk to Skagen, in the company of local police who had come down to meet them. There, they were accommodated in several of the town's resort hotels, where they ate steak and drank wine on credit with a relish that their hosts found vastly entertaining. 'All food was a joy to us,' Courtenay Dickinson recounted. 'If I were a poet, I could find no better or [more] deserving theme than the food at Skagen.'

Two miles down the coast, the *Igotz Mendi* remained wedded to the sand at dawn the following day, and Leutnant Karl Rose was becoming increasingly desperate. That morning, as newspapers across Europe published details of the *Wolf*'s extraordinary fifteen-month raiding mission and heroic return to Kiel,

Rose had watched the salvage tug *Viking* retire back to port in Skagen, its captain having given up hope of profiting from this maritime mishap. The gale blowing in from the west had become even fiercer, and the Spanish crew were becoming agitated at the groaning and cracking noises that the damaged collier was emitting as she shifted around on the sand.

Rose now knew that his gambit of setting free his prisoners had failed, and that the Danish Government would not extricate him from this imbroglio. The previous afternoon, after the last of the prisoners had gone, the cruiser *Heimdal* had arrived on the scene and its first officer had boarded the *Igotz Mendi* and confirmed to Rose that it would not permit the salvage tug to pull him off the sand. In desperation, Rose had sent Leutnant Adolf Wulff back to the Højen lighthouse in a launch, to telephone the German consulate in Copenhagen and summon help. But the ocean was now so treacherous that Wulff could not get back to the ship.

When a German U-boat surfaced near the stranded collier at 8.30 am, the saga of the *Igotz Mendi* threatened to spiral into a military confrontation between Denmark and Germany. The submarine had been dispatched soon after Leutnant Wulff's telegraph message reached Karl Nerger in Kiel, and it now attempted to make wireless contact with the prize ship. But the *Heimdal*'s captain blocked the U-boat's transmissions with a jamming signal, and Rose watched helplessly as it sank from view and departed.

The Spanish crew were now so alarmed by the weather – and by the increasingly tense stand-off between the Germans and the Danish – that they begged Rose to release them, and just after midday he flagged the *Diana* to call in the Skagen lifesavers once more. Over several hours, the longboats braved the violent sea to remove twenty-eight of the Spaniards, although Rose refused to allow Captain Ugalde, his chief engineer or first officer Gervasio Susasta – who was still facing trial in Germany – to disembark. That night, with all but three of the prisoners safely on land, Danish Navy officials in Copenhagen resolved to hand the ship back to its Spanish crew – a task they decided to delegate to local police in order to avoid a military incident.

As it turned out, the police were saved from this difficult duty by the natural elements, for the storm that had pounded the *Igotz Mendi* for two days grew so violent during the night that at 3 am Leutnant Rose was forced to signal the *Heimdal* that his crew required rescuing. The indefatigable lifesavers of Skagen were thus roused from their beds to make a third trip out to the Spanish ship, and after being thrown back several times by the huge waves, retrieved the last twenty-six men and delivered them to the police waiting on the beach just after midday.

In the midst of the rescue, a second and larger German U-boat suddenly surfaced 200 yards from the collier, and the *Heimdal* fired three warning shots across the submarine's bow – the first and only time that the Danish Navy fired on a German warship in the First World War. By then, however, the drawn-out debacle had reached its end for Karl Rose, along with his hopes of an Iron Cross and a captain's promotion. That afternoon, he and his men were marched through the main street of Skagen at gunpoint until they reached the Karstens Hotel, where they spent a comfortable night under armed guard before being assembled the following morning in the chill of Skagen's main street.

Stan and Mary Cameron had emerged from their hotel to watch the scene. The German crewmen seemed remarkably cheerful – they had told the police that sitting out the war in a Danish internment camp was a far more favourable prospect to them than being assigned to a U-boat or a destroyer in the North Sea. Stan Cameron caught a glimpse of Karl Rose's stony face amid the throng as the Germans were marched off to the railway station. The once vainglorious *leutnant* now looked utterly crestfallen, and when their eyes briefly met, Cameron could not suppress a rueful smile.

12

HONOUR AND DEFEAT

A blizzard descended on Kiel two days after the *Wolf* returned to its harbour, and the raider lay at anchor blanketed in a frosting of white. While the crew celebrated their return in the town's taverns or went home to their families, the prisoners remained aboard and became living exhibits in a floating tourist attraction, visited by parties of schoolchildren, groups of women and dignitaries of various rank asking incessant questions in broken English. Alfred Clarke was washing his handkerchiefs in an officer's room one afternoon when Prince Henry of Prussia poked his head through the doorway, saluted, and continued on his way.

The sickest of the prisoners, including Roy Alexander, were sent quickly to military hospitals, but the rest endured several days of waiting to learn which of Germany's prison camps would be their new homes. Proving that his black humour had survived the voyage, Tom Meadows approached the *Wolfchen*'s pilot, Paul Fabeck, one morning several days after they had docked. The New Zealand skipper noted that it was 27 February, precisely one year since he had been imprisoned aboard the *Wolf* in the Indian Ocean. He told Fabeck that this milestone surely deserved some formal recognition, and as a consequence he wanted to place a formal request with the Kaiser for an Iron Cross. 'Preferably First Class,' Meadows added, 'although if that's too difficult, Second Class will do.'

On 28 February, the prisoners from neutral countries were transferred to a German cruiser to be repatriated to their various home ports, and the following morning those remaining were assembled for the last time on the raider's deck in the pre-dawn hours. It was an unexpectedly emotional moment for some, for they had forged deep friendships with the German crew and felt a sense of loss now that they were finally leaving the ship. Sergeant Alcon Webb had already presented Dr Hermann Hauswaldt with a letter, written in his best curlicued script. 'Sir,' it stated, 'I desire to express to you and your Junior Medical Officer my thanks, and gratitude, for your courtesy and kindness to Corporal O'Grady and myself during the period we have worked under your supervision. I hope, Sir, that you and your medical colleagues will have health and prosperity and enjoy a well-deserved rest after such a long and arduous voyage.'

Roy Alexander had experienced his own violently contradictory emotions as he lay on the deck of a launch being shipped to hospital two days earlier, watching the *Wolf* fade from view. 'I suddenly realised I had grown to respect and admire that bulky black ship,' he recalled. 'I thought of her almost as if I had been one of the crew, instead of merely a prisoner.'

At 4 am on 1 March, the captured merchant and military officers were marched off the *Wolf* into the snow-caked streets of Kiel, the first time they had set foot on land since coming aboard the raider. Carrying their meagre belongings in cases and tote bags, they were led to the railway station and taken by train to Karlsruhe internment camp, 370 miles south near the French border. Civilians and ordinary seamen left the ship a few hours later on a train for other camps scattered across central and northern Germany. The scenes that flashed past them bore witness to the toll that more than three years of warfare had exacted on the country. Passing through Warburg, Alec Donaldson spotted a Red Cross train full of wounded German soldiers from the front and was shocked by their vacant stares and abject condition. They were, he thought, 'the personification of hopeless misery and blank despair'.

In London and Berlin, news of the raider's extraordinary reappearance in Kiel had been released by the British censor four days earlier, just as reports of the *Igotz Mendi*'s stranding began emerging from Denmark. The confluence of events had set off a propaganda war between the Admiralty and the *Admiralstab* that, within a remarkably short time, turned press coverage of the *Wolf*'s exploits into a hazy concoction of claims, denials, rumours and outright fabrications.

It began with a dramatic but entirely spurious statement from the German Government claiming that the *Wolf* had sunk or damaged 210,000 tons of Allied shipping, including the 28,000-ton Japanese battle-cruiser *Haruna,* an armoured cruiser and several British troop transports, which had been destroyed with the loss of 'a great number of men'. Scoffing at such claims, the Admiralty retorted that no British warship had been damaged by the *Wolf*, and the Japanese Government refuted the claim about the *Haruna*. But British and American newspapers were soon publishing equally creative fabrications. In one, which appeared on page six of *The Times* under the heading 'German Sea Atrocity', a Red Cross official claimed that the Chinese crew of the *Turritella* had been murdered en masse by the ship's German prize crew a year earlier. According to this story, the tanker was scuttled with bombs while the Chinese were still trapped below in the engine room. The Germans, it was reported, were now on trial for murder in India.

An erroneous report in the *Manchester Guardian* and several other newspapers claimed that the raider had encountered such a massive British Navy presence in the North Sea that she had been forced to turn back and land her prisoners in the Adriatic port of Pola (presumably then transporting them hundreds of miles overland to Germany). Newspaper editorials applauded the

Royal Navy's sterling work in bringing this about, unaware that the blockade had effectively been dismantled in early December 1917 when the 10th Cruiser Squadron was quietly redeployed as a convoy escort. The Admiralty was planning to replace the blockade with a massive minefield barrage off Scotland and Norway, but deployment of the mines had not yet started and the *Wolf* and *Igotz Mendi* had slipped through in the interregnum.

The British Government, not surprisingly, declined to correct the error and refused to confirm how many ships the *Wolf*'s minefields had destroyed. But the War Office was forced to concede that the raider had captured at least eleven ships – it named the *Turritella, Wordsworth, Jumna, Dee, Winslow, Beluga, Encore, Wairuna, Matunga, Hitachi Maru* and *Igotz Mendi* – and taken their crews and passengers prisoner. The story appeared on page three of the *New York Times* and circulated around the world, becoming embellished along the way with garbled details gleaned from the rescued prisoners of the *Igotz Mendi*, who were tracked down to their hotel rooms in Skagen by enterprising journalists.

One correspondent dispatched a report claiming that the *Wolf* had sunk a Japanese steamship called the '*Taksimara*', which was 'full of yellow persons who howled'. The *New York World* sent its Berlin correspondent, Cyril Brown, to Copenhagen to track down Stan Cameron and secure his story. In Madrid, anxious wives and mothers of the *Igotz Mendi*'s crew, some of them clad in mourning black, turned up at the offices of *El Sol* newspaper seeking information about loved ones they had assumed were dead. The *San Francisco Examiner* sent out reporters to the family homes of the city's thirty missing seamen to inform them their loved ones had turned up in Denmark or Germany.

In Berkeley, the Balch family – who were in the process of seeking adoption papers for four-year-old Edris Cameron – were startled by a telegram from Stan Cameron informing them that he, Mary and Juanita were still alive and resting in an obscure Scandinavian seaside resort. Mary sent a telegram to her parents in Australia that said simply, 'All is well. Letter will follow.'

The *Igotz Mendi* itself had, in the interim, become the centre of an international incident, for Germany was reported to have lodged a formal complaint with Denmark about the internment of Karl Rose and his crew. German newspaper editorials were denouncing the Danish Government, insisting that the Spanish freighter was a legitimate war prize and demanding that Denmark not only return the ship and its crew but also pay massive financial compensation or face 'disagreeable consequences'. An article in the *Washington Post* speculated that the two countries might go to war over the issue. The *New York Times* published an editorial sardonically suggesting that if Germany was entitled to compensation, Denmark should file a counter-claim for the 216 Danish freighters sunk by German U-boats so far during the war.

From his internment-camp dormitory in Aarlborg, northern Denmark, Karl Rose wrote a quixotic letter of complaint to the Danish minister of Foreign Affairs, disputing the legalities of his imprisonment. But Denmark was adamant that the *Igotz Mendi* was effectively a German warship that had violated neutral territory. Rose's blunder in running the ship aground had been mocked in the Danish press – 'Tourist Season Starts Early' was one headline – and the *leutnant* was a dejected and bitter man. In the first week of March, Rose was permitted to return to Skagen to preside over the funeral of a German seaman drowned off the coast, and while there he made the mistake of granting an interview to a journalist from the newspaper *Politiken*.

'For me, this stranding is almost in the nature of a tragedy,' he admitted, before berating the Danish Government for refusing to let the salvage tugs come to his aid. Rose was perplexed that Gervasio Susasta was being hailed as a hero for throwing the German prize crew's bombs off his ship. Couldn't everyone see the man was a criminal? And he was equally confounded that Tom Rees had told Danish newspapers that conditions in the *Wolf*'s prison quarters were intolerable. 'Throughout their journey there was not a complaint,' he protested. 'We gave the prisoners the same food as we had, we did everything in our power to make their lives as tolerable as possible . . . It has saddened me greatly since to see interviews in the Danish Press where the prisoners declared the opposite.'

But Rose, once a patriotic true believer in the Kaiser's naval elite, reserved his most bitter reflections for the war itself, which he now viewed with the same cynical detachment as Theodor Plivier. He remarked towards the end of the interview:

> It was strange for me to handle prize goods worth millions of marks every day, yet my salary was a mere 300 marks a month. On that sum, my wife and son could just survive in Hamburg. Businessmen, speculators on the stock market and neutrals have made fortunes on the war, whereas we that fought didn't get any of the booty, only the honour. Honour – well . . . For the time being I'm an interned officer in Aarlborg. This is the result of fifteen months of service and a kind of stress one can only take once in a lifetime!

His naval career ruined, Rose lived out the war in prison and returned to the sea as a merchant officer with the Hamburg-America line, whose records offer no clue as to his later life.

His bête noire, Gervasio Susasta, was an international hero by the time the *Igotz Mendi* returned to Spain in May 1918. Press reports lauded his courage, and the British Board of Trade presented him with a silver cup. In a reciprocal honour, Spain's lifesaving association bestowed its own bravery medal on Jens Kruse, leader of the Danish rescue boats. The *coup de grâce* in the affair was delivered several months later when a Swedish Court of Arbitration ruled that the Danish Government had been entirely justified in declining to assist Leutnant Rose. The Danish Foreign minister, however, tactfully kept the court ruling secret 'in order not to irritate the German Government'.

* *

Tom Rees, meanwhile, was only too happy to spur on the Allied war effort with some gratuitous Hun-bashing. Arriving back in London in the first week of March 1918, Rees obligingly put his name to a tendentious press article that depicted the *Wolf*'s crew as a bunch of bumbling amateurs and described Karl Nerger as a coward who quaked and stuttered with fear as he stood on the raider's bridge. Published under Rees's name, it offered this colourful description: 'The captain was a typical Hun, surly and continually bullying his officers and men. . . . He would hurl insults at an officer in front of everybody and seemed to have no gentlemanly instincts. He would never attempt to stop anything but the most inoffensive little ships that were likely to be unarmed. He sank a little French schooner one day and I remember he turned quite white, and trembled, when he discovered that this craft had two guns on board.'

Given that Rees was not even aboard the *Wolf* when the *Maréchal Davout* was sunk, it was a remarkably vivid account.

Throughout his illness, Rees had clung to his hidden notes of the *Wolf*'s minefields and armaments, and had managed to retrieve them before fleeing the *Igotz Mendi*. In a series of briefings at naval-intelligence headquarters, he passed the information on to the Admiralty, which immediately wired the details to Singapore, Australia and New Zealand. Australian Navy officials had already swept the area around Gabo Island, and in Singapore no ships had been reported mined, leading the Admiralty to suggest that the *Wolf*'s minefield had been destroyed by the monsoonal tides. But Rees's information was particularly valuable to New Zealand, for it gave precise locations and sizes for each minefield off the country's north and south islands.

Although six months had elapsed since the New Zealand Defence minister had asked navy officials to create a fleet of minesweepers, Captain Percival Hall-Thompson had so far found only two fishing trawlers suitable for the job. The crews for these ships had been thrown together so hastily that the captain of one, Scottish-born merchant skipper John Freeland, was given only twenty-four hours' notice of his new posting. Freeland had worked briefly on minesweepers in Aberdeen at the beginning of the war, but his experiences off New Zealand proved so terrifying that he would quit after less than four months. Sent out to the site of the *Port Kembla* sinking in February, Freeland's boat had nearly been blown out of the water twice in the course of deactivating four mines. The new information from London suggested that there were still thirty mines unaccounted for in those waters and another twenty-five lurking off the northern cape. Despite this, Hall-Thompson continued to issue a shipping alert that assured ship captains they faced only a 'slight' danger as long as they stayed in water deeper than 100 fathoms.

On 4 March, a mine from the *Wolf*'s northern field washed ashore on Great Barrier Island, near Auckland, having drifted 200 miles south, but Hall-Thompson did not send one of his trawlers north to begin sweeping until nearly two months later. The minesweeping crew were four weeks into their work – they had exploded four mines off Cape van Diemen – when the steamship *Wimmera*, carrying seventy-five passengers and seventy-six crew, struck a mine off the northern cape just after dawn on 27 June and sank. Twenty-six people were killed, two of them children.

During an inquiry into the tragedy, Hall-Thompson continued to insist that the minefield was 'not a menace to navigation' so long as ship captains stayed in deep water. He blamed the sinking on the *Wimmera*'s captain, Herbert Kell, who had apparently failed to heed the warning to stay within the 100-fathom line. The head of the *Wimmera* inquiry agreed with Hall-Thompson, and his critical findings ruined Captain Kell's reputation; the skipper himself was unable to offer a defence, having drowned after making sure most of his passengers reached the lifeboats. Hall-Thompson, however, enjoyed a long career in the British Navy after his unhappy tenure in New Zealand and was later promoted to admiral.

Roy Alexander commented after the war that merchant skippers such as Kell may well have felt genuine confusion about the danger from mines because of the false stories of sabotage and internal explosion spread by the Australian and New Zealand governments during 1917. 'Seen from all angles,' Alexander concluded, 'the Tasman Sea activities of the *Wolf* revealed hopeless incapacity on the part of the Australian administrators – an incapacity so hopeless that it remains almost incredible.'

In Australia, some measure of the confusion that existed was demonstrated by a near-disastrous incident in January 1918 when Rear-Admiral Yamaji's ship the *Hirado* sailed straight through the area off Gabo Island that was still being swept for mines – apparently because the admiral had received no adequate warning of the danger. By then, relations between the Australian and Japanese navies had reached an absolute nadir, for during his trip to Fiji to interrogate Count Felix von Luckner, Yamaji had again refused to help join the search for the *Wolf*, offering the lame excuse that 'searching among reefs is rather awkward to us'. Furious, the Australian Rear-Admiral William Creswell sent an official complaint to London in February 1918, accusing Yamaji of sabotaging their efforts to find the *Wolf* by twice refusing to assist, and quoting the Japanese rear-admiral's glib dismissal of the raider threat. 'It is now possible that the *Encounter* was despatched too late,' Creswell complained. 'But in any case her chances of tracking the raider were grievously diminished by having to do the work single-handed.'

As confused as government and navy officials were, the Australian and New Zealand public remained even more so, because their governments refused to confirm any press accounts of the *Wolf*'s minefields. In Melbourne, the Naval Board said it preferred to maintain 'a discreet silence'. The editor of the *Sun*, consistent to the end, published an editorial asserting that 'it is improbable that the *Wolf* was the minelayer'. The *Argus* newspaper was less complaisant, berating the Hughes government for its censorship and questioning how long it had known about the *Wolf*'s role in the ship sinkings that had for so long been blamed on sabotage.

'It will be thought that the shipping community at least should have been informed . . .' the newspaper argued. 'On the other hand, it will be asked: if the authorities were ignorant, what was the reason for so remarkable an ignorance in those who have such facilities for knowledge?' After months of being kept in the dark, the newspaper noted caustically, the Australian public had discovered the truth from the German Government.

* *

The details of the *Wolf*'s minefields were dispatched to Australia just as Lieutenant D. W. Drysdale arrived back in Melbourne from his exhaustive investigation of Carl Newman and the other 'foreigners' living on the coast near the site of the *Cumberland* disaster. Drysdale had managed to interview the elusive German-born fisherman and judged him to be 'an impudent, cunning man'; furthermore, every person the lieutenant had spoken to in neighbouring towns suspected that Newman had 'some secret reason' for going out to sea in his boat.

Drysdale's opinions should have been rendered redundant by the information just wired from the Admiralty, which confirmed that Newman had played no role whatsoever in the sinking of the *Cumberland*. Despite this, the fisherman was confronted at his home six weeks later, on 23 April, by a defence-intelligence officer, Captain William Trainor, who served him with an Alien Restriction Order compelling him to move inland and cease fishing. 'It is some damned funny business,' Newman retorted angrily. 'I know someone has been talking to the military about me but I will get even. I will not live inland. They can lock me up if they like . . . I am a well-known fisherman and have lived in these parts for nearly thirty years and reared a big family, and this is what you get for doing your duty.' Trainor promptly arrested Newman for failing to comply with the order and took him by train to the Victoria Military Barracks in Melbourne, where he was imprisoned.

Stripped of all rights to legal representation or due process, and unaware that he had been exonerated by two previous investigations, Newman made several plaintive attempts from his cell to summon help. In his semi-literate scrawl, he wrote a note offering £50 to anyone who could prove he had been disloyal to Australia, and asked his jailers to publish it in the *Age* newspaper at his expense, which they declined to do. He signed his name to a handwritten statement, written by a military police officer, in which he offered to sell his boat and donate the proceeds to a charity for returned soldiers. His family, meanwhile, had no idea where he was or why he had been arrested. In a letter addressed to the Defence department a week after he was taken away, one of Newman's daughters-in-law politely asked, 'if you could kindly furnish me with a little information as to the whereabouts of Mr [Carl] Newman Senior who was taken from his wife and family on April 23. . . . We don't know what the charge was against him and are quite overcome with the peculiar circumstances.'

Eight years earlier, Newman had helped the state government map the Gippsland coastline – a project that had inspired him to draw up his own plans for defending the area from military invasion. At his suggestion, police returned to his home and found the plans under his bed. Newman cited them as evidence of his patriotism and wrote a note to the head of military intelligence saying, 'Sir, Could i be of any servis to you in any way lett me know.' But his fate had already been determined, for several days earlier Brigadier-General R. E. Williams had recommended Newman's internment, citing the numerous complaints made against him, his large boat, his suspicious fishing trips and 'certain activities on the part of the enemy', all of which were deemed to make him 'a considerable menace' to the nation. By August, the fisherman was imprisoned in the government's 'German Concentration Camp' at Holdsworthy, west of Sydney, 600 miles away from his family.

Carl Newman became one of 6000 inmates crowded into Holdsworthy's wood and canvas barracks, which had been built without beds, chairs or tables. Many prisoners ate their meals on the floor, washed without hot water and slept on straw-stuffed sacks infested with vermin, for whatever furniture existed in the barracks was built by the prisoners at their own expense. Stoves were prohibited, even though the winter nights dropped below freezing point; in summer, the temperature topped forty degrees Celsius and dust storms often rendered food inedible. Although the prisoners had built restaurants, theatres and sporting areas to ameliorate their misery, the camp was riven with factions and feuds, for its inmates were drawn from many nations and included petty criminals, German troops from Asian garrisons and hundreds of captured sailors. A criminal protection racket in the camp had sparked a riot two years earlier in which one man was beaten to death and nineteen others were injured.

In August 1918, Newman's wife Louisa wrote to the Defence department asking for permission to live in the camp with her husband until the war ended, as they had been married for thirty-three years and 'it is the first time we have been parted'. The request was refused; wives visiting the camp were in fact only permitted to speak to their husbands through two wire-mesh barriers, between which guards patrolled back and forth. Such dehumanising conditions sparked a mass protest by more than a thousand internees during Newman's stay there, at the height of which the water mains were torn up and filled with sewage from the latrines. But by an extraordinary stroke of luck, Newman was released because of a clerical error in August 1919 – he had been mistaken for another inmate, George Newmann – and returned to his home. Long after the war ended, he was still being forced to take weekly boat rides to the mainland to report to local police.

Reviewing Newman's case after his release, a military-intelligence officer completely exonerated him, saying that the investigations that resulted in his imprisonment had failed to show any substantial evidence that he had ever engaged in disloyal actions or even remarks. 'It is true that there are many letters accusing Newman of suspicious movements,' the review said, 'but in no single case does there appear to be any satisfactory proof.' The fisherman had in many ways been fortunate – he was able to return home and resume his life. More than four thousand other 'enemy aliens' who had been resident in Australia were deported back to Germany between 1919 and 1920; a further 201 had already died in the concentration camps, some by committing suicide. The year after Newman was released, the Australian Government changed the Immigration Act to ban Germans, Bulgarians, Austrians or Turks from entering the country for five years.

The severity of those measures was applauded by some South African politicians, who demanded similar draconian laws in their own country and drew up legislation to deport all German-born citizens. That bill was defeated in June 1919, but only after a rancorous debate in which one MP described Germans as 'the spawn of hell'. By then, more than one and a half thousand interned German immigrants had 'volunteered' to be repatriated, having suffered financial and personal ruin; many took their South African-born wives and children to Germany with them. 'Hardships may probably be entailed,' commented Nelson Palmer of the Durban Vigilance Association, '. . . [but] I think it is fair. They get married for better or worse and must put up with the consequences.'

* *

For a few months at least in 1918, Karl Nerger became the most feted war hero in Germany. A photograph of the *Wolf*'s commander was emblazoned across the entire front page of the newspaper *Das Illustrierte Blatt*, and each of the five German states bestowed on him their highest military honour – a distinction that only a handful of men, including the Kaiser himself, had ever earned. The Berlin publishing house August Scherl offered Nerger a lucrative contract to write his memoir of the voyage, and on 26 March the captain and his crew were honoured by a full military parade through the streets of Berlin, presided over by Empress Augusta and recorded for posterity by movie cameras.

Cheering crowds choked the streets as Nerger and his men marched through the arch of the Brandenburg Gate and were escorted by a phalanx of helmeted soldiers past the Imperial Palace, where the empress and her grandchildren waved from a balcony. An official reception at the famed Busch Circus was opened by the emperor's brother, Prince Heinrich, commander-in-chief of the Baltic fleet. Wagner was played, film footage of the *Wolf* was screened and Karl Nerger spoke about his exploits. The crew spent the day swept up in a dizzying whirl of adulation. 'Women belonging to "patriotic societies" distributed flowers,' recalled Theodor Plivier. 'The city gave us a dinner and Kempinski [a famous restaurant] supper. In Busch Circus, in the theatre foyer and in the zoo we were almost suffocated by vast crowds of patriotic ladies thronging around us.'

Nerger's book, *SMS Wolf*, was rushed to the printers several months later and became a German best-seller that enjoyed multiple paperback printings. It was a book constrained in its detail by wartime censorship and the speed with which it was written; and although its tone was avowedly patriotic, Nerger made no outsized claims about sinking British troop transports or Japanese destroyers, and wrote with surprising affection about the men, women and children he had captured. The book was so widely distributed that Australian troops found mud-splattered copies of it in bunkers abandoned by retreating German troops on the Western Front. Capitalising on its success, the publisher quickly followed it with *Wolfchen: In an Aircraft Over Three Oceans*, by Matthaus Stein and Paul Fabeck. Leutnant Ernst Szielasko also knocked out a 127-page memoir, *15 Months as a Prize Officer on Board SMS Wolf*.

By the time these stirring tales were published, however, Germany was already sliding towards defeat and revolution. The *Admiralstab*'s grand strategy of starving the British into submission had become a lost cause even before the *Wolf* sailed back into Kiel, for the freighter convoys introduced by the British had nullified the U-boat campaign. Germany, not Britain, was a nation in collapse as the war dragged on. Supplies of both food and agricultural fertiliser had gradually been choked, first by the blockade and then by the entry of the United States into the war, which shut off direct American trade to Germany. While Allied forces on the Western Front were being reinforced by thousands of fresh American troops, weary German soldiers were absconding to loot British supply dumps for food scraps.

Theodor Plivier went home to Berlin to find his mother 'shrunken' and thin. His father had died only a few weeks earlier after the Admiralty's death notice for the *Wolf*'s crew arrived in the mail, the final devastating blow for an old man whose two other sons had already been crippled by war service, one physically and one mentally. Looking at a photograph of his father taken shortly before his death, Plivier noticed 'swollen finger-joints, his suit hanging loose on his emaciated body, his collar much too large around his neck'. When Plivier opened his knapsack to unpack the food he had pilfered from the *Wolf* – canned milk, corned beef and tinned fish – his mother said sorrowfully, 'If we'd had that a few weeks earlier, father would still have been here.' The suggestion that the old man starved to death may be coloured by emotion, for there is considerable argument about whether any German citizen actually died because of food shortages during the war. But Plivier's rage against the navy can only have been heightened by the thought that while he had been detained on board the *Wolf* for propaganda purposes, his father was dying of grief. By the time he finished his eight weeks' leave and returned to Wilhelmshaven – to take up a new post on a minesweeper at fifty pfennigs a day – Plivier's transformation into a revolutionary communist was complete.

Karl Nerger, too, was assigned to the minesweepers, as chief of the squadron in the North Sea – a curiously undistinguished job for such a celebrated war hero. Nerger's achievements had enabled him to erase at least one social stigma, for the Kaiser had finally granted him a dispensation to marry Marie and legitimise their four children. But his lack of status in the navy hierarchy remained; during the Berlin celebrations, Marie and the children had been hidden away in the cheering crowd, forbidden to approach him. And whereas the commander of the *Moewe*, the aristocratic Nikolaus Dohna-Schlodien, became aide-de-camp to the emperor himself, Nerger – a teacher's son from the middle classes – was appointed commander of a naval unit derisively known as 'the louse squadron'.

Posted to Wilhelmshaven, Nerger was on hand to witness the ignominious collapse of the German navy at the end of 1918, which lit the fuse of social revolution and forced the abdication of the Kaiser. With its armies facing defeat in France and the Balkans, Germany was forced to seek a negotiated peace in the final days of September 1918, yet Admiral Reinhard Scheer demanded his 80,000 men stage one last glorious, suicidal battle with the Royal Navy in the English Channel. It was a reprehensible plan, which Scheer concealed from the Kaiser and the government, and it sparked a mass mutiny in Wilhelmshaven among the crews of more than a dozen warships, who cut anchor cables, sabotaged searchlights, barricaded themselves below deck or refused to board. The jailing of the mutineers triggered a mass rally of sailors and workers in Kiel, who marched through the town singing 'The Internationale' and chanting '*frieden und brot!*' ('freedom and bread!'), arriving at the docklands to confront a phalanx of naval officers who fired on them, killing nine and injuring more than thirty. Enraged, the workers took over the warships and ultimately the town itself, demanding the emperor's abdication.

In Wilhelmshaven, Theodor Plivier was among the mutineers who walked off the ships in sympathy on 6 November, fomenting a march of 6000 people on the headquarters of Admiral Günther von Krosigk. The commander of Germany's largest naval base was forced into a humiliating capitulation, agreeing to free the jailed seamen, negotiate better working conditions and even suspend the requirement that enlisted men salute officers in the town. The rebellions quickly spread to Cologne, Hanover, Dresden and

Frankfurt, blossoming into worker revolts. By 9 November, more than a hundred thousand workers from Berlin's factories had taken to the city's streets, revolutionaries occupied the Reichstag and the socialist Karl Liebknecht was declaring from the balcony of the Imperial Palace that the rule of the royals had ended in Germany. The following day in the Busch Circus – where Nerger and his men had been feted only seven months earlier – the Social Democrat Party announced a provisional socialist government as the Kaiser fled by train to the Netherlands. Germany signed an armistice with the Allies twenty-four hours later, ending a war that had killed a total of more than sixteen million soldiers and civilians.

* *

It was a peace that came too late for some of the men who had been imprisoned on the *Wolf*. Private William Malthouse, one of the Australian soldiers captured from the *Matunga*, was already suffering severe gastritis when he arrived at Güstrow internment camp near Berlin in the bitter cold of March 1918. Malthouse was fifty-four years old and wrote letters to the Red Cross from the camp hospital, begging for warm clothing and saying he was fearful of enduring winter in the camp. His last letter to the Red Cross, as winter approached in October 1918, said, 'I am still in hospital. They cannot seem to do anything for me. My years are against me.' He died six weeks later, a month after the war ended.

Another Güstrow inmate taken from the *Matunga*, the furnace stoker Richard Turner, spent six months at the camp suffering from malarial fever until he was repatriated to a Red Cross hospital in Switzerland in September 1918. He died there on 9 December, and his landlocked sailor's grave can still be found in the Commonwealth war cemetery at Vevey on the shores of Lake Geneva.

Turner's ever-stoic and cheerful captain, Alec Donaldson, wrote to the Red Cross from Clausthal internment camp, high in the Harz Mountains of northern Germany, to report that he was fighting fit and wanted to order a new uniform. 'Don't believe all you hear about our hardships on the "Wolf",' he told the Australian Red Cross official Mary Chomley. 'We did not fare badly there.' After his release and return to Australia in early 1919, Donaldson professed that he had put on weight while held by the Germans and thought that 'short rations' might be good for the health.

Others endured a far more brutal experience. James Donnelly, a New Zealand sailor from the *Wairuna* who was sent to the Mecklenburg camp on the Baltic Sea, became a slave labourer in the salt mines of Saxony and came home with bayonet wounds in his thigh. Eric Minns, the launch boy of the *Matunga*, celebrated his fifteenth birthday in Güstrow and was put to work with other prisoners building the Hamburg–Lübeck rail link. 'My heart is not broken yet,' he wrote to his parents, 'but I think it soon will be if they keep me here much longer.'

Minns remained the youngest Australian prisoner of war in the First World War and endured another eight months of deprivation before he was liberated. His young shipmate Keith Harris was released earlier, but in grimmer circumstances: Harris was working on the rail line when a passing train blasted him with hot steam, burning his face so badly that he had to be repatriated to Geneva by the Red Cross.

Gerald Haxton was imprisoned at the Holzminden camp in northern Germany, where he listed his next of kin as 'W. S. Maugham, Bath Club, London'. When Somerset Maugham returned to Britain from his spying duties in Russia in late 1917, he was told that his young lover had been lost at sea aboard the *Hitachi Maru*. But the two men were reunited in 1919 and resumed their relationship (despite the novelist's recent marriage), embarking on a series of extraordinary treks and boat journeys together through China, Burma, Vietnam and Borneo in the years 1919–22. It was on one of those trips that Haxton introduced Maugham to the lawyer Courtenay Dickinson and his wife Mabel, who had returned to Singapore after the war.

Mabel Dickinson's fondness for liquor had not waned, for she was popularly known in Singapore as the 'Gin Queen' and held court every Saturday at the Hotel de l'Europe. In his conversations with the Dickinsons, Maugham learned of a local scandal involving a woman from the expatriate British community, Ethel Proudlock, who had been charged with murder after shooting dead her lover on the verandah of her home. Dickinson had been her solicitor, and Maugham appropriated the lawyer's detailed account of the case for one of his most popular melodramas, *The Letter*, which became a film starring Bette Davis in 1940. Among the minor characters in the play is a talkative, vivacious lawyer's wife whose cocktail making is legendary across the entire Malay peninsula. When he finished the play, Maugham sent Mrs Dickinson a typewritten copy with the inscription, 'To Mrs Dick, Here is the play which I owe so much to you.' Somerset Maugham and Gerald Haxton would remain lovers until Haxton's death from tuberculosis and the ravages of alcoholism in 1944.

The hardships of the voyage and imprisonment may well have hastened the death of many of those who were aboard the *Wolf*: Frederick Trayes died only four years after his escape from the *Igotz Mendi*; tuberculosis claimed the medical officer Alcon Webb in 1932, aged forty-eight; and Ross Ainsworth, chief engineer of the *Matunga*, was only fifty-two when he died of a stroke while still working for the Burns Philp line. Major John Flood returned to Papua New Guinea after the war with his wife Rose, taking up a private medical practice there, but a heart attack claimed him in 1929 at the age of forty-five. Rose Flood returned to her native Britain, where she lived in Southampton until her death from breast cancer in 1941, aged fifty-six. After her death, relatives discovered among her possessions a silver ornamental cup engraved with the words 'In Memory of a Trip Around the World, SMS *Wolf*, August 6 1917–February 24 1918'. The family was unable to establish who had given her the gift.

Tom Rees was awarded an MBE for risking his life to bring back a detailed report on the *Wolf*, and upon his return to New

Zealand as second officer of the steamer *Komata* he asked the Union Steamship Company whether it could pay some form of compensation for the ten months he had been imprisoned by the Germans and the nearly two months he had spent in London. The company sent him a cheque for £30 to cover his 'out-of-pocket expenses', equivalent to seven weeks' wages for a second officer – an amount Rees expressed considerable disenchantment over. Later, he sent a letter to the Australian prime minister, Billy Hughes, applying for the £2000 reward that Hughes had generously offered for information leading to the conviction of those responsible for the *Cumberland* sinking. But the government ruled that Rees was ineligible for the reward because no one had been convicted.

'I am directed to inform you that the matter has received consideration,' the prime minister's secretary informed him, 'but it is not considered that any reward is payable . . .'

Rees – who would remain a merchant seaman past his seventieth birthday – was not the only survivor of the *Wolf*'s exploits who felt shabbily treated by officialdom. Sailors from the *Matunga* who returned to Australia in early 1919, after nearly eighteen months of extreme hardship, were gratified to learn that the Burns Philp line had agreed to pay them for their time in captivity. But the company's penny-pinching accountants paid them at minimal seaman's rates and deducted from their wages the cost of uniforms sent to them in Germany's internment camps. In New Zealand, Captain John Freeland suffered such severe stress from his four-month minesweeping stint that by late 1920 he was hospitalised with heart trouble in Auckland General Hospital; when he died the following year, aged forty-eight, government officials in New Zealand were still refusing to accept responsibility for his health problems.

* *

Some of the more colourful myths that swirled around the *Wolf* became so fixed in the public imagination that eyewitnesses sometimes emerged to corroborate them. By the end of the war, many citizens of Australia were convinced they had seen the *Wolfchen* flying above their homes – a shared illusion sparked by erroneous newspaper reports that the German warplane had flown a reconnaissance mission over Sydney in mid-1917.

The source of this myth may well have been the *Wolfchen*'s flight officer, Matthaus Stein, who appears to have boasted to the prisoners aboard the *Wolf* that he had been ordered to take the seaplane over Sydney Harbour, to assess the number of warships stationed there during the raider's minelaying mission off Australia. Although the story was a flagrant fabrication – not only was the *Wolf* too far away from Sydney for such a flight to be possible, but the seaplane was dismantled during the raider's entire two-week sojourn in the Tasman Sea – many prisoners came to believe it. When Frederick Trayes and John Flood recounted it to journalists in London, a rash of newspaper headlines about this 'Seaplane Over Sydney Harbour' followed in Australia. In the ensuing weeks, police received more than twenty sightings of aircraft over the country's eastern states, and others came forward to swear that they had seen the *Wolfchen* during July 1917.

The story was largely forgotten until 1927, when Matthaus Stein arrived in Sydney as chief officer of the German steamer *Main* and was invited to speak at the German Club. Stein had visited Sydney before the war and had a number of friends from that visit in the audience. Perhaps overcome by the hospitality, he gave a colourful speech in which he not only repeated his account of flying over Sydney but claimed to have been armed with bombs. 'While flying above the city,' he said expansively, 'I could not help thinking of my friends below. I was glad at the time that it was not necessary to release the bombs . . .' A vigorous exchange of letters followed in the city's newspapers, with Roy Alexander and Alec Donaldson pouring scorn on Stein's story while others recounted the eyewitness reports of those who were certain they had seen Stein's aircraft in the skies above Australia. 'To this day,' Alexander later remarked, 'they recall how our city was spared by the chivalrous airman.'

A more poignant myth attached itself to the story of Alec Clelland and Arthur Steers, the *Turritella* crewmen who had escaped the *Wolf* in the shark-infested waters off Sunday Island in June 1917. The fate of the men became a source of intense speculation among the prisoners after they learned from the German crew that the calendar in the island's house had been found opened to the correct date. Fritz Witschetzky recalled that even he and his crewmen nursed a fervent hope that the two men had made it to shore and been rescued. By the time the *Wolf* returned to Germany, a story had circulated among the prisoners and crew that one of the men had been eaten by a shark while the other had reached the island, living a Robinson Crusoe existence until he was rescued by a passing Japanese steamer and returned to New Zealand. Stan Cameron claimed to have seen a wireless report confirming the rescue during a visit to the *Wolf*'s radio operators; others attributed the story to a crewman from the *Storebror*. Captain Tom Meadows heard it from a German officer and reported it to the Red Cross after he was interned in Germany.

In May 1918, Clelland's mother, Annie, wrote from her home in Limerick to Tom Meadows at Clausthal, begging him for further information. The New Zealander replied a month later, recounting the strange incident of the calendar and the rumour that had swept the raider of the rescue by a Japanese ship. 'What truth there was in this rumour I could not find out but it was freely circulated around the ship,' Meadows wrote. '. . . I would not falsely raise your hopes but until the Island has been searched there is no reason to believe your son did not safely reach the shore. There was food in abundance and plenty of fresh water on the Island and the sea was swarming with fish[;] it would have been possible for them to live for any length of time.'

At the Admiralty's request, the New Zealand Navy training ship *Amokura* was sent to the Kermadec Islands in late May

1918. For more than a week, the ship visited every major island in the group, and its crew landed on Sunday Island three times to search for any evidence of the two missing seamen. Nothing was found. The 'Robinson Crusoe' story lived on, however – Witschetzky heard it for the first time while talking to a merchant seaman in 1921, by which time it had been further embellished. In this version, the stranded seaman had not only been rescued but given a £1000 reward by the British Government for information about the *Wolf*. Annie Clelland continued to send letters to government officials imploring them to search nearby islands, but her son Alec was never seen again.

* *

Stan and Mary Cameron were finally reunited with their daughter Edris in San Francisco three months after their escape from the *Igotz Mendi*. The couple had remained in Copenhagen for six weeks, in part to recuperate and in part so that Stan could brief United States Navy officials about the *Wolf*'s raiding mission. During that time, Cyril Brown of the *New York World* interviewed him for a lengthy series of articles, which were published shortly after the Camerons arrived back in the United States in May 1918, having summoned the courage to make the Atlantic crossing back to New York.

It was not until 21 May that the Camerons returned to the Berkeley home of the Balch family, who had been caring for Edris. In the year since they had sailed for Australia, Stan's hair had turned almost completely white, his weight had dropped to 131 pounds and his once-boyish features had become sunken and etched with lines. Mary was also thin, and she wore a large floppy hat to disguise her still-regrowing hair. Despite his fragile physical state, however, the enterprising Stan had negotiated to have his ghostwritten story serialised in the California magazine *Sunset* and published as a book by George H. Doran and Co. of New York. He had also lined up a job in Seattle with the newly established United States Shipping Board, where he was to supervise 300 trainee merchant skippers at a newly built facility on the city's harbour. After only a week in California, the family uprooted themselves and moved north to Washington, the state where Stan was born in 1883.

For all his anger at the trauma his wife and daughter had been put through aboard the *Wolf*, Cameron took pains in interviews to make it clear that Karl Nerger and his crew had behaved with decency. In his serialised articles in the *New York World*, he spoke of his respect for Nerger and the friendships he had developed with the German officers; interviewed by the *Oakland Tribune*, he said the Germans had treated his family 'exceptionally well' under the circumstances.

It was a conciliatory attitude that may have been unwelcome with the war still raging and American troops being killed on the Western Front, for some journalists felt a compelling need to embellish his accounts. The *Seattle Post-Intelligencer* reported that the raider's crew used 'a fully equipped motion picture outfit [that] recorded almost daily the doings of the Cameron family aboard the German sea raider', citing this as evidence that the Germans were merely pretending to be humane for propaganda purposes.

In the *San Francisco Chronicle*, Cameron was quoted as saying that the Germans were merciless sadists who threw dead prisoners overboard on a daily basis and regularly discussed in front of him whether or not to execute his family. 'The insufferable heat of the tropics, the monotonous sweeping back and forth over the same stifling waters, the heartbreaking sight of prisoners, emaciated and blackened, tossed over the rails was our daily routine,' he reportedly claimed. The same story offered a colourful description of Leutnant Rose stabbing a crewman with his sword and then parading up and down the deck of the *Igotz Mendi* with the blade dripping blood. The journalist who penned these remarkable scenes went on to become a well-known writer of pulp fiction; the sword dripping with blood later appeared in other newspaper accounts, although the identity of the German officer wielding it changed in some to 'Willie' von Auerswald.

Cameron's book, which was published only a few months after he arrived back in the United States, mentioned nothing of these shocking incidents. Cyril Brown had pounded it out in record time, sticking faithfully to Stan's fair-minded view of the Germans and of Nerger in particular. Only the title, *Ten Months in a German Raider*, reflected the haste with which it was written. The family had actually been prisoners for seven months.

The Camerons returned to Berkeley in the early 1920s, and Stan resumed his career as a skipper aboard freighters. Mary sailed with him to Europe in 1925, leaving both her children behind this time, in Alameda. But after Stan gave up the sea for good in 1926, the couple moved to the Compton area of Los Angeles and he became an industrious entrepreneur, launching a car-rental firm and learning chemistry so that he could open a paint-manufacturing business and later a maritime laboratory. In the 1940s, he invented an electrostatic paint to keep barnacles off ships – an idea inspired by his time aboard the *Wolf* and tested by the United States Navy. At the age of sixty-seven, he was awarded a patent for the invention and earned himself a write-up in the *Los Angeles Times*.

At Long Beach boat jetty, the Camerons kept a converted Portuguese man-o'-war called the *Charlotte S*, which was their primary place of socialising. In his old age, Stan became known as 'Cap Cameron' , for he maintained the boat fastidiously, sailed every weekend and at home slept in a custom-built ship's berth installed in his bedroom. Mary remained fiercely devoted to him until her death in 1970, at the age of eighty; Stan died four years later. Despite their shared love of the sea, they had never again attempted to sail to Australia.

EPILOGUE

As a feat of military seamanship, the voyage of the *Wolf* was so singular as to justify Admiral Holtzendorff's claim that it would never be repeated. Karl Nerger kept his ship at sea for 444 days and travelled more than 64,000 miles in one unbroken voyage, equivalent to nearly three circumnavigations of the earth, without pulling in to any port. He traversed three of the four major oceans and evaded the combined navies of Britain, France, Japan, Australia and the United States, while carrying out a military mission that sank or damaged thirty ships, totalling more than 138,000 tons. When he returned to port, he had lost only a handful of crew and prisoners and had maintained extraordinary discipline on a ship crowded at times with nearly 750 men, women and children.

Yet the lustre of Nerger's fame faded quickly and other commerce-raiders soon eclipsed the *Wolf* in the public's imagination. When the war was over, it was Karl von Müller of the *Emden* and Felix von Luckner of the *Seeadler* who were lionised in books and magazine articles. Müller, the gallant kamikaze who led 130 of his men to a blazing death and later tried to tunnel his way out of a British internment camp, was dubbed 'The Last

Gentleman of War' by one biography. Luckner, of course, created his own mythology, inventing an elaborate story of the *Seeadler* being wrecked by a Pacific tsunami. After the war, he travelled the world giving colourful accounts of his exploits and tearing telephone books in half to demonstrate his strength. Henry Ford presented him with a car, the city of San Francisco made him an honorary citizen and in 1938, after he arrived in Australia aboard his yacht the *Sea Devil* as an emissary of Adolf Hitler, Prime Minister Joseph Lyons greeted the swashbuckling count at Parliament House in Canberra.

Karl Nerger, by comparison, withdrew from the public and watched his accomplishments belittled as the history of the war was written by its victors. The official British history of the war at sea, *Naval Operations*, credited the *Wolf* with sinking just twelve ships in nearly fifteen months. Its author, Henry Newbolt, praised Nerger for his 'energy, ingenuity and humanity' but went on to dismiss the entire German raider program as futile:

> The interference which they had aimed at was presumably such as raiders may effect by setting up a panic, or at least the feeling of uncertainty, in great ports of shipment, so that masters refuse to sail, bankers withhold trade credits, wharves, warehouses and railway sidings become congested with goods which cannot be transported; and as the result of all this economic and strategic arrangements are broken down or dangerously delayed. No such dislocation was effected even to the smallest degree by the German raiders, and the steadily progressive nature of their failure would seem to indicate either that the effort was ill-timed, or that it was ill-designed.

Australia's official naval historian, Arthur Jose, was similarly dismissive in his 1928 account, *The Royal Australian Navy*, making the unflattering accusation that Nerger had inflated his achievements with bombastic claims and 'a good deal of rodomontade'. 'Nerger was a brave and skilful leader, but he took fifteen months to catch fourteen vessels, most of them small,' Jose wrote. '. . . Safety is procurable on easy terms when one persists in haunting unfrequented waters and shunning contact with nine out of every ten vessels sighted.'

Such accounts were shaped by the desire of Allied military leaders to tailor the historical record to their own self-image. Even Arthur Jose – who had himself served as a navy censor during the war – waged a constant battle with navy officials who were trying to stymie the publication of anything that might, in his words, 'hurt the feelings of the British Government, the Admiralty, any Australian politician . . . or the US or Japanese Governments'. Jose's censored official history was finally published thirteen years after he had started it, but only after the official government historian, C. E. W. Bean, had accused the historian of anti-military bias.

Only in 1940 would British military officials acknowledge, in a classified official review, that the German raiders of the First World War caused significant loss and disruption, sinking more than 600,000 tons of shipping, holding up trade for lengthy periods and immobilising large numbers of Allied cruisers in distant waters. 'Under the circumstances,' it concluded, 'it seems extraordinary that they were not used on a larger scale.'

Nerger's reputation was besmirched further by Theodor Plivier, who established himself as a writer of politically charged realist prose with his 1930 book *Des Kaisers Kulis*, a lacerating yet poetic recreation of his First World War navy service. Plivier depicted Nerger as an isolated and ascetic loner, 'a dry mathematician who escaped the pursuit and pitfalls of the enemy, not by speed, but by the incredible slowness of our ship's movements . . . He fired no shot, he eschewed reckless feats of arms and heroism and only acted where all seemed perfectly safe.'

As a former gunner, of course, Plivier owed his life to his former captain's extraordinary restraint and discipline, and his contradictory feelings about Nerger are evident later in the book, when he acknowledges Nerger as a peerless officer whose achievement was 'without parallel'. Like many dedicated communists,

Plivier was destined to spend his life grappling with disillusion. When *Des Kaisers Kulis* was burned in public by the Nazis, he was forced to leave Germany and settle in Russia. There, his best-selling 1945 novel *Stalingrad* ran foul of the communist censors because of its pitiless descriptions of warfare, compelling him to break with the communists and return to West Germany. He died in 1955, leaving a considerable body of work and a school named after him in Berlin.

For Karl Nerger, the rise of the Nazis had even more regrettable consequences. Nerger was fifty-seven when Hitler was elected chancellor of Germany and had spent the fifteen years since the war living in relative obscurity. He had quit the navy almost immediately after the end of the war and taken a job with the industrial conglomerate Siemens, moving to Berlin to run factory security at one of its subsidiaries. When the Nazis came to power, however, he was feted once again as a war hero. A year before the Second World War began, he travelled to Kiel for a twentieth-anniversary reunion of more than a hundred and fifty officers and crew from the *Wolf*; over three days, they met at the naval barracks, dined together, laid a wreath at a memorial for dead crewmen and were honoured by the crew of the torpedo-boat *Wolf*, which had inherited the raider's name. A year later, he joined a gathering of military heroes at a Nazi ceremony commemorating the twenty-fifth anniversary of the Battle of Tannenberg, and was honoured with the rank of 'rear admiral retired'.

Nerger was by then a white-haired sixty-four-year-old, and it is easy to imagine how seductive such recognition was to a man who had been ill rewarded during his naval career and belittled after it. When Siemens had promoted him in 1938 to head of factory security for the company's two principal operations, Siemens Schuckertwerke and Siemens & Halse, he joined the upper management of a company that was enmeshed with the Nazi regime. Siemens executives had financially supported Hitler's rise to power, and the company employed forced labour in its factories from the Auschwitz, Buchenwald and Sachsenhausen concentration camps. Nerger's immediate superior, Wolf-Dietrich von Witzleben, was among the most senior executives in the company. After the war, Siemens claimed it had no choice but to cooperate with the Nazis and had treated its forced labourers humanely.

Whether Nerger helped to run the company's labour camps is far from clear, although some historians have suggested that as head of factory security for Siemens it would have been an unavoidable part of his duties. Traces of Nerger's life suggest complicity with the Nazis: in 1936, he bought a villa in Potsdam at a knock-down price from a Jewish family who had been forced to flee Germany; he participated in a civil organisation involved in factory security; he signed letters with the obligatory 'Heil Hitler!'. His role in the labour camps, if any, did not survive in the company records.

When the Russians swept through Berlin in August 1945, Nerger was arrested and thrown in the Sachsenhausen concentration camp, accused of being a member of military counter-intelligence. He was then seventy years old. In stories passed down through his family, it was claimed that Nerger's wife, Marie, died after being beaten by a Russian soldier while trying to stop his arrest. In fact, Marie Nerger died of typhus four months after her husband was taken away by the Russians. Nerger himself survived for nearly eighteen months in Sachsenhausen, a grim and terrible place in the aftermath of the war.

The camp records show that Nerger died in January 1947, a month before his seventy-second birthday, from cachexia – a disease of malnutrition. Sixteen years after his death, however, his fifty-six-year-old son, Dr Hans Nerger, received a letter from Heinz Masuch, a former inmate of Sachsenhausen. 'Dr Nerger,' the letter stated, 'you have a right to know the full truth about the death of your father, a truth which is so cruel that when I myself recall that awful time a feeling of hate rises in me against those who were to blame . . .'

Masuch went on to reveal that he had befriended Nerger in Sachsenhausen, coming to rely on him as a wise counsel in the vicious and predatory environs of the barracks. But the old man was ill and weak from lack of food, and he became the target of another inmate, Wilhelm Wagner, who ran an extortion and theft racket in league with the Russian guards. When Nerger refused to hand over his last remaining good pair of shoes in the freezing winter of early 1947, Wagner had viciously beaten him over the head with an iron bar.

'Dr Nerger!' Masuch said. 'I'm sorry if I have caused great pain to you with the truth, but since I had your address, it was not possible for me to conceal it. You must be assured that your Father was always and will remain for me and for a great many of his suffering comrades an irreproachable model.'

Four years later, Masuch succeeded in pressuring the German police into prosecuting Wagner for his crimes inside Sachsenhausen. In April 1967, the forty-seven-year-old ex-soldier appeared before a jury in Freiburg charged with extortion, robbery and bodily injury causing death. During the hearings, a former German Army colonel who had been in Sachsenhausen confirmed that Nerger had been admitted to the infirmary with an injury, but said he could not recall the precise cause of death. For his part, Wagner vehemently denied all the allegations. He was acquitted of Nerger's killing but sentenced to five years' imprisonment for his attacks on other inmates.

It was, strangely enough, one of Nerger's former prisoners who did most to revive the memory of his seamanship and his honourable conduct as a naval captain. In 1937, Roy Alexander published a colourful recreation of his experiences as a captured seaman entitled *The Cruise of the Raider Wolf*. It was the only eyewitness account of the voyage that stayed in print beyond its author's lifetime. Alexander was so effusive in his praise of Nerger's achievements that when the book reached its fourth printing, in 1941, he was forced to write a new preface, for by then a more ruthless breed of German commerce-raiders was at large under the Nazi flag, and anti-German sentiment was again running hot. Two raiders, the *Orion* and the *Komet*, had fired on the passenger-ship *Rangitane* off New Zealand in 1940, killing sixteen people, including six women passengers. A year later, the raider *Kormoran* would sink the Australian light-cruiser HMAS *Sydney* off Western Australia, killing all 645 of her crew.

Alexander remained steadfast in his praise, however, saying he could not imagine Nerger perpetrating the murderous deeds of the *Orion* and the *Komet*. 'Karl August Nerger,' he avowed, 'is one of the greatest seamen this world has known.'

Like so many of the *Wolf*'s survivors, Alexander was not destined for a long life, even though he gave up the sea for a more sedentary career as a journalist, author and broadcaster. In 1949, he checked himself in to the Mont Park mental hospital in Melbourne seeking treatment for a 'neurotic temperament', and two years later he was jailed in the country town of Ballarat on unspecified charges that may well have stemmed from his heavy drinking. He died in 1952, aged fifty-three, from liver disease.

Alexander was one of many ex-prisoners from the *Wolf* who, before he died, had sought out some of his former captors. While still working as a merchant seaman, he visited Hamburg and looked up a former crewman of the raider, who took him to his home for dinner. There, Alexander was amused to see that pride of place on the living-room wall was reserved for a walking stick fashioned out of a shark's spine.

Fritz Witschetzky, the *Wolf*'s gunnery officer, was serving on a German cruiser stationed in Oslo in 1921 when he ran across a seaman who had been one of the 'neutrals' from the *Winslow*, and they shared a nostalgic drink.

Ernst Szielasko may well have kept in contact with Stan Cameron, for a portrait photograph of Szielasko in uniform was found among Cameron's collection of *Wolf* memorabilia after he died.

Kapitänleutnant Karl Schmehl, in addition, remained in contact with Norman Pyne from the *Matunga*, sending him postcards from Germany 'in remembrance of good days and bad days on board'. They all shared the memory of an extraordinary voyage that had largely been lost to history.

When the war ended, SMS *Wolf* was seized by the French Government as part of German war reparations and recommissioned as a passenger-freighter. Renamed the *Antinous*, she returned to the very same Pacific trade routes where she had caused havoc and death only a few years earlier. In 1924, the French surrealist poet Paul Éluard, fleeing an unhappy love triangle in which he was ensnared with his wife Gala and the German Dadaist painter Max Ernst, boarded the *Antinous* in Marseilles for a six-month cruise to the East. Upon crossing the Pacific towards Tahiti, Éluard inadvertently conjured forth the ship's dark history when he wrote a poem evoking the numbing repetition of the voyage:

> Days so slow, days of rain . . .
> days of eyes closed to the sea's horizon
> Of hours all alike, days of captivity.

After more than a decade of uneventful peacetime service, the old freighter was finally scuttled in 1931.

Appendices

I

THE *WOLF*'S SPECIFICATIONS

Original name: *Wachtfels*
Builder: Flensburger Schiffbau-Gesellschaft
Launch date: 8 March 1913
Registered tonnage: 5809
Length: 442.9 feet
Breadth: 56.1 feet
Engine: 2800-horsepower, three-cylinder, triple-expansion steam engine; one propeller
Maximum speed: 10.5 knots
Range: 42,000 nautical miles at nine knots
Weapons: Seven 5.9-inch guns; three two-inch guns; four single-tube torpedo launchers; sixteen torpedoes; 465 mines; Friedrichshafen 33e aircraft
Source: *German Raiders: A History of Auxiliary Cruisers of the German Navy 1895–1945*, by Paul Schmalenbach

Wolfchen
Model: Friedrichshafen 33e two-seater reconnaissance biplane with twin seafloats
Engine: Benz Bz III six-cylinder, 150 horsepower
Wingspan: 54.9 feet
Length: 34.3 feet
Weight: 2222.3 pounds
Maximum speed: 73.9 mph
Initial climb: 3280 feet in 17.5 minutes
Armaments: None

II

LIST OF SHIPS SUNK AND MINED BY THE *WOLF*

Ship name	Tonnage	Captured/ mined	Location	Date
Matheran (Britain)	7654	Mined	Off Cape Town	26 January 1917
Tyndareus (Britain)	10,516	Mined	Off Cape Agulhas	6 February 1917
Worcestershire (Britain)	7175	Mined	Off Colombo	17 February 1917
Cilicia (Britain)	3750	Mined	Off Cape Town	18 February 1917
Perseus (Britain)	6728	Mined	Off Colombo	21 February 1917
Turritella (Britain)	5528	Captured	Indian Ocean	27 February 1917
Jumna (Britain)	4152	Captured	Indian Ocean	1 March 1917
Wordsworth (Britain)	3509	Captured	Indian Ocean	11 March 1917
Dee (Mauritius)	1169	Captured	Indian Ocean	30 March 1917
C. de Eizaguirre (Spain)	4376	Mined	Off Cape Town	25 May 1917
Wairuna (New Zealand)	3947	Captured	South Pacific	2 June 1917
City of Exeter (Britain)	9373	Mined	Off Bombay	11 June 1917
Winslow (United States)	567	Captured	South Pacific	16 June 1917
Unkai Maru (Japan)	3188	Mined	Off Bombay	17 June 1917
Mongolia (Britain)	9505	Mined	Off Bombay	23 June 1917
Cumberland (Australia)	9471	Mined	Off Gabo Island, South-East Australia	6 July 1917
Beluga (United States)	508	Captured	South Pacific	9 July 1917

Encore (United States)	651	Captured	South Pacific	15 July 1917
Okhla (Britain)	5288	Mined	Off Bombay	29 July 1917
Matunga (Australia)	1618	Captured	South Pacific	6 August 1917
City of Athens (Britain)	5604	Mined	Off Cape Town	10 August 1917
Bhamo (Britain)	5244	Mined	Off Cape Town	26 August 1917
Port Kembla (New Zealand)	4700	Mined	Off Wellington	18 September 1917
Hitachi Maru (Japan)	6557	Captured	Indian Ocean	26 September 1917
Igotz Mendi (Spain)	4648	Captured	Indian Ocean	10 November 1917
Croxteth Hall (Britain)	5072	Mined	Off Bombay	17 November 1917
John H. Kirby (United States)	1395	Captured	Indian Ocean	30 November 1917
Maréchal Davout (France)	2192	Captured	Atlantic Ocean	15 December 1917
Storebror (Norway)	2050	Captured	Atlantic Ocean	4 January 1918
Wimmera (New Zealand)	3021	Mined	Off North Cape, New Zealand	27 June 1918

Frank Mace, with lit cigarette, astride one of the *Wolf*'s mines near New Plymouth, New Zealand, June 1919. (© Puke Ariki: PHO2009-156)

Other Mine Incidents

Mines laid by the *Wolf* often detached from their anchor chains and drifted on the ocean currents for months, even decades, before floating ashore. Here is a list of the known mine incidents that are not included in the table.

21 February 1918: Washed up near Falmouth, north-east Tasmania, and exploded.

25 April 1918: Sunk by rifle fire from SS *Kouri* 100 miles east of Sydney.

11 August 1918: Secured off south-eastern Australia by SS *Kilbaha* and exploded.

September 1918: Drifted into shore ten and a half miles south of Colombo, Ceylon, and exploded, killing fifteen people and injuring 150 others who had gathered to watch.

7 November 1918: Sunk by rifle fire off south-eastern Australia by SS *Bodalla*.

Date unknown: Floated into shore at Baa Atoll, northern Maldives, and exploded when a fisherman hit it with a stick. A dozen villagers killed or injured.

10 January 1919: Exploded after hitting rocks near Awakino, north-west New Zealand, shattering windows of nearby houses.

30 January 1919: Pulled ashore near Levin, New Zealand, by a town local using his motorbike and some rope. Destroyed by navy officials.

23 February 1919: Sunk by rifle fire off south-eastern Australia by SS *Aeon*.

21 April 1919: Exploded while being pulled ashore by three men using a horse-drawn cart at Port Waikato, north-west New Zealand. All three were killed, along with their horses.

22 May 1919: Washed up near Port Stephens, north of Sydney, and exploded by rifle fire.

29 May 1919: Exploded after striking rocks near Gabo Island.

21 June 1919: Pulled from the surf by a farmer with horse and dray near New Plymouth, on New Zealand's north-west coast. Locals posed for photographs with the mine until customs officials destroyed it two days later.

1 September 1919: Washed up and destroyed on beach at Cooktown, far-north Queensland.

10 October 1919: Exploded by rifle fire from SS *Tarcoola* off south-eastern Australia.

December 1919: Towed ashore by two Aboriginal people at Dove Island in the Torres Strait. Later destroyed.

19 February 1920: Found washed ashore on central New South Wales coast and destroyed.

19 February 1921: Found washed ashore at Noosa Heads on the Queensland coast.

24 October 1929: Swept up by trawler *Koraaga* off south-eastern Australia.

11 December 2008: Found washed ashore near Karamea, on the western coastline of New Zealand. Bomb Squad called in, although it was thought the mine was no longer active.

III

LIST OF THE *WOLF*'S CREW

Name	Class	Rank
Abheiden	Naval Yard Division	Obermaschinistenmaat
Adam	Naval Ratings Division 1 and 2	Bootsmannsmaat
Albert	Naval Ratings Division 1 and 2	Bootsmannsmaat
Angermann	Naval Yard Division	Maschinistenanwärter
Angerstein	Naval Yard Division	Oberheizer
Anrehm	Naval Ratings Division 1 and 2	Matrose
Antweiler	Naval Ratings Division 1 and 2	Obermatrose
v. Auerswald	Officer	Leutnant zur See
Backstein	Naval Ratings Division 1 and 2	Feuerwerksmaat
Baltes	Naval Yard Division	Oberheizer
Bartl	Mines Division	Minenoberheize
Behrends	Naval Ratings Division 1 and 2	Obermatrose
Beier	Naval Ratings Division 1 and 2	Obermatrose
Beierl	Naval Yard Division (did not return)	Obermechanikersmaat
Bein	Naval Ratings Division 1 and 2	Obermatrose
Bendel	Second Torpedo Division	Torp'oberbootsmannsmaat
Berner	Naval Yard Division	Obermaschinistenmaat
Bernhard	Naval Ratings Division 1 and 2	Obermatrose
Berten	Mines Division	Minenoberheize
Bettighofer	Second Torpedo Division	Torp'oberbootsmannsmaat
Biester	Naval Yard Division	Obersanitätsgast
Birg	Naval Ratings Division 1 and 2	Obermatrose
Bögholz	Second Torpedo Division	Torpedooberheizer
Böhmler	Naval Ratings Division 1 and 2	Matrose
Bohn	Naval Ratings Division 1 and 2	Matrose
Böhnes	Naval Yard Division	Ober-F.T.-Gast
Bölte	Naval Ratings Division 1 and 2	Bootsmannsmaat
Borchard	Naval Yard Division	Oberheizer

Bothe	Naval Yard Division	Oberheizer
Brandes	Naval Ratings Division 1 and 2	Obermatrose
Brandes	Officer	Kapitänleutnant
Brandt	Naval Ratings Division 1 and 2	Obermatrose
Braune	Naval Ratings Division 1 and 2	Feuerwerksmaat
Braunholz	Naval Yard Division	Oberheizer
Breschke	Naval Ratings Division 1 and 2	Obermatrose
Bruckner	Naval Yard Division	Ober-F.T.-Gast
Bruder	Mines Division (did not return)	Minenobermatrose
Bruer	Naval Ratings Division 1 and 2	Obermatrose
Brunhörn	Naval Ratings Division 1 and 2	Obermatrose
Bruns	Naval Yard Division	Oberheizer
Buchholz	Naval Ratings Division 1 and 2	Obermatrose
Büfing	Naval Ratings Division 1 and 2	Obermatrose
Bülow	Naval Ratings Division 1 and 2	Obermatrose
Burgass	Naval Ratings Division 1 and 2	Steuermannsmaat
Burmeister	Deck officer	Maschinist Seewehr II
Büttner	Naval Ratings Division 1 and 2	Obermatrose
Clar	Naval Yard Division	Maschinistenanwärter Oberheizer
Coerper	Naval Yard Division	Oberheizer
Cron	Naval Yard Division	Zimmermannsgast
Cruse	Naval Yard Division	Maschinistenanwärter Oberheizer
Dages	Naval Ratings Division 1 and 2	Obermatrose
Dallmann	Naval Yard Division	Obermaschinistenmaat
Däumer	Naval Yard Division	Maschinistenanwärter Oberheizer
Dengel	Naval Yard Division	Maschinistenanwärter Oberheizer
Dennert	Naval Ratings Division 1 and 2	Obermatrose
Diederich	Naval Yard Division	Maschinistenanwärter Oberheizer
Dietrich	Officer	Torpedoleutnant
Doll	Naval Yard Division	Oberschuhmachersgast
Dormanns	Second Torpedo Division	Torpedooberheizer
Draunsfeld	Naval Yard Division	Maschinistenanwärter Oberheizer

Drentel	Naval Ratings Division 1 and 2	Obermatrose
Duis	Naval Ratings Division 1 and 2	Matrose
Eckerlin	Naval Ratings Division 1 and 2	Obermatrose
Ehrig	Naval Yard Division	Obermaschinistenmaat
v. Eiken	Naval Ratings Division 1 and 2	Obermatrose
Einfalt	Naval Ratings Division 1 and 2	Obermatrose
Elvert	Naval Ratings Division 1 and 2	Obermatrose
Erhardt	Naval Ratings Division 1 and 2	Obermatrose
Fabeck	Deck officer	Flugmeister
Fischer	Naval Ratings Division 1 and 2	Obermatrose
Fitzeck	Naval Yard Division	Obermaschinistenmaat
Folkmann	Naval Yard Division	Maschinistenanwärter Oberheizer
Förster	Naval Yard Division	Maschinistenanwärter Oberheizer
Frank	Naval Ratings Division 1 and 2	Obermatrose
Frenz	Naval Ratings Division 1 and 2	Obermatrose
Frisch	Naval Yard Division	Ober-F.T.-Gast
Fuchs	Naval Ratings Division 1 and 2	Obermatrose
Ganter	Naval Yard Division	Obermaterialienverwalt'maat
Gast	Mines Division	Minenobermatrose
Gatzlaff	Second Torpedo Division	Torpedoobermatrose
Gehrke	Mines Division	Minenoberheize
Geiser	Naval Ratings Division 1 and 2	Matrose
Geyer	Naval Ratings Division 1 and 2	Obermatrose
Gildenberg	Naval Yard Division	F.T.-Maat
Göbels	Mines Division	Minenoberheize
Gottmann	Naval Ratings Division 1 and 2	Obersignalgast
Grab	Naval Yard Division	Maschinistenanwärter Oberheizer
Gramberg	Naval Ratings Division 1 and 2	Obermatrose
Grimm	Naval Ratings Division 1 and 2	Obermatrose
Grimm	Naval Ratings Division 1 and 2	Obermatrose
Gronow	Naval Yard Division	Maschinistenanwärter Oberheizer
Groschowski	Naval Yard Division	Maschinistenanwärter Oberheizer

Gross	Naval Ratings Division 1 and 2	Bootsmannsmaat
Grübel	Naval Ratings Division 1 and 2	Obermatrose
Grüneberg	Naval Ratings Division 1 and 2	Obermatrose
Gutzmans	Naval Ratings Division 1 and 2	Matrose
Haag	Naval Yard Division	Maschinistenanwärter Oberheizer
Haffe	Naval Ratings Division 1 and 2	Oberbootsmannsmaat
Hain	Naval Yard Division	Ober-F.T.-Gast
Halder	Naval Ratings Division 1 and 2	Obermatrose
Hampe	Mines Division (did not return)	Minenobermatrose
Händler	Second Torpedo Division	Torpedooberheizer
Hansen	Naval Ratings Division 1 and 2	Matrose
Dr Hauswaldt	Officer	Marineoberassist'arzt d. R.
Heidemann	Naval Yard Division	Obersanitätsmaat
Heidenreich	Naval Ratings Division 1 and 2	Obermatrose
Heidmann	Naval Yard Division	Zimmermannsgast
Heine	Second Torpedo Division	Torpedoobermatrose
Heining	Naval Yard Division	Obermechanikersgast
Heinrichsmeyer	Mines Division	Minenoberheize
Heitzmann	Deck officer	Bootsmann
Hellemeyer	Officer	Marinezahlmeister
Hellmann	Naval Yard Division	F.T.-Maat
Hennig	Naval Yard Division	Maschinistenanwärter Oberheizer
Hessling	Naval Ratings Division 1 and 2	Obermatrose
Hildenbrande	Second Torpedo Division	Torpedoobermatrose
Hilker	Naval Ratings Division 1 and 2	Oberfeuerwerksmaat
Hinrichs	Naval Yard Division	Zimmermannsmaat
Hoffmann	Mines Division	Minenobermatrose
Hollern	Deck officer	Steuermann
Hopp	Naval Ratings Division 1 and 2	Obermatrose
Huch	Mines Division	Minenoberheize
Hünecke	Mines Division	Minenoberheize
Jacob	Deck officer	Torpeder
Jacobsen	Naval Yard Division	Obermaschinistenmaat
Jädecke	Naval Ratings Division 1 and 2	Obermatrose

Jans	Naval Ratings Division 1 and 2	Obermatrose
Kalm	Naval Ratings Division 1 and 2	Obermatrose
Karpfseer	Naval Ratings Division 1 and 2	Obermatrose
Kemper	Mines Division	Minenoberheize
Kersten	Mines Division	Minenoberheize
Kiel	Naval Ratings Division 1 and 2	Obersignalgast
Kienaft	Naval Ratings Division 1 and 2	Obermatrose
Kienast	Officer	Oberleutnant zur See
Kilian	Naval Yard Division	Obersegelmachersgast
Kimmerle	Naval Ratings Division 1 and 2	Obermatrose
Kinau	Mines Division	Minenbootsmannsmaat
Kirschhöfer	Naval Ratings Division 1 and 2	Matrose
Kirschner	Naval Ratings Division 1 and 2	Matrose
Klewenhagen	Naval Yard Division	Maschinistenanwärter Oberheizer
Knopf	Naval Ratings Division 1 and 2	Obermatrose
Koniezni	Naval Ratings Division 1 and 2	Obersignalgast
König	Naval Ratings Division 1 and 2	Obermatrose
König	Naval Yard Division	Obermaschinistenmaat
König	Naval Ratings Division 1 and 2	Obermatrose
Korbach	Naval Yard Division	Verwaltungsschreiber
Kranz	Naval Ratings Division 1 and 2	Matrose
Kravatzo	Naval Ratings Division 1 and 2	Obermatrose
Krietsch	Naval Ratings Division 1 and 2	Obermatrose
Krietsch	Naval Ratings Division 1 and 2	Obermatrose
Krönauer	Second Torpedo Division	Torp'oberbootsmannsmaat
Kulbars	Naval Ratings Division 1 and 2	Obermatrose
Kummer	Naval Yard Division	Maschinistenanwärter Oberheizer
Kunz	Naval Yard Division	Maschinistenanwärter Oberheizer
Kurfürlt	Naval Ratings Division 1 and 2	Obermatrose
Kurre	Naval Yard Division	Schreiber
Lange	Naval Ratings Division 1 and 2	Obersteuermannsmaat
Lange	Naval Ratings Division 1 and 2	Obermatrose
Langewald	Naval Ratings Division 1 and 2	Obermatrose
Lanken	Naval Ratings Division 1 and 2	Obermatrose

Lankow	Naval Ratings Division 1 and 2	Obermatrose
Lassow	Naval Ratings Division 1 and 2	Bootsmannsmaat
Lau	Naval Yard Division	Obermaschinistenanwärter
Leimbach	Second Torpedo Division	Torpedooberheizer
Lerchmacher	Naval Ratings Division 1 and 2	Matrose
Loedel	Naval Yard Division	Obersanitätsgast
Lohmann	Mines Division	Minenoberheizer
Löwenkam	Naval Yard Division	Obersegelmachersgast
Lück	Naval Yard Division	Maschinistenanwärter Oberheizer
Lührs	Naval Ratings Division 1 and 2	Obermatrose
Maleska	Second Torpedo Division	Torpedooberheizer
Manz	Naval Yard Division	Maschinistenanwärter Oberheizer
Marbach	Naval Yard Division	Obermalersgast
Martins	Naval Ratings Division 1 and 2	Matrose
Mathics	Naval Yard Division	Maschinistenanwärter Oberheizer
Mau	Mines Division	Minenbootsmannsmaat
Metelmann	Naval Ratings Division 1 and 2	Obermatrose
Methling	Naval Ratings Division 1 and 2	Oberbootsmannsmaat
Meyer	Deck officer	Marineobermaschinist
Meyer	Naval Ratings Division 1 and 2	Matrose
Meyer	Naval Ratings Division 1 and 2	Obermatrose
Meyer	Naval Ratings Division 1 and 2	Obermatrose
Meyer	Naval Ratings Division 1 and 2	Obermatrose
Meyer	Naval Ratings Division 1 and 2	Obermatrose
Mickley	Naval Yard Division	Obermaschinistenmaat
Milde	Naval Ratings Division 1 and 2	Obermatrose
Milz	Naval Ratings Division 1 and 2	Obersignalgast
Möller	Naval Ratings Division 1 and 2	Obermatrose
Moreth	Naval Yard Division	Maschinistenanwärter Oberheizer
Möser	Naval Ratings Division 1 and 2	Obermatrose
Muche	Naval Yard Division	Bäckersgast
Müller	Naval Yard Division	Bottelier

Müller	Naval Yard Division	Maschinistenanwärter Oberheizer
Nachtigall	Naval Ratings Division 1 and 2	Obermatrose
Nerger	Officer	Fregattenkapitän
Neumann	Naval Yard Division	Zimmermannsgast
Niemann	Naval Ratings Division 1 and 2	Obermatrose
Niemeyer	Naval Yard Division	Maschinistenanwärter Oberheizer
Niemojewsky	Naval Ratings Division 1 and 2	Obermatrose
Nisius	Naval Ratings Division 1 and 2	Obermatrose
Nissen	Naval Yard Division	Obermaschinistenmaat
Nolte	Naval Ratings Division 1 and 2	Matrose
Ohage	Naval Ratings Division 1 and 2	Obermatrose
Ohlmann	Naval Yard Division	Maschinistenanwärter Oberheizer
Orlowsky	Naval Yard Division	Maschinistenanwärter Oberheizer
Patzsch	Naval Ratings Division 1 and 2	Obersignalgast
Paukl	Naval Ratings Division 1 and 2	Obermatrose
Peitz	Naval Ratings Division 1 and 2	Matrose
Petznick	Naval Ratings Division 1 and 2	Bootsmannsmaat
Peuert	Naval Yard Division	Maschinistenanwärter Oberheizer
Pfeiffer	Naval Yard Division	Maschinistenanwärter Oberheizer
Pfeilstücker	Second Torpedo Division	Torpedooberheizer
Piezarek	Deck officer	Torpedomaschinist
Plivier	Naval Ratings Division 1 and 2	Obermatrose
Podziadlowski	Naval Ratings Division 1 and 2	Obermatrose
Politt	Naval Ratings Division 1 and 2	Matrose
Pöplow	Naval Yard Division	Oberheizer
Porrepp	Naval Ratings Division 1 and 2	Obermatrose
Priemer	Naval Ratings Division 1 and 2	Obermatrose
Przigoda	Naval Ratings Division 1 and 2	Obermatrose
Przybyla	Naval Ratings Division 1 and 2	Obermatrose
Przylutzki	Mines Division	Minenobermatrose
Rabe	Naval Yard Division	Maschinistenanwärter Oberheizer

Reimers	Naval Ratings Division 1 and 2	Obermatrose
Reintsema	Mines Division	Minenoberheize
Rentzelmann	Naval Ratings Division 1 and 2	Bootsmannsmaat
Reuter	Naval Yard Division	Ober-F.T.-Gast
Richter	Naval Ratings Division 1 and 2	Obermatrose
Rieck	Naval Ratings Division 1 and 2	Bootsmannsmaat
Riede	Mines Division	Minenobermatrose
Riehl	Naval Yard Division	Maschinistenanwärter Oberheizer
Ringel	Naval Ratings Division 1 and 2	Hoboistenmaat
Ritter	Naval Ratings Division 1 and 2	Obermatrose
Rose	Officer	Leutnant zur See d. R.
Röseler	Naval Ratings Division 1 and 2	Obermatrose
Roth	Naval Yard Division	Maschinistenanwärter Oberheizer
Rothaupt	Naval Yard Division	Maschinistenanwärter Oberheizer
Rott	Second Torpedo Division	Torpedoobermatrose
Ruffenach	Naval Yard Division	Obermechanikersgast
Dr Runze	Officer	Feldhilfsarzt
Sabrowsky	Naval Ratings Division 1 and 2	Obermatrose
Sachse	Naval Ratings Division 1 and 2	Obersignalgast
Sarnowosky	Naval Ratings Division 1 and 2	Obermatrose
Schade	Deck officer	Steuermann
Schäfer	Naval Yard Division	Oberheizer
Schaller	Naval Yard Division	Oberheizer
Schaub	Naval Ratings Division 1 and 2	Obermatrose
Scheitl	Naval Ratings Division 1 and 2	Matrose
Schibalsky	Naval Ratings Division 1 and 2	Obermatrose
Schiefelbein	Naval Yard Division	Maschintstenmaat
Schilinski	Naval Yard Division	Heizer
Schindler	Naval Ratings Division 1 and 2	Obermatrose
Schlottfeld	Deck officer	Maschinist Seewehr II
Schmehl	Officer	Kapitänleutnant d. R.
Schmeller	Naval Yard Division	Heizer
Schmidt	Naval Yard Division	Heizer
Schmidt	Naval Yard Division	Oberschneidersgast

Schmidt	Naval Ratings Division 1 and 2	Obermatrose
Schmidt	Naval Ratings Division 1 and 2	Obermatrose
Schmidt	Naval Ratings Division 1 and 2	Obersignalgast
Schmidt	Mines Division	Minenoberheize
Schoch	Naval Ratings Division 1 and 2	Obermatrose
Schönberg	Naval Ratings Division 1 and 2	Obermatrose
Schröder	Naval Yard Division	Obermaschinistenmaat
Schröder	Naval Yard Division	Heizer
Schuch	Naval Yard Division	Ober-F.T.-Gast
Schuhmacher	Mines Division	Minenbootsmannsmaat
Schüle	Mines Division	Minenbootsmannsmaat
Schulte	Naval Yard Division	Bäckersgast
Schulz	Mines Division	Minenoberheize
Schulze	Second Torpedo Division	Torpedooberheizer
Schünemann	Second Torpedo Division	Torpedoober maschin'maat
Schwab	Naval Ratings Division 1 and 2	Obermatrose
Schwarz	Naval Ratings Division 1 and 2	Bootsmannsmaat
Schwarz	Naval Yard Division	Maschinistenanwärter Oberheizer
Seifert	Naval Ratings Division 1 and 2	Matrose
Seiler	Naval Yard Division	Obermaschinistenmaat
Skaeb	Naval Ratings Division 1 and 2	Obermatrose
Steenblock	Naval Ratings Division 1 and 2	Obermatrose
Steffen	Naval Ratings Division 1 and 2	Obermatrose
Stein	Officer	Vizeflugmeister
Stein	Mines Division	Minenoberheize
Steinhäuser	Naval Ratings Division 1 and 2	Obermatrose
Steinmeyer	Naval Ratings Division 1 and 2	Obermatrose
Stendtner	Naval Yard Division	Oberheizer
Stoll	Naval Ratings Division 1 and 2	Matrose
Streiber	Naval Ratings Division 1 and 2	Obermatrose
Strömer	Naval Ratings Division 1 and 2	Obermatrose
Stüven	Mines Division (did not return)	Minenoberheizer
Sund	Naval Yard Division	Obermaschinistenmaat
Surhoff	Naval Yard Division	Obermaschinistenmaat
Sus	Naval Yard Division	Oberheizer

Szielasko	Officer	Leutnant zur See d. R.
Tanz	Naval Ratings Division 1 and 2	Obermatrose
Teuchert	Naval Ratings Division 1 and 2	Obersignalgast
Thomas	Naval Yard Division	Obermaschinistenmaat
Thrun	Second Torpedo Division	Torpedooberheizer
Tielking	Naval Ratings Division 1 and 2	Obermatrose
Tietz	Naval Ratings Division 1 and 2	Obermatrose
Trunk	Second Torpedo Division	Torp'oberbootsmannsmaat
Turner	Naval Ratings Division 1 and 2	Steuermannsmaat
Turulski	Naval Ratings Division 1 and 2	Obermatrose
Uhl	Naval Yard Division	F.T.-Maat
Vaders	Naval Yard Division	Obermaschinistenmaat
Veith	Naval Ratings Division 1 and 2	Obermatrose
Vetten	Naval Yard Division	Obermaschinistenmaat
Viert	Naval Ratings Division 1 and 2	Bootsmannsmaat
Vissering	Officer	Leutnant zur See d. R.
Vogelsang	Naval Ratings Division 1 and 2	Obermatrose
Voigt	Naval Ratings Division 1 and 2	Obermatrose
Volk	Naval Ratings Division 1 and 2	Oberwachtmeistermaat
Volk	Naval Yard Division	Oberheizer
Volk	Naval Ratings Division 1 and 2	Obermatrose
Volk	Naval Ratings Division 1 and 2	Obermatrose
Vollmer	Second Torpedo Division	Torpedoober maschin'maat
Voss	Naval Ratings Division 1 and 2	Signalmaat
Vosseler	Naval Ratings Division 1 and 2	Obermatrose
Wagner	Mines Division	Minenoberheize
Wähling	Mines Division	Minenobermatrose
Waldner	Naval Ratings Division 1 and 2	Obermatrose
Walter	Naval Ratings Division 1 and 2	Obermatrose
Warnstedt	Naval Ratings Division 1 and 2	Matrose
Weber	Naval Ratings Division 1 and 2	Obermatrose
Weber	Mines Division	Torpedermaat
Wehmhöner	Naval Ratings Division 1 and 2	Obermatrose
Wehrenberg	Naval Ratings Division 1 and 2	Obermatrose
Weiss	Naval Ratings Division 1 and 2	Bootsmannsmaat
Wenzel	Naval Ratings Division 1 and 2	Matrose

Westhoven	Naval Yard Division	Oberheizer
Wieduwilt	Deck officer	Maschinist
Wienicke	Naval Yard Division	Oberheizer
Wiesner	Naval Yard Division	Ober-F.T.-Gast
Wilken	Mines Division	Minenoberheize
Wilkening	Naval Ratings Division 1 and 2	Obermatrose
Wimmer	Naval Yard Division	Oberheizer
Wirz	Naval Ratings Division 1 and 2	Matrose
Wischmannski	Naval Ratings Division 1 and 2	Obermatrose
Witschetzky	Officer	Oberleutnant zur See
Woerle	Naval Yard Division	Oberheizer
Wolff	Naval Yard Division	Sanitätsmaat
Wölki	Second Torpedo Division	Torpedoober maschin'maat
Wulff	Officer	Leutnant zur See d. R.
Wunram	Naval Ratings Division 1 and 2	Obersteuermannsmaat
Zabel	Mines Division	Torpedermaat
Zimmer	Naval Yard Division	Oberheizer
Zimmermann	Naval Ratings Division 1 and 2	Obermatrose

IV

LIST OF THE *WOLF*'S PRISONERS

The following is a list of all prisoners captured by the *Wolf* who are known to the authors.

Turritella
Christie, A. D.
Clelland, Arthur
Davies, John E.
Heck, John Henry
Meadows, Tom G. (Captain)
Rosen
Steers, Alec

Jumna
Barus, Albert
Boshing, Robert
Buckingham, Robert
Burns, Robert
Cook, Archibald
Cuthbert, James
Dearmid
Elliot
Fraser, Alex F.
Gordon, William
Mallon, James
Maneriff
McAlpine, William
McGenghlin, Bernard
McLaren
Meese, George
Mitchell, Thomas
Mortimer
Pearce, Alfred C.
Potts, Mathie
Raby, C. R.
Ragau, John
Sterling, William
Steven
Ware, William
Wickmann, William Shaw (Captain)

Wordsworth
Bowman, A.
Burman, James
Campbell, Alexander
Cannisers
Cuthill
Davies, Frank
Day
Doolan
Forsyth
Forsyth, J.
Hickson, James
James, J. T.
Jenkins, James
Keegans, William
Llloyd, Jim
Lynch
Mackay
McAsoll
McDonald
McRae, John
Morrison, Kenneth
Mowforth, J.
Robinson, F.
Shields, John W. (Captain)
Strahan
Waugh, A.
Whyte
Williams
Winston
Winton, B.

Dee
Acland, Heise
Bohmer, R.
Boucary, S.
Castel, F.
Choron
Desveaux, P.
Emanuel, A.
Ivanoff
Joliconre, Henry
Latour
Marton, Jean
Pachelet, R.
Raoul, C.
Roth, J.
Rugg, John (Captain)
Seewatione

Wairuna
Alexander, Roy H. J.
Baird, G.
Ball, R.
Bish, J. E.
Campbell, W. G.
Carroll, J. W.
Claridge, C. J.
Coleman, J. E.
Currie, A. S.
Curtis, G.
Daniels, Arthur
Doherty, W.
Donnelly, James
Donovan, Richard
Evans, J. B.
Fornberg, John

Franklin, George
Gilliard, S.
Good, M.
Hickling, C.
Holden, R. W.
Ibister, P.
Johansson, Emil
Jones, Percy P.
Kenny, Peter
Littlemore, S.
Llloyd, L.
Macdonald, R.
Matthews, R. C.
McDonald, H.
McGaughey, R.
McKenzie, R.
McLeod, A.
Muir, T. W.
Murphy, T.
Murray
Olsen, L.
Patterson, A.
Quinn, A.
Quinn, James A.
Rees, Thomas R.
Ross, Harry
Saunders, Harold C. (Captain)
Saunders, J. D.
Stennan, W.
Thompson, A.

Winslow
Andersen, Axel A.
Ashford, Robert Watson
Christianson, Christian Peter
Jennings, J.
Morney, T.
Murukama, Y.
Nelson, A.
Nelson, Charles
Nillson, Johan
Nordstrom, Olaf Peter
Trudgett, Robert (Captain)

Beluga
Anderson, Carl G.
Bennett, Nathaniel M.
Buckhard, M.
Cameron, John Stanley (Captain)
Cameron, Juanita
Cameron, Mary
Johnson, Axel
Lindholm, Bertel
Martin, John
Morris, John
Netherwood, Richard L.
Neves, J
Parra, Daniel

Encore
Bindberg, Oscar
Emery, V.
Fox, John
Grau, Axel
Henry, Victori
Hilborn, John A.
Jenssen, Jens
Jorgensen, H. R.
Kasklow, J. Olsen
Korman, Gottlieb
Olsen, Anton (Captain)
Ube, F.

Matunga
Ainsworth, Alexander Ross
Berry, O.
Bliss, A. J. C.
Brocker, John W.
Bruce, H.
Burnett, John
Butler, James
Caress, J.
Casey, F.
Clancy, E.
Dickson, W.
Donaldson, Alec (Captain)
England, J.
Foley, M.
Goulding, Jack
Harris, Keith
Hayes, W.
Hayson, C.
Heffernan, J.
Hilder, C.
Jackson, H.
Jensen, J.
Jones, O.
Kelly, T.
Lynch, R.
Mackenzie, Agnes
McBride, William
McCaw, J.
McHutchinson, J.
McNaughton, A.
Minns, Eric
Moon, J.
Ord, M.
Perryman, G.
Peterson, G.
Pyne, Norman
Rae, S.
Simmons, A.
Smith, H. L.
Sweeney, F.
Taylor, R.
Turner, R.
Wells, A.
Wilson, F.
Wood, J.
Passengers
Burnett, J.
Cains, A. W.
Chambers, George R.
Clancy, Edward
Flood, John Wellesley
Flood, Rose
Green, George
Jackson, H.
Kennedy
Laycock, Frank
Macintosh, P. H. M.
Malthouse, William
Marshall, H. J.
McEnnally, William
Noble, Edward G.
O'Grady, James
Pearce, Rupert
Strangman, Cecil Lucius
Symes, D.
Wayland, J. H.
Webb, Alcon

Hitachi Maru
Kuziraoka, Kameno
Suetsugu, Kuraichi
Tominaga, Seizu (Captain)
Rest of crew unknown
Passengers
Allday, Gordon H.
Bartlett, G.
Benson, Barker Rutter
Benson, Mary Marie
Clarke, Alfred F.
Covil, Reginald Alan
Crawley, C. R.

Cross, Alexander William
Dickinson, Courtenay
Garland, B. D.
Haxton, Gerald
Hodges, R. B.
Joseph, Kiam Leuw
Chong Ah Sing
Konagei, Kiyoshi
Long, Marie Elsonore
Menson, Leonie
Patterson, Denis Ford
Purdom, W. August
Sawyer, Bruce
Shiraishi, Kenkichi
Stopani, W. A.
Trayes, Frederick George
Trayes, Jessie Mary
Whittaker, Mabel F.
Youn, Yap Fong

Igotz Mendi
Aberasturi, Antonion
Alzarez, Marmil A.
Arostigni, Mariano
Barrona, Julian
Bertomen, Jan D.
Bertomen, Jose R.
Buiston, Jose R.
Carlos, Thomas
Galdo, Dionicir R.
Gonzalez, Jose A.
Gorrono, Jesus
Gracia, Anton P.
Ibarouto, Alejo G.
Igarza, Manuel C.
Lardin, Franco M
Lareno, Ricardo
Lopez, Antonio C.
Lopez, Jesus N.
Lopez, Jose
Lopez, Nazario
Ondora, Jose M.
Onvorsa, Joaquin
Porrsia, Romnaldo B.
Prista, Victor M.
Susasta, Gervasio
Ugaldo, Rosalio U.
Ugalde, Quintín (Captain)
Zabala, Eusebio
Zubin, Leandro H.

John H. Kirby
Blom, John Arnold (Captain)
Colstad, Adolph
Moore, Edward
Olssen, Ole
Rest of crew unknown

Maréchal Davout
Brett, Louis (Captain)
Rest of crew unknown

Storebror
Captain and crew unknown

Every endeavour has been made to contact relatives and descendants of those who were aboard SMS *Wolf*. Anyone wishing to contact Richard Guilliatt or Peter Hohnen with additional information about the voyage of the *Wolf* can email them at guilliatt.hohnen@gmail.com.

ACKNOWLEDGEMENTS

Any book that requires five years of research owes its existence to a great many more people than its authors, and this one is no exception. We are deeply indebted to a multitude of far-flung assistants who helped us amass the details of this story, often for little or no personal reward.

In particular, we want to express our profound gratitude to those descendants of the *Wolf*'s crew and prisoners who gave us access to private family archives that yielded a trove of unpublished photographs, letters and journals from the voyage.

In Los Angeles, Walt Coburn – son of Juanita Coburn (née Cameron) and grandson of Stan and Mary Cameron – cheerfully handed over his mother's entire collection of photographs and other memorabilia from the voyage, asking for nothing in return other than a good bottle of Australian Shiraz.

In Braunschweig, Dr Christian Hauswaldt was similarly generous with the photographic collection of his late father, Dr Hermann Hauswaldt, and patiently answered our many questions over several years of correspondence – waiting until late in 2008 to reveal that he still possessed his father's ninety-year-old handwritten medical log from the ship.

Also in Germany, several of Kapitän Karl Nerger's descendants – his great nephew Klaus Nerger, his grandsons Uwe and Axel, and his great-grandson Wolf-Christian Nerger – proved overwhelmingly generous with information and photographic material about their remarkable ancestor.

Sigrid Könneke very kindly provided us with a typed copy of the unpublished diary written by her father, Albert Wieduwilt, during his tenure as a senior engineer aboard the *Wolf*.

Bruce Pyne, son of the late Norman Pyne, provided photographs from his father's collection but sadly passed away before our book was published. We are indebted to his son Michael for permission to use this material. Greg Minns was similarly generous in providing photographs and newspaper clippings relating to his late grandfather, Eric Minns.

Richard Bell travelled from his home in France to England to investigate essential details about his mysterious great aunt, Rose Flood (née Coombes).

In Victoria, Frank Newman provided valuable insights into the life of his grandfather, Carl Newman.

In New Zealand, Rachel Watson supplied important details about the minesweeping career of her grandfather, Captain John Freeland.

A number of historians and professional researchers gave generously of their time and expertise. Among them was Ian Affleck, recently retired senior photographic curator of the Australian War Memorial; by extraordinary coincidence, Ian purchased at auction in 2005 a wonderful collection of more than two hundred photographs taken aboard the *Wolf*, which can now be viewed on the Australian War Memorial website. His colleague Ashley Ekins also gave us important assistance. Darren Watson, author of a historical study of the Carl Newman case, helped us research the details of that sad episode. Dr Frank Cain, senior lecturer at the Australian Defence Force Academy, guided us on issues of Australia's intelligence agencies. Patricia Worth worked tirelessly to locate files in the National Library and the National Archives in Canberra, and Jenny Gleeson provided her expertise as a professional librarian.

In Wellington, Joanne Whittle did an outstanding and exhaustive job of combing through the files of the New Zealand National

Archives and the Wellington City Archives to locate and collate important material. Her partner, Dr Aaron Fox, formerly of the New Zealand Defence Force, offered many helpful suggestions.

We would also like to thank Emilie Kolb at the Department of German Studies, University of Sydney, genealogist Judith Edmonds, Georgia Harvey, Peter Gill and Neil Smith AM.

Mackenzie Gregory, a former lieutenant-commander in the Royal Australian Navy and convenor of the invaluable website Ahoy – Mac's Web Log (http://ahoy.tk-jk.net), was a fount of knowledge on naval matters and provided valuable commentary on the manuscript.

In Britain, Roger Nixon conducted extensive file research for us in the National Archives in Kew.

In Germany, we were assisted by genealogist Andrea Bentschneider, whose search for descendants of Kapitän Karl Nerger benefitted from an eerie coincidence when she was herself contacted by Uwe Nerger, who was researching the life of his grandfather. Guenther Klugermann also conducted genealogical research and obtained a copy of the Wolf's 'war diary' from the German military archives in Freiburg.

Professor Wilfried Feldenkirchen of Friedrich Alexander University in Nuremberg kindly assisted with material on Karl Nerger's post-war career at Siemens. Horst Bredow, founder and executive director of the German U-Boat Museum in Cuxhaven, tracked down the ninety-year-old war-service records of many *Wolf* crew members and officers. The naval historian Dr Werner Rahn helped us locate valuable source material.

In Denmark, Brigadier General Michael Clemmesen of the Royal Danish Defence College was extraordinarily helpful in providing documents from the Danish naval archives, along with translations and guidance on Danish military matters. Martin Prag visited the Skagen Museum on our behalf and located extensive files and photographs of the Igotz Mendi incident. The Skagen Museum's curator, Hans Nielsen, kindly gave us permission to use images from his collection.

In Spain, our search for news reports on the *Igotz Mendi* was assisted by Helena Carvajal, Dolores Jimenez and Margareta Moreno, who also translated those clippings.

In South Africa, Dr Andrew Conder helped us locate records from the military archives and parliamentary transcripts.

In the United States, the Californian genealogist Margaret Posehn gave us tremendous assistance in tracking down Walt Coburn, the only living descendant of Stan and Mary Cameron. Emeritus Professor Paul G. Halpern of Florida State University also offered the guidance of a professional historian.

For locating and translating foreign-language documents, we are grateful to Erica and Fumi Shaw, Nadine Helmi, Katharina Rentschler, Yona Pössnecker, Justin Whitney, Britte Sorensen and Susanne Gross.

We would like to sincerely thank the literary agents Mark Lucas in London and Kathleen Anderson in New York for finding a home for this project in their respective countries. Nikki Christer and Kevin O'Brien at Random House Australia went the extra mile for us in editing and preparing the book for publication, and we would also like to thank Bill Scott-Kerr at Transworld in the United Kingdom, and Martin Beiser at Free Press in the United States for their input.

Finally, this book might never have been published if our agent, Mary Cunnane, had not introduced the authors and shepherded us expertly to the right publishers. Many thanks, Mary.

* *

There are many people who helped me get started on this long and arduous voyage, a true odyssey with many hardships and frustrations as well as serendipitous happenings and incredible coincidences. But, first of all, I should like to pay tribute to the memory of two great Australian historians, Professors Manning Clark AC and John D. Ritchie AO. When I was a student at the Australian National University in Canberra, they instilled and reinforced in me a love for Australian and British history.

Another student of theirs (far more distinguished), Professor Iain McCalman AO, suggested in the course of a chance meeting in a coffee shop in Margaret River that I submit the *Wolf* story to his agent, Mary Cunnane.

High on my gratitude list also is Professor Michael Morgan, neurosurgeon extraordinaire, whose gifted hands saved my life when I underwent surgery for a cerebral aneurysm.

The idea of researching the *Wolf*'s unique voyage came to me on a motoring trip from Perth to Broome in 2002 when I stopped in Geraldton to view the monument to the sinking of HMAS *Sydney* in 1941 by a second-generation German raider, *Kormoran*. It set me thinking about stories I had heard in my childhood from my father's mother about a very successful raider of the First World War, SMS *Wolf*, which had captured her younger brother's ship *Matunga* while she was en route from Brisbane to Rabaul, New Guinea. From August 1917 until March 1918, my grandmother's family, the Ainsworths, believed that their relative Ross had died at sea when the *Matunga* disappeared in an 'oceanic earthquake' – the widely published explanation at the time. They were eventually informed that he was a prisoner of war in Germany, like countless other families around the world who also believed their loved ones had been lost at sea, when in fact they had been captured by the *Wolf*. I often pondered how my great-uncle survived those long months in the Hell Hole and later in a German prison camp; the Ainsworth family motto, *Spero meliora* ('I hope for better things'), was probably never so sorely tested.

My first breakthrough in seeing the human-interest value of this story came when I discovered that a New Zealand diver, Mike Fraser, had learned about the *Wolf*'s activities while stationed as a meteorologist on the Kermadec Islands north of New Zealand. Mike – who lost his right forearm to a white pointer while diving in 1992 – had obtained copies of the memoirs written by the *Wolf*'s commander, Kapitän Karl August Nerger, and gunnery officer Fritz Witschetzky. Remarkably, neither of those books had ever been published in English, and Mike had arranged for them to be translated as a private initiative. Those books set me searching for other first-hand accounts, particularly on the German side. Back in the 1990s, when living in Canberra, I had purchased books on the *Wolf* by two Australians, Alec Donaldson – captain of my great-uncle's ship the *Matunga* – and Roy Alexander, who had written a colourful account of his adventure as a prisoner in the Hell Hole.

Mike Scanlon and Joanne Crawford of the *Newcastle Herald* newspaper were instrumental in helping me locate descendants of the Gregory family and piece together Mary Cameron's early family history.

I started this research while living in Western Australia, and those I would like to specifically thank for helping me to see the potential of this story are Carrol Adams, Paddy Bergin, Greg Colgan (of documentary-maker Electric Pictures Pty Ltd), Susan Groom, Stuart and Jacoba Hohnen, Helen Laing, Carey Watkin and Susann Anna.

My children, Emma, Amelia and Julian, have sustained me throughout by their faith that I could bring this mission to a successful conclusion. I thank them for their confident urging: 'We know you have it in you, Dad.'

And, finally, I would like to record my gratitude to my Muse, Victoria Christie, for constant inspiration, encouragement and advice, sometimes in periods of great stress.

Peter Hohnen

* *

First and foremost, I would like to thank Peter Hohnen for allowing me to come aboard *The Wolf*, a project that had already absorbed a great deal of his energy, time and financial resources when we first met in April 2006. As co-authors, we make an unlikely pair, but somehow it worked. I am grateful to Deborah Tobias for her legal advice and extremely flexible billing system. And, for their patience and forbearance, I am indebted to my wonderful family – Susan, Jess and Pia – in a way I suspect they'll never let me forget.

Richard Guilliatt

REFERENCES

Abbreviations used in this section

APH: Australian Parliamentary Hansard
BMAG: Bundesarchiv Militärarchiv, Germany
BPH: British Parliamentary Hansard
DID: Director of the intelligence division of the naval staff, London
MAD: Marinministeriets Archiv, Denmark
NAA: National Archives of Australia
NANZ: National Archives of New Zealand
NARSSA: National Archives and Records Service of South Africa
NAUK: National Archives of the United Kingdom
NID: Naval-intelligence division
NLA: National Library of Australia
SAPH: South African Parliamentary Hansard

The notation 'Nerger diary' refers to the BMAG file entitled 'Kriegstagebuch des Kommandos SMS "Wolf"' (War Diary of the Commander of SMS 'Wolf' – in other words, the captain's log), by Fregattenkapitän Karl August Nerger, RM99/785, held at the Kriegsarchiv der Marine, Freiburg, Germany.

The notation 'Admiralty file' refers to the NAUK file entitled 'Cruise of the German Auxiliary Cruiser "Wolf"', ADM137/3910, held at the Public Record Office, Kew, United Kingdom.

Part 1

Chapter 1: The Black Raider

P. 3 *'The thrill of war'*: *San Francisco Chronicle*, 12 April 1917, p. 1.
3 *Details of Camerons' early life*: From author interviews with Cameron family descendants and New South Wales marriage certificate 1908/002235. Additional details from 'I Remember', an unpublished family history by Mary Cameron's sister, Jean Shaw Peterson, and from undated newspaper articles collected by Stan Cameron and held by his grandson, Walter Coburn.
4 *'terrifying ordeal'*: *San Francisco Examiner*, 7 June 1909, p. 1.
5 *'extraordinary wages'*: *Oakland Tribune*, 17 May 1917, p. 15.
5 *'boiling down the bodies'*: *The Times*, 16 April 1917; *Washington Post*, 21 April 1917.
5 *Seldom have I gone to sea under more favourable circumstances'*: Cameron, p. 12.
5 *'like many Americans he was ambivalent'*: Cameron himself did not write of this, but a crewman aboard the *Wolf* later wrote in his diary that the American skipper 'continued to say that people in the west of America were particularly enraged about the war and that a civil war will probably break out there. He did not believe that American troops would be sent to the European theater.' (Wieduwilt, pp. 25–6).
7 *'happy as could be'*: Cameron, p. 15.
8 *'By God'*: Ibid., p. 17.
9 *'Suddenly she threw both her arms'*: Ibid., p. 20.
10 *'Captain, I take charge'*: Ibid., p. 21.
13 *'Tell your wife'*: Ibid., pp. 30–31.
16 *'The sea for miles around us'*: Ibid., pp. 33–34.

Chapter 2: Suicide Ships

P. 18 *Details of* Lusitania *sinking*: From Bailey and Ryan, pp. 128–46.
18 *'"divine" plan'*: Best, p. 145.
19 *'Right, Justice and the Spirit of Peace'*: *The Times*, 17 October 1907, p. 3.
20 *'grass would sooner or later grow'*: Ferguson, p. 86.
20 *'It's starvation'*: Fisher, p. 135.
20 *'key to victory'*: Tirpitz, p. 419.

20 *Naval rules of engagement and commerce war:* For further discussion, see Bailey and Ryan, pp. 26–46; Best, pp. 67–74; Phillipson, pp. 348–71; Howard, Andrepoulos and Shulman, pp. 116–28; Tirpitz, pp. 576–9.

21 *'unscrupulously outraged'*: Tirpitz, p. 578.

22 *'wanton recklessness'*: Ibid., p. 405.

22 Lusitania *reaction: New York Times*, 11 May 1915, p. 4; Bailey and Ryan, pp. 226–44.

23 *'paralysed the commerce'*: *Manchester Guardian*, 21 June 1864, cited in Fox, p. 229.

24 *'It is almost in our heart'*: Cited in *New York Times*, 11 November 1914, p. 1.

24 *'without parallel'*: *Chicago Tribune*, 11 November 1914, p. 2.

24 *'suicide ships'*: Plivier, p. 172. The nickname '*Himmelfahrtsdampfer*' literally means 'ascension steamer' and is a play on '*Hilfskreuzer*' or 'auxiliary cruiser', *Christi himmelfahrt* being the day of Christ's ascension to heaven. We have adopted the colloquial meaning: suicide ship.

24 *Commerce-raider campaign:* For further discussion of the rationale, see Mantey, pp. 139–42, and Schmalenbach, pp. 132–8.

26 *Press coverage of* Appam *and* Moewe: *New York Times*, 2 February 1916, p. 1; also 5 February 1916, p. 1.

26 *'fateful decision'*: Beesly, p. 145.

27 Belgravia *details:* Schmalenbach, p. 136; Witschetzky, pp. 13–22.

27 *'A victorious end'*: Halpern, pp. 328–9.

29 *'it is absolutely essential'*: Mantey, p. 238.

29 Wolf*'s operational orders:* From Admiralty document 'Review of German Cruiser Warfare 1914–1918', NAUK, ADM275/22.

30 *'I wish you luck'*: Mantey, p. 368.

30 *'Nerger oversaw the work'*: Witschetzky, pp 28–31; Plivier, p. 226.

32 *Description of Witschetzky:* Plivier, p. 244.

32 *'A great bunch of guys'*: Witschetzky, p. 15.

33 *'unutterably stupid'*: Plivier, p. 109.

33 *'Do you think I carried wine-buckets'*: Ibid., p. 224.

35 *Room 40:* Role in First World War detailed in Tuchman, pp. 3–24, and at length in Beesly.

37 *'lucky star'*: Nerger (Admiralty translation), p. 3.

37 *'the loneliest man on board'*: Plivier, p. 248.

38 *'The admirals sent him to the sky-tripper'*: Ibid., p. 226.

41 *Details of* Matheran *sinking:* From transcripts of evidence, 'Wreck Enquiry – SS *Matheran*', NARSSA, 78/17/23/2.

41 *Details of anonymous postcard and seizure of* Tasmanic*:* From Admiralty cable, 28 January 1917, Admiralty file.
42 *'As a matter of courtesy'*: Lord Burnham quoted in Sanders and Taylor, p. 30.
42 *British war censorship:* For details, see Ferguson, pp. 212–47; Sanders and Taylor, pp. 15–54; Rose, pp. 10–41.
42 *'If the people really knew'*: Cited in Knightley, p. 109.
42 *German atrocities and the Bryce Report:* For further discussion, see Knightley, pp. 83–4; Williams, pp. 39–80; Ponsonby, Chapter 23.
43 *'the military masters': New York Times*, 15 June 1917, p. 1.
43 *Every German a potential spy:* British War Office dispatch quoted in the *Argus*, 7 July 1917, p. 15.
43 *Internment and anti-German sentiment in South Africa:* For details, see Minutes of Evidence, Select Committee on Enemies Repatriation and Denaturalization Bill, 10 April 1919, SAPH; *Cape Times*, 30 January 1917, p. 1; *The Times*, 14 May 1915, p. 5; *New York Times*, 16 May 1915, p. 4.
44 *Newspaper editorials:* Cited in *Cape Times*, 15 February 1917, p. 7.
46 *'It's strange'*: Nerger diary, 20 February 1917.
47 *Madras Government statement:* Reported in *Times of Ceylon*, 26 February 1917.
47 Worcestershire *sinking*: For press discussion, see *Times of Ceylon*, 24 February 1917, 6 March 1917; *Madras Mail*, 26 February 1917.

Chapter 3: Wartime Secrets

P. 51 *Dispatch from British naval commander at Aden:* Telegram, 5 March 1917, Admiralty file.
52 *Details of* Turritella *minelaying and capture:* From Mantey, pp. 315–24.
52 *'a report on the* Wolf*'*: DID cable, 6 March 1917, Admiralty file.
52 *Details of impact of the German U-boat campaign:* From Halpern, pp. 335–51.
53 *Keynes's warning:* Ferguson, p. 327.
53 *'ended horrifically'*: Schmalenbach, p. 24.
54 *Details of* Moewe*'s impact:* From 'Review of German Cruiser Warfare 1914–1918', NAUK, ADM275/22; *Los Angeles Times*, 18 January 1917, p. III4; *Washington Post*, 9 April 1917, p. 1; *New York Times*, 11 January 1917, p. 2, 1 April 1917, p. E4 and 8 April 1917, p. 3.

54 *'I simply cannot understand'*: *The Times*, 7 April 1917, p. 5.
55 *Hughes's statement:* APH, 6 March 1917.
55 *Cook's statement:* APH, 8 March 1917.
55 *'a very strong impression'*: BPH, 21 February 1917.
56 *Miniature submarines: New York Times*, 28 January 1917, p. SM43. Other reports: *Washington Post*, 14 March 1917, p. 1; *Los Angeles Times*, 30 March 1917, p. 12 and 11 May, p. I11.
56 *'the manufacturing of these sensations'*: *Christian Science Monitor*, 22 March 1917, p. 10.
56 *'absolute transparency'*: *The Times*, 22 February 1917, p. 8.
56 *'send a squadron to the Coast of Queensland'*: Foreign Office cable, 14 March 1917, Admiralty file.
57 *'unspeakably useless'*: Bromby, p. 20.
57 *Australia's paltry defences:* For details, see Jose, pp. 336–74.
58 *Massey's criticism:* NANZ, ACHK16558, G2, 39.
58 *'It is sometimes necessary'*: Jose, p. 338.
59 *Details of ship redeployments:* Ibid., pp. 310–14, 338–9.
59 *'Some of the sailors'*: Report by Major W. H. Bingham, 16 March 1917, Admiralty file.
60 *'Prisoners claim'*: Undated cable, Admiralty file.
60 *'One single armed merchantman'*: Quotation and details of ship deployments from 'Review of German Cruiser Warfare 1914–1918', NAUK, ADM275/22. Also Newbolt, pp. 209–15.
61 *Details of* C. de Eizaguirre *disaster:* From *Cape Times*, 29 May 1917, p. 7, and 8 June 1917, p. 5.
61 *'Is this the same old spot?'*: DID notation, 26 May 1917, Admiralty file.
62 *Richard Reading:* Quoted in *Times of India*, 4 July 1917, pp. 7–8.
63 *Norman Brookes's response:* Brookes, pp. 85–9.
63 *Details of* Mongolia *tragedy:* From *Sydney Morning Herald*, 31 July 1917, pp. 7–8; *Times of India*, 30 June 1917; also Norman Brookes and Richard Reading accounts, cited above.
65 *'A boatload of men wearing helmets'*: *Morning Post*, 23 April 1917; other false sightings taken from NID cables in Admiralty file.
65 *Report of Indian prisoners:* From NID cable, 5 July 1917, Admiralty file.
66 *'According to the Chinese crew'*: Briefing note, 29 May 1917, Admiralty file.
67 *'a single U-boat could destroy every warship'*: The warning came from Captain Arthur Gordon-Smith in a memo on 17 January 1917, NAA, MP1049/1, 1920/0128.

68 *'the British Navy's Pacific commander'*: Cable from Captain M. Segrave, 12 July 1917, Admiralty file.

Chapter 4: Edge of the World

P. 69 *'The crew on board doesn't feel like working'*: Wieduwilt, p. 12.
69 *Albert Wieduwilt:* Biographical details provided by his family.
70 *'The sailors made gloomy faces'*: Witschetzky, p. 144.
72 *'Seamen covered in blood'*: Ibid., pp. 113–14.
73 *'We had a ten-minute pause in our labours'*: Plivier, p. 246.
73 *'Perhaps it wasn't the gunnery officer's fault'*: Ibid., p. 246.
74 *Description of Meadows, Wickmann and Shields:* Witschetzky, pp. 107–8, 128.
75 *Description of Southern Ocean crossing:* Nerger diary, 31 March to 17 April 1917; Witschetzky, pp. 134–5.
75 *'Niggers'*: This epithet was used freely at the time. Stan Cameron and Roy Alexander both described the black occupants of the Hell Hole as 'niggers' in their published memoirs. Another prisoner, Captain Alec Donaldson, complained in his memoir that the hammock next to his was occupied by 'a Mauritius nigger, who stank like a pole-cat and snored like a hog.' (*Fifty Years Too Soon*, p. 227.)
76 *Strained relations between Rugg and his crew:* Nerger, p. 11 (Admiralty translation); Witschetzky, pp. 133–4.
76 *Marton's anger:* Alexander, pp. 84–5.
76 *'Fritz Witschetzky had begun pondering the absurdity of the voyage'*: Witschetzky, pp. 148–50.
77 *'Our heads buzzed'*: Plivier, pp. 255–6.
78 *Sunday Island history:* Norton, pp. 21–4, 160–89.
79 *'Black night'*: Witschetzky, p. 160.
80 Wairuna *crew details:* Alexander, pp. 16–20.
80 *Harry Ross:* Details from Australian Imperial Force service file NAA, B2455/8037812.
80 *Tom Rees:* Details from Wellington City Archives, file AF004:7/4.
81 *'uncoded wireless communication was still permitted'*: Jose, pp. 346–8.
82 *'Meadows unleashed a barrage of abuse'*: Witschetzky, p. 177.
82 *'We shall return to Germany'*: Alexander, p. 25.
83 *Clelland and Steers escape:* Details from ibid., pp. 34–5.
84 *'Trudgett wept openly'*: Described in 'Hell Holes on Land and Sea' by Robert D. Trudgett, *Sunset* magazine, May 1919.
84 *'Trudgett's crewmen had told him'*: Nerger diary, 20 June 1917.

85 *'incandescent with rage'*: Alexander, pp. 38–40.
85 *Story of the calendar:* Witschetzky, pp. 170, 182–3.
86 *'The prisoners, in that ghastly light'*: Alexander, p. 52.
87 *Description of minelaying off Gabo Island:* Witschetzky, pp. 191–2; Nerger diary, 3–4 July 1917; Alexander, pp. 55–9.
88 *'just finishing his breakfast porridge'*: Details of *Cumberland* sinking from the transcript and appendices to the enquiry into sinking of SS *Cumberland*, NAA, MP1049/1, 1917/153.
89 *'fully illustrates that her explosion occurred from inside'*: Report of Rear-Admiral Yamaji, 8 July 1917, NAA, AWM36, Bundle 22/9, Item 653289.
89 *Details of censorship and rumours:* APH, 11 July 1917; *The Age*, 12 July 1917, p. 7.
90 *Henry Maiden's role:* Detailed in the transcripts of enquiry into sinking of SS *Cumberland*, NAA, MP1049/1, 1917/153.
90 *'An undercover agent'*: Ibid.
90 *The detaining of the* Tasmanic*:* Detailed in Cain, p. 95.
90 *'Everything points to foul play'*: APH, 11 July 1917.
90 *'the first intimation of the presence of the raider'*: Selheim memorandum, 29 March 1917, NAA, MP16/1, 1917/100.
90 *'Prime Minister Hughes had himself initially acknowledged'*: APH, 11 July 1917.
90 *Government reward offered: Argus*, 20 July 1917, p. 6.
91 *'I naturally thought'*: Nerger, pp. 13–14 (Admiralty translation).
91 *'In any case, it is to be kept from the people'*: Wieduwilt, p. 24.
91 *'Proud England'*: Ibid., p. 21.

Part 2

Chapter 5: Juanita's War

P. 95 *'Witschetzky stooped to talk'*: Witschetzky, pp. 202–3.
96 *'Stan Cameron was discomfited'*: Stan Cameron's collection of photos from the *Wolf* included one showing Juanita sitting on the shoulders of a German sailor. He had written on the back, 'Whoah, Bill!'
96 *'Mary had asked Nerger to transmit a wireless message'*: Alexander, p. 75.
97 *Details of Mary's breakdown:* Cameron, pp. 38–41.
97 *'Owing to the experience'*: Ibid., pp. 38–9.
98 *'highly strung and courageous'*: Ibid., p. 38.
98 *'admitted to the ship's hospital'*: Handwritten notation in the medical journal of Dr Hermann Hauswaldt, 20 July 1917. Translated for the authors by Dr Christian Hauswaldt, his son.

98 *'Oh, how nice it is'*: Szielasko, p. 57.
98 *'She was a very smart and bright little girl'*: Ibid., p. 51.
99 *'the time of her life'*: Cameron, p. 28.
99 *'A "Dreikäsehoch" she was'*: Nerger, p. 59 (2000 edition).
100 Wolfchen *crash:* Nerger diary, 12 July 1917.
100 *'He was her "dear Paul"'*: Nerger, p. 60 (2000 edition).
100 *'narrowly escaped a tribe of headhunters'*: Szielasko, pp. 58–60; also *Washington Post*, 26 November 1905, p. 1, and 6 December 1905, p. 13.
100 *'a grudging mutual admiration'*: Cameron, pp. 45–8.
101 *'a very agreeable man to talk to'*: Ibid., p. 53.
101 *'One can get used to it'*: Cameron, 'The Sea Wolf's Prey', *Sunset* magazine, September 1918, p. 21.
101 *'just stepped out of a bandbox'*: Cameron, pp. 53–4.
101 *'a splendid chap with honest, straight opinions'*: Nerger, p. 63 (2000 edition).
102 *'It was more than a chair'*: Alexander, pp. 82–3.
103 *'pulling out a knife'*: Ibid., p. 72; Szielasko, pp. 35–6.
103 *Trudgett incident:* Alexander, p. 88.
103 *'ripe'*: Ibid., p. 122.
104 *'Plivier recalled the shortness of breath'*: Plivier, p. 252.
105 *'Burns Philp Rabaul'*: Jose, p. 348.
105 Matunga *details:* Donaldson, *Amazing Cruise*, pp. 54–60.
106 *'Strangman and Flood would later say that they were warned'*: Prisoner statements taken aboard the *Wolf*, 20 August 1917, BMAG, RM99/790.
106 *'could have been captured by the* Wolf*'*: Intelligence note, 12 July 1917, Admiralty file.
106 *'They brightly told me'*: Donaldson, *Fifty Years Too Soon*, p. 220.
107 *'VHV to VHB'*: Jose, p. 348.
107 *'Good morning, Captain Donaldson!'*: Donaldson, *Fifty Years Too Soon*, pp. 222–3; Nerger, p. 70 (2000 edition).
108 Matunga *cargo manifest:* NAA, MP1049/1, 1917/0183.
109 *'It was probably 8:30 pm'*: Cameron, pp. 58–9.
110 *Auerswald incidents:* Alexander, pp. 82–3; Cameron, pp. 64–5.
111 *Flood biographical details:* From registers of births and marriages in Ireland and Australia; also *Adelaide Advertiser*, 26 March 1929, p. 15 and John Flood's service record, NAA B2455/4039255.
111 *Conditions in Rabaul:* Mackenzie, pp. 207–18.
112 *'Miss Agnes was not the least interested'*: Szielasko, p. 72; Nerger, p. 78 (2000 edition); Alexander, p. 124.

112 Matunga *revelries:* Alexander, p. 113; Cameron, 'The Sea Wolf 's Prey', *Sunset* magazine, September 1918, p. 23.
113 *'evilly beautiful'*: Alexander, p. 117.
113 *Hauswaldt's intervention:* Cameron, pp. 64–5.
115 *Details of shooting incident in Offak Bay:* Alexander, pp. 125–6; Cameron, pp. 72–5; Nerger, p. 17 (Admiralty translation).
115 *'Damn funny, captain'*: Donaldson, *Fifty Years Too Soon*, p. 231.
116 *'suspected these newcomers to be Germans cleverly disguised'*: 'The Sea Wolf 's Prey', *Sunset* magazine, September 1918, p. 23.
117 *'the acme of inhumanity'*: Cameron, p. 81.
118 *'She's a bloody good riddance'*: Donaldson, *Fifty Years Too Soon*, p. 236.

Chapter 6: The Enemy Within

P. 119 *'Rampant'*: Cited in *Australian Dictionary of Biography 1891–1939*, p. 82, available online at http://adbonline.anu.edu.au/adbonline.htm.
120 *Special Intelligence Bureau:* For a history, see Cain, pp. 1–43.
120 *'Pickle the Spy'*: Munro-Ferguson in a letter to Britain's secretary of state for the colonies, Walter Long, 24 August 1917, NLA, MS696/1074.
121 *Details of Cumberland enquiry and Jones's role:* From the transcript and appendices to the enquiry into sinking of SS *Cumberland*, NAA, MP1049/1, 1917/153.
121 *Anti-German paranoia in Australia:* For details, see Scott, pp. 105–67.
122 *Public sightings of strange ships and aircraft:* Collected in the NAA file MP1049/1/0, 1917/0218.
122 *'we found that they were savage and inhuman'*: Lewis, p. 69.
122 *'Australia's grave danger from within'*: *Mirror*, 24 February 1917, p. 9.
122 *Story of attack on film crew:* Ibid., p. 14.
123 *'cold as sea-ice'*: Hungerford, p. 317.
123 *'more British than the people of Great Britain'*: APH, 10 September 1919.
123 *'racial war'*: Fitzhardinge, p. 33.
123 *Details of Australia's wartime censorship and enemy-alien laws:* Scott, pp. 57–167; Cain, pp. 106–39.
124 *'Delays abounded and increased'*: Quoted in Scott, p. 80.
124 *'not a single case of German espionage within Australia would be substantiated'*: Scott, pp. 141–2.
125 *'unholy alliance'*: Fitzhardinge, p. 214.

125 *'the Kaiser's "cunning men"'*: *Argus*, 9 August 1917, p. 8.
125 *Hughes's use of censorship and his relationship with Steward:* For details, see Cain, pp. 7, 117–19; also Munro-Ferguson's letter to Walter Long, 24 August 1917, NLA, MS696/1074.
126 *'No evidence of these conspiracies'*: Cain, pp. 10–15, 81–4.
126 *'he would soon take to carrying a pistol'*: Fitzhardinge, p. 289.
126 *'I firmly believe that there is a directing hand'*: *Sun*, 19 August 1917.
127 *'its interim report'*: Transcript and appendices of enquiry into sinking of SS *Cumberland*, NAA, MP1049/1, 1917/153.
127 *Cook's statement: Mirror*, 8 September 1917.
127 *'wire stories were published'*: *New York Times*, 3 July 1917; *Sun*, 18 August 1917 and 2 October 1917.
128 *'no German mine layers or submarines have been reported'*: *New York Times*, 14 August 1917, p. 14.
128 *South African reaction to* City of Athens *sinking: Cape Times*, 13 August 1917, p. 6, and 14 August 1917, p. 6.
129 *'a raider was probably at large'*: Cable from Prime Minister Hughes to Governor-General and Navy, 31 August 1917, NAA, MP1049, 1917/0183; secret memorandum from navy secretary to Hughes, 1 September 1917, ibid.
129 *'it was presumed raider* Wolf *was in these waters'*: Intelligence note, 4 September 1917, Admiralty file.
129 *'point[s] to the presence of the Raider'*: Intelligence note, 9 September 1917, Admiralty file.
129 *'The results of the investigations show conclusively'*: Jones report dated 11 September 1917, contained in transcript and appendices to enquiry into sinking of SS *Cumberland*, NAA, MP1049/1, 1917/153, along with reports by Warren and Lyle.
130 *'So far as I can summarise'*: Yamaji to Australian Naval Board, 11 September 1917, NAA, MP1049, 1917/0183.
131 *'"dislike and distrust" of the Australians'*: Munro-Ferguson in a letter to Walter Long, 25 October 1917, NLA, MS696/970.
131 *Australian Navy's bitter complaint:* Secret report by Rear-Admiral William Creswell, 21 February 1918, NAA, AWM36, 32/2.
131 *'expert opinion'*: Brocklebank, p. 17.
131 *'The cause of the disaster'*: *The Dominion*, 19 September 1917.
132 *'improbable'*: Navy Office cable, 20 September 1917, NANZ, ADOE16612/M1, 13/384.
132 *Hall-Thompson's reply*: 21 September 1917, NANZ, N1 8/30.
132 *'It is just possible'*: Hall-Thompson to Marine Department, NANZ, ADOE16612/M1, 13/374.

134 *Von Luckner's adventures:* For a full recounting, see Bade, *Sea Devil*; also Jose, pp. 365–7, and *Sun*, 8 October and 19 October 1917.

134 *'refused to answer'*: BPH, 10 July 1917; *Argus*, 10 August 1917, p. 7.

135 *'a gang of spies'*: Naval Staff Office memo, 10 September 1917, NAA, MP1049, 1917/0183.

135 *'a quantity of high explosive substance'*: Finding of magistrate W. G. Riddell, 28 September 1917, NANZ, ADOE16612/M1, 13/374.

135 *'INTERN THE GERMANS'*: *Sun*, 28 September 1917, p. 5.

135 *Press reports of inquiry: New Zealand Times*, 28 September 1917; *New Zealand Herald*, 1 October 1917; *Argus*, 3 October 1917.

136 *New regulations on the wharves:* Letter from Hall-Thompson to the minister for Defence, 15 October 1917, NANZ, ADOE16612, 20/169M1.

136 *New Zealand reaction and arrest of crewman: New Zealand Herald*, 20–22 September, 1 and 4 October 1917.

136 *'unable to find a cause'*: *Sun*, 29 September 1917, p. 5.

137 *'if drastic steps are not taken'*: Ibid., 3 October 1917, p. 5.

138 *'the British Government complained'*: *Argus*, 23 February 1918, p. 8.

138 *'They seemed to point unerringly'*: *Sydney Morning Herald*, 12 October 1917, p. 7.

138 *'The censor-germ which has possessed ministers'*: *Sun*, 12 October 1917, p. 4.

139 *Newspaper editorials*: *Sun*, 9 October 1917, p. 5; *Sydney Morning Herald*, 16 October 1917, p. 6. Other reaction: *Sun*, 11 and 19 October 1917.

139 *'army of invasion'*: *Mirror*, 8 September 1917.

139 *'*The Times *reported Australia's ship losses as examples of sabotage'*: *The Times*, 24 September 1917, p. 13.

140 *'little hope was entertained for their survival'*: *San Francisco Chronicle*, undated newspaper clipping from Stan Cameron's collection.

140 *'An* in memoriam *to the crew'*: *Rabaul Record*, October 1917.

140 *Crew of the* Wordsworth *listed as drowned*: Memo to registrar general, 6 April 1918, Admiralty file.

140 *'Could you not tell one now'*: Letter from Elizabeth Pearce, 15 October 1917, NAA, MP1049, 1917/0183.

Chapter 7: Message in a Bottle

P. 142 *'a light blue chiffon dress'*: Witschetzky, p. 240.

142 *'After dinner, we were all treated to quite a sight'*: Witschetzky, p. 239.

143 *'What is Frau Flood wearing tonight?'*: Ibid.

143 *'My God, where do I accommodate them?'*: Szielasko, p. 66.

143 *'the Garden of Eden before Eve showed on the job'*: Cameron, p. 42.

143 *'particularly good-looking ones'*: Alexander, p. 186.

144 *'That changed her mind'*: Nerger, p. 78 (2000 edition).

144 *'I see your Commandant is heading for Singapore'*: Recalled in Witschetzky, p. 241.

146 *'Nerger noted in his log'*: Nerger diary, 26 August 1917.

148 *'several of the crew were court-martialled'*: Details of the HMAS *Psyche* from Feakes, pp. 193–5; Jose, pp. 218–21; 'HMAS Psyche' by Dudley Ricketts, undated article by former crewman, accessible at www.navyhistory.org.au/hmas-psyche-1915.

148 *'Permission not granted! I repeat – do not open fire'*: Witschetzky, p. 244.

149 Psyche *encounter:* For other descriptions, see Cameron, pp. 86–7; Nerger, p. 18 (Admiralty translation); Nerger diary, September 2–3 1917.

149 *'He may have been tired'*: Alexander, p. 145. In his official history of the Royal Australian Navy, Arthur Jose dates the encounter as the night of 3 September and says the *Psyche*'s position on that night raises some doubt as to whether she was the warship the *Wolf* nearly fired on. But Nerger's war diary shows the incident happened on the night of 2 September, when the ships would have passed each other.

150 *'Japan had four destroyers on regular patrol'*: Newbolt, Vol. 4, p. 225.

152 *Norman Pyne's account: Evening Post*, 27 November 1929; *New Zealand Herald*, 12 April 1930.

153 *Details of Meadows incident:* Alexander, p. 149; Nerger diary, 5 September 1917; Witschetzky, pp. 247–8.

155 *'Nerger appeared at the bridge rail'*: Alexander, pp. 151–2.

155 *'cheery, good-hearted chaps'*: Alexander, p. 138.

156 *'Nerger calculated'*: Nerger diary, 10 September 1917.

157 *'Albert Wieduwilt had recalibrated his calculations'*: Wieduwilt, p. 35.

157 *'Theodor Plivier was among the dissidents'*: Plivier, pp. 274–5.

158 *'The organiser of the theft was court-martialled'*: Witschetzky, p. 222.

158 *'The flood of language that flowed down on the unlucky sailor'*: Alexander, p. 76.

159 *'We're slaving for the insurance companies'*: Plivier, p. 254.

Chapter 8: Scandal and Mutiny

P. 160 *'who had married only three weeks earlier'*: Shiraishi, p. 17.

161 *'one of Maugham's most famous plays'*: The play was *The Letter* (see Chapter 12).

161 *'he realised almost immediately what was about to happen'*: Shiraishi, p. 36.

161 *'Five bells had just gone'*: Trayes, p. 14.

163 Wolf *'s attack on* Hitachi Maru*:* See Appendix to Nerger diary, 'Beschießung des Japanischen Dampfers "Hitachi Maru" am 26.IX.1917'; Nerger, pp. 18–22 (Admiralty translation); Trayes, pp. 11–25; Clarke, pp. 8–14; Wieduwilt, pp. 35–8; Witschetzky, pp. 251–6; letter from Courtenay Dickinson to colleague Howard Mundell, 17 March 1918, Admiralty file.

164 *'Most of us thought the end had come'*: Trayes, p. 23.

164 *'a new type of Hun'*: Ibid., p. 26.

165 *'Alfred Clarke was surprised'*: Clarke, pp. 32–3.

165 *'Tominaga explained that he had been following the procedure for evading U-boat attack'*: Nerger, p. 19 (Admiralty translation).

165 *Drinking habits of William Cross and Mabel Whittaker:* Szielasko, pp. 36–7; Cameron, p. 112; Witschetzky, p. 257.

166 *'pink silk petticoats bordered with lace'*: Nerger, p. 121 (2000 edition).

166 *Gerald Haxton biographical details:* From Maugham, pp. 17–21; Meyers, pp. 96–115; Haxton's United States Army registration card, No. 12-2-18-A.

167 *'full of charm and full of liquor, in almost equal parts'*: Quoted in Maugham, p. 50.

167 *'he looked as if he could have done with that Tahiti cocktail'*: Alexander, pp. 202–3.

168 *'the most beautiful track or road I have ever seen'*: Witschetzky, p. 264.

170 *'precocious, merry chit-chat'*: Szielasko, p. 57.

170 'Lieber Gott, mach mich fromm': Nerger, p. 64 (2000 edition).

172 *'surprised to see that Rose was drunk'*: Letter from Courtenay Dickinson to Howard Mundell, 17 March 1918, Admiralty file.

172 *'a snob and man who did not know the meaning of the word gentleman'*: Cameron, p. 105.

172 *'I wonder that the Germans didn't cut off the little girl's ears and nose'*: Witschetzky, p. 268.
172 *'The Germans are not thieves'*: Clarke, p. 26.
173 *'What do you expect?'*: Cameron, p. 107.
173 *'rather unusual exhibition of the European male torso'*: Trayes, p. 33.
174 *'The gentlemen officers "called on her"'*: Wieduwilt, p. 37.
174 *'soothing the fears'*: Alexander, p. 211.
174 *'very partial'*: Cameron, p. 127.
175 *'It had been my lot to hear much scandal'*: Alexander, p. 198.
175 *'This woman was a beast of the lowest'*: Inscription written by Mary Cameron on the back of a photograph of Rose Flood and other prisoners aboard the *Wolf*. (Photograph supplied by Walt Coburn.)
177 *Axel Johnson's death:* Nerger diary, 12 October 1917; Cameron, p. 114. Dr Hermann Hauswaldt's journal records that Johnson suffered 'violent bleeding from his nose and eyes' but states no cause of death. Stan Cameron recalls that he was told Johnson had 'heart trouble'.
178 *'There was a perpetual crowd around the bit of paper'*: Plivier, p. 255.
179 *'The patient, normally a big man'*: Alexander, p. 195.
180 *'We, the undersigned'*: Trayes, p. 55.
181 *'The people on the whole were about as merry as mutes at a funeral'*: Letter from Courtenay Dickinson to Howard Mundell, 17 March 1918, Admiralty file.
181 *'all-pervading, loathsome smell of sweating Eastern humanity'*: Clarke, p. 45.
182 *'she stared down her attacker'*: Hasegawa, pp. 143–4.
183 *'an outbreak of war'*: Nerger diary, 7 November 1917.
183 *'The first bomb erupted'*: See Hasegawa, and Cameron, pp. 122–3; Trayes, pp. 63–5; Clarke, pp. 50–2.
185 *'She was a real ray of sunshine'*: Szielasko, p. 58.
185 *'Theodor Plivier overheard Dierck Butendrift'*: Plivier, p. 278.
186 *'If Bülow won't, then he won't'*: Ibid., p. 258.
187 *'brandishing a pistol and screaming abuse at them'*: Clarke, pp. 90–1.
187 *'Nerger professed he would have shot any man'*: Recounted by Wolf-Christian Nerger, Nerger's great-grandson, in email correspondence with authors.
187 Clarke, p. 91.

Part 3

Chapter 9: A Speck on the Ocean

P. 191 *'It is a solitary speck on the boundless ocean'*: Lord Curzon to the House of Lords, BPH, 29 October 1917.

192 *'the Admiralty's commander in Singapore had wired London'*: Telegram dated 26 October 1917, NAA, MP1049, 1917/0183.

192 *'But the sultan regarded the Suvadiva natives as "ignorant"'*: DID briefing note, 27 November 1917, Admiralty file.

193 *'It is considered probable that ships reported were* WOLF *and* HITACHI MARU*'*: Telegram dated 27 November 1917, Admiralty file.

193 *Allied naval strength in Indian Ocean:* For details, see Newbolt, pp. 224–5.

193 *Shortage of ships:* Detailed in cable to the Admiralty from the senior naval officer, Egypt, 7 December 1917, Admiralty file.

194 *Success of the convoys:* For details, see Halpern, pp. 364–5.

194 *'they might already be close to Germany'*: NID briefing note, undated, Admiralty file.

194 *'The chances are altogether against a minelayer'*: *Argus*, 16 October 1917, p. 4.

194 *'HMAS* Una *reported a seismic disturbance'*: Letter from Captain C. T. Glossop to superintendent of Navigation, Sydney, 12 October 1917, NAA, MP1049, 1917/0183.

195 *'extraordinary laxity'*: *Argus*, 8 October 1917, p. 7.

195 *'hardly appears necessary'*: Summary sheet of New Zealand Navy telegrams, NANZ, AAYT8499, N20, 6iii/TRW.

195 *'Raider may be anywhere in the Indian Ocean'*: Cable dated 19 December 1917, Admiralty file.

195 *'the mines had been anchored too deeply'*: 'Review of German Cruiser Warfare 1914–1918', p. 20, NAUK, ADM 275/22. The complete disappearance of the *Wolf*'s 110 mines off Singapore remains a mystery. After the war, Germany announced that the Japanese battle-cruiser *Haruna* had been disabled by one of the mines – a claim that was emphatically denied by the Japanese Navy but that can still be found on some official naval websites (see, for instance, the United States Navy website www.history.navy.mil). Nerger's war diary on 6 September 1917, two days after the mines were laid, records a distress signal from the British freighter *Brodholme* off Singapore, and Fritz Witschetzky claimed in his book that one ship was sunk and another damaged by the mines (Witschetzky, pp. 246–7). However, the authors were unable to find any

evidence supporting these claims. An Admiralty memo on 16 April 1918 reported that minesweepers had failed to locate any of the mines and concluded they had 'probably been destroyed by the monsoon'.

196 *'even the ship's owners remained unaware'*: Shiraishi, p. 30; *Yomiuri Shimbun*, 28 December 1917, p. 5.

196 *'giant octopus'*: The giant octopus was reported in *Yomiuri Shimbun*, 21 and 22 December 1917, p. 5.

197 *'No further information regarding* Wolf': Cable dated 24 December 1917, Admiralty file.

197 *'reckless extremists, peace cranks, disloyalists and pro-Germans'*: *Argus*, 13 November 1917, p. 5.

197 *Details of violence surrounding conscription campaign:* Fitzhardinge, pp. 289–96.

198 *'The Sydney manager of Burns Philp complained'*: Letter from Walter Lucas to Captain Hugh Thring, 11 December 1917, NAA, MP1049, 1917/0183.

198 *'Cumming pointedly remarked'*: 'Finding and Recommendation, Preliminary Inquiry into the Circumstances Attending the Reported Disappearance of the British Steamship "Matunga"', 19 October 1917, NAA, MP1049, 1917/0183.

199 *Carl Newman biographical details:* Authors' interview with Carl Newman's grandson, Frank Newman; Carl Newman's marriage certificate, 14 February 1885; Australian Government file on the Newman case, NAA, MP16.1/1917/100.

199 *'if submarines ever worked on the coast of Australia'*: Letter from L. Travers, 5 February 1917, NAA, MP16.1/1917/100.

200 *'blow up half the shipping around our coast'*: Letter from W. B. Smith, 21 July 1917, ibid.

200 *'loyal and law-abiding'*: Unsigned report to Naval Staff Office, Melbourne, 20 August 1917, ibid.

201 *Richardson's role in seizing codes:* For background, see Jose, pp. 380–1.

201 *'he is not involved in any improper practices'*: Report of Captain J. T. Richardson, 31 October 1917, NAA, MP16.1/1917/100.

201 *'gossip is plentiful'*: Letter from Judge J. B. Box, 7 November 1917, NAA, MP1049/1, 1921/0307.

201 The Age*'s report:* 4 January 1918.

201 *'the naturalised German is more dangerous'*: Report of Lieutenant D. W. Drysdale, 12 March 1918, NAA, MP1049/1/1921/0307.

202 *'like sardines packed in a tin'*: Alexander, pp. 248–9.

203 *'The mad riot of music was accompanied by irritating shrieks of laughter'*: Clarke, p. 45.
203 *'Flood was incredulous'*: Nerger, p. 124 (2000 edition).
204 *'The hatred of some of these people'*: Ibid.
204 *'Many of us were highly incensed'*: Cameron, p. 128.
205 *'a somewhat embarrassing incident'*: Nerger, p. 114 (2000 edition).
205 *'O Death! Where is thy sting?'*: Alexander, p. 212.
206 *'Her presence entailed the constant ingress, egress and regress of German sailors'*: Letter from Courtenay Dickinson to Howard Mundell, 17 March 1918, Admiralty file.
206 *'Her fondness for liquor'*: Witschetzky, p. 291.
206 *'the only able-bodied man'*: *Oakland Tribune*, 22 May 1918, p. 2.
207 *'first class passengers on a modern liner'*: Cameron, p. 129.
207 *'Trayes promptly reported him to Leutnant Rose'*: Trayes, p. 128.
208 *'The German* leutnant *always sat next to a "friend"'*: Cameron, p. 150.
208 *'you actually covet the food another person is eating'*: Ibid.
208 *'All throughout the trip this man had behaved like a dog in a manger'*: Ibid., p. 160.
208 *'"servile" and unworthy of a British officer'*: Diplomatic cable from the British embassy in Copenhagen to the Admiralty, 5 March 1918, Admiralty file.
209 *Poem:* Recalled by Szielasko, p. 100.
209 *'a very artful piece of shamming'*: Letter from Courtenay Dickinson to Howard Mundell, 17 March 1918, Admiralty file.
211 *'we would think of Spain and freedom'*: Cameron, pp. 131–2.
214 *'never sounded merrier or more blissful'*: Witschetzky, p. 293.
214 *'Our thoughts were of home'*: Wieduwilt, p. 46.
214 *'a dismal farce'*: Trayes, p. 111.
216 *'Others were covered with skin eruptions'*: Alexander, p. 223.

Chapter 10: End Run

P. 217 *'Prisoners on board German raider'*: Cable dated 15 January 1918, Admiralty file.
219 *'Local natives had provided detailed descriptions'*: Cable dated 12 January 1918, ibid.
219 *Hall-Thompson's difficulties finding minesweepers:* Detailed in letter from the chief surveyor of ships dated 7 March 1918, NANZ, ADOE16612, M1, 25/911.

220 *'he reassured shipping officials that danger from the mines was "slight"'*: Trade-route warning dated 18 January 1918, NANZ, AAYT8499, N20, 6iv, TRW.
220 *'I have a right to know if Rupert is alive or dead'*: Letter from Elizabeth Pearce, 31 December 1917, NAA, MP1049, 1917/0183.
220 *'the Minister, whilst sympathising deeply'*: Letter from George Macandie, 2 January 1918, ibid.
221 *'The vessel was doing war work'*: *Sun*, 18 January 1918.
221 *Laura McBride's letters to New Zealand Government and navy officials, and details of Burns Philp's response:* NANZ, ADOE16612, M1, 20/61.
221 *'we do not want the Germans to find out'*: Letter from George Macandie to Elizabeth Pearce, 31 January 1918, NAA, MP1049, 1917/0183.
222 *'practically public all over Australia'*: Letter from deputy chief censor to the Department of Defence, 5 February 1918, ibid.
223 *'a minefield laid by the German raider* Wolf*'*: *Argus*, 10 August 1917, p. 7.
224 *'I seemed to have become almost German'*: Alexander, p. 233.
225 *'even the sinking of the neutral* Storebror *was "quite right"'*: Ibid, p. 235.
225 *Robert Trudgett's account of conversations with Adolf Wulff:* *Sunset* magazine, May 1919, p. 31.
225 *'Are the trams still running in George Street, mate?'*: Interview with Eric Minns, *Sun*, 7 May 1974, p. 14.
225 *'Minns was convinced that the Germans simply turned a blind eye'*: Ibid.
226 *'We all liked "Mines"'*: Donaldson, *Amazing Cruise*, p. 96.
226 *'I am well and on the* Wolf*'*: *Sunset* magazine, May 1919, p. 32.
227 *'His flesh had gone puffy and rotten'*: Alexander, p. 213.
227 *'At first it was only little pockets around my teeth'*: Plivier, p. 256.
228 'Igotz Mendi*'s plates had been scraped bare of paint'*: Alexander, p. 237.
230 *'It would have been extremely favourable'*: Nerger diary, 18 January 1918.
230 *'It seemed that she could appear at will'*: Cameron, p. 132.
231 *'Stan, there's a cruiser with four funnels just ahead'*: Ibid., pp. 142–4.
233 *'It was not for me, Captain Rose'*: Ibid., p. 146.
234 *'The wind was raging for hours'*: Trayes, p. 138.
234 *'We were so cold and hungry'*: *Newcastle Herald* article, undated, from Stan Cameron collection.

236 *'no longer "quite right in the head"'*: Alexander, p. 240.
237 *'It was a shock to see Webb's condition'*: Alexander, p. 245.
239 *'The loss of my ship to the enemy'*: Witschetzky, p. 307.
240 *'There is only a small chance of getting through without being seen'*: Nerger diary, 5 February 1918.
240 *'It was better to be a live prisoner-of-war in Germany'*: Alexander, p. 250.
242 *'swathed in rags to keep out the cold'*: Plivier, p. 289.
242 *'he was still throwing SOS messages overboard'*: A message evidently thrown overboard by Meadows in the North Sea on 10 February was retrieved off the coast of Norway more than two weeks later. British officials in Bergen notified the Admiralty by cable on 1 March, by which time it was too late to intercept the *Wolf*.
242 *Movements and composition of the Grand Fleet*: From Jose, pp. 279–84, 299–302; Newbolt, pp. 205–9; Halpern, pp. 403–5.
244 *'Nerger with auxiliary cruiser* Wolf*'*: Nerger diary, 17 February 1918.
245 *'When does the first letter from you come?'*: This is an extract from Nerger's personal diary written at 2 am on the morning of 18 February 1918. According to his family, it is the only remnant of the diary – as distinguished from his official captain's war diary – that has survived. Translation provided to the authors by Nerger's grandson, Uwe Nerger.

Chapter 11: Stranded

P. 247 *'The cold fog, the great bergs of ice floating by the ship'*: Trayes, p. 144.
248 *'dead easy'*: Letter from Courtenay Dickinson to Howard Mundell, 17 March 1918, Admiralty file.
249 *'I'm not afraid'*: *Sunset* magazine, November 1918, p. 43.
250 *'There was no fog to help the enemy'*: Trayes, p. 150.
251 *'By eerie coincidence'*: Mantey, p. 308. Mantey's official history claims that the letters were postmarked at the precise hour that Nerger dropped anchor on 17 February 1918, but both Witschetzky and Plivier say the letters were sent to their families in January.
252 *'I cordially welcome you'*: Mantey, p. 310.
253 *'the crew were forbidden from leaving the ship'*: Clarke, p. 116; Donaldson, *Amazing Cruise*, p. 116.
253 *'Sergeant Alcon Webb counted at least ninety warships'*: Statement of Alcon Webb, 22 October 1918, NAA, MP1049/1, 1921/0307.

254 *'It seems that things are not looking good with you'*: Nerger personal diary entry (from the only remnant that has survived), 18 February 1918. Translated for the authors by Uwe Nerger.

255 *'Something had caused considerable dissatisfaction'*: Clarke, p. 117.

255 *'The highest military order that the nation had to bestow'*: Plivier, p. 291.

256 *'For the last year, mysterious news'*: Translation of Holtzendorff statement, 23 February 1918, Admiralty file.

257 *'The Igotz Mendi had been even luckier than the* Wolf*'*: Jose (p. 303) records that the 2nd Light-Cruiser Battle Squadron was on convoy duty between Britain and Norway from 18 to 21 February 1918.

257 *'There is no hope left'*: Trayes, p. 156.

257 *'Just the weather I want'*: Cameron, p. 155.

258 *'I think I just felt her smell the bottom'*: Ibid., p. 156.

260 *'You people can cut the noise now'*: Ibid, p. 158.

261 *'Leutnant Wulff had . . . sent a telegram to Karl Nerger'*: Much of this chronology of events is drawn from the April 1918 Danish Navy report '*Depecher vedrørende tysk (spansk) Damper Igotz Mendi's Stranding udfor Højen d. 24/2 1918*' ('Reports about German (Spanish) steam ship Igotz Mendi's stranding off Hojen on 24 February 1918'), file number M38, MAD.

261 *'But Lagoni already knew there was something amiss'*: Handwritten report of Captain Otto Lagoni, 10 March 1918, MAD, M38.

262 *'one of Juanita Cameron's abandoned Kewpie dolls'*: Cameron, p. 162.

262 *'he suddenly ran into the redoubtable Mabel Whittaker'*: Letter from Courtenay Dickinson to Howard Mundell, 17 March 1918, Admiralty file.

263 *'Kapitän, Kapitän, wake up'*: Cameron, p. 164.

264 *'a fallen enemy'*: Trayes, p. 164.

265 *'All food was a joy to us'*: Letter from Courtenay Dickinson to Howard Mundell, 17 March 1918, Admiralty file.

266 *'In desperation, Rose had sent Leutnant Adolf Wulff back'*: Report of the first officer of the *Heimdal*, 25 February 1918, MAD, M38.

266 *'Danish Navy officials in Copenhagen resolved to hand the ship back'*: Clemmesen, p. 63.

267 *'The indefatigable lifesavers of Skagen'*: *Dansa Søfartstidende* (*Nautical Times*), 7 March 1918, p. 53.

267 *'a second and larger German U-boat suddenly surfaced'*: Clemmesen, p. 63.

Chapter 12: Honour and Defeat

P. 268 *'Prince Henry of Prussia poked his head through the doorway'*: Clarke, p. 125.

269 *'Preferably First Class'*: Nerger, p. 115 (2000 edition).

269 *'Sir, I desire to express to you'*: Handwritten letter of Sergeant Alcon Webb, 19 February 1918. Copy kindly given to the authors by Hermann Hauswaldt's son, Dr Christian Hauswaldt.

269 *'I suddenly realised I had grown to respect and admire that bulky black ship'*: Alexander, p. 254.

270 *'the personification of hopeless misery'*: Donaldson, *Amazing Cruise*, p. 131.

270 *'a great number of men'*: Translation of German Government announcement, 26 February 1918, Admiralty file.

270 *'German Sea Atrocity'*: *The Times*, 9 March 1918, p. 6.

270 *'An erroneous report in the* Manchester Guardian*'*: *Manchester Guardian*, 26 February 1918. See also *The Times*, 27 February, p. 6.

271 *'The story appeared on page three of the* New York Times*'*: *New York Times*, 28 February 1918, p. 3. See also *Washington Post*, 26 February, p. 4, and *Chicago Tribune*, 27 February, p. 3.

271 *'full of yellow persons who howled'*: Press cable dated 26 February 1918, Admiralty file.

271 *'All is well. Letter will follow'*: *Newcastle Herald* article, undated, from collection of Stan Cameron.

272 *'Denmark should file a counter-claim'*: *Washington Post*, 7 March 1918, p. ES1; *New York Times*, 8 March 1918, p. 1, and 9 March 1918, p. 12.

272 *'Tourist Season Starts Early'*: *Skagens Avis* (*Skagens News*), 25 February 1918, p. 13.

272 *'For me, this stranding is almost in the nature of a tragedy'*: *Politiken* (*Policy*), 9 March 1918, p. 5.

273 *'It was strange for me to handle prize goods worth millions of marks'*: Ibid, p. 6.

273 *'Press reports lauded his courage'*: *The Age*, 4 March 1918.

273 *Spanish lifesaving association bravery medal:* The Medalla de la Sociedad Española de Salvamento de Náufragos, on display at Skagen's lifesaving museum.

273 *'in order not to irritate the German Government'*: Cable from

Sir Ralph Paget to Foreign Secretary Arthur Balfour, 18 September 1918, Admiralty file.

274 *'The captain was a typical Hun'*: 'Nine Months on the Raider "Wolf"', T. E. Rees, source and date unknown, from collection of Stan Cameron.

274 *'the* Wolf*'s minefield had been destroyed by the monsoonal tides'*: Report of Vice-Admiral F. C. J. Tudor, 5 March 1918, Admiralty file.

275 *'Freeland's boat had nearly been blown out of the water'*: Details from affidavit of J. Freeland, 22 December 1920, Auckland City Council Archives, ACC275 Box 33, Record No 20-322; *New Zealand Herald*, 13 July 1921.

275 *'Hall-Thompson continued to issue a shipping alert'*: Transcript of Hall-Thompson's testimony to *Wimmera* inquiry, 2 August 1918, NANZ, AAYT8499, N20/11.

275 *'Hall-Thompson did not send one of his trawlers north to begin sweeping until nearly two months later'*: Affidavit of minesweeper captain Charles Kiely, 20 July 1918, ibid.

275 *'not a menace to navigation'*: Transcript of Hall-Thompson's testimony, 2 August 1918, ibid.

276 *'Seen from all angles'*: Alexander, p. 65.

276 *'the admiral had received no adequate warning'*: Memo on the files of Sir Ronald Munro-Ferguson, 18 February 1918, NLA, MS696/1013.

276 *'searching among reefs is rather awkward to us'*: 'Report of Japanese Refusal to Co-Operate with the Naval Board', Rear-Admiral William Creswell, 21 February 1918, NAA, AWM36, 32/2.

276 *'It is now possible that the* Encounter *was despatched too late'*: Ibid.

276 *'a discreet silence'*: *Argus*, 27 February 1918, p. 6.

276 *'it is improbable that the* Wolf *was the minelayer'*: *Sun*, 2 March 1918.

276 *'It will be thought that the shipping community at least should have been informed'*: *Argus*, 28 February 1918, p. 4.

277 *'an impudent, cunning man'*: Report of Lieutenant D. W. Drysdale, 12 March 1918, NAA, MP1049/1, 1921/0307.

277 *'It is some damned funny business'*: Report of Captain W. P. Trainor, 4 May 1918, NAA, MP16/1, 1917/100.

278 *'if you could kindly furnish me with a little information'*: Letter from Mrs J. G. Newman, stamped 4 May 1918, ibid.

278 *'Sir, Could i be of any servis to you'*: Handwritten letter by Charles Newman, 9 May 1918, ibid. Newman's plans for defending the coast are detailed in the same file.

278 *'a considerable menace'*: Memo to the Department of Defence from Brigadier-General R. E. Williams, 3 May 1918, ibid.

279 *Details of Holdsworthy:* From Fischer, pp. 199–228. The camp's name bears a confusing resemblance to the nearby suburb of Holsworthy.

279 *'it is the first time we have been parted'*: Letter from Louisa Newman to the military-intelligence office, 6 August 1918, NAA, MP16/1, 1917/100.

279 *'in no single case does there appear to be any satisfactory proof'*: Typewritten report by H. A. Thomas, undated, ibid.

280 *Statistics on deportations and deaths in custody:* See Fischer, pp. 280–302, and Scott, pp. 114–67.

280 *Details of South African deportation debates:* From the *Cape Times*, 15 March, 5 April and 20 June 1919.

281 *'The crew spent the day swept up in a dizzying whirl of adulation'*: Details drawn from silent film footage held at the Kriegsarchiv der Marine, Freiburg, Germany.

281 *'Women belonging to "patriotic societies" distributed flowers'*: Plivier, p. 292.

282 *'Theodor Plivier went home to Berlin'*: Plivier, pp. 293–4.

282 *'Marie and the children had been hidden away'*: Recounted to the authors by Wolf-Christian Nerger.

283 *'the louse squadron'*: Plivier, p. 296.

283 *Details of the German Navy mutinies of 1918:* From Horn, pp. 198–266.

284 *'I am still in hospital'*: Letter of William Malthouse to Mary Chomley, 23 October 1918, NAA, AWM1DRL428, 00022/190162.

284 *'Don't believe all you hear about our hardships'*: Letter of Alec Donaldson to Mary Chomley, 21 June 1918, NAA, AWM1DRL428, 54/7.

285 *'My heart is not broken yet'*: Letter of Eric Minns, 14 June 1918, courtesy of the Minns family.

286 *'Gin Queen'*: Recounted in 'How Murder on the Veranda Inspired Somerset Maugham', by Norman Sherry, *Sunday Times Magazine*, 22 February 1978, pp. 12–16.

286 *'To Mrs Dick, Here is the play which I owe so much to you'*: Ibid.

286 *Further details on Haxton and Maugham:* Meyers, pp. 122–65.
287 *'an amount Rees expressed considerable disenchantment over':* Memo of general manager, Union Steamship Company of New Zealand, 17 July 1918, Wellington City Archives, AF004.7.4.
287 *'it is not considered that any reward is payable':* Letter from the secretary of the Prime Minister's department, 30 May 1919, NAA, MP1049/1, 1918.0284.
287 *'the company's penny-pinching accountants':* Letter of Laura McBride to Sir James Allen, 13 October 1919, NANZ, ADOE16612, M1, 20/61.
287 *'still refusing to accept responsibility for his health problems': New Zealand Herald*, 13 July 1921.
288 *'Seaplane Over Sydney Harbour': Argus*, 16 March 1918, p. 9; *The Age*, 16 March 1918.
288 *'While flying above the city': Sydney Morning Herald*, 18 October 1927, p. 11.
288 *'they recall how our city was spared':* Alexander, p. 79.
289 *'What truth there was in this rumour I could not find':* Letter from Tom Meadows to Mrs A. Clelland, 21 June 1918, NANZ, ADOE16612, M1, 20/116.
290 *'Nothing was found':* Cable from Navy Office, Wellington, 11 June 1918, ibid.
291 *'exceptionally well':* Stan Cameron interviewed by *Oakland Tribune*, 23 May 1918, p. 2.
291 *'a fully equipped motion picture outfit': Seattle Post-Intelligencer*, undated news clipping from collection of Stan Cameron.
291 *'The insufferable heat of the tropics': San Francisco Chronicle*, undated news clipping from collection of Stan Cameron.
292 *'he was awarded a patent for the invention': Los Angeles Times*, 7 April 1952, p. 30.

Epilogue

P. 293 *'The Last Gentleman of War':* This was the title given to an English translation of the 1979 book by the German author R. K. Lochner (Annapolis, Naval University Press, 1988). Lochner's original title was *Die Kaperfahrten des kleinen Kreuzers Emden* (*The Raiding Mission of the Small Cruiser Emden*).
294 *'Prime Minister Joseph Lyons greeted the swashbuckling count': Canberra Times*, 4 June 1938, p. 2.
294 *'The interference which they had aimed at':* Newbolt, Vol. 4, p. 226.
294 *'a good deal of rodomontade':* Jose, p. 364.

294 *'Nerger was a brave and skilful leader'*: Ibid., p. 352.
295 *'hurt the feelings of the British Government'*: Letter from Arthur Jose to C. W. Bean, 25 January 1921, NAA, AWM39, CA7039.
295 *Bean's criticism:* Contained in a letter to the Defence Department dated 29 September 1926, ibid.
295 *'it seems extraordinary that they were not used on a larger scale'*: 'Review of German Cruiser Warfare 1914–1918', NAUK, ADM 275/22.
295 *'a dry mathematician'*: Plivier, p. 248.
296 *'a school named after him'*: Plivier changed the spelling of his name to Plievier after fleeing Germany in 1933.
296 *'a twentieth-anniversary reunion'*: *Nordische Rundschau* (*Northern Review*), 25 February 1938.
296 *'promoted him in 1938 to head of factory security'*: Details from Karl Nerger *curriculum vitae* in Siemens archives, provided by Professor Wilfried Feldenkirchen. For more on Siemens, see Wiesen, *West German Industry*.
296 *Siemens:* In 2007, two of Nerger's grandsons, Uwe and Axel Nerger, set out to explore their grandfather's past with the help of a German television crew. The resulting documentary, entitled *Was Their Grandfather A Nazi?*, was screened in Germany in August 2007. In it, the two men revealed details of Nerger's role at Siemens and investigated his internment at Sachsenhausen. The historian Rolf Schmolling was quoted as saying that the head of factory security for a company such as Siemens often acted as an intermediary between the company and the Gestapo. The documentary concluded that Nerger knew of and must have condoned the suffering of enforced workers.
297 *'you have a right to know the full truth'*: Letter from Heinz Masuch to Dr Hans Nerger, 26 October 1963. Letter provided to authors by Wolf-Christian Nerger.
298 *'the forty-seven-year-old ex-soldier appeared before a jury in Freiburg'*: *Allgemeine Zeitung* (*General News*), 26 April 1967.
299 *'one of the greatest seamen this world has known'*: Alexander, p. 254.
299 *'neurotic temperament'*: Details of Alexander's hospitalisation from an affidavit sworn by his brother, 14 November 1952, New South Wales Supreme Court probate records.
300 *'in remembrance of good days and bad days on board'*: Postcard, date obscured, provided to authors by Norman Pyne's son, Bruce.
300 *'fleeing an unhappy love triangle'*: McNab, pp. 57–63.

BIBLIOGRAPHY

Alexander, Roy, *The Cruise of the Raider 'Wolf'*, Sydney, Angus & Robertson, 1941 (4th edition)

Bade, James, *Sea Devil: Count von Luckner in New Zealand and the Pacific*, Wellington, Steele Roberts, 2006

Bailey, Thomas A. and Paul B. Ryan, *The Lusitania Disaster*, New York, The Free Press, 1975

Bean, C. E. W., *Anzac to Amiens, Vol. IX*, Ringwood, Penguin Books, 1993

Beesly, Patrick, *Room 40: British Naval Intelligence 1914–18*, London, Hamish Hamilton, 1982

Best, Geoffrey, *Humanity in Warfare*, New York, Columbia University Press, 1980

Brocklebank, Laurie W., *The Failure to Detect the German Raider Wolf in New Zealand Waters in 1917*, Honours History Paper, Palmerston North, Massey University, 1991

Bromby, Robin, *German Raiders of the South Seas*, Sydney, Doubleday, 1985

Brookes, Dame Mabel, *Memoirs*, South Melbourne, Macmillan, 1974

Brown, Stephen R., *Scurvy: How a Surgeon, a Mariner and a Gentleman Solved the Greatest Medical Mystery of the Age of Sail*, Melbourne, Penguin Books, 2003

Cain, Frank, *The Origins of Political Surveillance in Australia*, Sydney, Angus & Robertson, 1983

Cameron, John Stanley, *Ten Months in a German Raider*, New York, George H. Doran Company, 1918

Cecil, Hugh and Peter H. Liddle (eds), *Facing Armageddon: The First World War Experienced*, London, Lee Cooper, 1996

Clarke, Alfred, *To Kiel in the German Raider Wolf – and After*, Colombo, The Times of Ceylon Company, 1920

Clemmesen, Michael H., *The Danish Armed Forces 1909–1918*, Copenhagen, Royal Danish Defence College, 2007

Cruttwell, C. R. M. F., *A History of the Great War, 1914–1918*, London, Oxford University Press, 1934

Davis, Lance E. and Stanley L. Engerman, *Naval Blockades in Peace and War: An Economic History Since 1750*, New York, Cambridge University Press, 2006
Donaldson, Captain A., *The Amazing Cruise of the German Raider 'Wolf'*, Sydney, New Century Press, 1941
Fifty Years Too Soon, Melbourne, Whitcombe & Tombs, 1948
Dove, Richard (ed.), *'Totally Un-English'?: Britain's Internment of 'Enemy Aliens' in Two World Wars*, New York, Rodopi, 2005
Feakes, Henry James, *White Ensign Southern Cross: A Story of the King's Ships of Australia's Navy*, Sydney, Ure Smith, 1951
Ferguson, Niall, *The Pity of War*, London, Penguin Books, 1998
Fischer, Gerhard, *Enemy Aliens: Internment and the Homefront Experience in Australia 1914–1920*, St Lucia, University of Queensland Press, 1989
Fisher, John Arbuthnot, *Memories and Records*, New York, George H. Doran, 1920
Fitzhardinge, L. F., *The Little Digger 1914–1952*, Sydney, Angus & Robertson, 1979
Fox, Stephen, *Wolf of the Deep: Raphael Semmes and the Notorious Confederate Raider CSS Alabama*, New York, Alfred A. Knopf, 2007
Freese, Barbara, *Coal: A Human History*, Sydney, Random House, 2005
Halpern, Paul G., *A Naval History of World War I*, Annapolis, Naval Institute Press, 1994
Hasegawa, Shin, *Hitachi Maru of the Indian Sea*, Tokyo, Chu-ko Bunko Publications, 1980
Hauswaldt, Dr Hermann, 'Ärztliches Tagebuch S.M.H. Wolf' ('Doctor's Diary S.M.H Wolf'), 4 February 1916–4 January 1918. Unpublished handwritten journal supplied to the authors by Dr Christian Hauswaldt. ('S.M.H.' stands for *Seine Majestaet's Hilfskreuzer* – His Majesty's Auxiliary Cruiser.)
Horn, Daniel, *The German Naval Mutinies of World War I*, New Brunswick, Rutgers University Press, 1969
Horne, Donald, *Billy Hughes: Prime Minister of Australia 1915–1923*, Victoria, Bookman Press, 1983
Horner, D. M. (ed.), *The Commanders*, Sydney, Allen & Unwin, 1984
Howard, Michael, George J. Andreopoulos and Mark R. Shulman (eds), *The Laws of War – Constraints on Warfare in the Western World*, New Haven, Yale University Press, 1994
Hoyt, Edwin P., *Raider Wolf: The Voyage of Captain Nerger, 1916–1918*, New York, Pinnacle Books, 1974
Hughes, Aneurin, *Billy Hughes*, Milton, John Wiley & Sons Australia Ltd, 2005
Hungerford, T. A. G., *Straightshooter*, Fremantle, Fremantle Arts Centre Press, 2003
Hurd, Archibald, *The Merchant Navy* (vols 1–3), The Naval & Military Press Ltd, East Sussex, and The Imperial War Museum, London, 2003 (facsimile edition)
Ireland, Bernard and John Keegan (ed.), *War at Sea 1914–45*, London, Cassell, 2002
Jensen, Peter R., *From the Wireless to the Web*, Sydney, University of New South Wales Press, 2000
Jose, Arthur W., *The Royal Australian Navy: The Official History of Australia in the War of 1914–1918, Vol. IX*, Sydney, University of Queensland Press, 1987 (11th edition)
Knightley, Philip, *The First Casualty – From the Crimea to Vietnam: The War Correspondent as Hero, Propagandist, and Myth-Maker*, New York, Harcourt Brace Jovanovich, 1975
Langewiesche, William, *The Outlaw Sea: Chaos and Crime on the World's Oceans*, London, Granta Books, 2004
Lewis, Brian, *Our War: A View of World War I from Inside an Australian Family*, Ringwood, Penguin Books, 1980

Luebke, Frederick C., *Bonds of Loyalty: German Americans and World War I*, De Kalb, Northern Illinois University Press, 1974

Macdougall, Tony (ed.), *War Letters of General Monash*, Potts Point, Duffy & Snellgrove, 2002

Mackenzie, S. S., *The Australians at Rabaul: The Official History of Australia in the War of 1914–1918, Vol. X*, Sydney, University of Queensland Press, 1987 (11th edition)

Mantey, E. F. W. von (ed.), *Der Kreuzerkrieg in den ausländischen Gewässern: Die deutschen Hilfskreuzer* (*The Cruiser War in Foreign Waters: The German Auxiliary Cruisers*), vol. III of *Der Krieg zur See 1914–1918*, Berlin, E. S. Mittler & Son, 1937

Marder, Arthur J., *From The Dreadnought to Scapa Flow, Vol. 1*, London, Oxford University Press, 1961

Maugham, Robin, *Conversations With Willie*, London, W. H. Allen, 1978

McNab, Robert, *Ghost Ships: A Surrealist Love Triangle*, New Haven, Yale University Press, 2004

Meade, Kevin, *Heroes Before Gallipoli*, Milton, Wiley, 2005

Meyers, Jeffrey, *Somerset Maugham: A Life*, New York, Random House, 2004

Nerger, Karl August, *SMS Wolf*, Berlin, August Scherl, 1918 (translated manuscript from archives of British Admiralty; additional translations from Beate Lauterbach and Michael Zehnpfennig (trs), Auckland, GTO Publisher, 2000)

Newbolt, Henry, *Naval Operations Vol. 4* and *Vol. 5*, East Sussex, The Naval & Military Press Ltd, and London, The Imperial War Museum, 2003 (facsimile edition)

Norton, Elsie K., *Crusoes of Sunday Island*, London, G. Bell & Sons, 1957

Panayi, Panikos, *The Enemy In Our Midst: Germans in Britain during the First World War*, Providence, Berg Publishers Limited, 1991

Perry, Roland, *Monash: The Outsider Who Won a War*, Sydney, Random House, 2004

Phillipson, Coleman, *International Law and the Great War*, London, T. Fisher Unwin Ltd, 1915

Plivier, Theodor, *The Kaiser's Coolies*, Margaret Green (trans.), New York, Alfred A. Knopf, 1931

Ponsonby, Arthur, *Falsehood in Wartime: Propaganda Lies of the First World War*, London, George Allen & Unwin, 1928

Rose, Tania, *Aspects of Political Censorship* (monograph), Hull, The University of Hull Press, 1995

Sanders, M. L. and P. M. Taylor, *British Propaganda During the First World War, 1914–1918*, London, Macmillan, 1982

Schmalenbach, Paul, *German Raiders: A History of Auxiliary Cruisers of the German Navy 1895–1945*, Annapolis, Naval Institute Press, 1979

Scott, Ernest, *Australia During the War: The Official History of Australia in the War of 1914–1918, Vol. XI*, Sydney, University of Queensland Press, 1989 (11th edition)

Shiraishi, Katsuhiko, *The Fate of the Abducted Lieutenant Commander*, Tokyo, Shimpusha Publishing, 2007

Singh, Simon, *The Code Book: The Secret History of Codes and Code-Breaking*, London, HarperCollins, 2000

Stein, Matthaus and Paul Fabeck, *Wolfchen: Im Fleugzeug über drei Weltmeeren (Wolfchen: In an Aircraft Over Three Oceans)*, Berlin, August Scherl, 1918

Stevens, David (ed.), *Maritime Power in the 20th Century, The Australian Experience*, Sydney, Allen & Unwin, 1998

Stone, Norman, *Europe Transformed 1878–1919*, London, Fontana Paperbacks, 1990

Strachan, Hew, *The First World War Volume I: To Arms*, Oxford, Oxford University Press, 2001

Szielasko, Ernst, *15 Monate Prisenoffizier an Bord SMS Wolf* (*15 Months as a Prize Officer Aboard SMS Wolf*), Berlin, Deutscher Lermittel-Verlag, 1918

Tampke, Jürgen and Colin Doxford, *Australia, Willkommen: A History of the Germans in Australia*, Kensington, New South Wales University Press, 2003

Tirpitz, Alfred Peter Friedrich von, *My Memoirs*, London, Hurst & Blackett Ltd, 1919

Trayes, F. G., *Five Months on a German Raider: Being the Adventures of an Englishman Captured by the 'Wolf'*, London, Headley Bros, 1919

Tuchman, Barbara, *The Zimmerman Telegram: How the USA Entered the Great War*, London, Constable and Company Ltd, 1959

Van der Vat, Dan, *Standard of Power*, Sydney, Random House, 2001

Walter, John, *The Kaiser's Pirates*, London, Arms & Armour Press, 1994

Watson, Darren, 'In The Shadow of the "Wolf": Enemy Activity and the Internment of a Gippsland Fisherman', Gippsland Heritage Journal, No. 24, 2000

Wieduwilt, Albert, 'Tagebuch geschrieben auf dem Hilfskreuzer SMS 'Wolf' (Diary Written on the Auxiliary Cruiser SMS 'Wolf'), 30 November 1916–24 February 1918, unpublished transcript of personal diary supplied by Wieduwilt family

Wiesen, S. Jonathan, *West German Industry and the Challenge of the Nazi Past*, Chapel Hill, University of North Carolina Press, 2001

Williams, John F., *German Anzacs and the First World War*, Sydney, University of New South Wales Press, 2003

Witschetzky, F., *Das Schwarze Schiff: Kriegs und Kaperfahrten des Hilfskreuzers 'Wolf'* (*The Black Ship: War and Commerce-Raiding on the Auxiliary Cruiser 'Wolf'*), Stuttgart, Union Deutsche Berlagsgesellschaft, 1921

INDEX